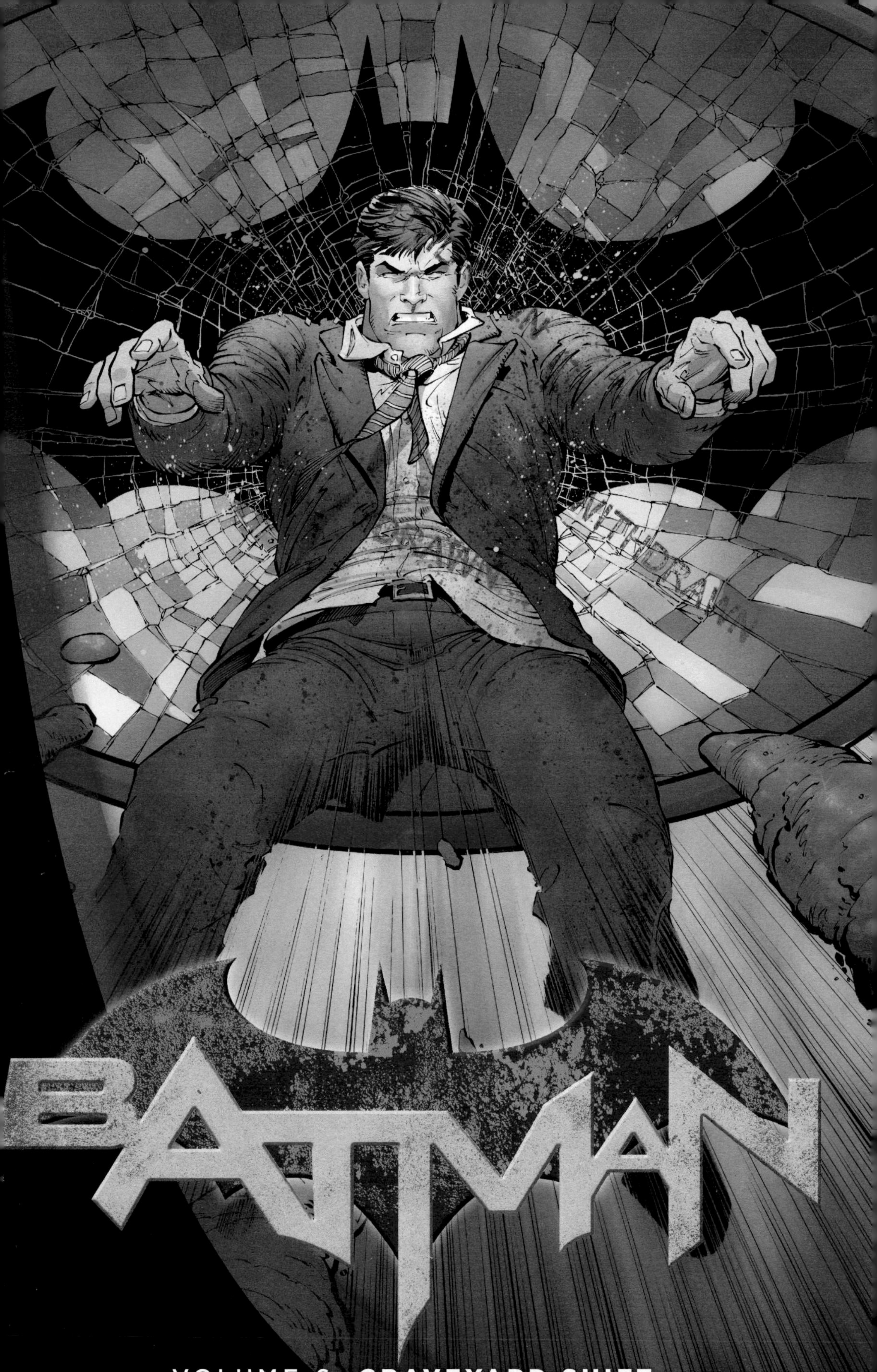
BATMAN

VOLUME 6 GRAVEYARD SHIFT

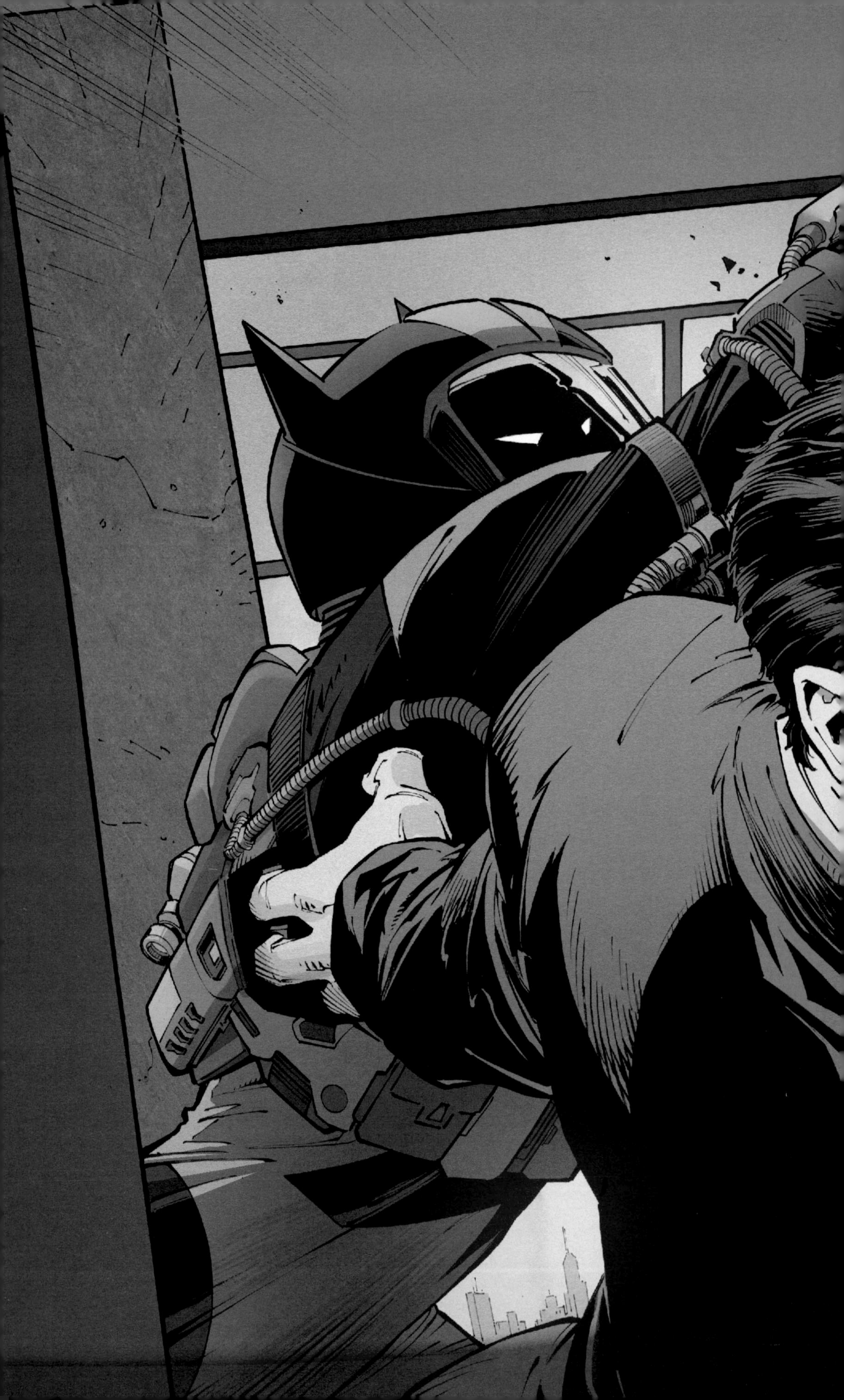

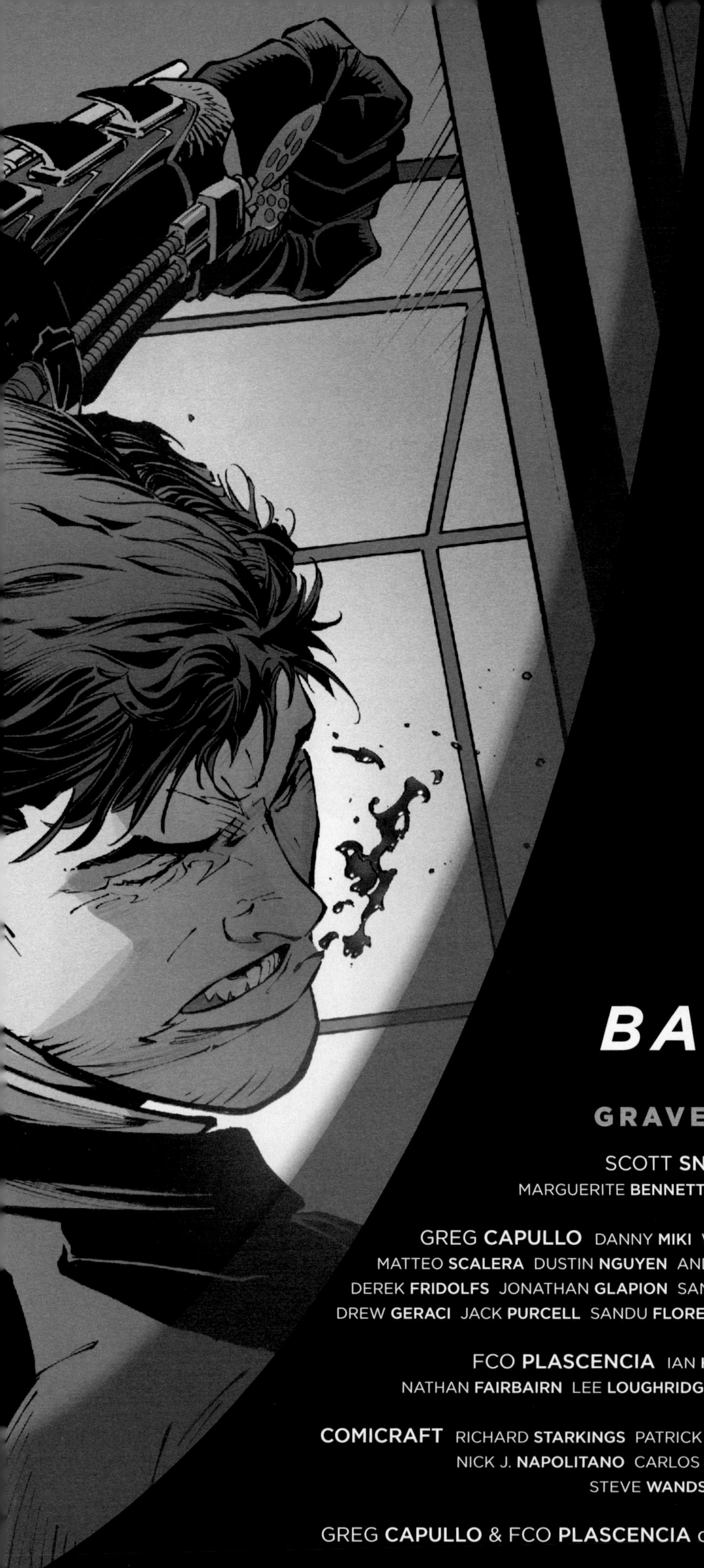

BATMAN

VOLUME 6

GRAVEYARD SHIFT

SCOTT **SNYDER** JAMES **TYNION IV**
MARGUERITE **BENNETT** GERRY **DUGGAN** writers

GREG **CAPULLO** DANNY **MIKI** WES **CRAIG** ALEX **MALEEV**
MATTEO **SCALERA** DUSTIN **NGUYEN** ANDY **KUBERT** ANDY **CLARKE**
DEREK **FRIDOLFS** JONATHAN **GLAPION** SANDRA **HOPE** CRAIG **YEUNG**
DREW **GERACI** JACK **PURCELL** SANDU **FLOREA** MARC **DEERING** artists

FCO **PLASCENCIA** IAN **HANNIN** BRAD **ANDERSON**
NATHAN **FAIRBAIRN** LEE **LOUGHRIDGE** JOHN **KALISZ** colorists

COMICRAFT RICHARD **STARKINGS** PATRICK **BROSSEAU** DAVE **SHARPE**
NICK J. **NAPOLITANO** CARLOS M. **MANGUAL** DEZI **SIENTY**
STEVE **WANDS** SAL **CIPRIANO** letterers

GREG **CAPULLO** & FCO **PLASCENCIA** collection cover artists

BATMAN created by BOB **KANE**

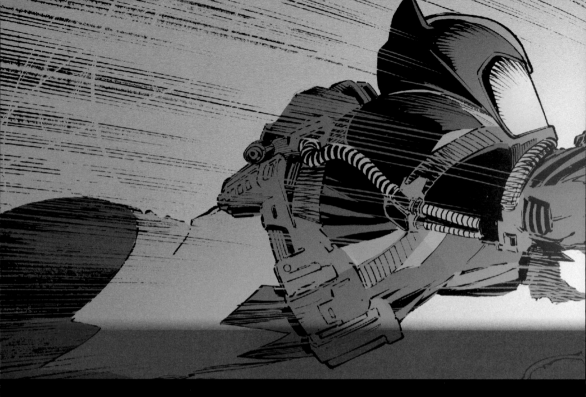

MIKE MARTS MARK DOYLE Editors – Original Series KATIE KUBERT Associate Editor – Original Series
MATT HUMPHREYS Assistant Editor – Original Series ROBIN WILDMAN Editor
ROBBIN BROSTERMAN Design Director – Books ROBBIE BIEDERMAN Publication Design

BOB HARRAS Senior VP – Editor-in-Chief, DC Comics

DIANE NELSON President DAN DIDIO and JIM LEE Co-Publishers GEOFF JOHNS Chief Creative Officer
AMIT DESAI Senior VP – Marketing and Franchise Management
AMY GENKINS Senior VP – Business and Legal Affairs NAIRI GARDINER Senior VP – Finance
JEFF BOISON VP – Publishing Planning MARK CHIARELLO VP – Art Direction and Design
JOHN CUNNINGHAM VP – Marketing TERRI CUNNINGHAM VP – Editorial Administration
LARRY GANEM VP – Talent Relations and Services ALISON GILL Senior VP – Manufacturing and Operations
HANK KANALZ Senior VP – Vertigo and Integrated Publishing JAY KOGAN VP – Business and Legal Affairs, Publishing
JACK MAHAN VP – Business Affairs, Talent NICK NAPOLITANO VP – Manufacturing Administration SUE POHJA VP – Book Sales
FRED RUIZ VP – Manufacturing Operations COURTNEY SIMMONS Senior VP – Publicity BOB WAYNE Senior VP – Sales

BATMAN VOL. 6: GRAVEYARD SHIFT

Originally published in single magazine form as BATMAN 0, 18-20, 28, 34, ANNUAL 2 © 2012, 2013, 2014 DC Comics. All Rights Reserved.
All characters, their distinctive likenesses and related elements featured in this publication are trademarks of DC Comics. MAD and
Alfred E. Neuman © and ™ E.C. Publications, Inc.The stories, characters and incidents featured in this publication are entirely fictional.
DC Comics does not read or accept unsolicited ideas, stories or artwork.

DC Comics, 1700 Broadway, New York, NY 10019
A Warner Bros. Entertainment Company.
Printed by RR Donnelley, Salem, VA, USA. 3/27/15. First Printing.

ISBN: 978-1-4012-5230-4

Library of Congress Cataloging-in-Publication Data

Snyder, Scott.
Batman. Volume 6, Graveyard shift / Scott Snyder ; illustrated by Greg Capullo.
pages cm
ISBN 978-1-4012-5230-4 (hardback)
1. Graphic novels. I. Capullo, Greg, illustrator. II. Title. III. Title: Graveyard shift.
PN6728.B36S687 2015
741.5'973—dc23

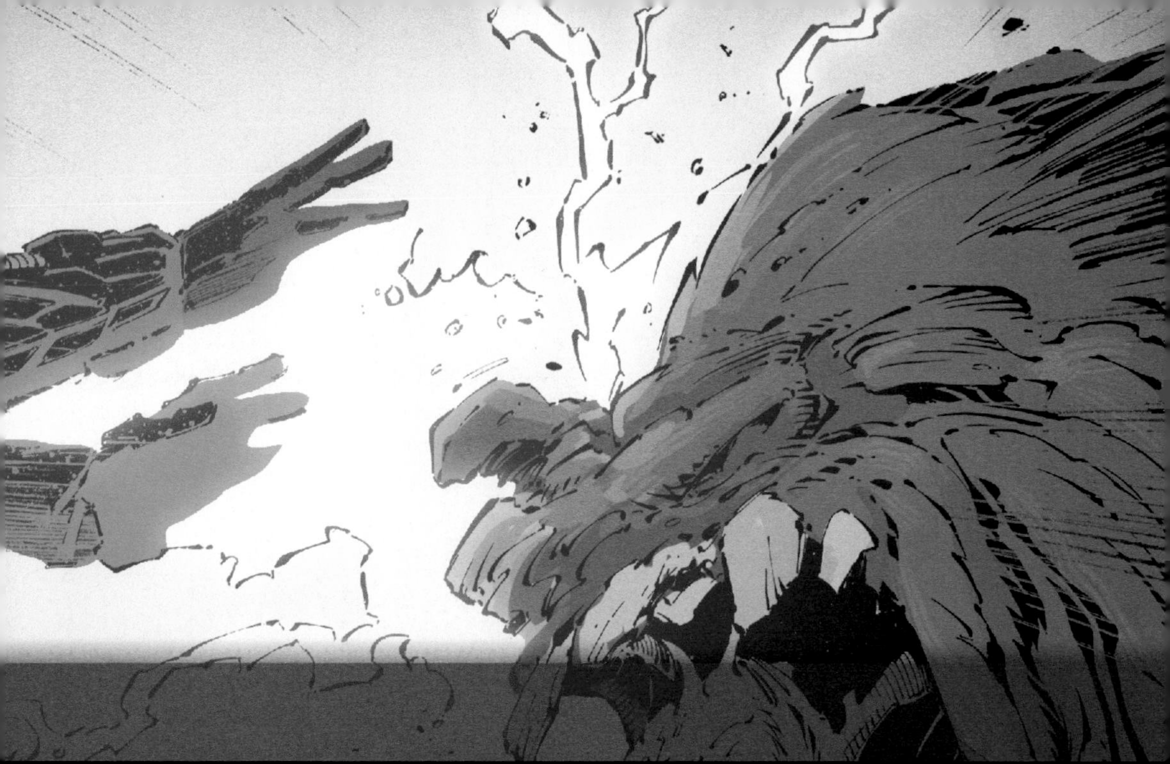

In these pages are a selection of exceptional standalone stories from Scott Snyder and Greg Capullo's acclaimed BATMAN, following the Dark Knight through his past and future and tying into ZERO YEAR, BATMAN INCORPORATED, BATMAN ETERNAL and more.

In the first of these lost tales, "Bright New Yesterday," readers flash back six years to the time now known as the Zero Year, when the newly returned Bruce Wayne was not yet calling himself Batman, but was already at work fighting Gotham's underworld. Likewise, "Tomorrow" and "Ages" explore the long-lasting effects of Batman's actions during the pivotal Zero Year.

Back in the present in "Resolve" and "Ghost Lights," Batman must process the death of his son and crime-fighting partner, Damian Wayne (whose tragic end in BATMAN INCORPORATED rocked all of Gotham's crime-fighters), before getting back to his detective roots in the mysteries "Nowhere Man" and "The Meek."

Finally, flashing forward to the near future in "Gotham Eternal," the Dark Knight and his new partner explore the darker world of BATMAN ETERNAL

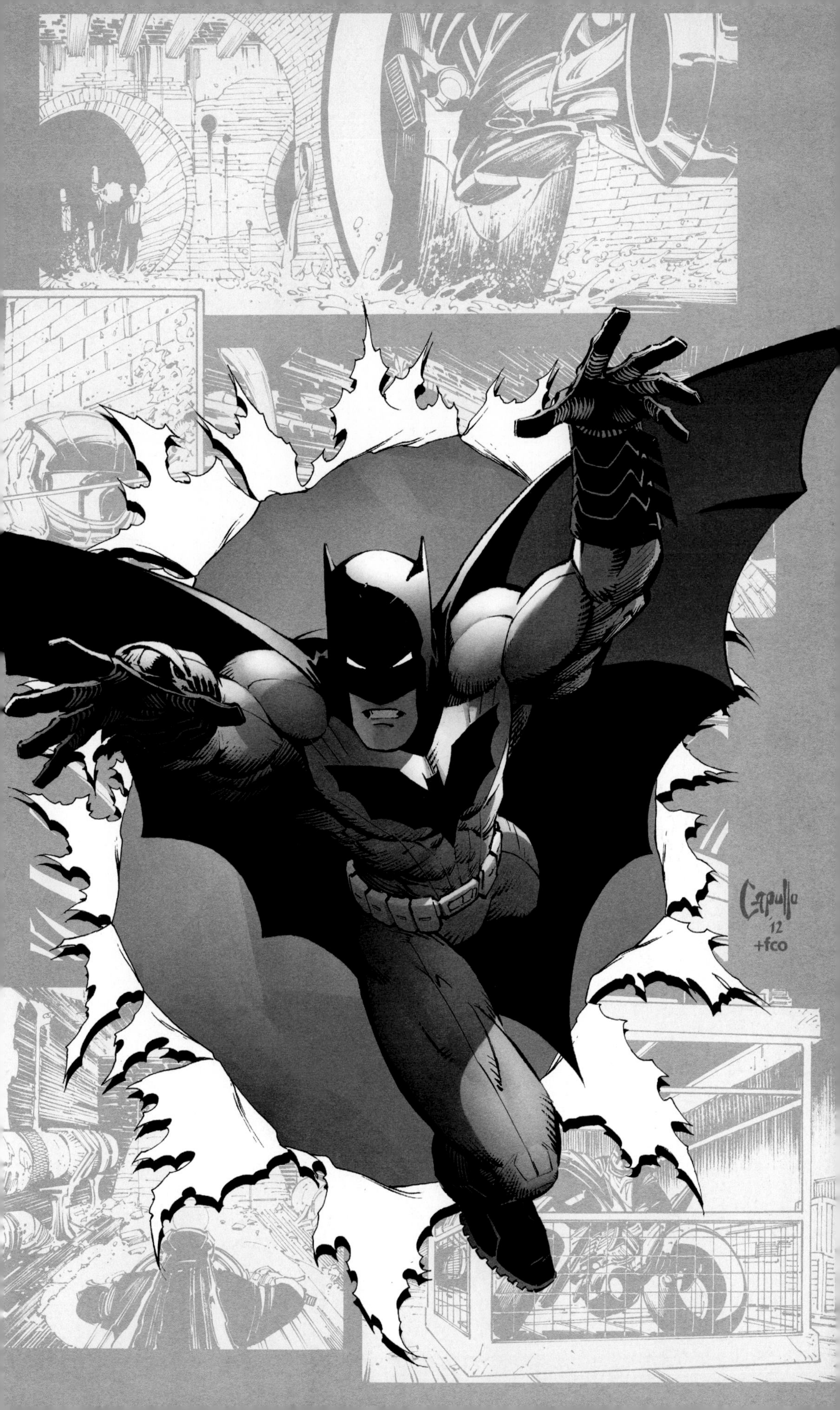
Capullo '12 +fco

BRIGHT NEW YESTERDAY

SCOTT SNYDER writer GREG CAPULLO penciller JONATHAN GLAPION inker FCO PLASCENCIA colorist cover by GREG CAPULLO and FCO PLASCEN

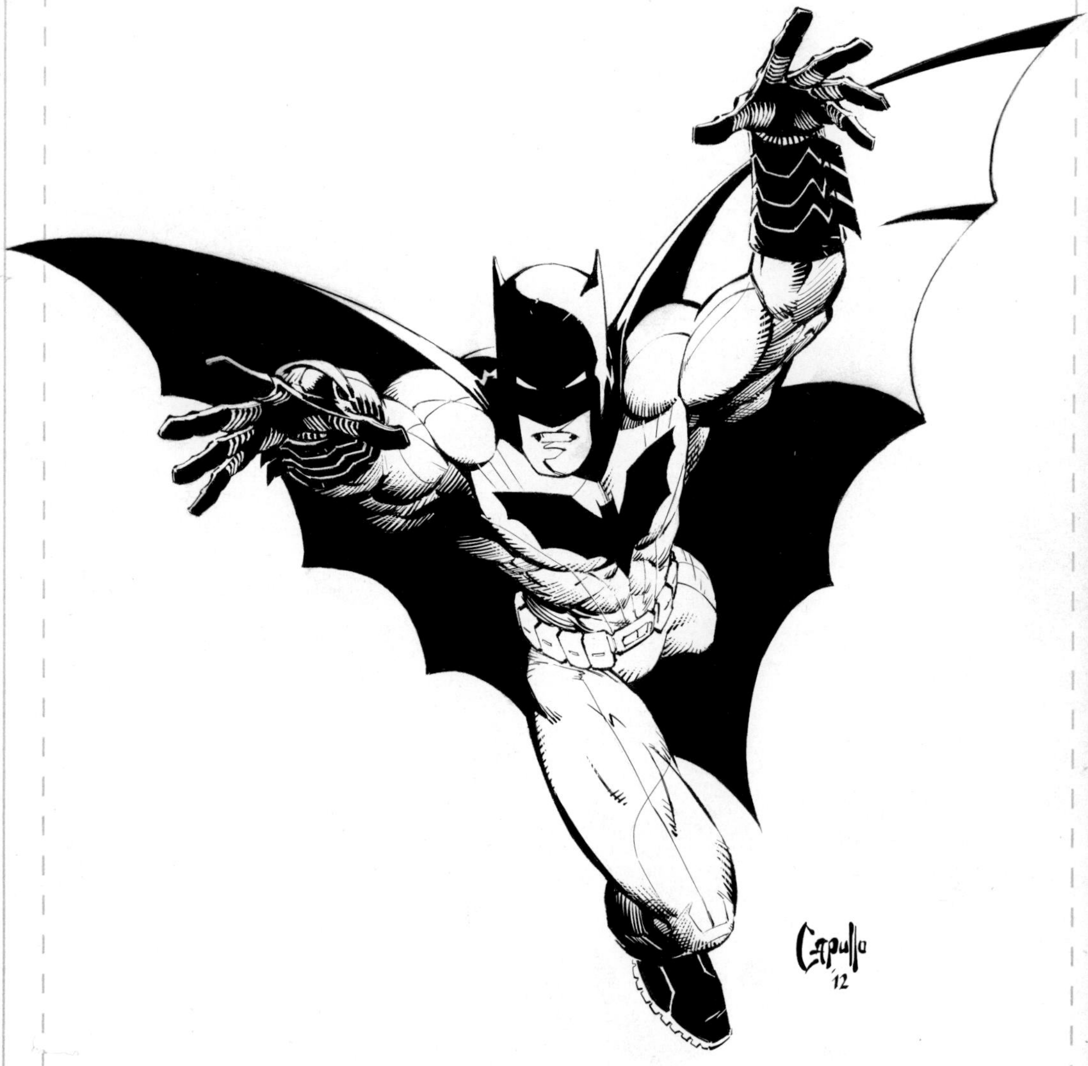
Capullo '12

MINIMUM BLEED 1/4 ALL AROUND

LIVE AREA

CROP

BLEED

PRINTED COVER SIZE: 6 5/8 X 10 3/16

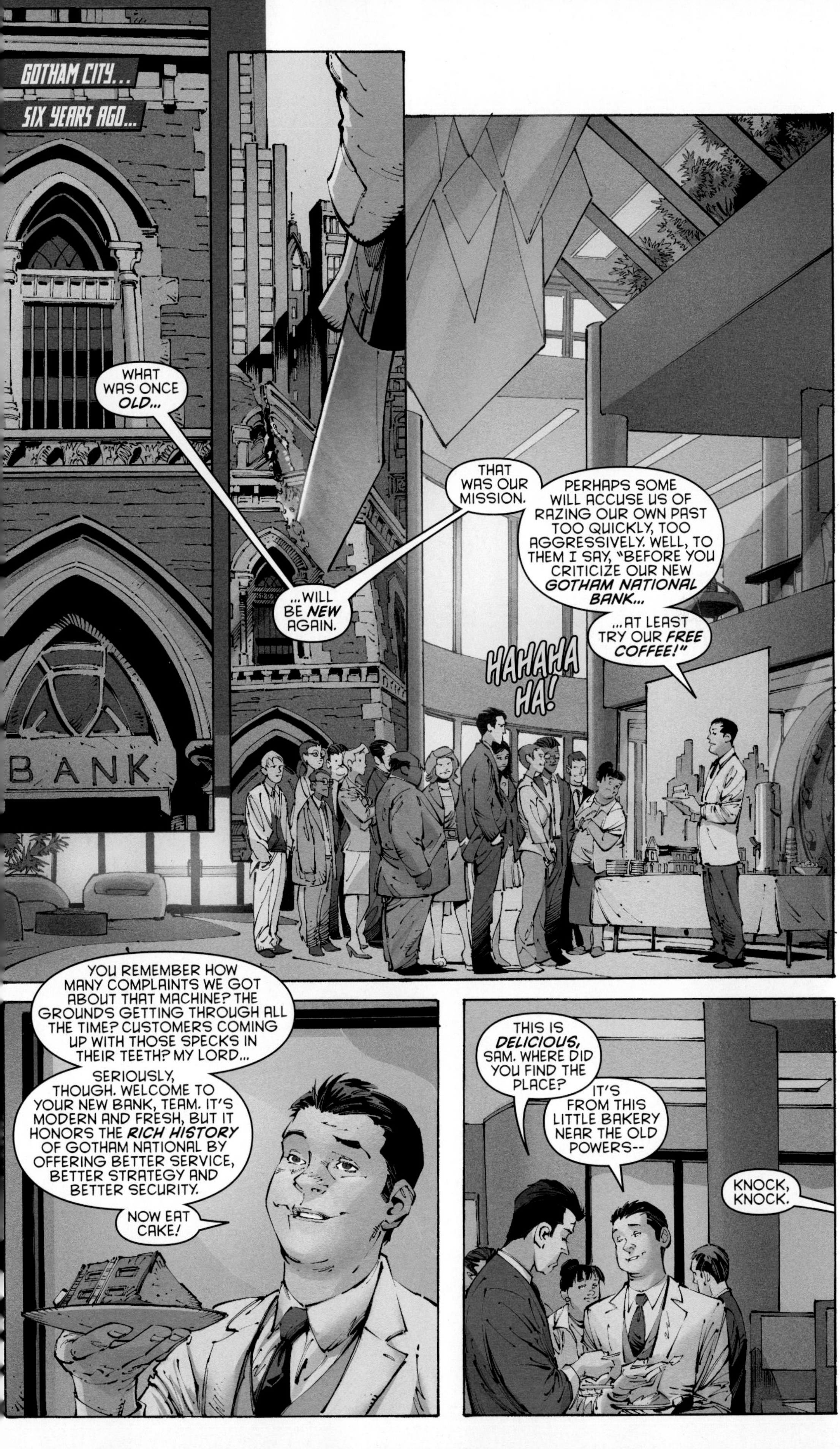
GOTHAM CITY...
SIX YEARS AGO...
WHAT WAS ONCE OLD...
...WILL BE NEW AGAIN.
THAT WAS OUR MISSION.
PERHAPS SOME WILL ACCUSE US OF RAZING OUR OWN PAST TOO QUICKLY, TOO AGGRESSIVELY. WELL, TO THEM I SAY, "BEFORE YOU CRITICIZE OUR NEW GOTHAM NATIONAL BANK...
...AT LEAST TRY OUR FREE COFFEE!"
HAHAHA HA!
BANK
YOU REMEMBER HOW MANY COMPLAINTS WE GOT ABOUT THAT MACHINE? THE GROUNDS GETTING THROUGH ALL THE TIME? CUSTOMERS COMING UP WITH THOSE SPECKS IN THEIR TEETH? MY LORD...
SERIOUSLY, THOUGH. WELCOME TO YOUR NEW BANK, TEAM. IT'S MODERN AND FRESH, BUT IT HONORS THE RICH HISTORY OF GOTHAM NATIONAL BY OFFERING BETTER SERVICE, BETTER STRATEGY AND BETTER SECURITY.
NOW EAT CAKE!
THIS IS DELICIOUS, SAM. WHERE DID YOU FIND THE PLACE?
IT'S FROM THIS LITTLE BAKERY NEAR THE OLD POWERS--
KNOCK, KNOCK.

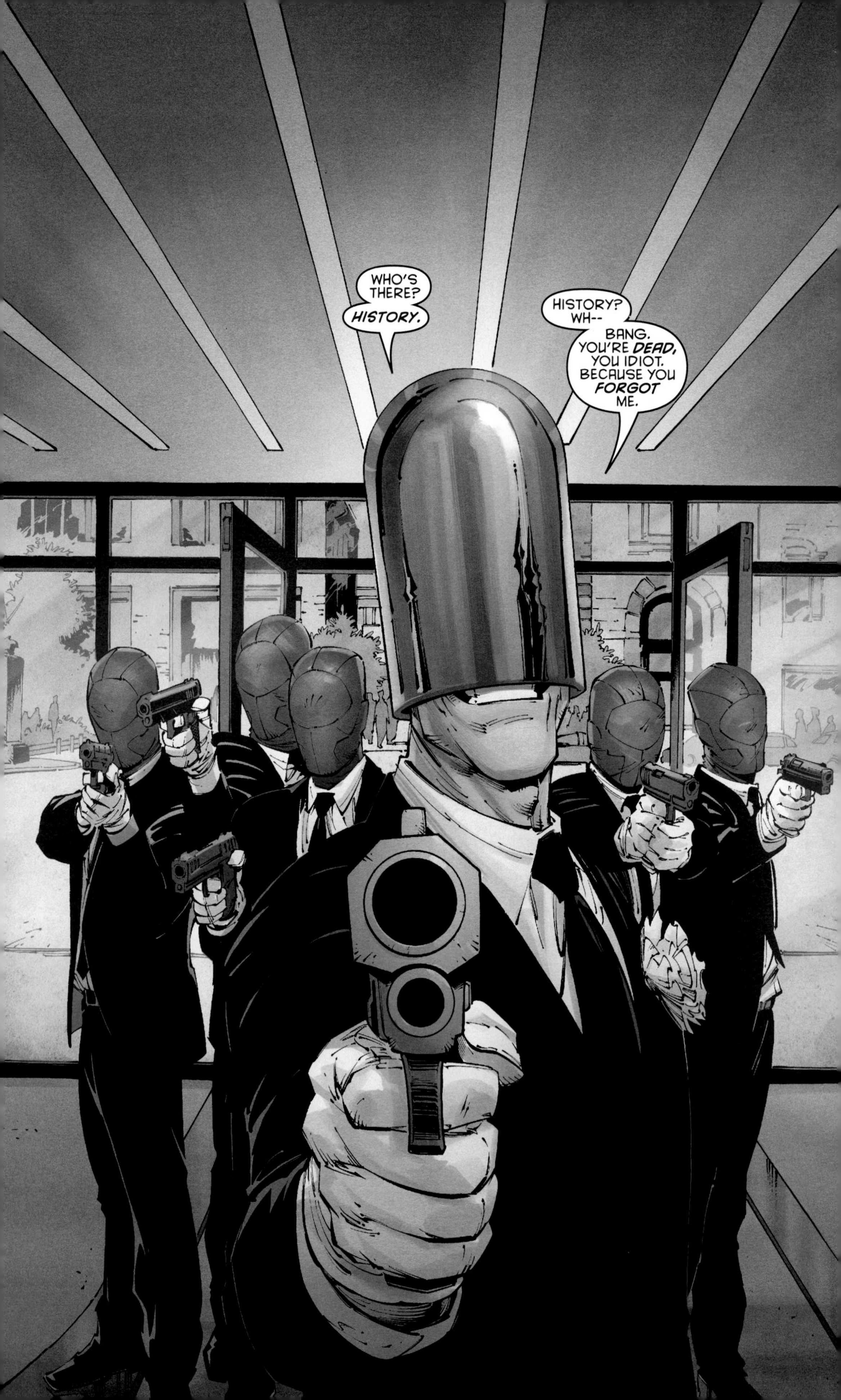
WHO'S THERE?
HISTORY.
HISTORY? WH--
BANG. YOU'RE DEAD, YOU IDIOT. BECAUSE YOU FORGOT ME.

SO REMEMBER YOUR HISTORY, LADIES AND GENTLEMEN.

AND HISTORICALLY, AT THE OLD GOTHAM NATIONAL, THE WAY IT WORKED WAS YOU GOT DOWN ON THE GROUND AND WERE AS QUIET AS *CHURCH MICE* AND WE DIDN'T DECORATE THE *WALLS* WITH YOU.

ALL RIGHT?

NOW, RED HOOD GANG-- *ROB THEM BLIND!*

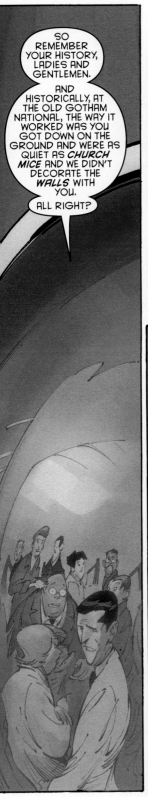

YOU... YOU HAVE *NO RIGHT!* HOW DID YOU GET IN HERE?

WITH *THIS* LITTLE DOODAD. MADE BY YOUR OWN SECURITY TEAM, STOLEN BY US.

IT'S ALREADY KNOCKED OUT YOUR VAULT CONTRACTION SYSTEM, YOUR SILENT ALARM, THAT BRAND NEW COFFEE MACHINE--THE ONE THAT KEEPS THE GROUNDS *IN* THE PACKETS--

BUT SEE I'M AFRAID YOU WEREN'T *LISTENING* TO MY HISTORY LESSON, MR. DEKE.

RED HOOD FIVE, PUT HIM DOWN.

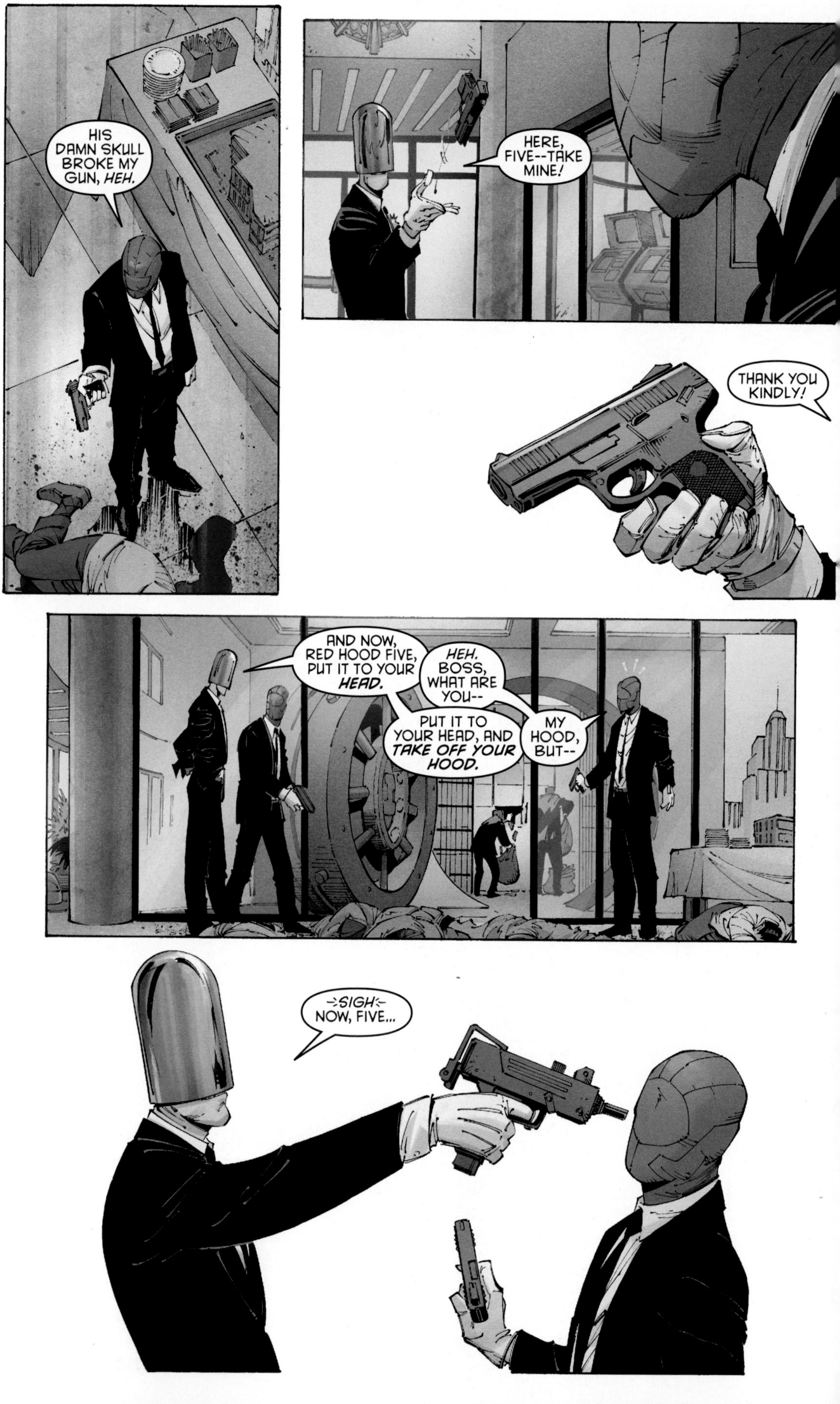
HIS DAMN SKULL BROKE MY GUN, *HEH.*
HERE, FIVE--TAKE MINE!
THANK YOU KINDLY!
AND NOW, RED HOOD FIVE, PUT IT TO YOUR *HEAD.*
HEH. BOSS, WHAT ARE YOU--
PUT IT TO YOUR HEAD, AND *TAKE OFF YOUR HOOD.*
MY HOOD, BUT--
-SIGH- NOW, FIVE...

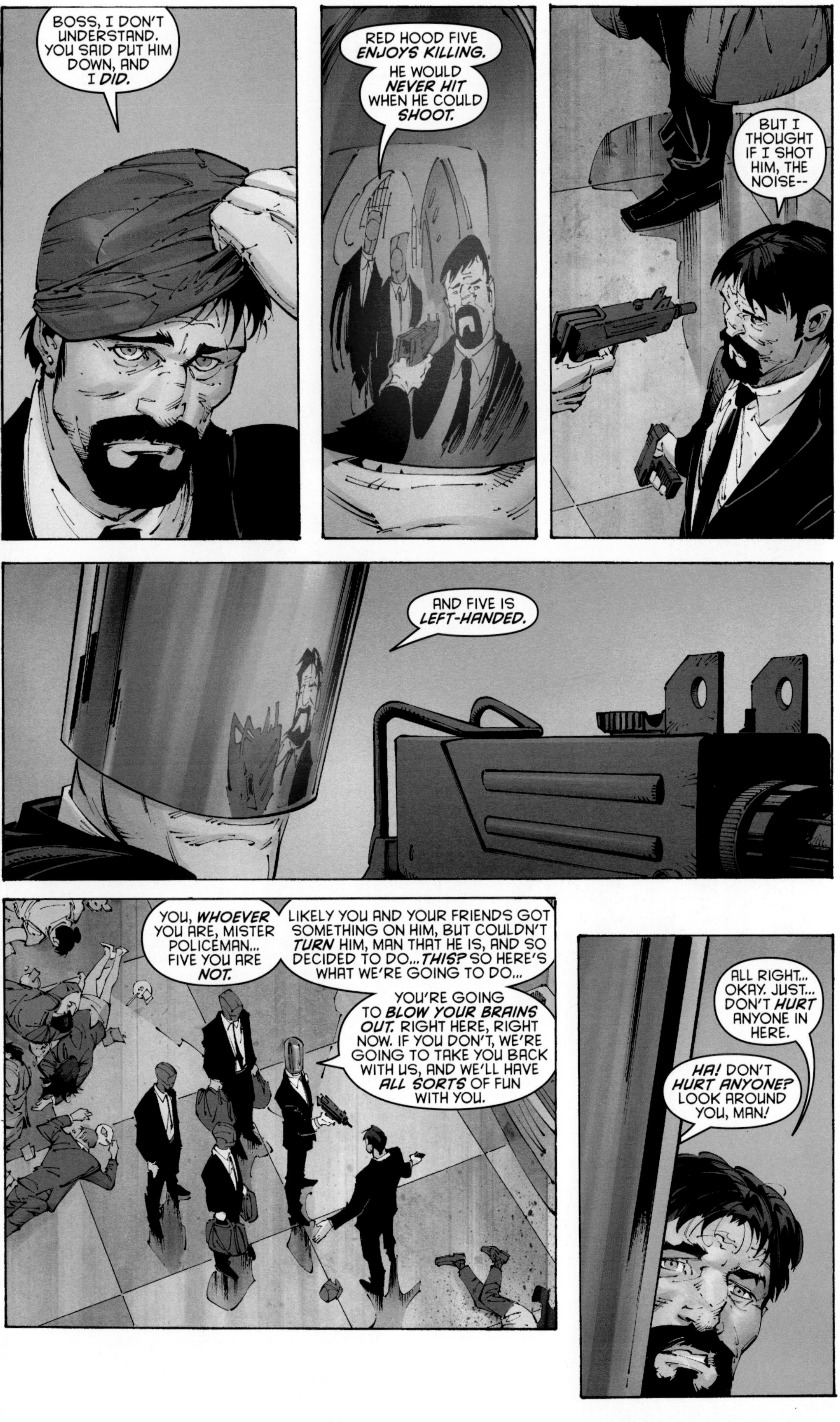

BOSS, I DON'T UNDERSTAND. YOU SAID PUT HIM DOWN, AND I DID.
RED HOOD FIVE ENJOYS KILLING.
HE WOULD NEVER HIT WHEN HE COULD SHOOT.
BUT I THOUGHT IF I SHOT HIM, THE NOISE--
AND FIVE IS LEFT-HANDED.
YOU, WHOEVER YOU ARE, MISTER POLICEMAN... FIVE YOU ARE NOT.
LIKELY YOU AND YOUR FRIENDS GOT SOMETHING ON HIM, BUT COULDN'T TURN HIM, MAN THAT HE IS, AND SO DECIDED TO DO...THIS? SO HERE'S WHAT WE'RE GOING TO DO...
YOU'RE GOING TO BLOW YOUR BRAINS OUT, RIGHT HERE, RIGHT NOW. IF YOU DON'T, WE'RE GOING TO TAKE YOU BACK WITH US, AND WE'LL HAVE ALL SORTS OF FUN WITH YOU.
ALL RIGHT... OKAY. JUST... DON'T HURT ANYONE IN HERE.
HA! DON'T HURT ANYONE? LOOK AROUND YOU, MAN!

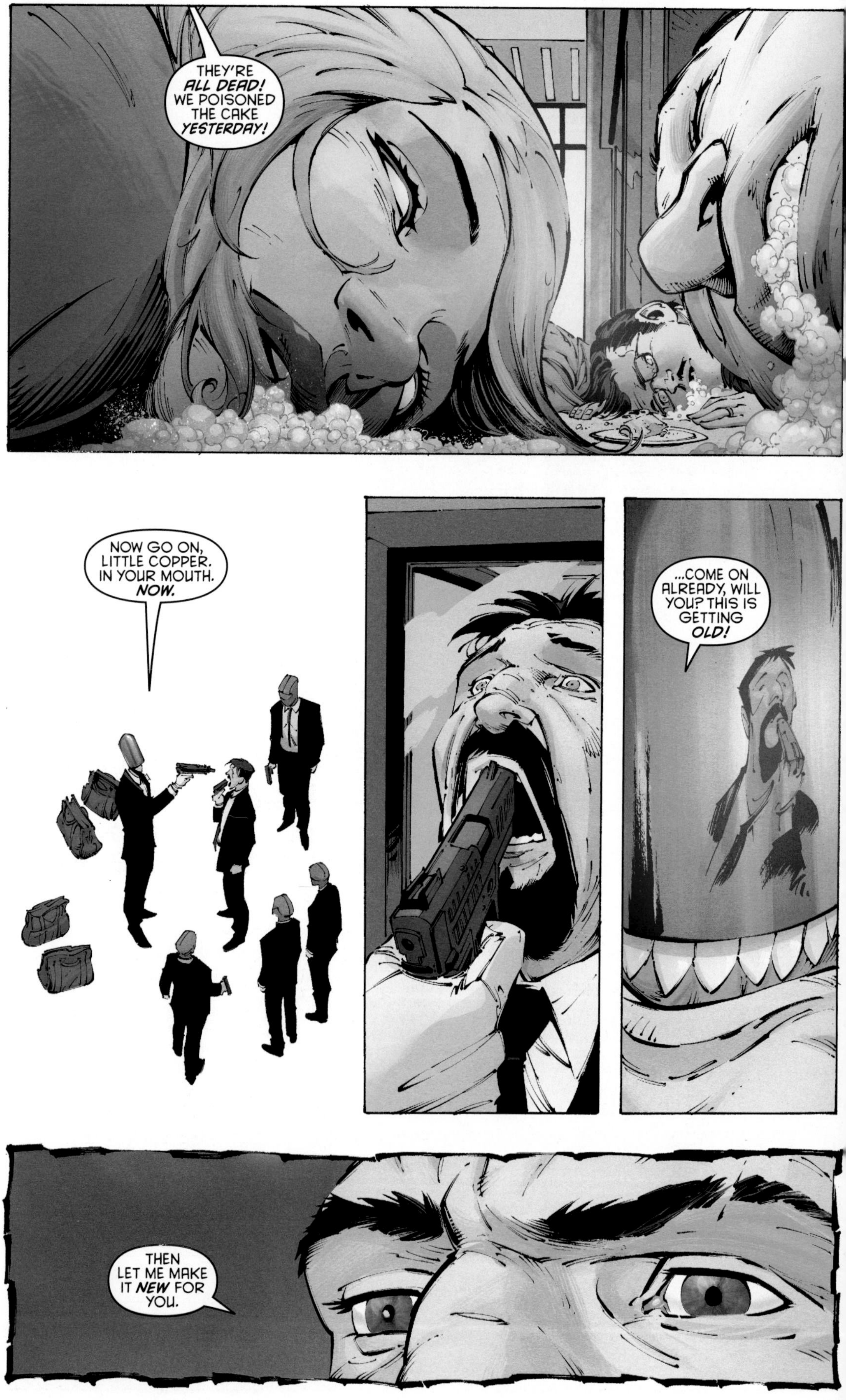

THEY'RE ALL DEAD! WE POISONED THE CAKE YESTERDAY!
NOW GO ON, LITTLE COPPER. IN YOUR MOUTH. NOW.
...COME ON ALREADY, WILL YOU? THIS IS GETTING OLD!
THEN LET ME MAKE IT NEW FOR YOU.

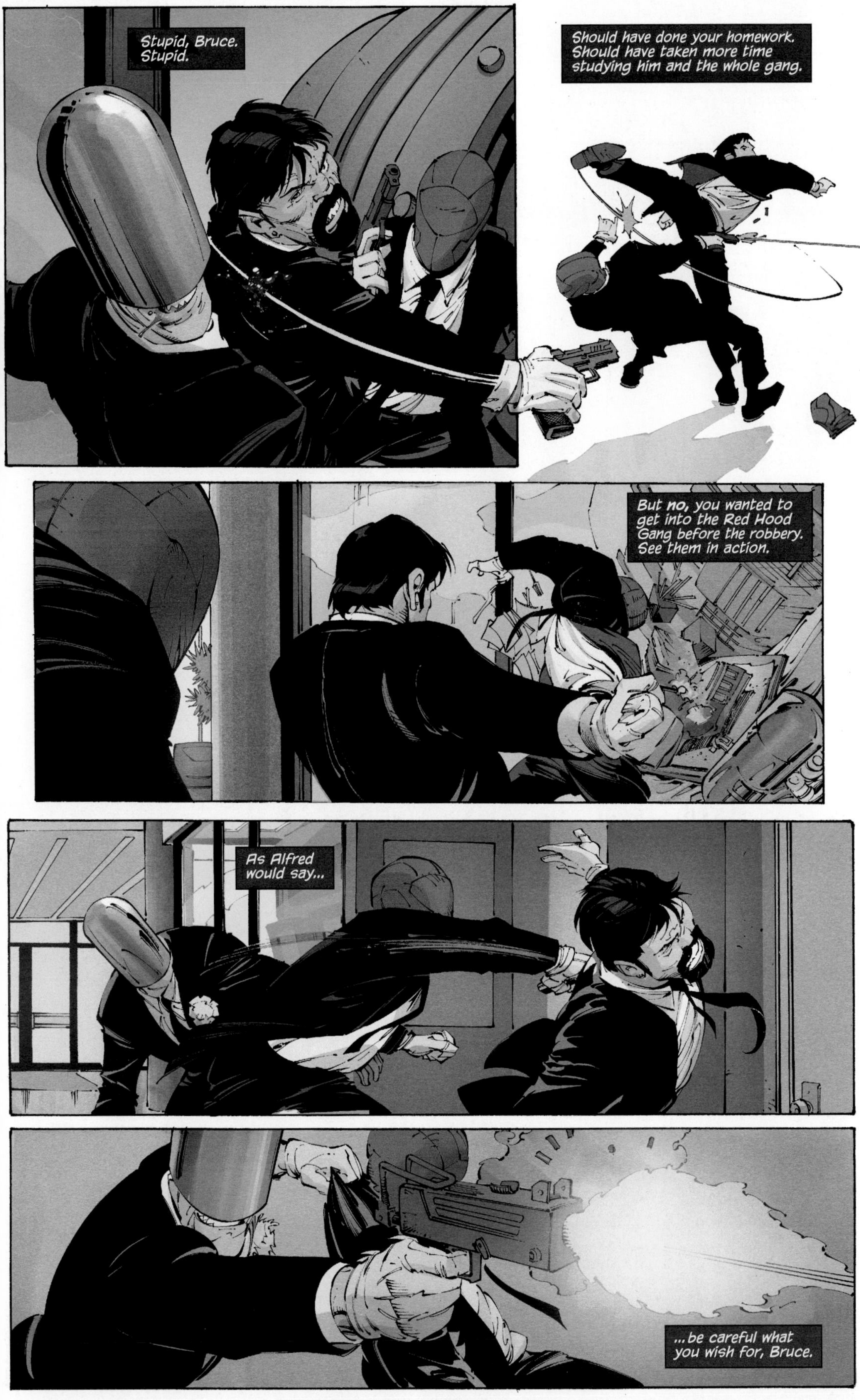
Stupid, Bruce. Stupid.
Should have done your homework. Should have taken more time studying him and the whole gang.
But no, you wanted to get into the Red Hood Gang before the robbery. See them in action.
As Alfred would say...
...be careful what you wish for, Bruce.

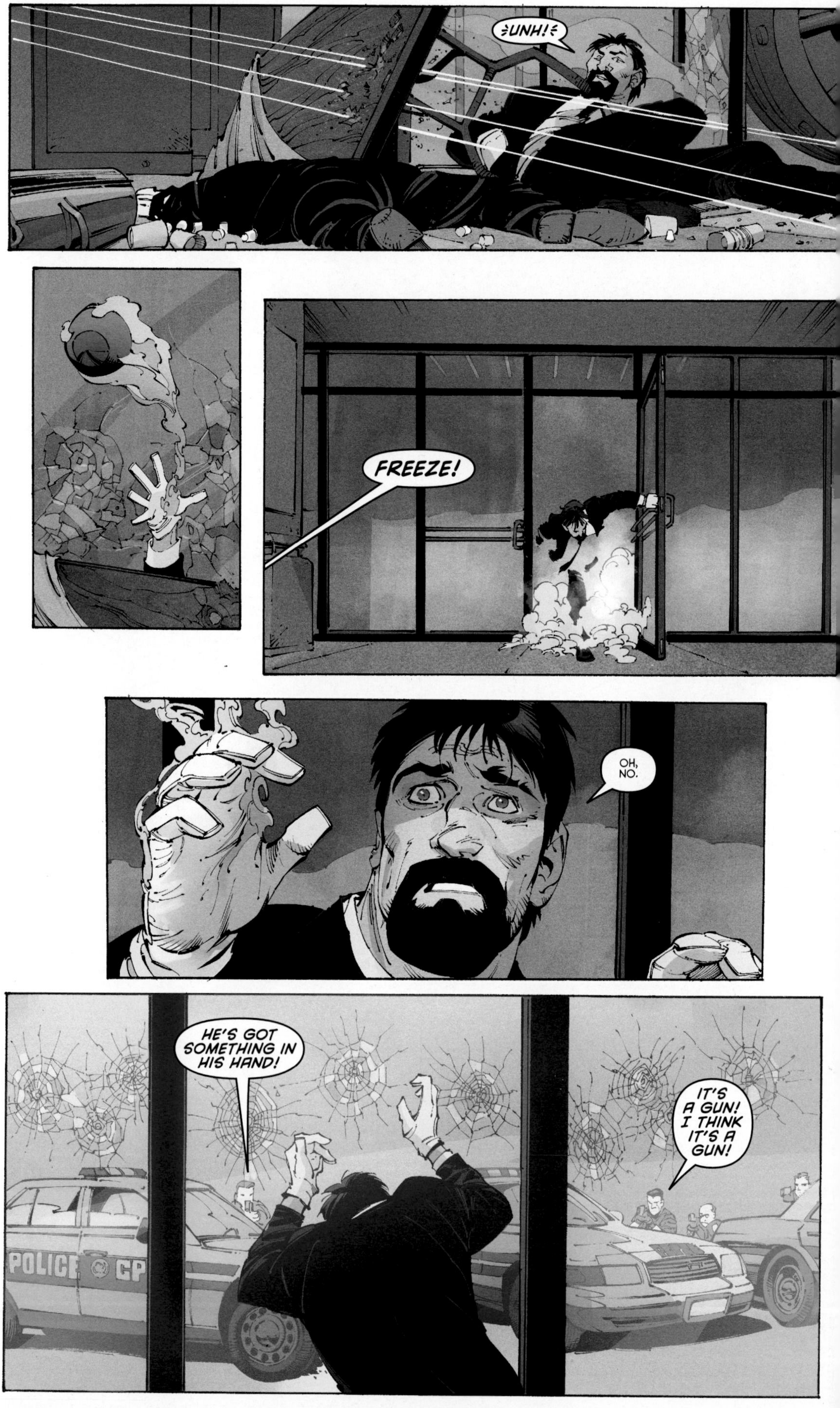
UNH!
FREEZE!
OH, NO.
HE'S GOT SOMETHING IN HIS HAND!
IT'S A GUN! I THINK IT'S A GUN!
POLICE GCPD

WELL, WELL... GOTHAM'S FINEST! KILL THEM ALL!

THEY'RE COMING OUT! FIRE! FIRE!

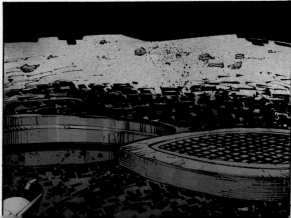

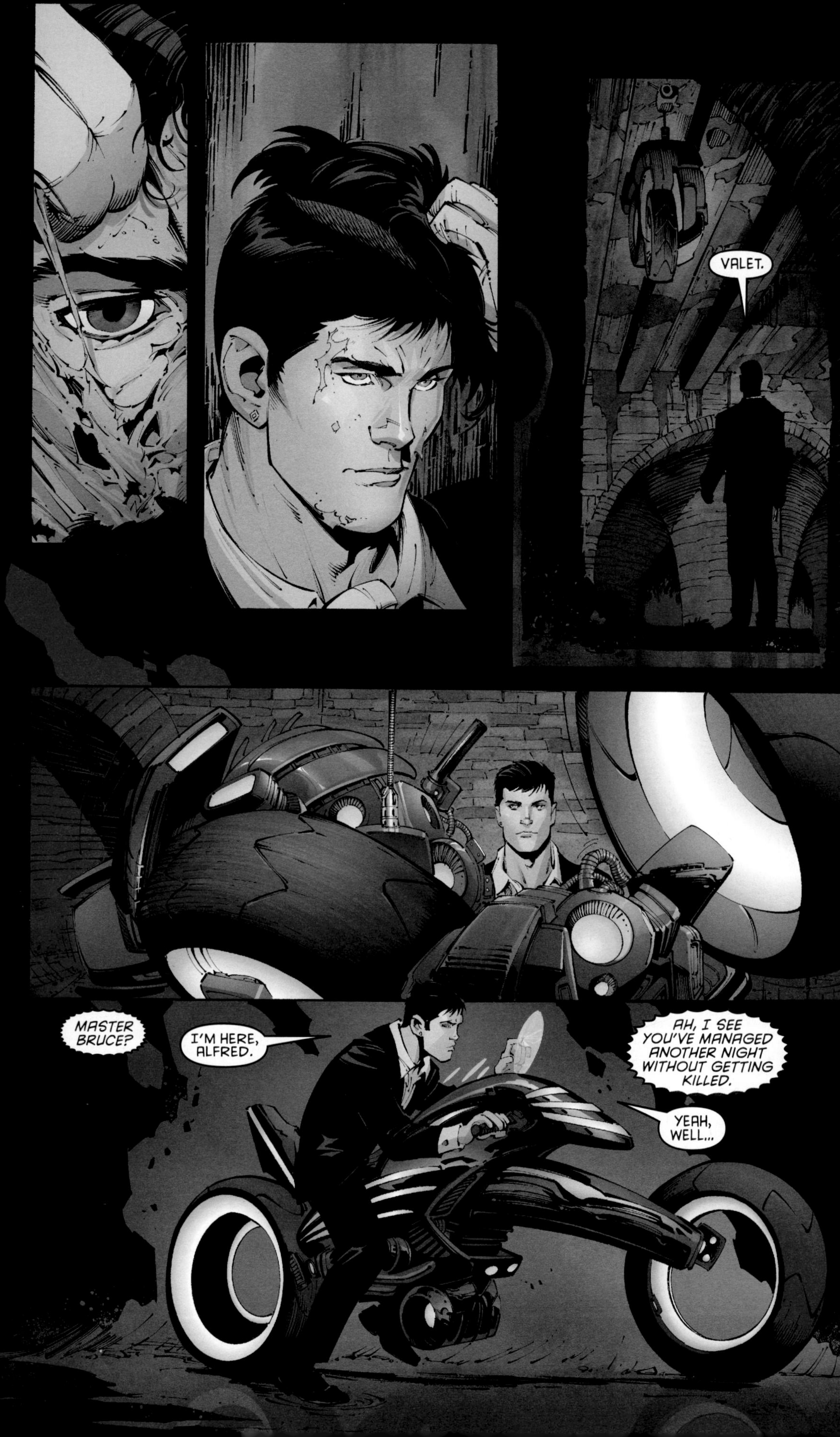
VALET.
MASTER BRUCE?
I'M HERE, ALFRED.
AH, I SEE YOU'VE MANAGED ANOTHER NIGHT WITHOUT GETTING KILLED.
YEAH, WELL...

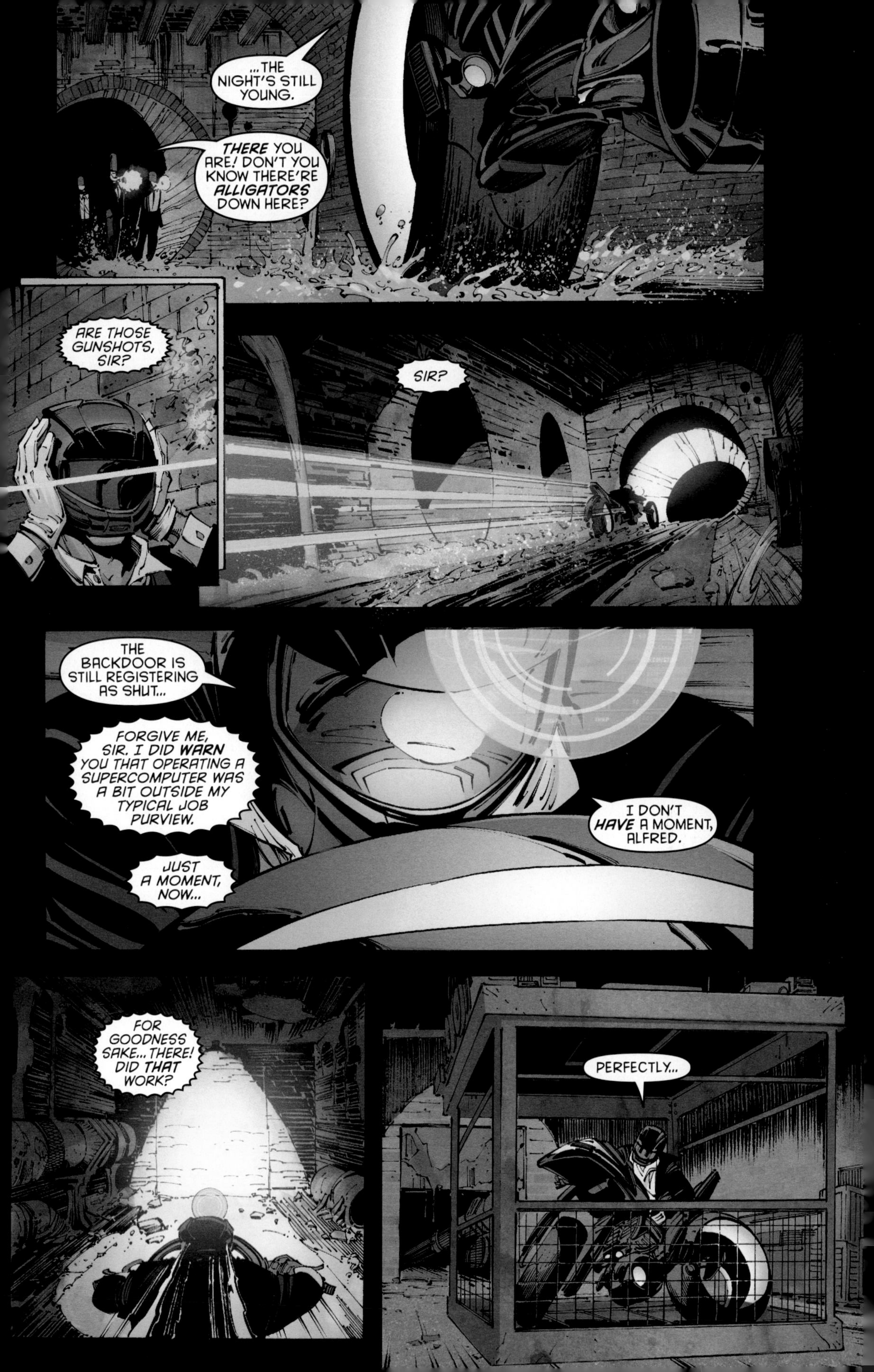
...THE NIGHT'S STILL YOUNG.
THERE YOU ARE! DON'T YOU KNOW THERE'RE ALLIGATORS DOWN HERE?
ARE THOSE GUNSHOTS, SIR?
SIR?
THE BACKDOOR IS STILL REGISTERING AS SHUT...
FORGIVE ME, SIR. I DID WARN YOU THAT OPERATING A SUPERCOMPUTER WAS A BIT OUTSIDE MY TYPICAL JOB PURVIEW.
JUST A MOMENT, NOW...
I DON'T HAVE A MOMENT, ALFRED.
FOR GOODNESS SAKE... THERE! DID THAT WORK?
PERFECTLY...

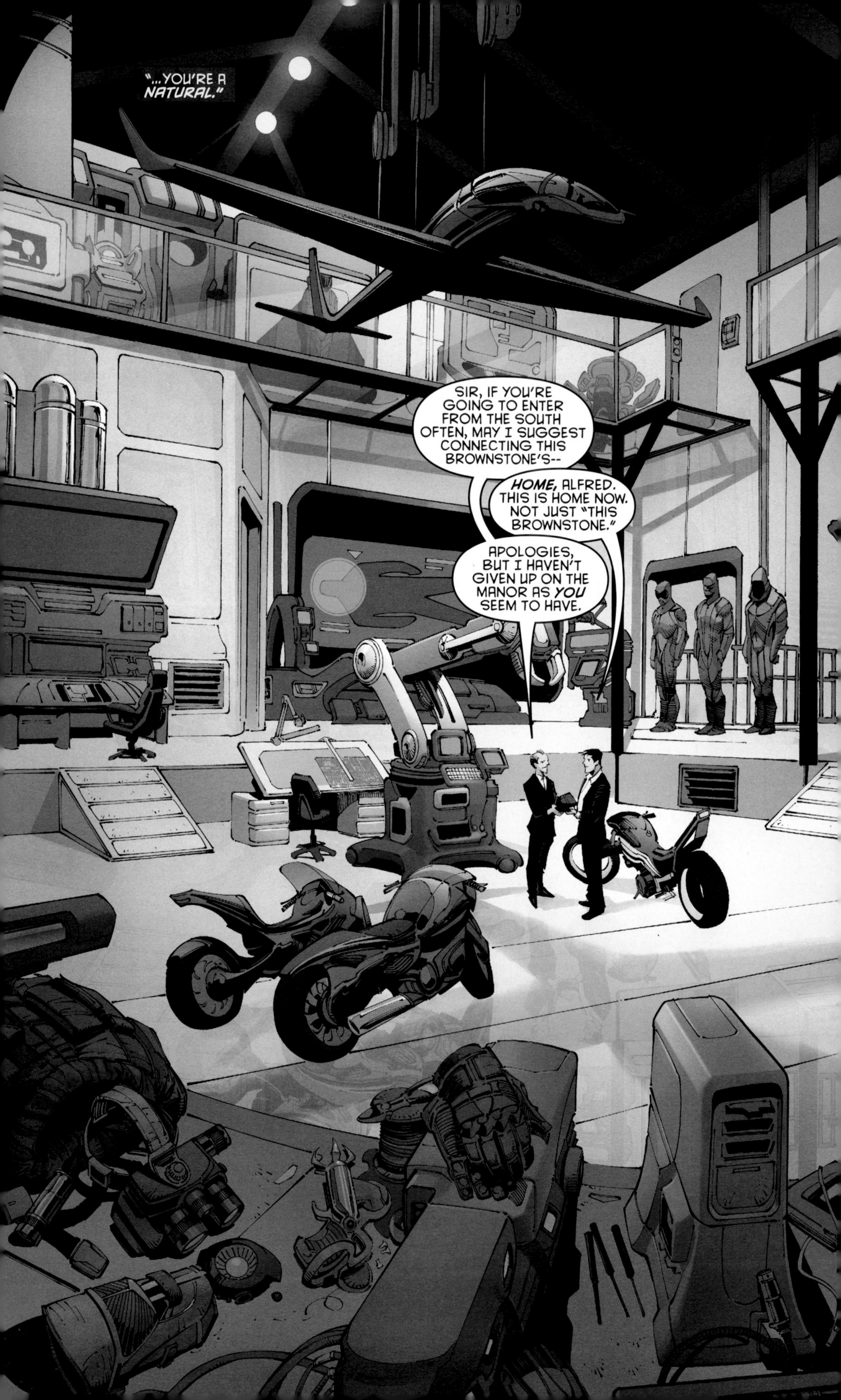
"...YOU'RE A NATURAL."
SIR, IF YOU'RE GOING TO ENTER FROM THE SOUTH OFTEN, MAY I SUGGEST CONNECTING THIS BROWNSTONE'S--
HOME, ALFRED. THIS IS HOME NOW. NOT JUST "THIS BROWNSTONE."
APOLOGIES, BUT I HAVEN'T GIVEN UP ON THE MANOR AS YOU SEEM TO HAVE.

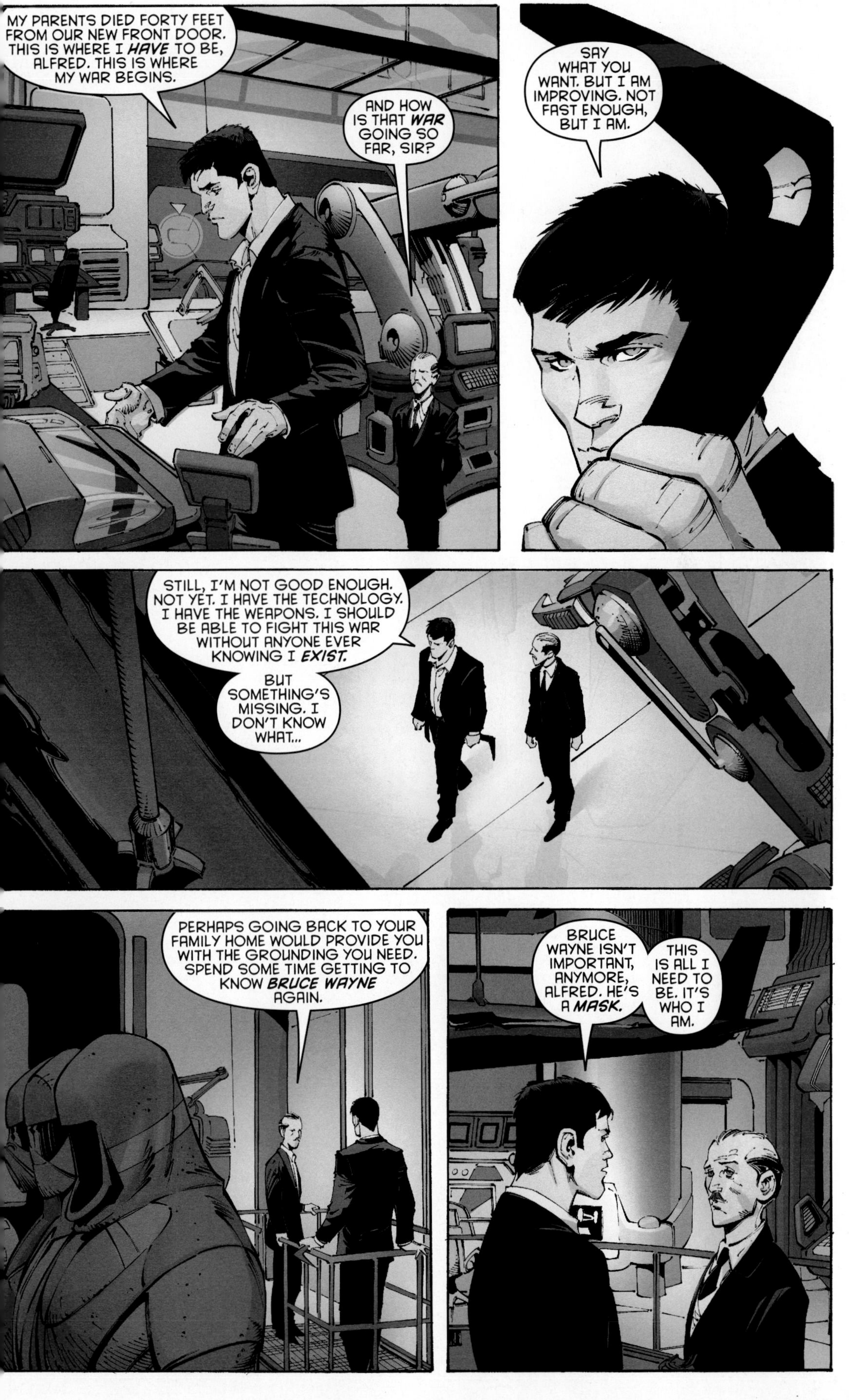

MY PARENTS DIED FORTY FEET FROM OUR NEW FRONT DOOR. THIS IS WHERE I *HAVE* TO BE, ALFRED. THIS IS WHERE MY WAR BEGINS.
AND HOW IS THAT *WAR* GOING SO FAR, SIR?
SAY WHAT YOU WANT. BUT I AM IMPROVING. NOT FAST ENOUGH, BUT I AM.
STILL, I'M NOT GOOD ENOUGH. NOT YET. I HAVE THE TECHNOLOGY. I HAVE THE WEAPONS. I SHOULD BE ABLE TO FIGHT THIS WAR WITHOUT ANYONE EVER KNOWING I *EXIST.*
BUT SOMETHING'S MISSING. I DON'T KNOW WHAT...
PERHAPS GOING BACK TO YOUR FAMILY HOME WOULD PROVIDE YOU WITH THE GROUNDING YOU NEED. SPEND SOME TIME GETTING TO KNOW *BRUCE WAYNE* AGAIN.
BRUCE WAYNE ISN'T IMPORTANT, ANYMORE, ALFRED. HE'S A *MASK.*
THIS IS ALL I NEED TO BE. IT'S WHO I AM.

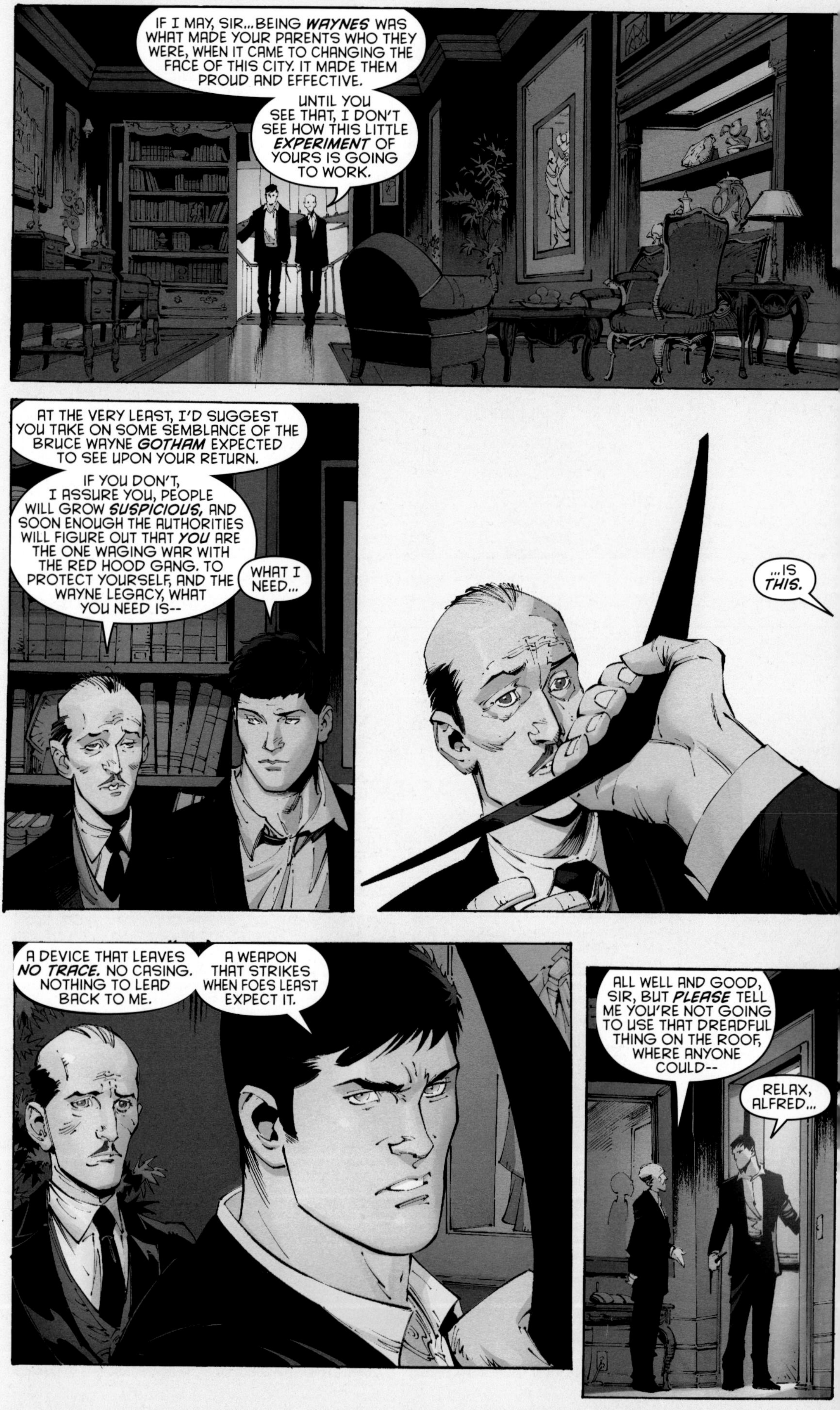
IF I MAY, SIR... BEING WAYNES WAS WHAT MADE YOUR PARENTS WHO THEY WERE, WHEN IT CAME TO CHANGING THE FACE OF THIS CITY. IT MADE THEM PROUD AND EFFECTIVE.
UNTIL YOU SEE THAT, I DON'T SEE HOW THIS LITTLE EXPERIMENT OF YOURS IS GOING TO WORK.
AT THE VERY LEAST, I'D SUGGEST YOU TAKE ON SOME SEMBLANCE OF THE BRUCE WAYNE GOTHAM EXPECTED TO SEE UPON YOUR RETURN.
IF YOU DON'T, I ASSURE YOU, PEOPLE WILL GROW SUSPICIOUS, AND SOON ENOUGH THE AUTHORITIES WILL FIGURE OUT THAT YOU ARE THE ONE WAGING WAR WITH THE RED HOOD GANG. TO PROTECT YOURSELF, AND THE WAYNE LEGACY, WHAT YOU NEED IS--
WHAT I NEED...
...IS THIS.
A DEVICE THAT LEAVES NO TRACE. NO CASING. NOTHING TO LEAD BACK TO ME.
A WEAPON THAT STRIKES WHEN FOES LEAST EXPECT IT.
ALL WELL AND GOOD, SIR, BUT PLEASE TELL ME YOU'RE NOT GOING TO USE THAT DREADFUL THING ON THE ROOF, WHERE ANYONE COULD--
RELAX, ALFRED...

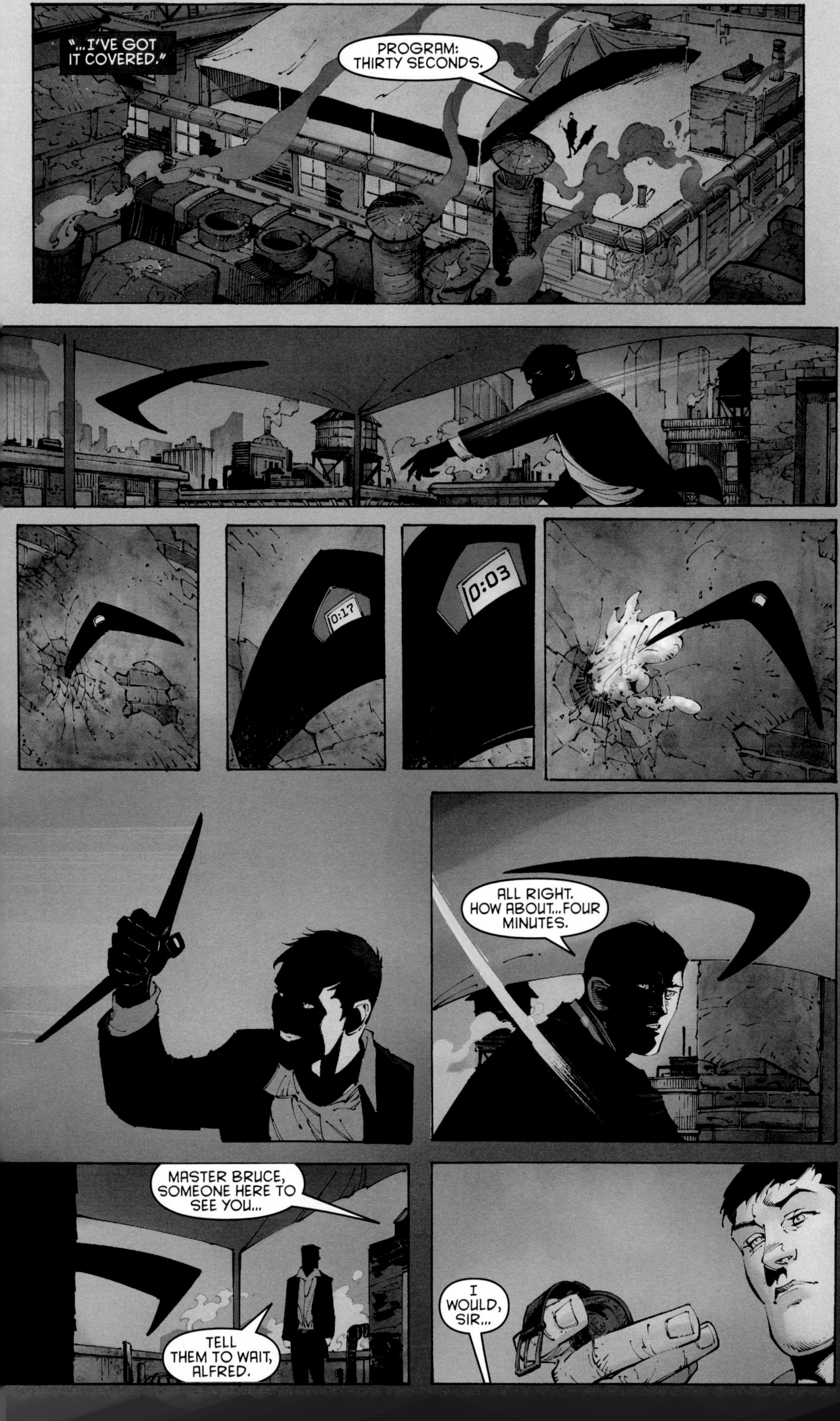
"...I'VE GOT IT COVERED."
PROGRAM: THIRTY SECONDS.
0:17
0:03
ALL RIGHT. HOW ABOUT...FOUR MINUTES.
MASTER BRUCE, SOMEONE HERE TO SEE YOU...
TELL THEM TO WAIT, ALFRED.
I WOULD, SIR...

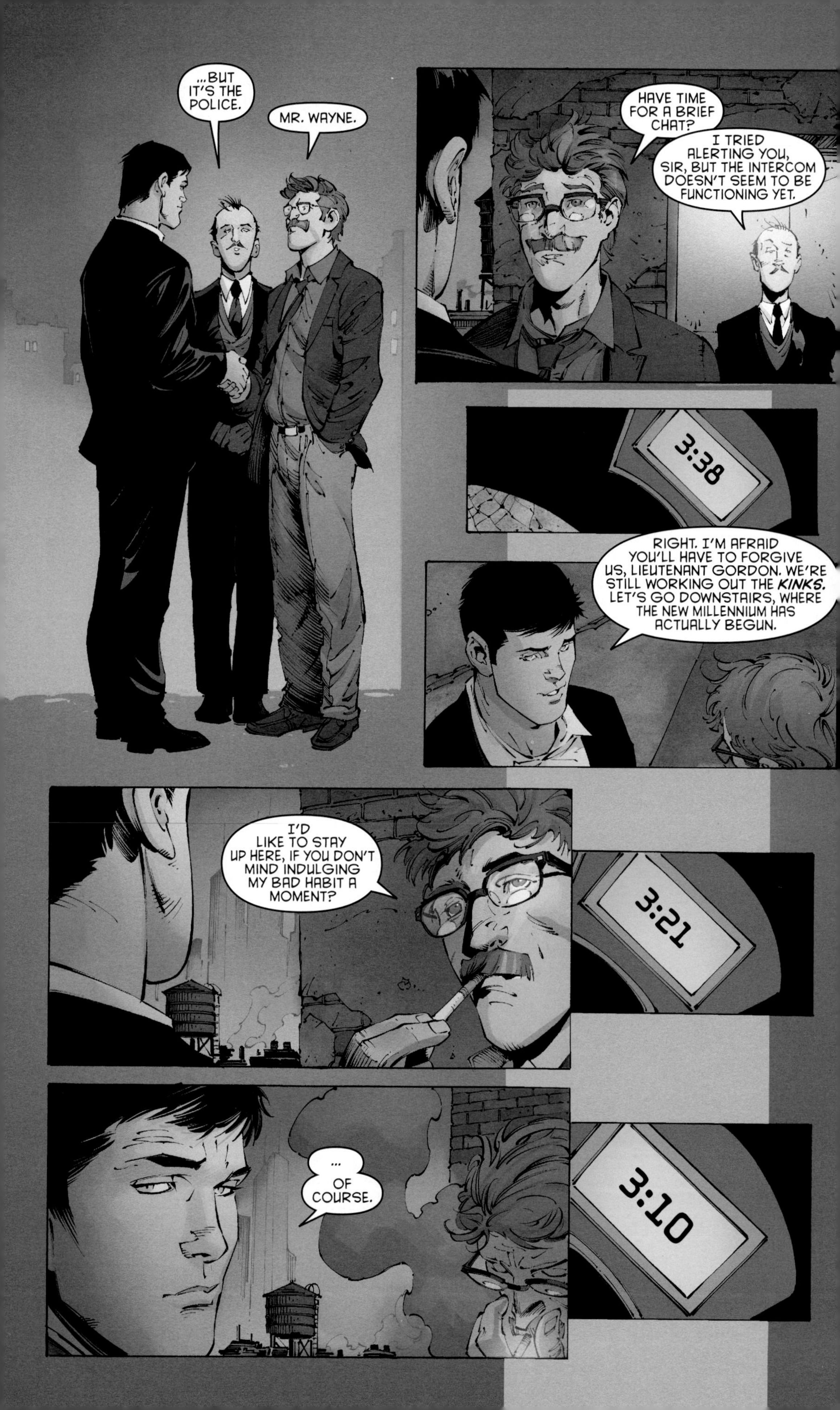

...BUT IT'S THE POLICE.
MR. WAYNE.
HAVE TIME FOR A BRIEF CHAT?
I TRIED ALERTING YOU, SIR, BUT THE INTERCOM DOESN'T SEEM TO BE FUNCTIONING YET.
3:38
RIGHT. I'M AFRAID YOU'LL HAVE TO FORGIVE US, LIEUTENANT GORDON. WE'RE STILL WORKING OUT THE *KINKS.* LET'S GO DOWNSTAIRS, WHERE THE NEW MILLENNIUM HAS ACTUALLY BEGUN.
I'D LIKE TO STAY UP HERE, IF YOU DON'T MIND INDULGING MY BAD HABIT A MOMENT?
3:21
... OF COURSE.
3:10

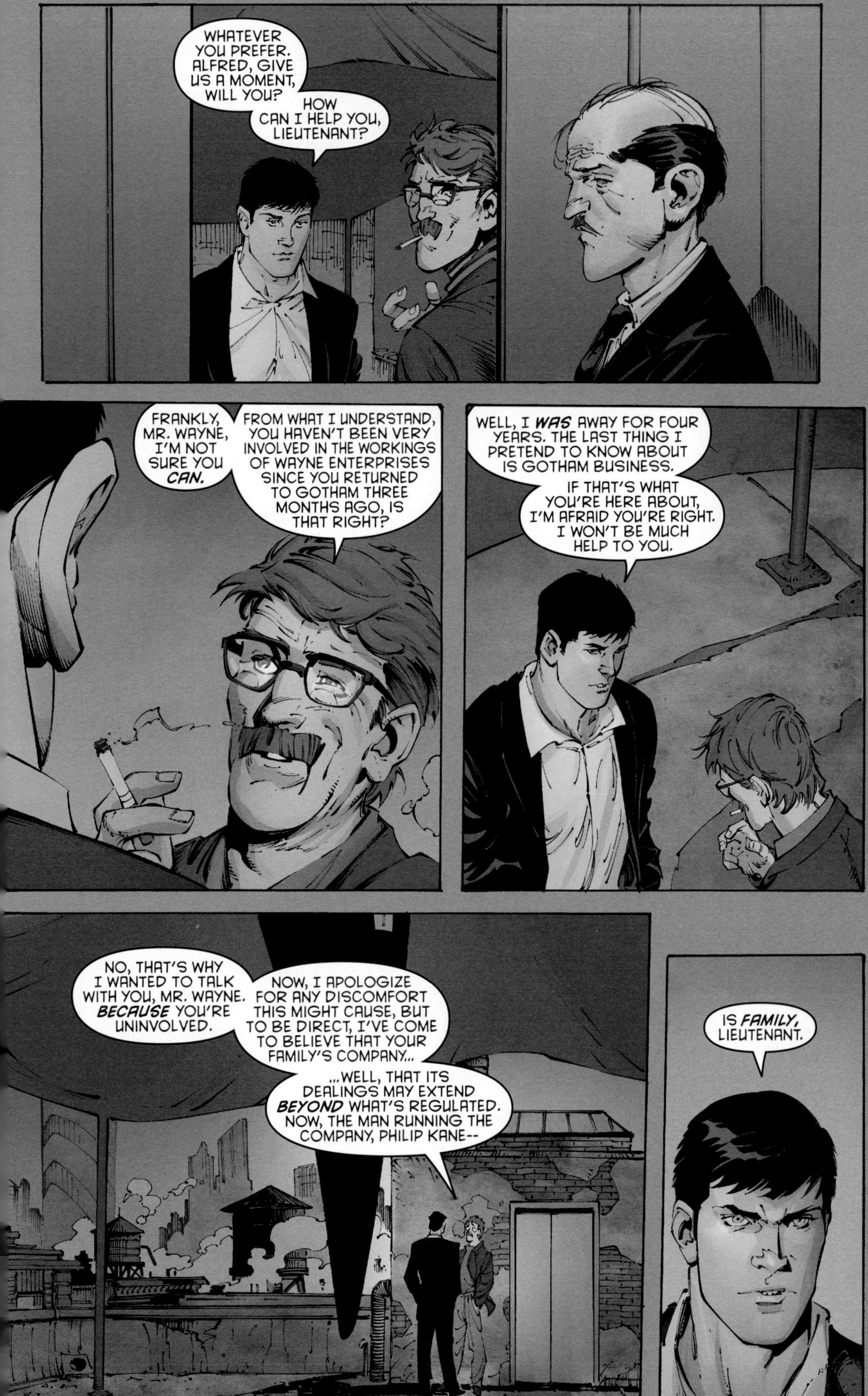
WHATEVER YOU PREFER. ALFRED, GIVE US A MOMENT, WILL YOU?
HOW CAN I HELP YOU, LIEUTENANT?
FRANKLY, MR. WAYNE, I'M NOT SURE YOU CAN.
FROM WHAT I UNDERSTAND, YOU HAVEN'T BEEN VERY INVOLVED IN THE WORKINGS OF WAYNE ENTERPRISES SINCE YOU RETURNED TO GOTHAM THREE MONTHS AGO, IS THAT RIGHT?
WELL, I WAS AWAY FOR FOUR YEARS. THE LAST THING I PRETEND TO KNOW ABOUT IS GOTHAM BUSINESS.
IF THAT'S WHAT YOU'RE HERE ABOUT, I'M AFRAID YOU'RE RIGHT. I WON'T BE MUCH HELP TO YOU.
NO, THAT'S WHY I WANTED TO TALK WITH YOU, MR. WAYNE. BECAUSE YOU'RE UNINVOLVED.
NOW, I APOLOGIZE FOR ANY DISCOMFORT THIS MIGHT CAUSE, BUT TO BE DIRECT, I'VE COME TO BELIEVE THAT YOUR FAMILY'S COMPANY...
...WELL, THAT ITS DEALINGS MAY EXTEND BEYOND WHAT'S REGULATED. NOW, THE MAN RUNNING THE COMPANY, PHILIP KANE--
IS FAMILY, LIEUTENANT.

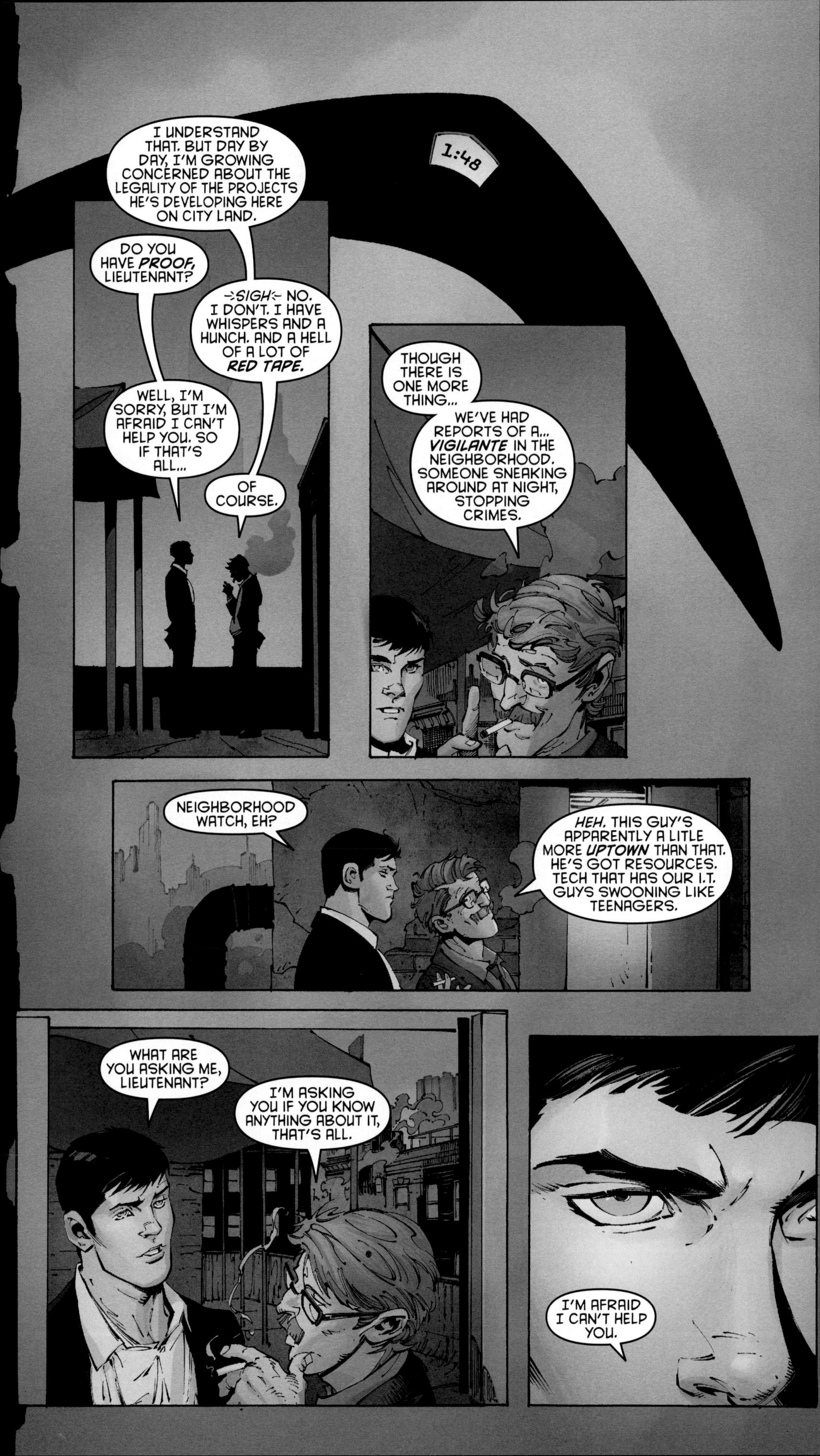

1:48
I UNDERSTAND THAT. BUT DAY BY DAY, I'M GROWING CONCERNED ABOUT THE LEGALITY OF THE PROJECTS HE'S DEVELOPING HERE ON CITY LAND.
DO YOU HAVE PROOF, LIEUTENANT?
-SIGH- NO. I DON'T. I HAVE WHISPERS AND A HUNCH. AND A HELL OF A LOT OF RED TAPE.
WELL, I'M SORRY, BUT I'M AFRAID I CAN'T HELP YOU. SO IF THAT'S ALL...
OF COURSE.
THOUGH THERE IS ONE MORE THING...
WE'VE HAD REPORTS OF A... VIGILANTE IN THE NEIGHBORHOOD. SOMEONE SNEAKING AROUND AT NIGHT, STOPPING CRIMES.
NEIGHBORHOOD WATCH, EH?
HEH. THIS GUY'S APPARENTLY A LITLE MORE UPTOWN THAN THAT. HE'S GOT RESOURCES. TECH THAT HAS OUR I.T. GUYS SWOONING LIKE TEENAGERS.
WHAT ARE YOU ASKING ME, LIEUTENANT?
I'M ASKING YOU IF YOU KNOW ANYTHING ABOUT IT, THAT'S ALL.
I'M AFRAID I CAN'T HELP YOU.

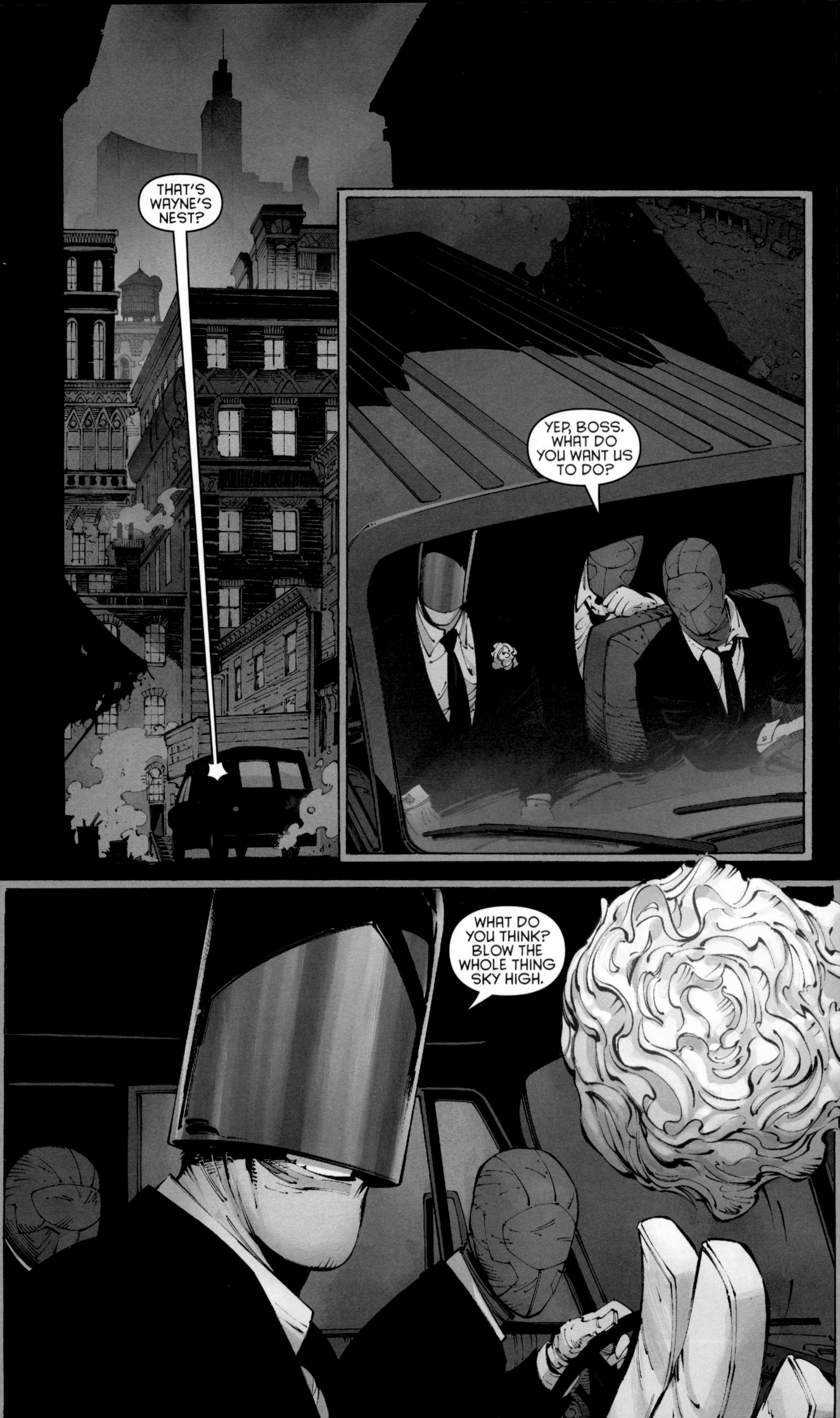
THAT'S WAYNE'S NEST?
YEP, BOSS. WHAT DO YOU WANT US TO DO?
WHAT DO YOU THINK? BLOW THE WHOLE THING SKY HIGH.

THE STORY CONTINUES IN BATMAN : ZERO YEAR

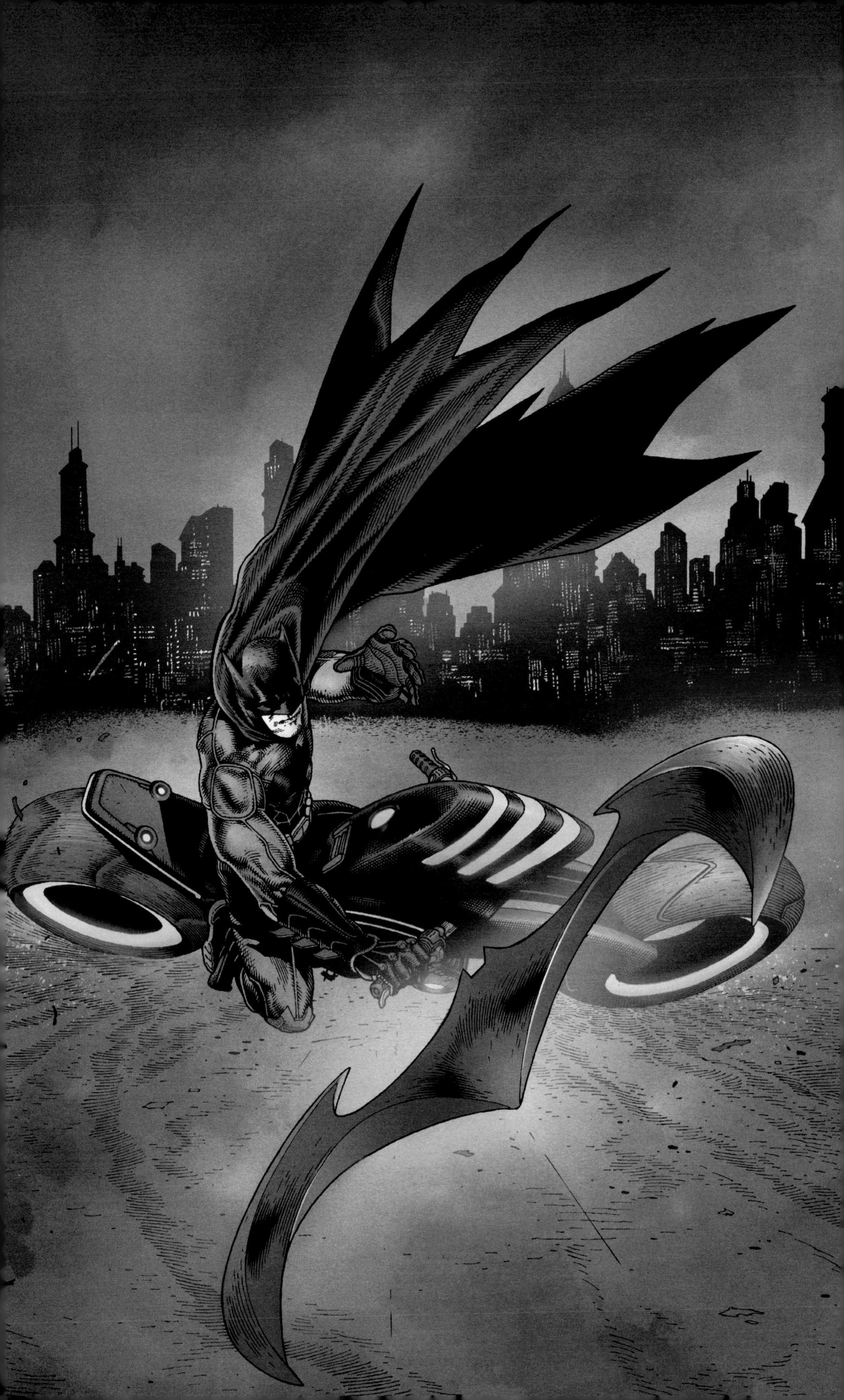

TOMORROW

JAMES TYNION IV writer ANDY CLARKE artist FCO PLASCENCIA colorist variant cover by ANDY CLARKE

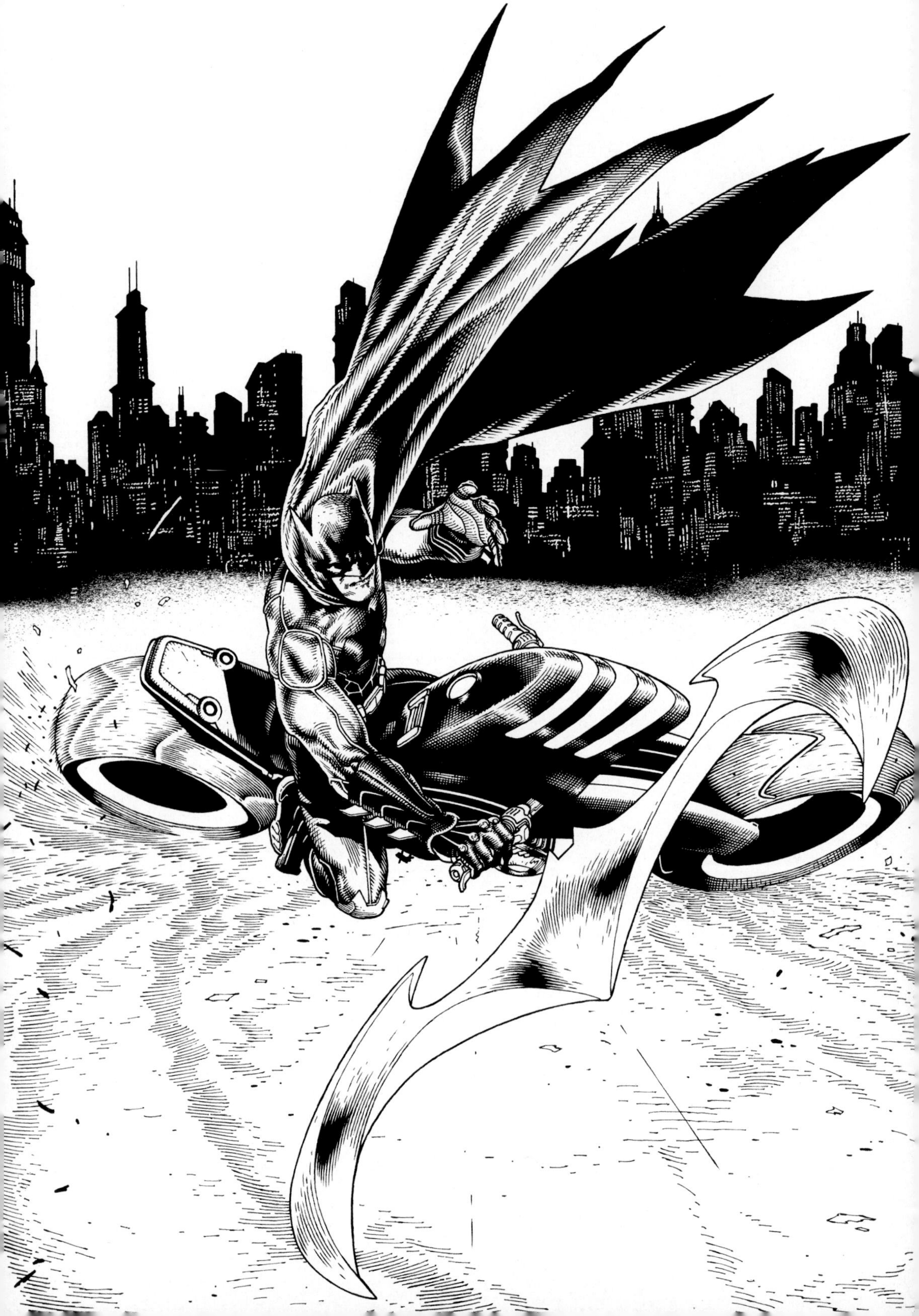

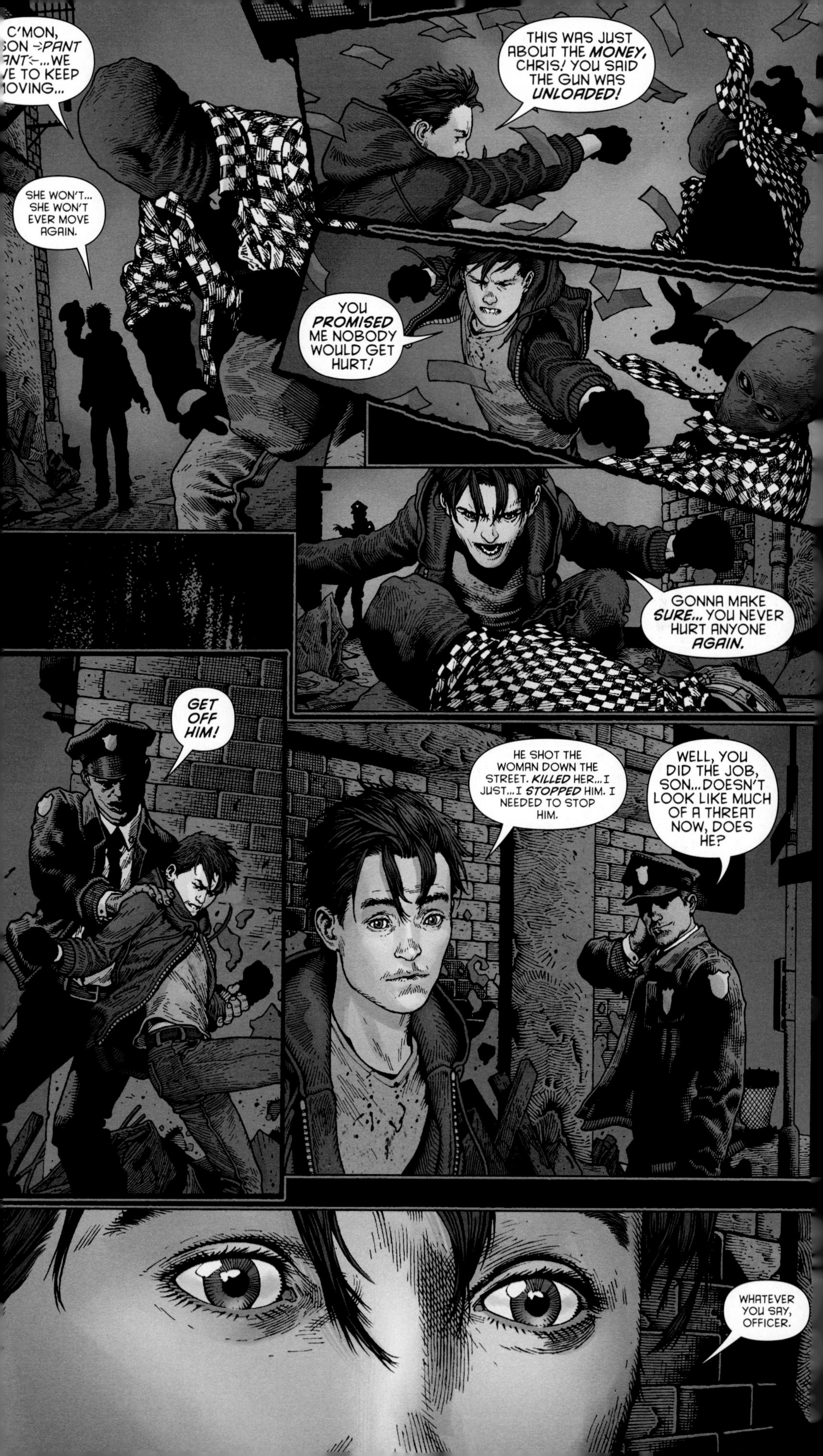

C'MON, SON ⇒PANT ANT⇐...WE VE TO KEEP OVING...
THIS WAS JUST ABOUT THE *MONEY,* CHRIS! YOU SAID THE GUN WAS *UNLOADED!*
SHE WON'T... SHE WON'T EVER MOVE AGAIN.
YOU *PROMISED* ME NOBODY WOULD GET HURT!
GONNA MAKE *SURE...* YOU NEVER HURT ANYONE *AGAIN.*
GET OFF HIM!
HE SHOT THE WOMAN DOWN THE STREET. *KILLED* HER... I JUST... I *STOPPED* HIM. I NEEDED TO STOP HIM.
WELL, YOU DID THE JOB, SON... DOESN'T LOOK LIKE MUCH OF A THREAT NOW, DOES HE?
WHATEVER YOU SAY, OFFICER.

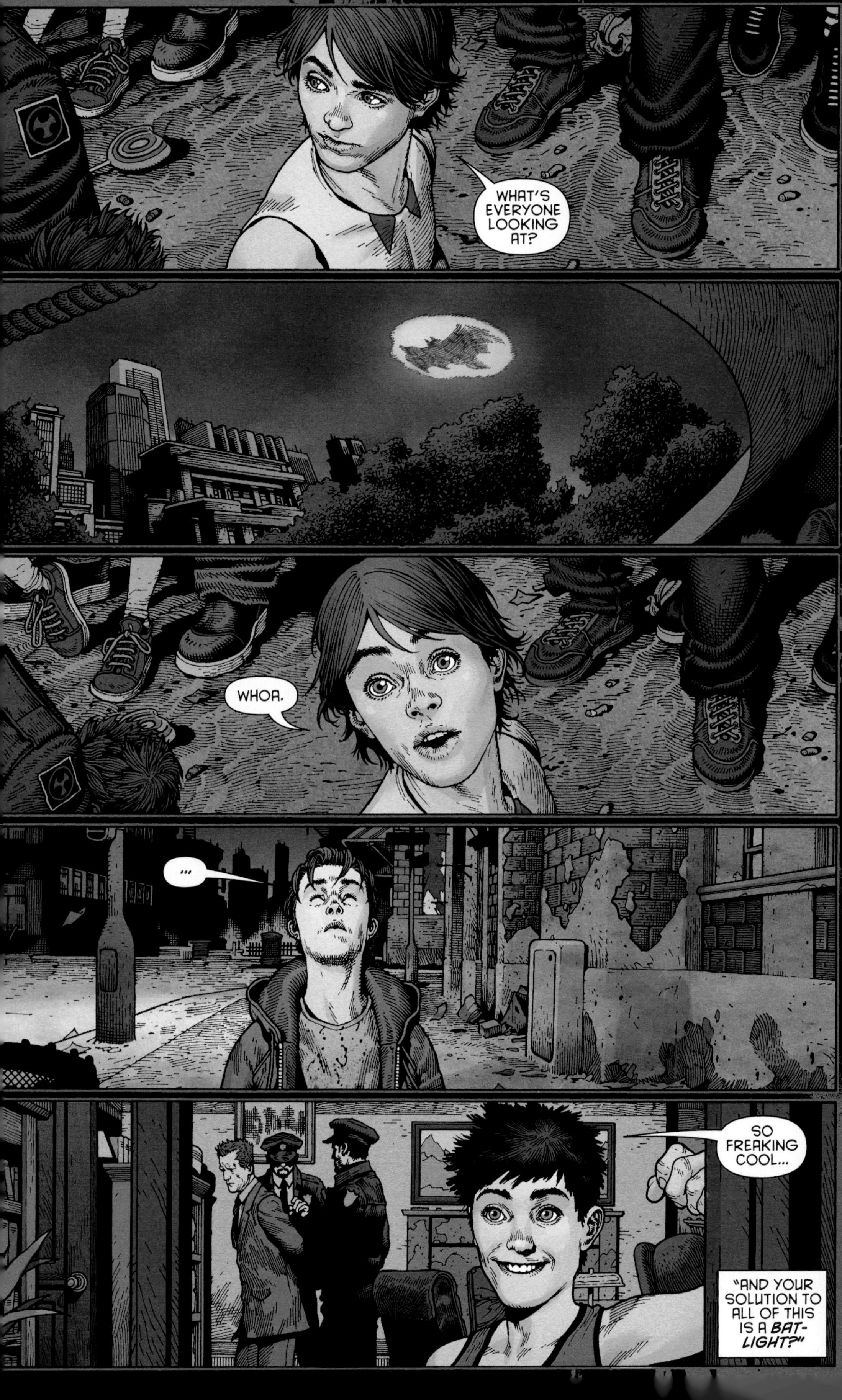

WHAT'S EVERYONE LOOKING AT?
WHOA.
...
SO FREAKING COOL...
"AND YOUR SOLUTION TO ALL OF THIS IS A *BAT-LIGHT?*"

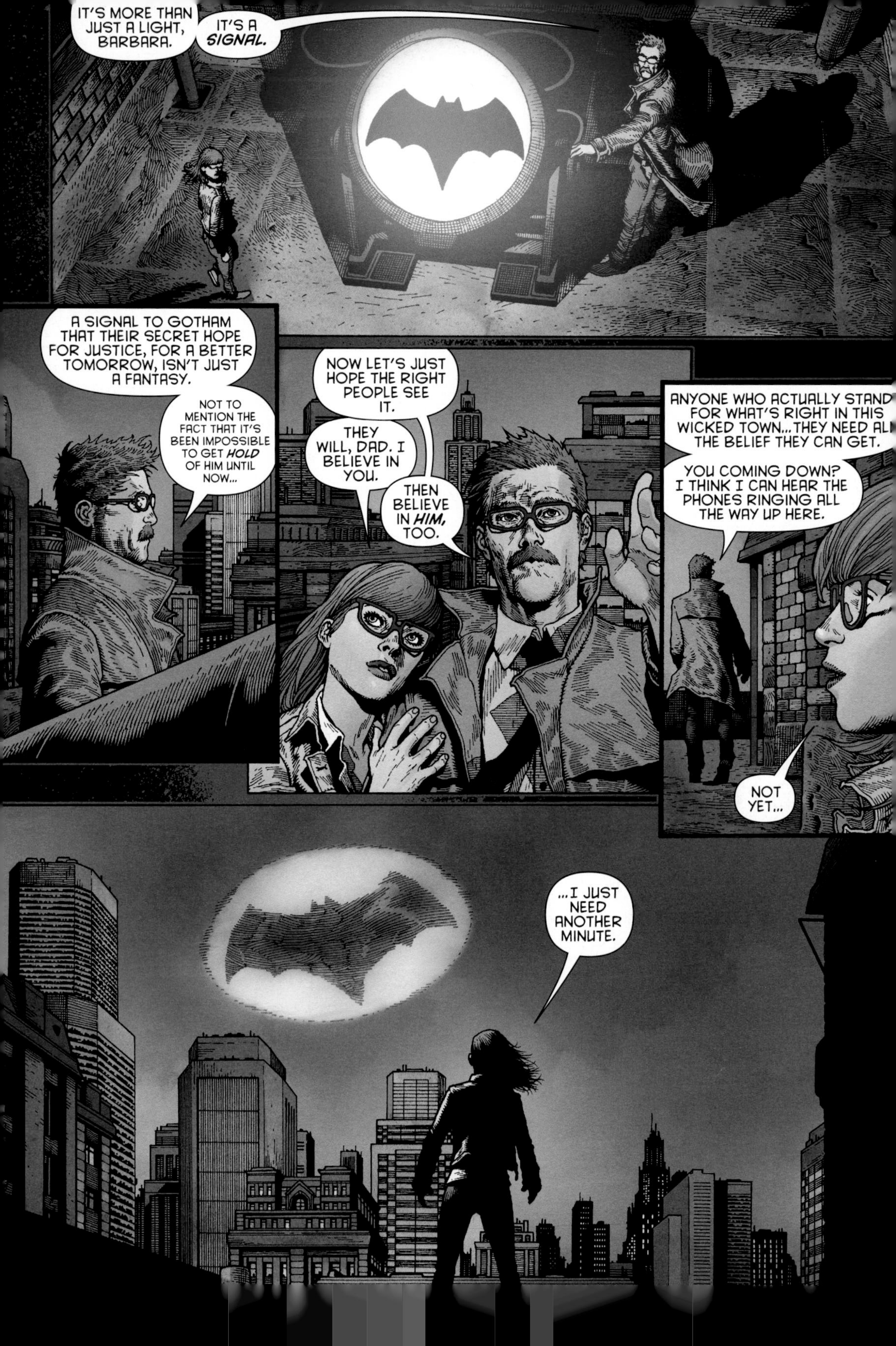
IT'S MORE THAN JUST A LIGHT, BARBARA.
IT'S A SIGNAL.
A SIGNAL TO GOTHAM THAT THEIR SECRET HOPE FOR JUSTICE, FOR A BETTER TOMORROW, ISN'T JUST A FANTASY.
NOT TO MENTION THE FACT THAT IT'S BEEN IMPOSSIBLE TO GET HOLD OF HIM UNTIL NOW...
NOW LET'S JUST HOPE THE RIGHT PEOPLE SEE IT.
THEY WILL, DAD. I BELIEVE IN YOU.
THEN BELIEVE IN HIM, TOO.
ANYONE WHO ACTUALLY STAND FOR WHAT'S RIGHT IN THIS WICKED TOWN... THEY NEED AL THE BELIEF THEY CAN GET.
YOU COMING DOWN? I THINK I CAN HEAR THE PHONES RINGING ALL THE WAY UP HERE.
NOT YET...
...I JUST NEED ANOTHER MINUTE.

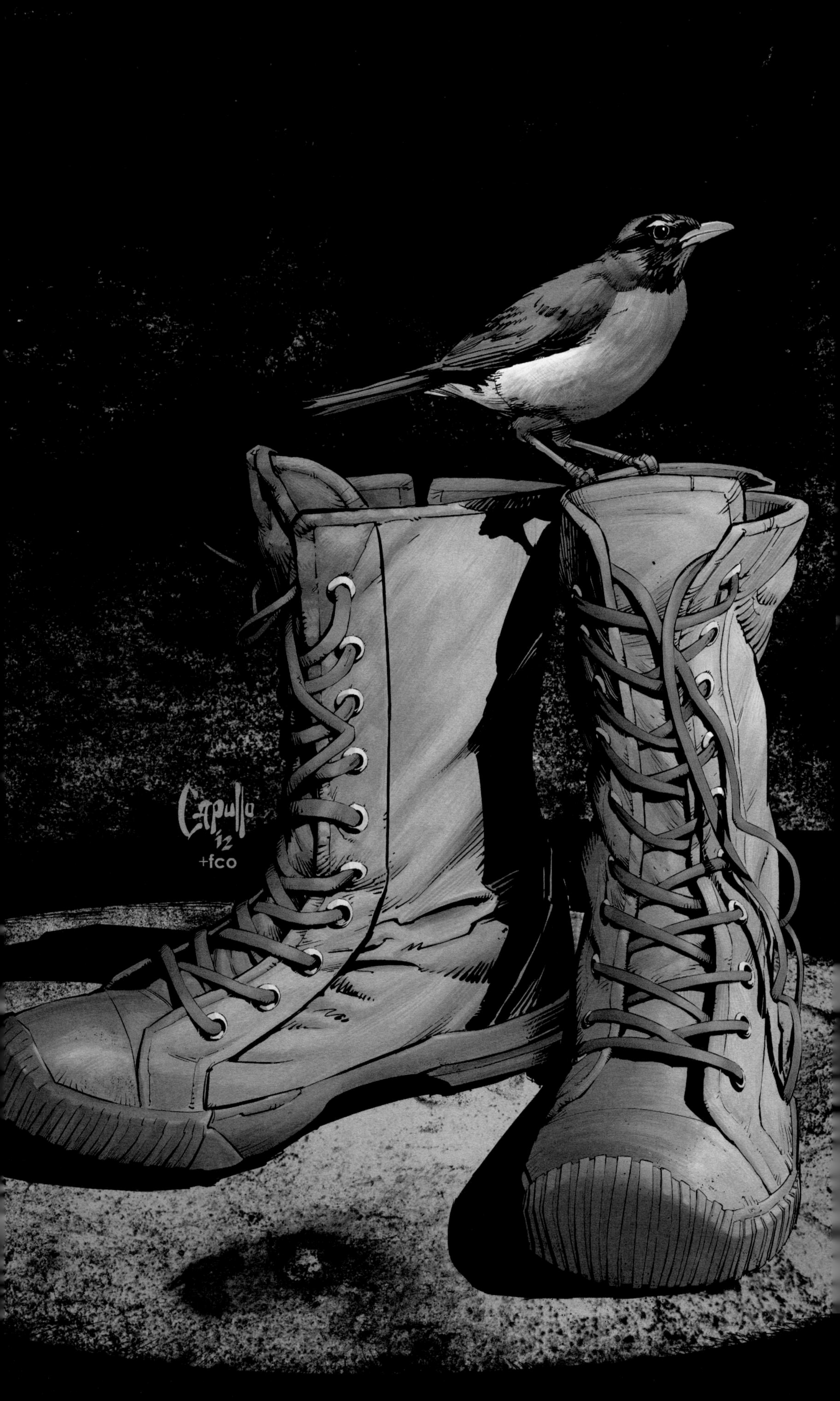
Capullo
'12
+fco

RESOLVE

Chapter One **SCOTT SNYDER** writer **ANDY KUBERT** penciller **SANDRA HOPE** inker **BRAD ANDERSON** colorist
Chapter Two **SCOTT SNYDER JAMES TYNION IV** writers **ALEX MALEEV** artist **NATHAN FAIRBAIRN** colorist
cover by **GREG CAPULLO & FCO PLASCENCIA**

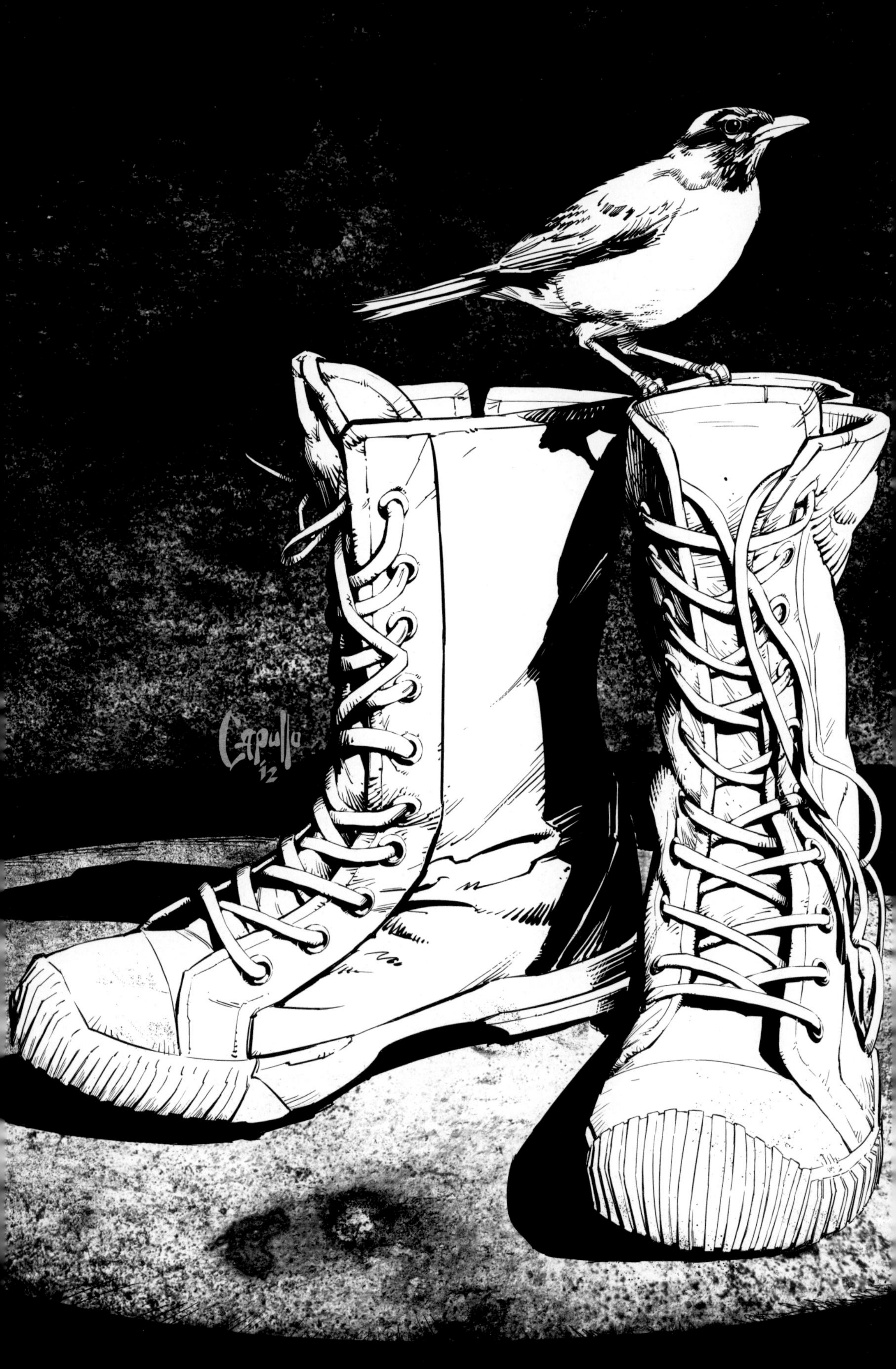
Capullo '12

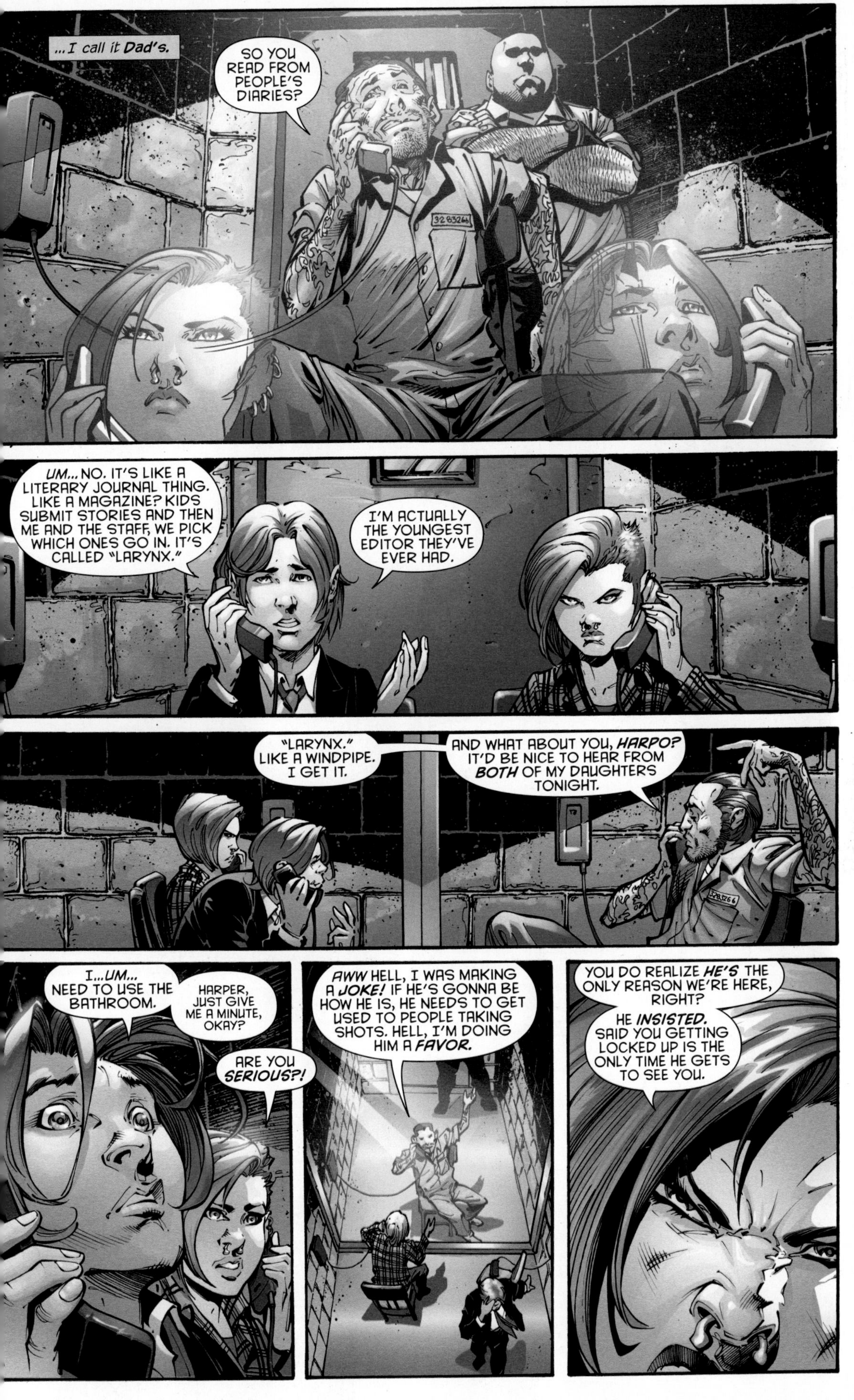

...I call it Dad's.
SO YOU READ FROM PEOPLE'S DIARIES?
UM... NO. IT'S LIKE A LITERARY JOURNAL THING. LIKE A MAGAZINE? KIDS SUBMIT STORIES AND THEN ME AND THE STAFF, WE PICK WHICH ONES GO IN. IT'S CALLED "LARYNX."
I'M ACTUALLY THE YOUNGEST EDITOR THEY'VE EVER HAD.
"LARYNX." LIKE A WINDPIPE. I GET IT.
AND WHAT ABOUT YOU, HARPO? IT'D BE NICE TO HEAR FROM BOTH OF MY DAUGHTERS TONIGHT.
I...UM... NEED TO USE THE BATHROOM.
HARPER, JUST GIVE ME A MINUTE, OKAY?
ARE YOU SERIOUS?!
AWW HELL, I WAS MAKING A JOKE! IF HE'S GONNA BE HOW HE IS, HE NEEDS TO GET USED TO PEOPLE TAKING SHOTS. HELL, I'M DOING HIM A FAVOR.
YOU DO REALIZE HE'S THE ONLY REASON WE'RE HERE, RIGHT?
HE INSISTED. SAID YOU GETTING LOCKED UP IS THE ONLY TIME HE GETS TO SEE YOU.

WHAT DID YOU DO TO GET IN HERE THIS TIME, ANYWAYS?

Pfft. LIKE YOU DON'T KNOW.

WHAT THE HELL IS *THAT* SUPPOSED TO MEAN?!

LOOK, I DON'T KNOW HOW YOU GOT YOUR *SPECIAL FRIEND* TO TARGET ME, BUT TELL HIM TO LAY OFF! YOU KNOW I'M SMALL FRY. HE SHOULD, TOO.

WHAT DO YOU MEAN MY *"SPECIAL FRIEND"*?

HEH, YOU LOOK JUST LIKE YOUR *MOTHER* WHEN YOU MAKE THAT FACE.

DON'T YOU *DARE* TALK ABOUT MY MOTHER!

HON, YOUR MOM WAS *HARDLY* THE SAINT YOU THINK SHE WAS. YOU KNOW DAMN WELL THE THINGS SHE DID--

TIME'S UP, MARCUS.

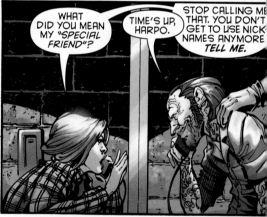

WHAT DID YOU MEAN MY *"SPECIAL FRIEND"*?

TIME'S UP, HARPO.

STOP CALLING ME THAT. YOU DON'T GET TO USE NICK-NAMES ANYMORE *TELL ME.*

MAYBE NEXT TIME, KID. GOTTA REST THE OLD *LARYNX.*

So, maybe this isn't the very definition of "safe," but I don't want to get Cullen any more upset than he already is.

I've been tracking *Batman* through Gotham for months. Ever since he told me in no uncertain terms to stop.

BEEEEEEP

Never have been all that good about people telling me what to do, really. And how *could* I stop?

It doesn't matter how many times he keeps moving his *black boxes* or encrypting his *code*. If Batman's electric footprint touches Gotham's grid...I can find him.

CLINK

Presuming I can get there, that is. Moving rooftop to rooftop isn't exactly the *easiest thing in the world.*

But these last few nights, I haven't been able to stop myself. If I'm being honest, it's because I'm worried. I've never seen him like this before.

And I'm *terrified* of what might happen next.

ANY MINUTE NOW...

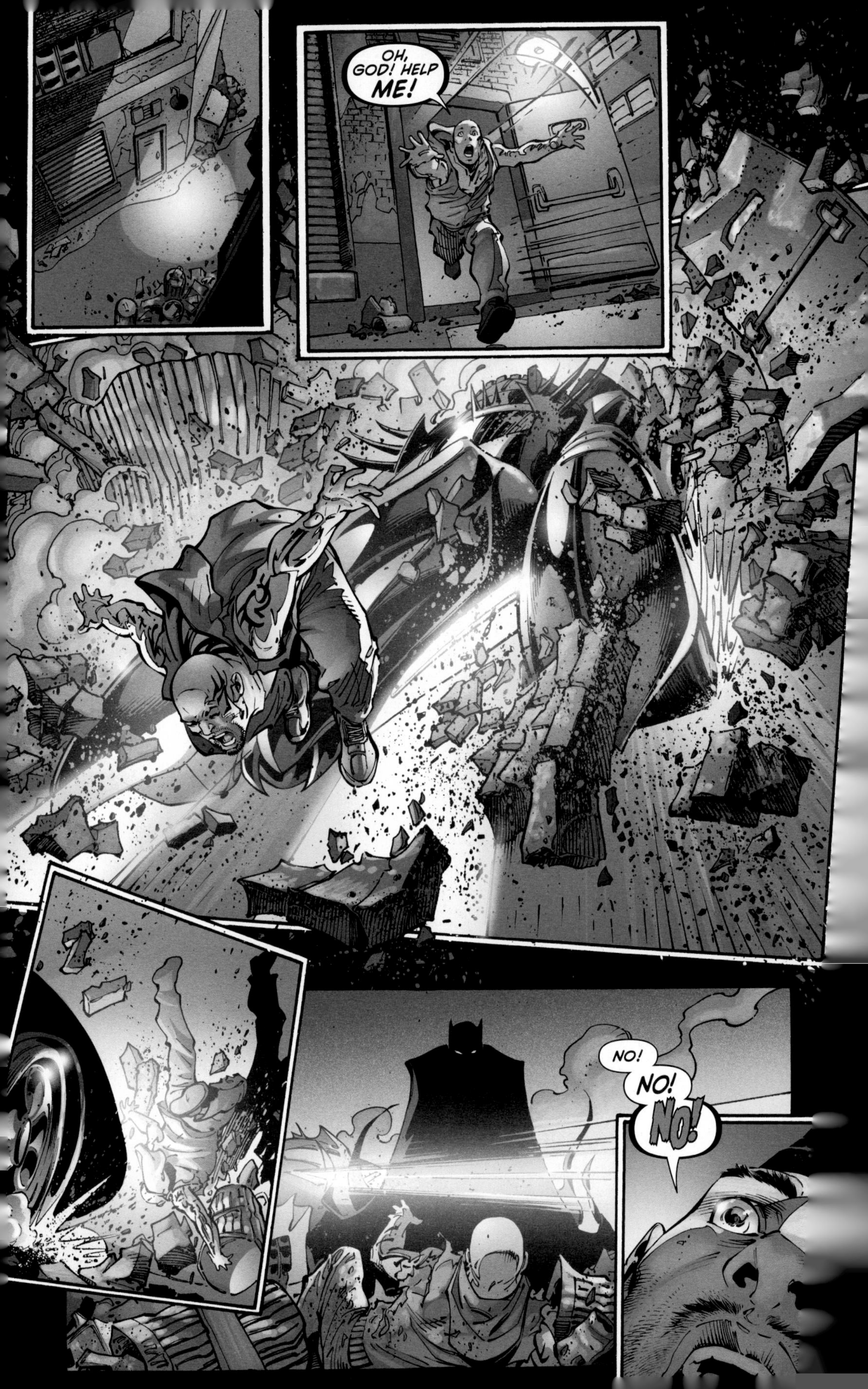
OH, GOD! HELP ME!
NO!
NO!
NO!

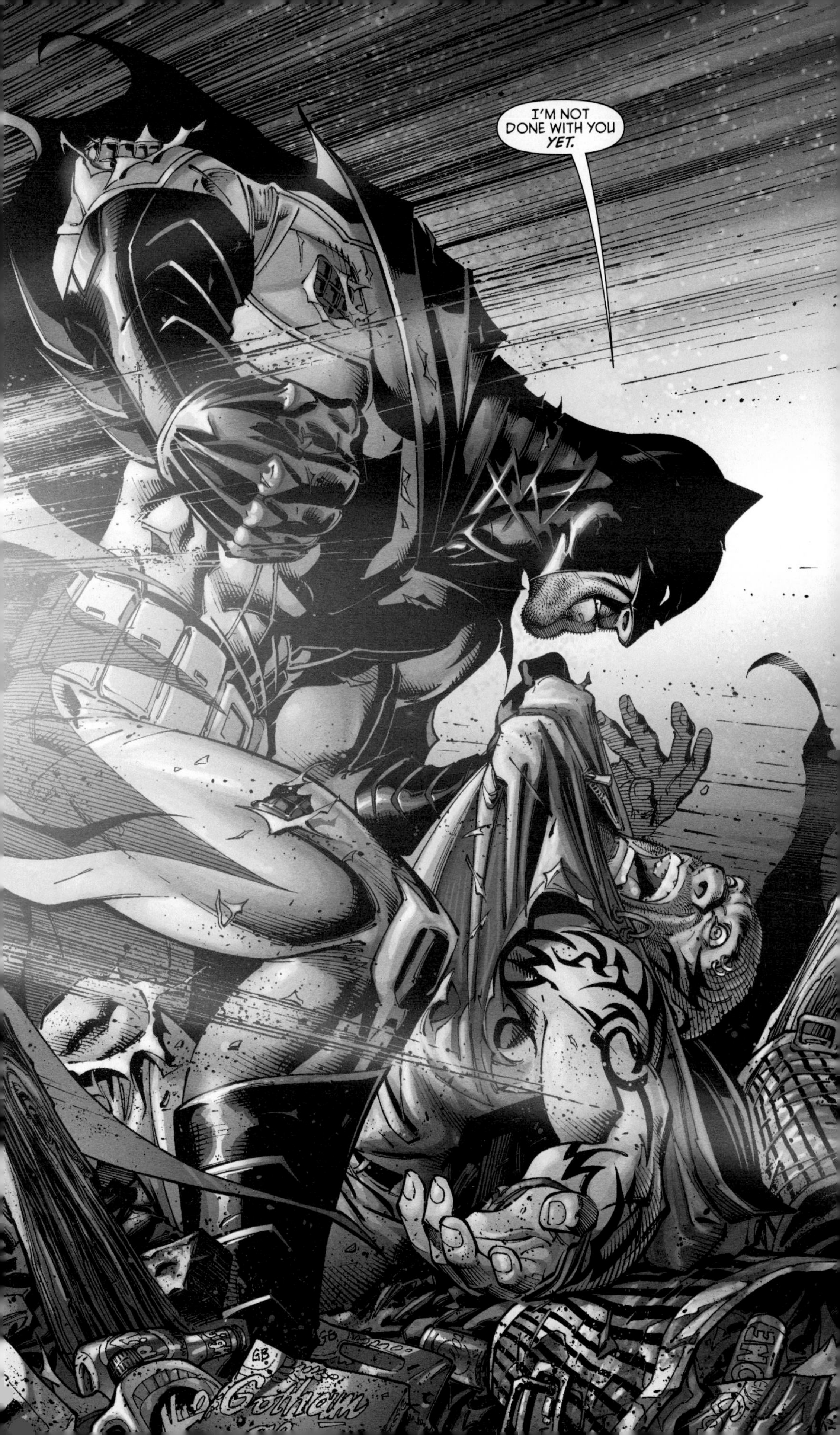
I'M NOT DONE WITH YOU *YET.*
Gotham

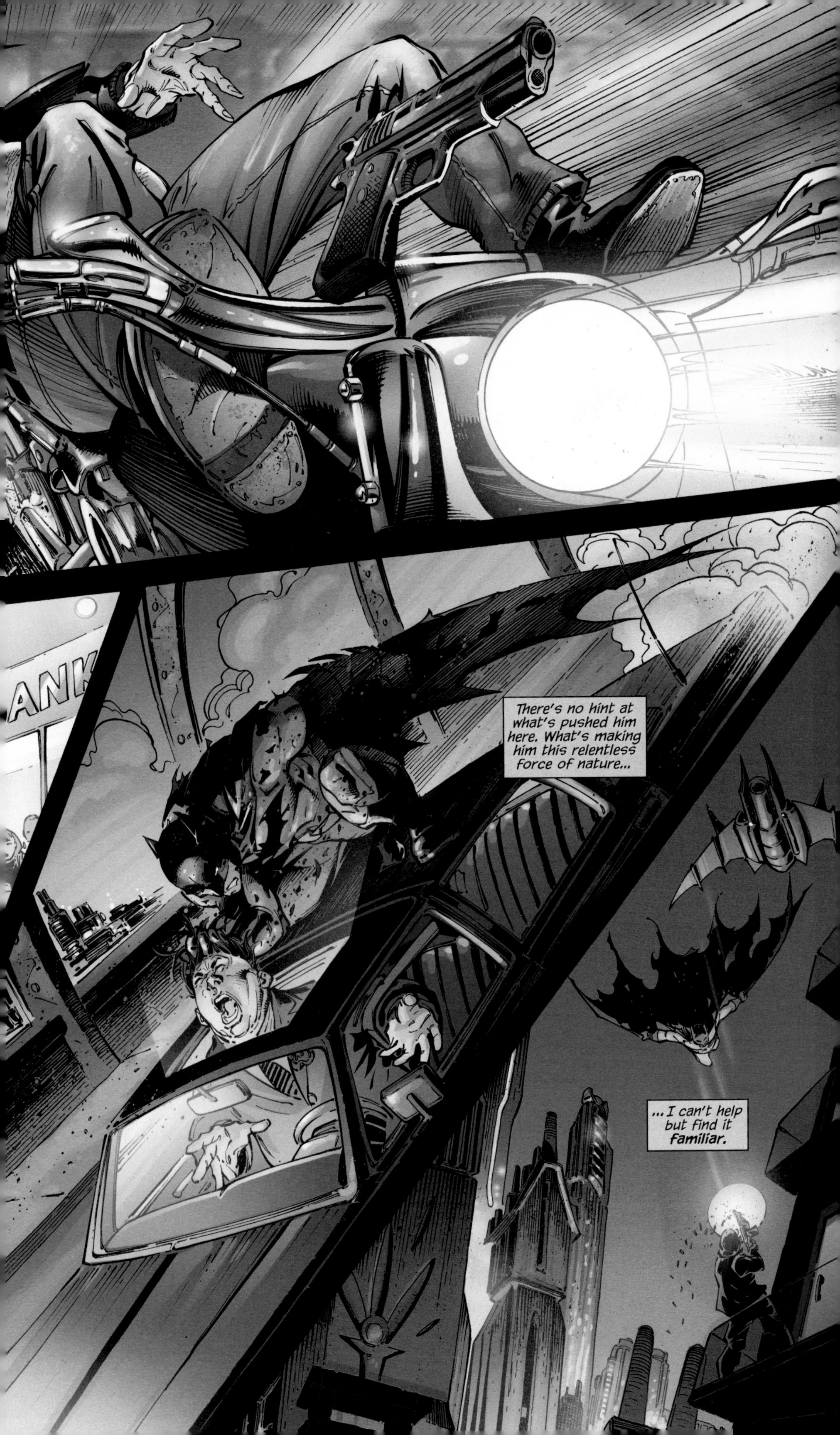
There's no hint at what's pushed him here. What's making him this relentless force of nature...
...I can't help but find it **familiar**.

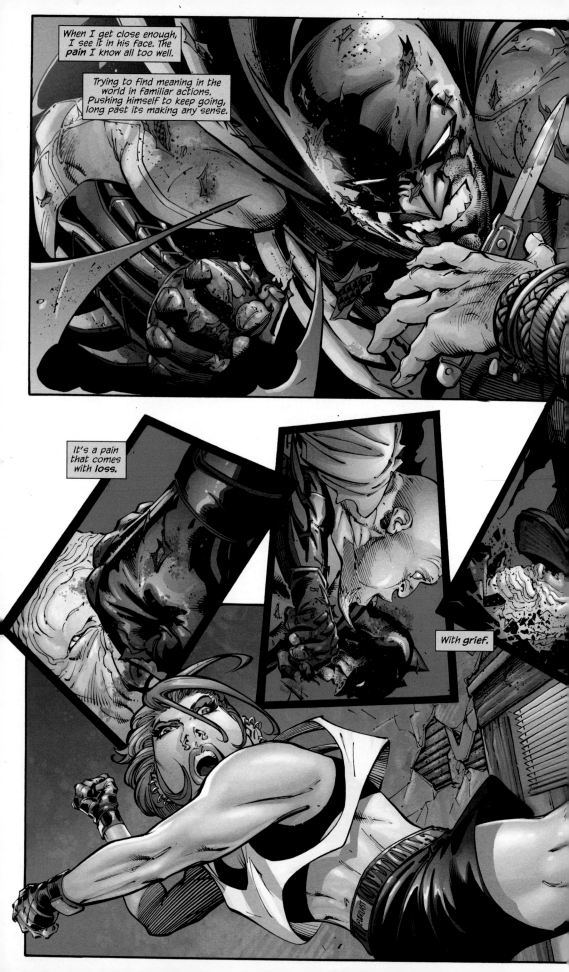

WAIT, WHAT ARE WE *TALKING* ABOUT?

BATMAN, CULLEN. WE'RE ALWAYS TALKING ABOUT BATMAN. THIS TIME IS NO *DIFFERENT.*

WELL, I'M NOT EXACTLY SURE THAT YOU WATCHING HIM FOR A FEW MONTHS MAKES YOU AN *EXPERT.*

I'M BEING *SERIOUS!*

EVERY DAY IT'S A LITTLE WORSE. YESTERDAY, I SAW HIM GET STABBED IN THE LEG BY A MUGGER...

I'M SURE HE GETS HIT LIKE THAT ALL THE TIME.

BY NINJA CYBORG ASSASSINS! NOT HALF-DRUNK, BACK ALLEY MUGGERS!

THE IDEA THAT SOME *NOBODY* COULD GET THAT CLOSE, AND HURT HIM...ACTUALLY *HURT* HIM...IT'S *TERRIFYING.*

HE'S *BATMAN!* HE'S GOING TO BE FINE.

YOU HAVEN'T SEEN HIM, CULLEN. HE'S GETTING SLOWER. HE'S MISSING PUNCHES... AND SO FAR HE'S JUST BEEN RUNNING UP AGAINST LOW-RENT

BUT ONE OF THESE NIGHTS, THAT WON'T BE THE

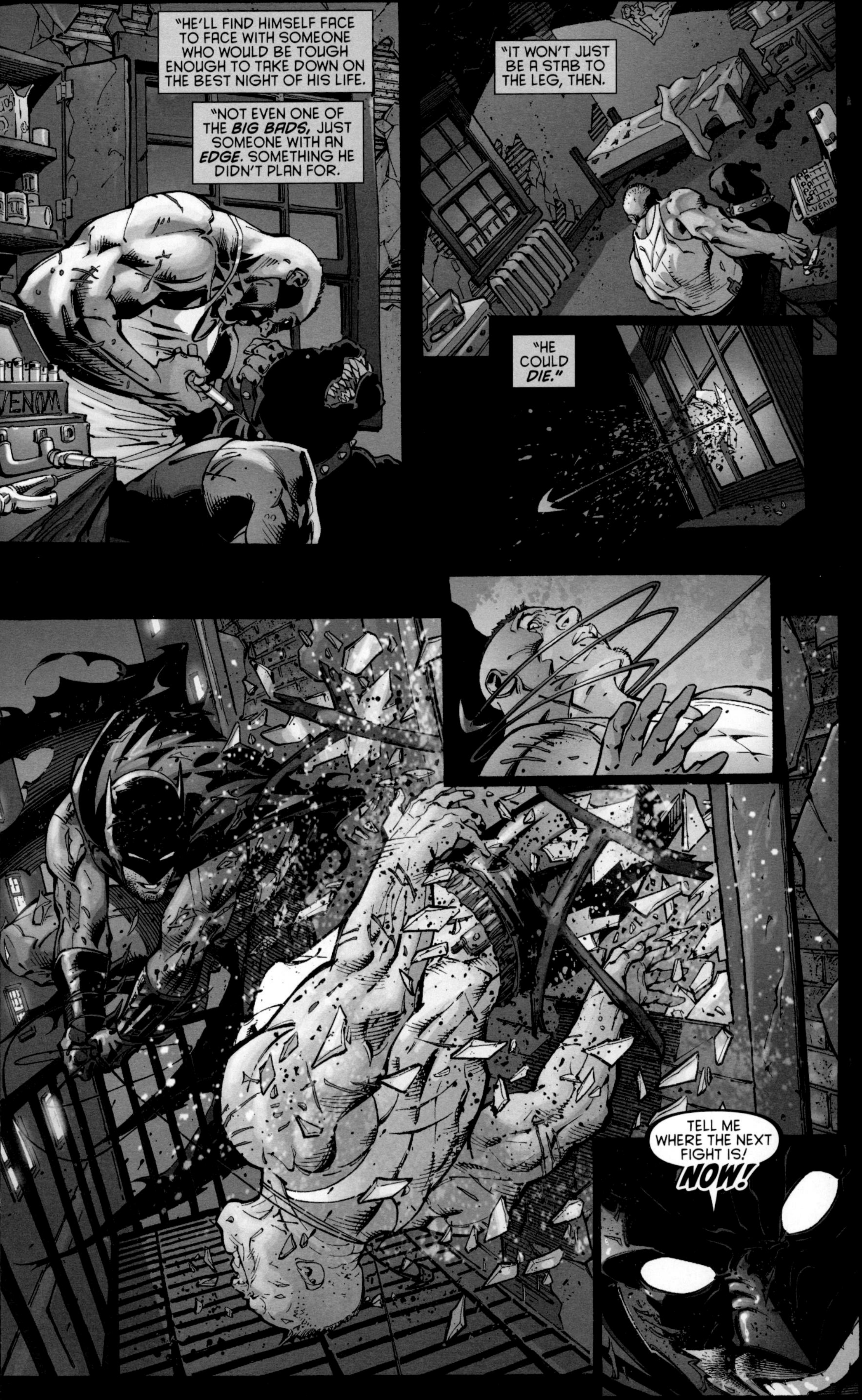
"HE'LL FIND HIMSELF FACE TO FACE WITH SOMEONE WHO WOULD BE TOUGH ENOUGH TO TAKE DOWN ON THE BEST NIGHT OF HIS LIFE.
"NOT EVEN ONE OF THE *BIG BADS,* JUST SOMEONE WITH AN *EDGE*. SOMETHING HE DIDN'T PLAN FOR.
VENOM
"IT WON'T JUST BE A STAB TO THE LEG, THEN.
"HE COULD *DIE."*
TELL ME WHERE THE NEXT FIGHT IS! NOW!

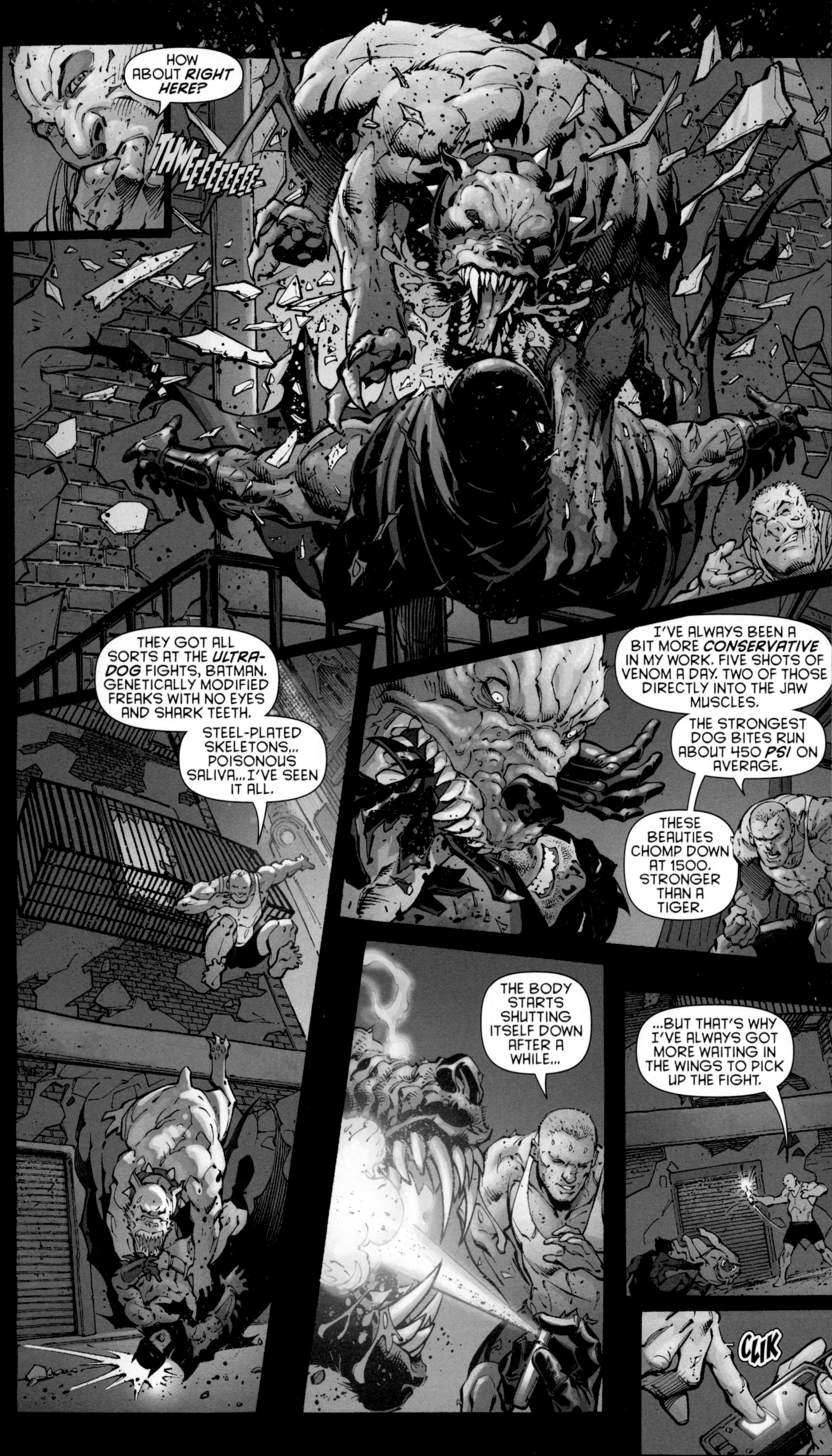
HOW ABOUT RIGHT HERE?
THWEEEEEEEEE
THEY GOT ALL SORTS AT THE ULTRA-DOG FIGHTS, BATMAN. GENETICALLY MODIFIED FREAKS WITH NO EYES AND SHARK TEETH.
STEEL-PLATED SKELETONS... POISONOUS SALIVA... I'VE SEEN IT ALL.
I'VE ALWAYS BEEN A BIT MORE CONSERVATIVE IN MY WORK. FIVE SHOTS OF VENOM A DAY. TWO OF THOSE DIRECTLY INTO THE JAW MUSCLES.
THE STRONGEST DOG BITES RUN ABOUT 450 PSI ON AVERAGE.
THESE BEAUTIES CHOMP DOWN AT 1500. STRONGER THAN A TIGER.
THE BODY STARTS SHUTTING ITSELF DOWN AFTER A WHILE...
...BUT THAT'S WHY I'VE ALWAYS GOT MORE WAITING IN THE WINGS TO PICK UP THE FIGHT.
CLIK

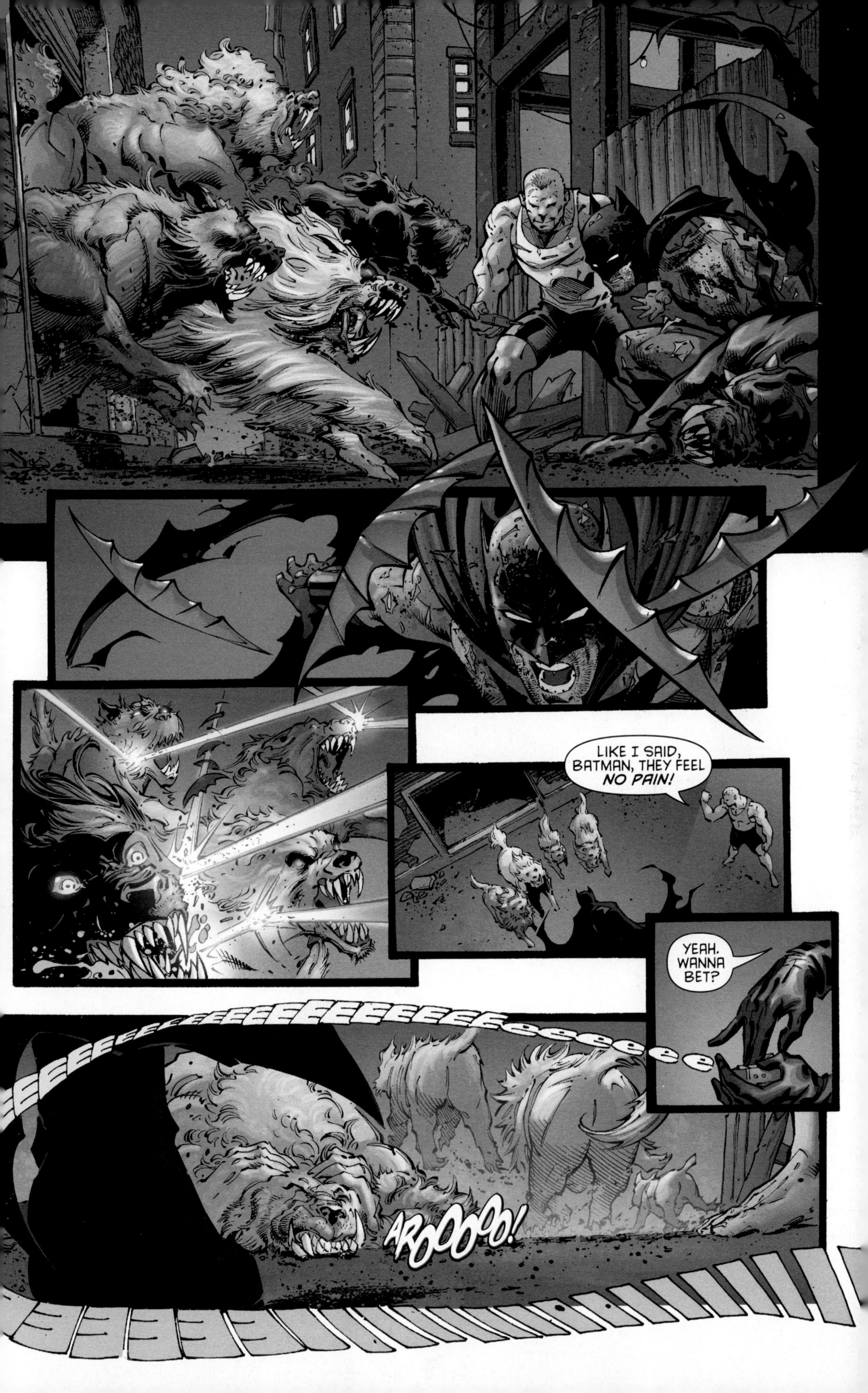
LIKE I SAID, BATMAN, THEY FEEL NO PAIN!
YEAH. WANNA BET?
EEEEEEEEEEEEEEEEEEEEEEEEEEEEEeeeeeeee
AROOOOO!

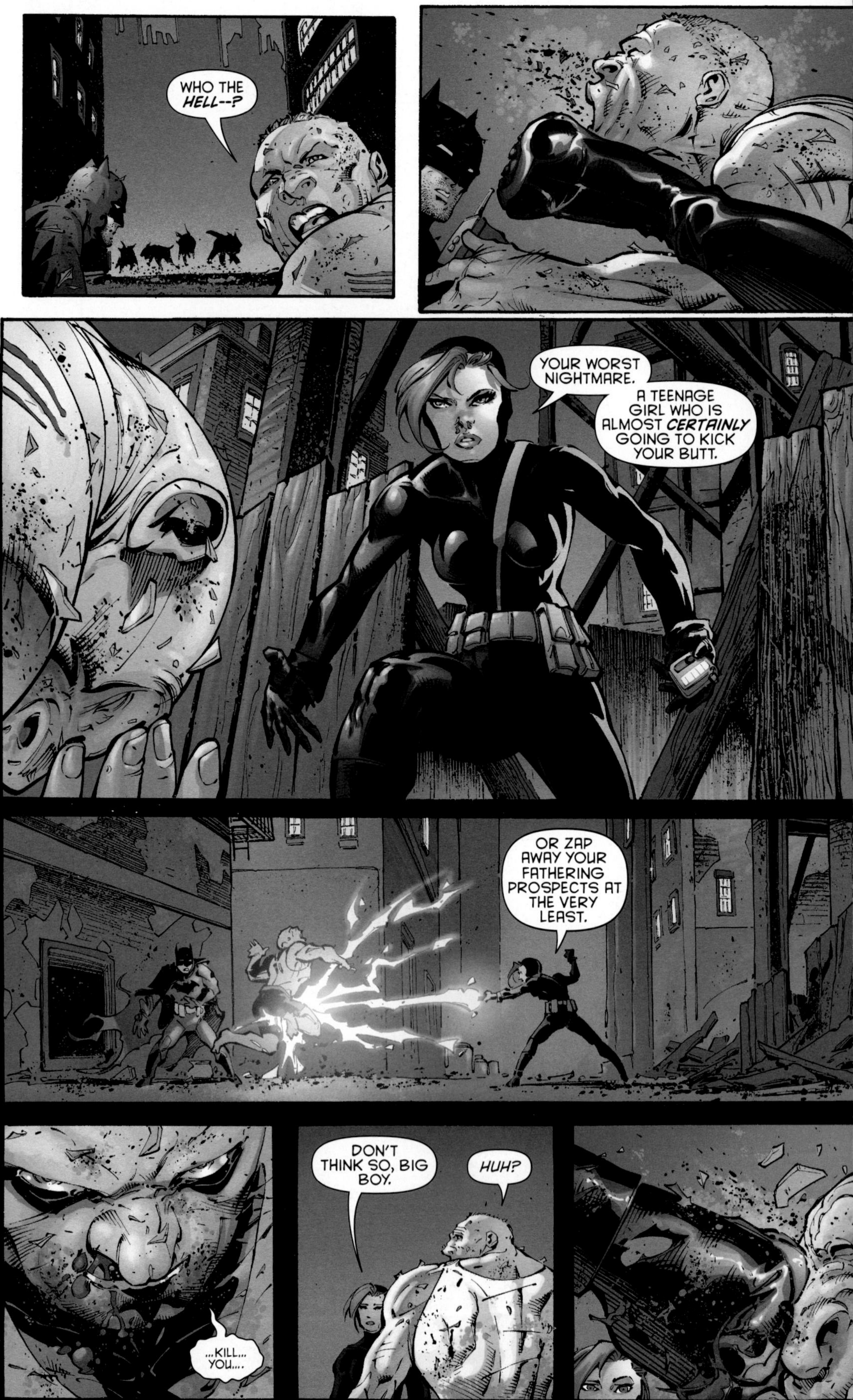
WHO THE HELL--?
YOUR WORST NIGHTMARE.
A TEENAGE GIRL WHO IS ALMOST CERTAINLY GOING TO KICK YOUR BUTT.
OR ZAP AWAY YOUR FATHERING PROSPECTS AT THE VERY LEAST.
...KILL... YOU....
DON'T THINK SO, BIG BOY.
HUH?

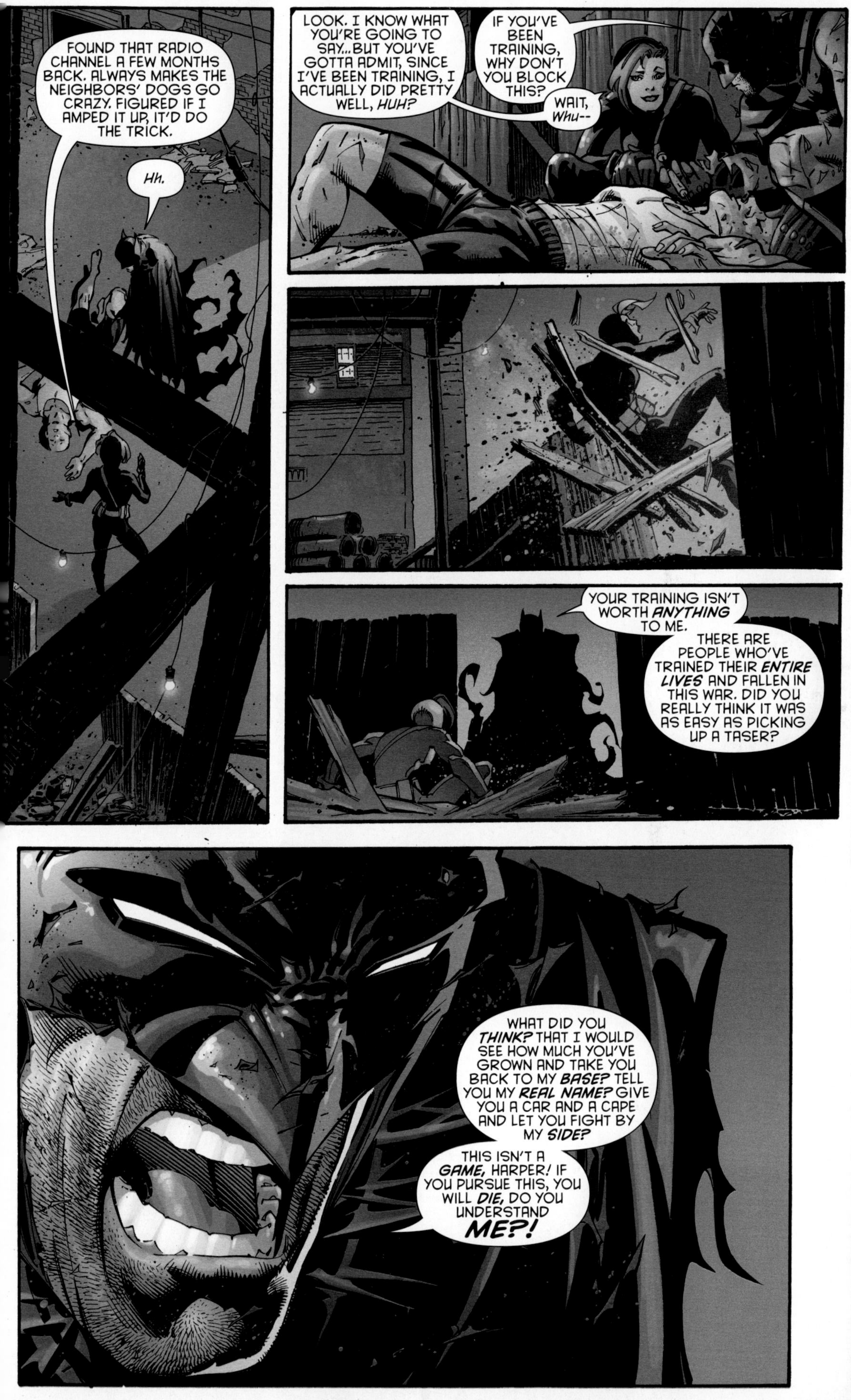
FOUND THAT RADIO CHANNEL A FEW MONTHS BACK. ALWAYS MAKES THE NEIGHBORS' DOGS GO CRAZY. FIGURED IF I AMPED IT UP, IT'D DO THE TRICK.
Hh.
LOOK. I KNOW WHAT YOU'RE GOING TO SAY...BUT YOU'VE GOTTA ADMIT, SINCE I'VE BEEN TRAINING, I ACTUALLY DID PRETTY WELL, HUH?
IF YOU'VE BEEN TRAINING, WHY DON'T YOU BLOCK THIS?
WAIT, Whu--
YOUR TRAINING ISN'T WORTH ANYTHING TO ME.
THERE ARE PEOPLE WHO'VE TRAINED THEIR ENTIRE LIVES AND FALLEN IN THIS WAR. DID YOU REALLY THINK IT WAS AS EASY AS PICKING UP A TASER?
WHAT DID YOU THINK? THAT I WOULD SEE HOW MUCH YOU'VE GROWN AND TAKE YOU BACK TO MY BASE? TELL YOU MY REAL NAME? GIVE YOU A CAR AND A CAPE AND LET YOU FIGHT BY MY SIDE?
THIS ISN'T A GAME, HARPER! IF YOU PURSUE THIS, YOU WILL DIE, DO YOU UNDERSTAND ME?!

I'M NOT AN *IDIOT*, BATMAN. I KNOW I'M NOT READY. NOT YET. BUT THAT DOESN'T MEAN I'M GOING TO STOP. YOU KNOW YOU CAN'T MAKE ME.

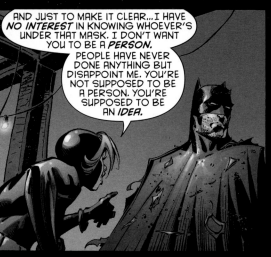

AND JUST TO MAKE IT CLEAR... I HAVE *NO INTEREST* IN KNOWING WHOEVER'S UNDER THAT MASK. I DON'T WANT YOU TO BE A *PERSON*.

PEOPLE HAVE NEVER DONE ANYTHING BUT DISAPPOINT ME. YOU'RE NOT SUPPOSED TO BE A PERSON. YOU'RE SUPPOSED TO BE AN *IDEA*.

BUT YOU CAN'T BE THAT IF YOU'RE *DEAD*. THAT'S WHY I STEPPED IN TONIGHT. YOU DO REALIZE THAT YOU COULD HAVE *DIED*, RIGHT? OR ARE YOU THAT FAR GONE?

YOU NEED TO FACE WHATEVER YOU'RE TRYING NOT TO FACE. YOU NEED TO DO IT *RIGHT NOW!*

BATMAN DOESN'T *GET* TO DIE.

I COULDN'T SIT BY AND WATCH MY HERO FALL IN SOME BACK ALLEY LIKE A COMMON THUG.

I DON'T *CARE* WHO YOU ARE. I DON'T CARE IF YOU APPROVE OF WHAT I'M DOING. BUT I'M DOING IT *BECAUSE* OF YOU.

AND YOU CAN JUST FREAKING *DEAL*.

AND DON'T PRETEND LIKE I'M *NOTHING* TO YOU, ALL RIGHT? I KNOW IT WAS YOU. I KNOW YOU LOCKED UP MY FATHER.

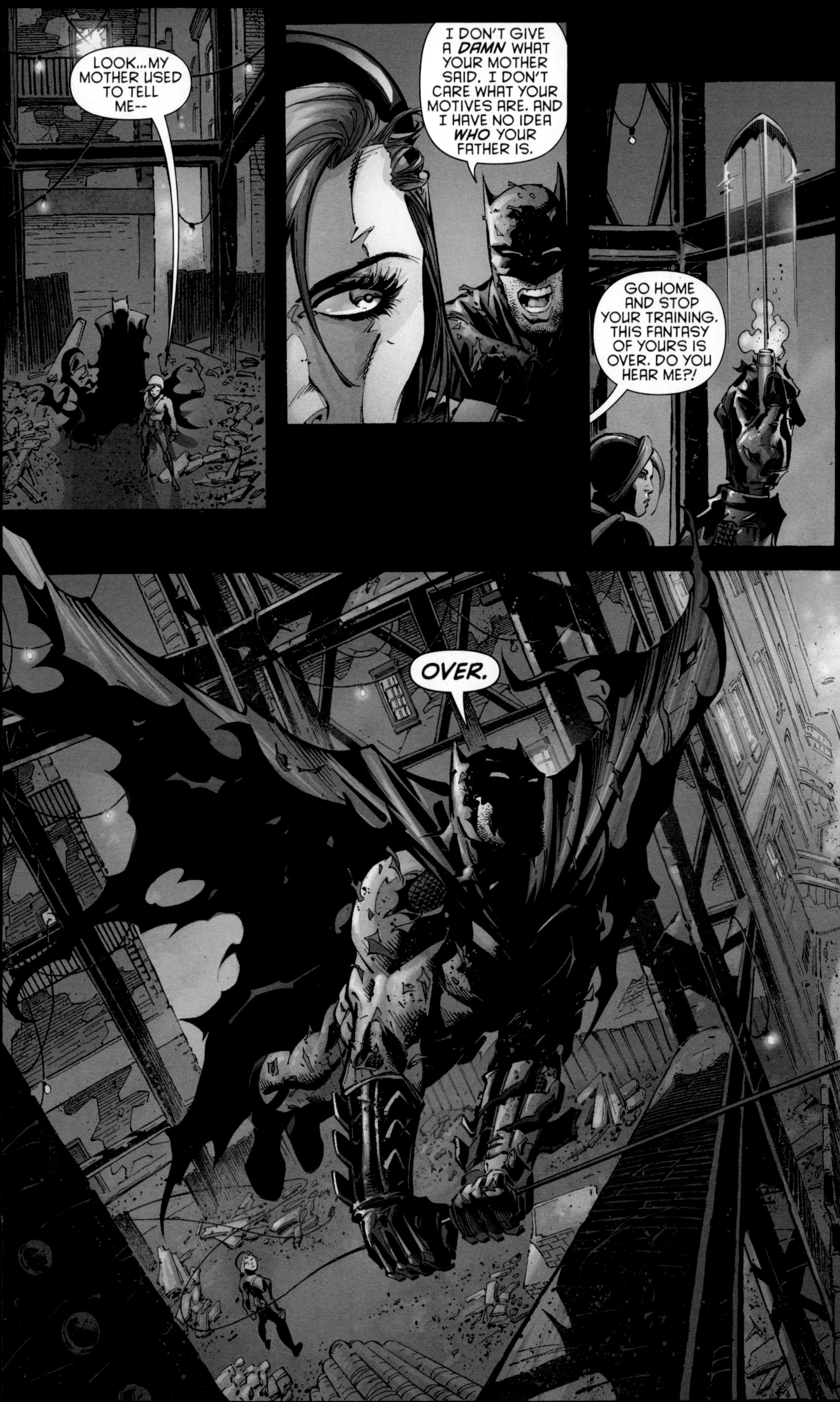

LOOK...MY MOTHER USED TO TELL ME--
I DON'T GIVE A DAMN WHAT YOUR MOTHER SAID. I DON'T CARE WHAT YOUR MOTIVES ARE. AND I HAVE NO IDEA WHO YOUR FATHER IS.
GO HOME AND STOP YOUR TRAINING. THIS FANTASY OF YOURS IS OVER. DO YOU HEAR ME?!
OVER.

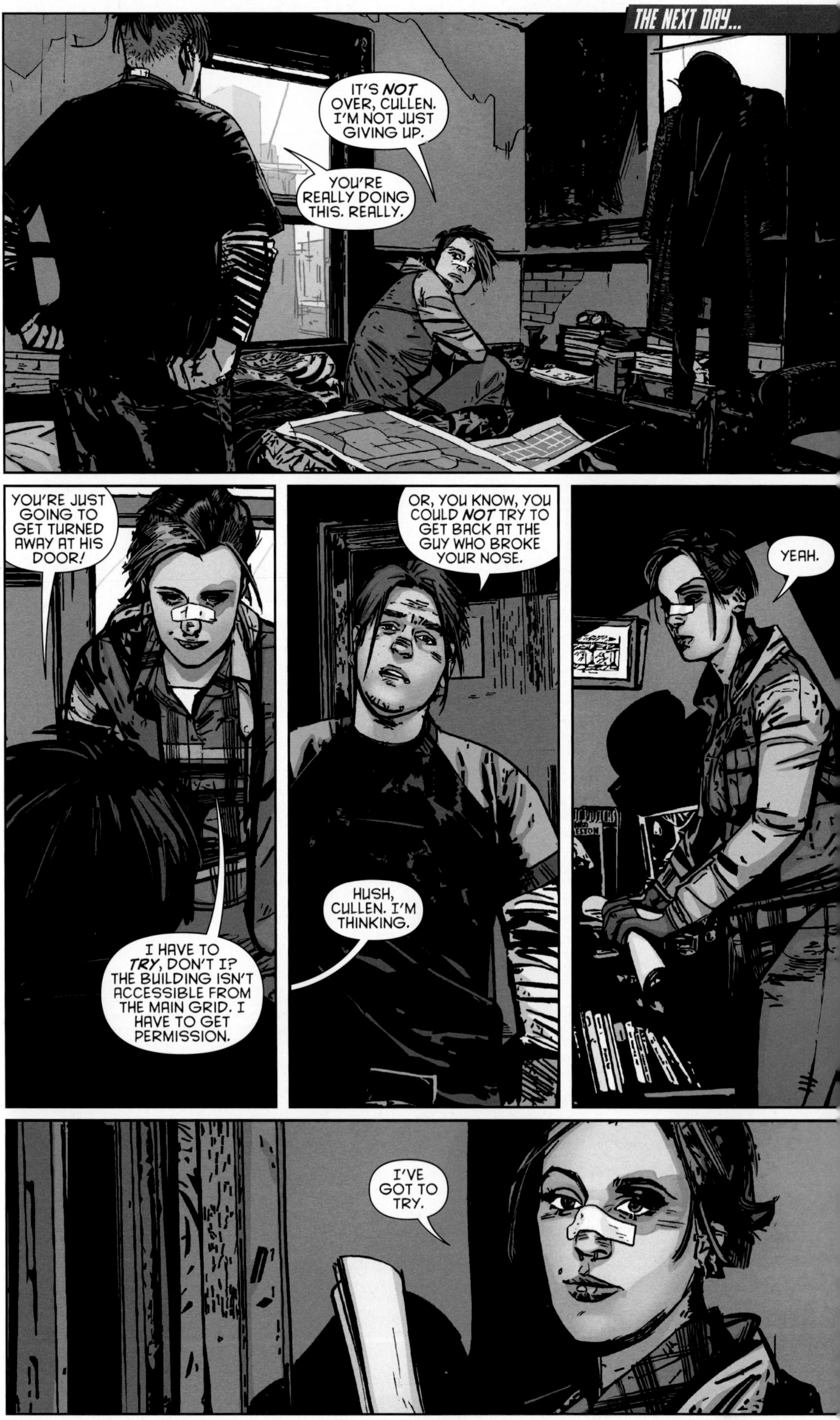
THE NEXT DAY...
YOU'RE REALLY DOING THIS. REALLY.
IT'S NOT OVER, CULLEN. I'M NOT JUST GIVING UP.
YOU'RE JUST GOING TO GET TURNED AWAY AT HIS DOOR!
I HAVE TO TRY, DON'T I? THE BUILDING ISN'T ACCESSIBLE FROM THE MAIN GRID. I HAVE TO GET PERMISSION.
OR, YOU KNOW, YOU COULD NOT TRY TO GET BACK AT THE GUY WHO BROKE YOUR NOSE.
HUSH, CULLEN. I'M THINKING.
YEAH.
I'VE GOT TO TRY.

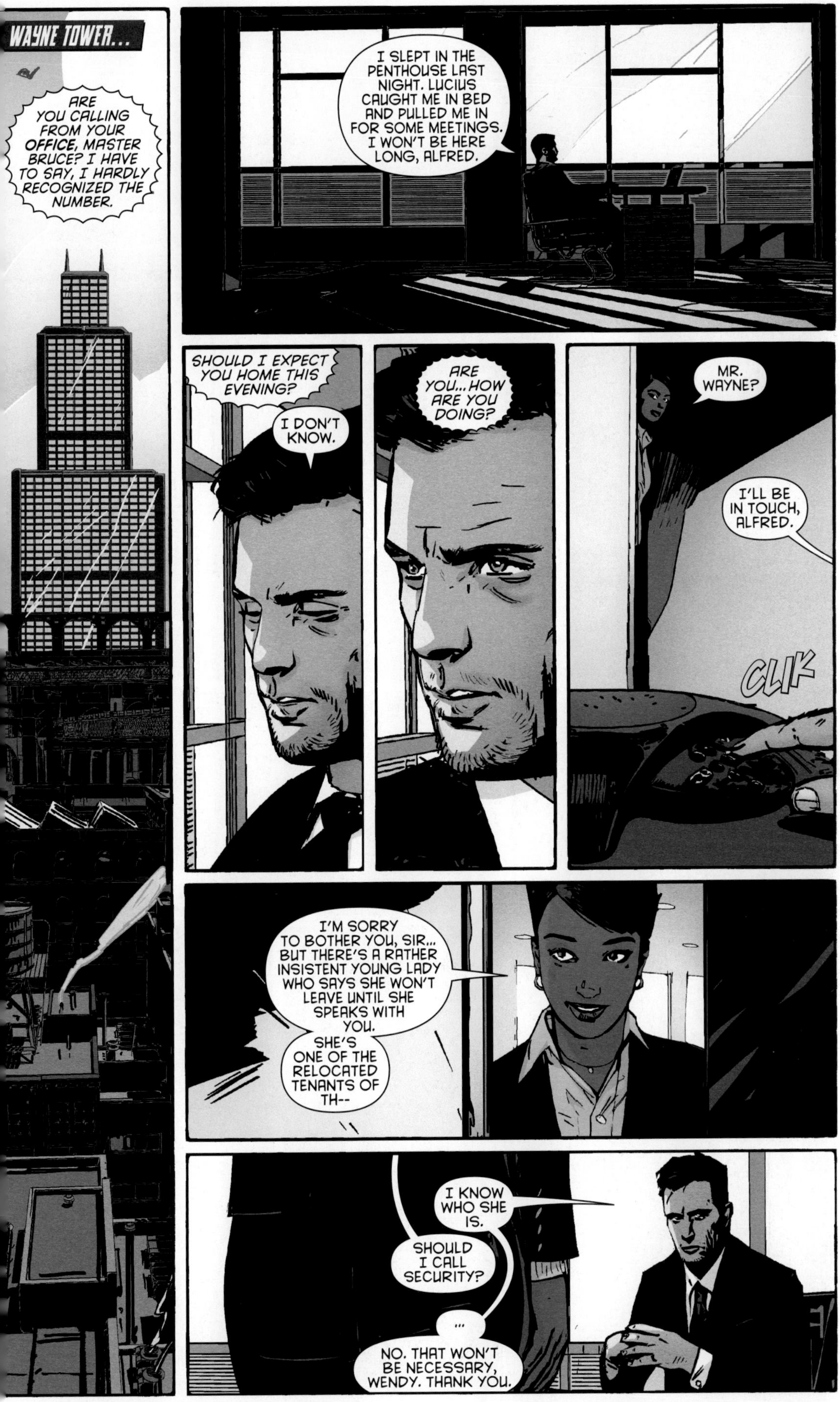

WAYNE TOWER...
ARE YOU CALLING FROM YOUR OFFICE, MASTER BRUCE? I HAVE TO SAY, I HARDLY RECOGNIZED THE NUMBER.
I SLEPT IN THE PENTHOUSE LAST NIGHT. LUCIUS CAUGHT ME IN BED AND PULLED ME IN FOR SOME MEETINGS. I WON'T BE HERE LONG, ALFRED.
SHOULD I EXPECT YOU HOME THIS EVENING?
I DON'T KNOW.
ARE YOU...HOW ARE YOU DOING?
MR. WAYNE?
I'LL BE IN TOUCH, ALFRED.
CLIK
I'M SORRY TO BOTHER YOU, SIR... BUT THERE'S A RATHER INSISTENT YOUNG LADY WHO SAYS SHE WON'T LEAVE UNTIL SHE SPEAKS WITH YOU.
SHE'S ONE OF THE RELOCATED TENANTS OF TH--
I KNOW WHO SHE IS.
SHOULD I CALL SECURITY?
...
NO. THAT WON'T BE NECESSARY, WENDY. THANK YOU.

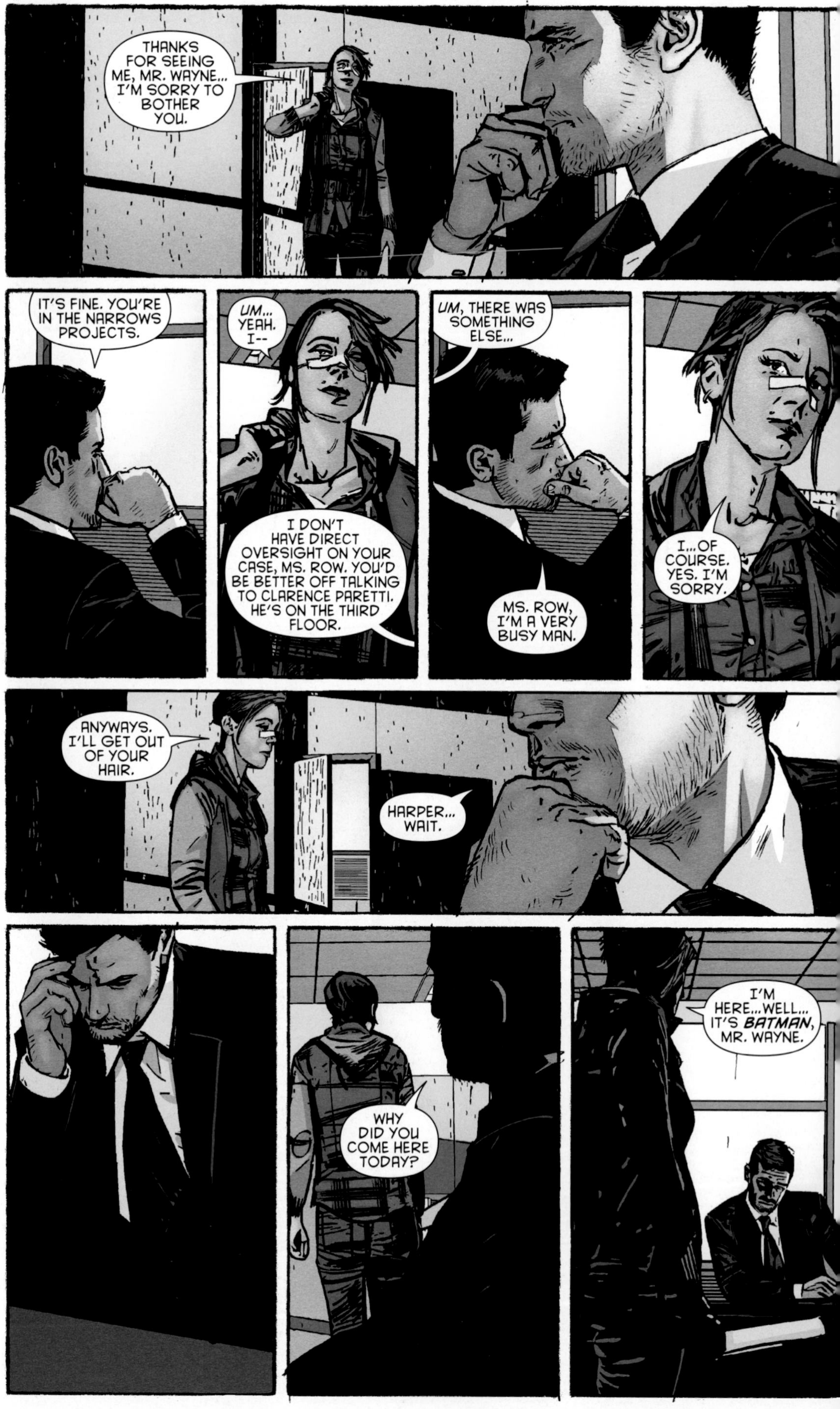
THANKS FOR SEEING ME, MR. WAYNE... I'M SORRY TO BOTHER YOU.
IT'S FINE. YOU'RE IN THE NARROWS PROJECTS.
UM... YEAH. I--
I DON'T HAVE DIRECT OVERSIGHT ON YOUR CASE, MS. ROW. YOU'D BE BETTER OFF TALKING TO CLARENCE PARETTI. HE'S ON THE THIRD FLOOR.
UM, THERE WAS SOMETHING ELSE...
MS. ROW, I'M A VERY BUSY MAN.
I... OF COURSE. YES. I'M SORRY.
ANYWAYS. I'LL GET OUT OF YOUR HAIR.
HARPER... WAIT.
WHY DID YOU COME HERE TODAY?
I'M HERE... WELL... IT'S BATMAN, MR. WAYNE.

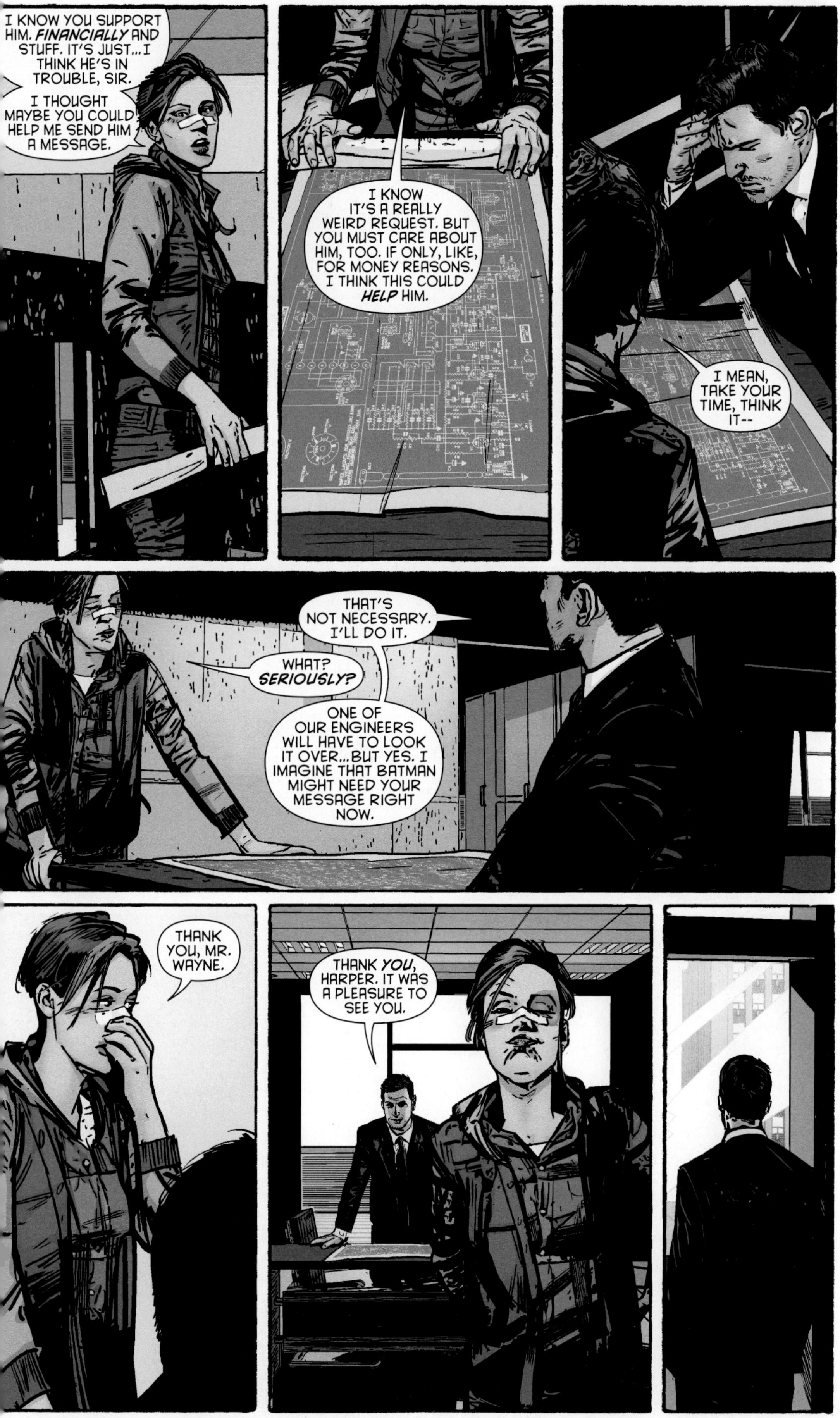

I KNOW YOU SUPPORT HIM. FINANCIALLY AND STUFF. IT'S JUST... I THINK HE'S IN TROUBLE, SIR.
I THOUGHT MAYBE YOU COULD HELP ME SEND HIM A MESSAGE.
I KNOW IT'S A REALLY WEIRD REQUEST. BUT YOU MUST CARE ABOUT HIM, TOO. IF ONLY, LIKE, FOR MONEY REASONS. I THINK THIS COULD HELP HIM.
I MEAN, TAKE YOUR TIME, THINK IT--
THAT'S NOT NECESSARY. I'LL DO IT.
WHAT? SERIOUSLY?
ONE OF OUR ENGINEERS WILL HAVE TO LOOK IT OVER... BUT YES. I IMAGINE THAT BATMAN MIGHT NEED YOUR MESSAGE RIGHT NOW.
THANK YOU, MR. WAYNE.
THANK YOU, HARPER. IT WAS A PLEASURE TO SEE YOU.

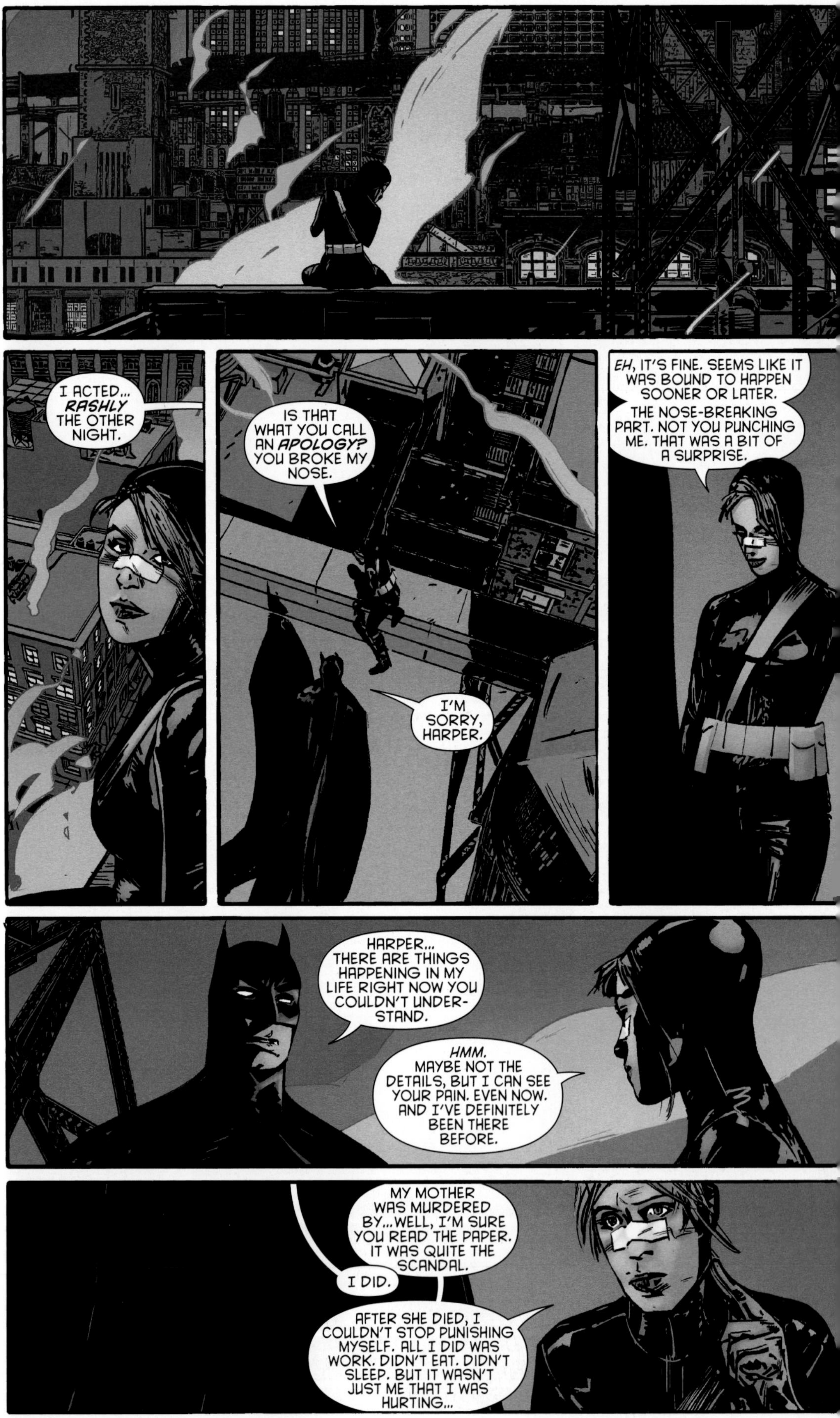
I ACTED... *RASHLY* THE OTHER NIGHT.
IS THAT WHAT YOU CALL AN *APOLOGY?* YOU BROKE MY NOSE.
I'M SORRY, HARPER.
EH, IT'S FINE. SEEMS LIKE IT WAS BOUND TO HAPPEN SOONER OR LATER.
THE NOSE-BREAKING PART. NOT YOU PUNCHING ME. THAT WAS A BIT OF A SURPRISE.
HARPER... THERE ARE THINGS HAPPENING IN MY LIFE RIGHT NOW YOU COULDN'T UNDER-STAND.
HMM. MAYBE NOT THE DETAILS, BUT I CAN SEE YOUR PAIN. EVEN NOW. AND I'VE DEFINITELY BEEN THERE BEFORE.
MY MOTHER WAS MURDERED BY...WELL, I'M SURE YOU READ THE PAPER. IT WAS QUITE THE SCANDAL.
I DID.
AFTER SHE DIED, I COULDN'T STOP PUNISHING MYSELF. ALL I DID WAS WORK. DIDN'T EAT. DIDN'T SLEEP. BUT IT WASN'T JUST ME THAT I WAS HURTING...

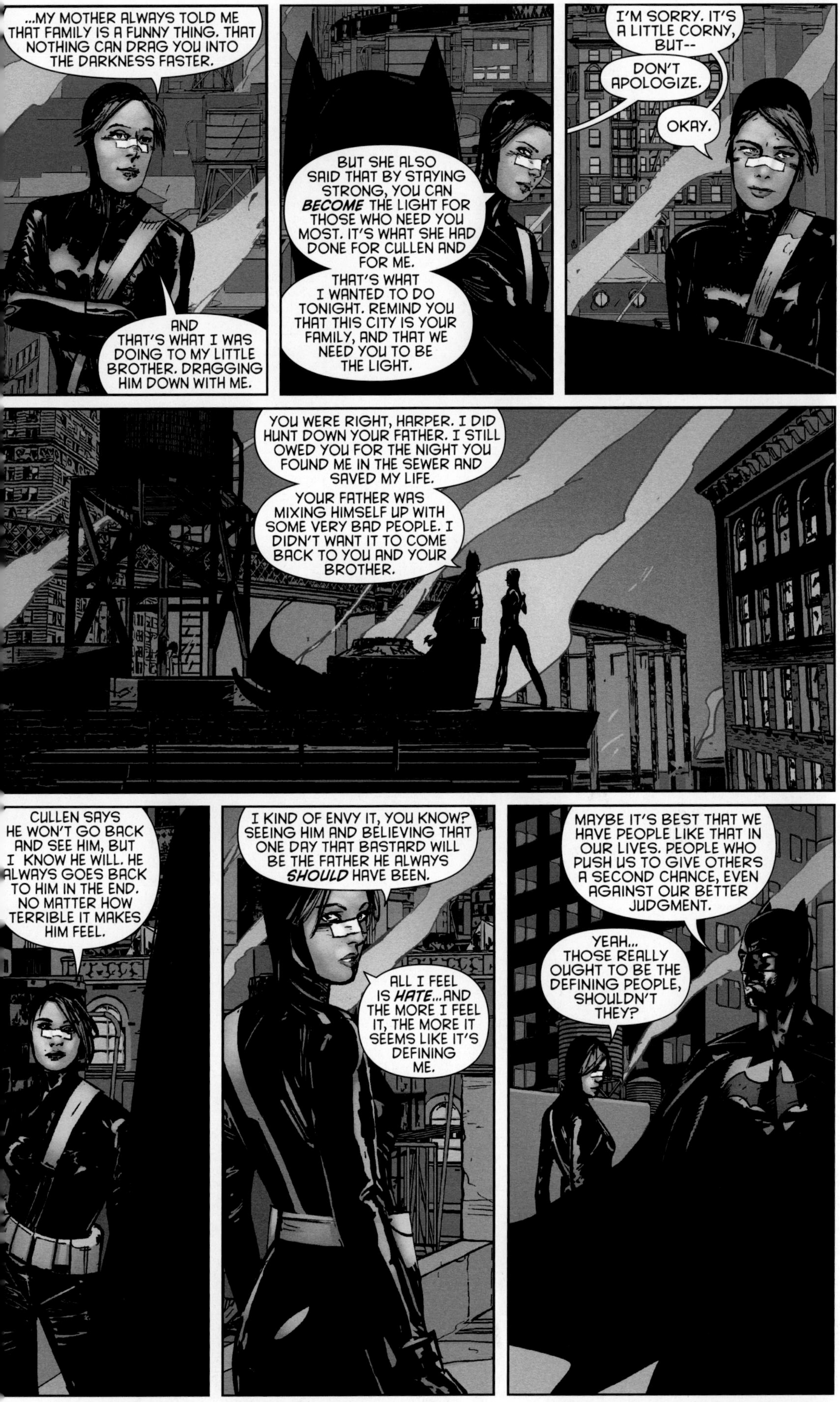
...MY MOTHER ALWAYS TOLD ME THAT FAMILY IS A FUNNY THING. THAT NOTHING CAN DRAG YOU INTO THE DARKNESS FASTER.
AND THAT'S WHAT I WAS DOING TO MY LITTLE BROTHER. DRAGGING HIM DOWN WITH ME.
BUT SHE ALSO SAID THAT BY STAYING STRONG, YOU CAN BECOME THE LIGHT FOR THOSE WHO NEED YOU MOST. IT'S WHAT SHE HAD DONE FOR CULLEN AND FOR ME.
THAT'S WHAT I WANTED TO DO TONIGHT. REMIND YOU THAT THIS CITY IS YOUR FAMILY, AND THAT WE NEED YOU TO BE THE LIGHT.
I'M SORRY. IT'S A LITTLE CORNY, BUT--
DON'T APOLOGIZE.
OKAY.
YOU WERE RIGHT, HARPER. I DID HUNT DOWN YOUR FATHER. I STILL OWED YOU FOR THE NIGHT YOU FOUND ME IN THE SEWER AND SAVED MY LIFE.
YOUR FATHER WAS MIXING HIMSELF UP WITH SOME VERY BAD PEOPLE. I DIDN'T WANT IT TO COME BACK TO YOU AND YOUR BROTHER.
CULLEN SAYS HE WON'T GO BACK AND SEE HIM, BUT I KNOW HE WILL. HE ALWAYS GOES BACK TO HIM IN THE END. NO MATTER HOW TERRIBLE IT MAKES HIM FEEL.
I KIND OF ENVY IT, YOU KNOW? SEEING HIM AND BELIEVING THAT ONE DAY THAT BASTARD WILL BE THE FATHER HE ALWAYS SHOULD HAVE BEEN.
ALL I FEEL IS HATE...AND THE MORE I FEEL IT, THE MORE IT SEEMS LIKE IT'S DEFINING ME.
MAYBE IT'S BEST THAT WE HAVE PEOPLE LIKE THAT IN OUR LIVES. PEOPLE WHO PUSH US TO GIVE OTHERS A SECOND CHANCE, EVEN AGAINST OUR BETTER JUDGMENT.
YEAH... THOSE REALLY OUGHT TO BE THE DEFINING PEOPLE, SHOULDN'T THEY?

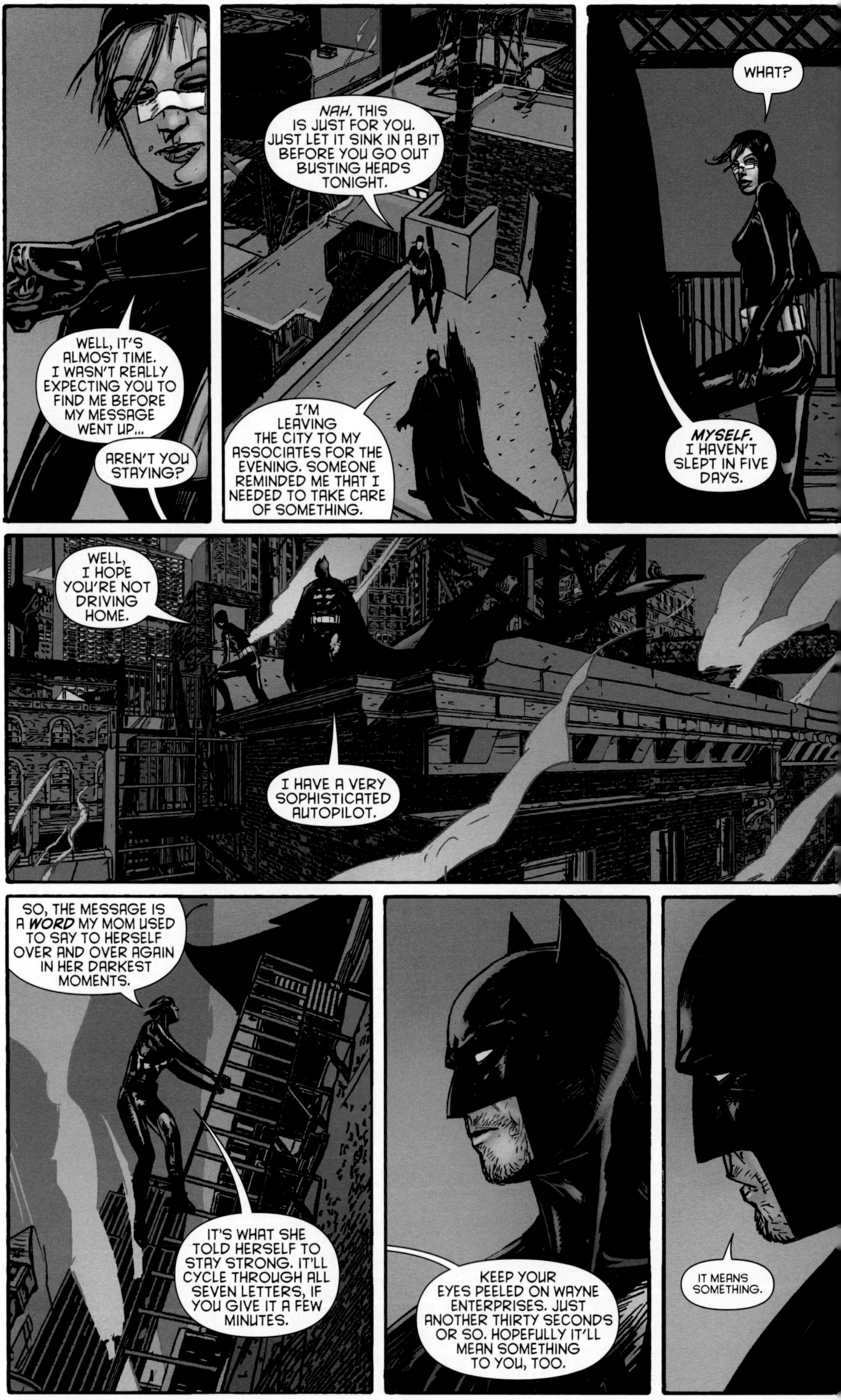
WELL, IT'S ALMOST TIME. I WASN'T REALLY EXPECTING YOU TO FIND ME BEFORE MY MESSAGE WENT UP...
AREN'T YOU STAYING?
I'M LEAVING THE CITY TO MY ASSOCIATES FOR THE EVENING. SOMEONE REMINDED ME THAT I NEEDED TO TAKE CARE OF SOMETHING.
NAH. THIS IS JUST FOR YOU. JUST LET IT SINK IN A BIT BEFORE YOU GO OUT BUSTING HEADS TONIGHT.
WHAT?
MYSELF. I HAVEN'T SLEPT IN FIVE DAYS.
WELL, I HOPE YOU'RE NOT DRIVING HOME.
I HAVE A VERY SOPHISTICATED AUTOPILOT.
SO, THE MESSAGE IS A WORD MY MOM USED TO SAY TO HERSELF OVER AND OVER AGAIN IN HER DARKEST MOMENTS.
IT'S WHAT SHE TOLD HERSELF TO STAY STRONG. IT'LL CYCLE THROUGH ALL SEVEN LETTERS, IF YOU GIVE IT A FEW MINUTES.
KEEP YOUR EYES PEELED ON WAYNE ENTERPRISES. JUST ANOTHER THIRTY SECONDS OR SO. HOPEFULLY IT'LL MEAN SOMETHING TO YOU, TOO.
IT MEANS SOMETHING.

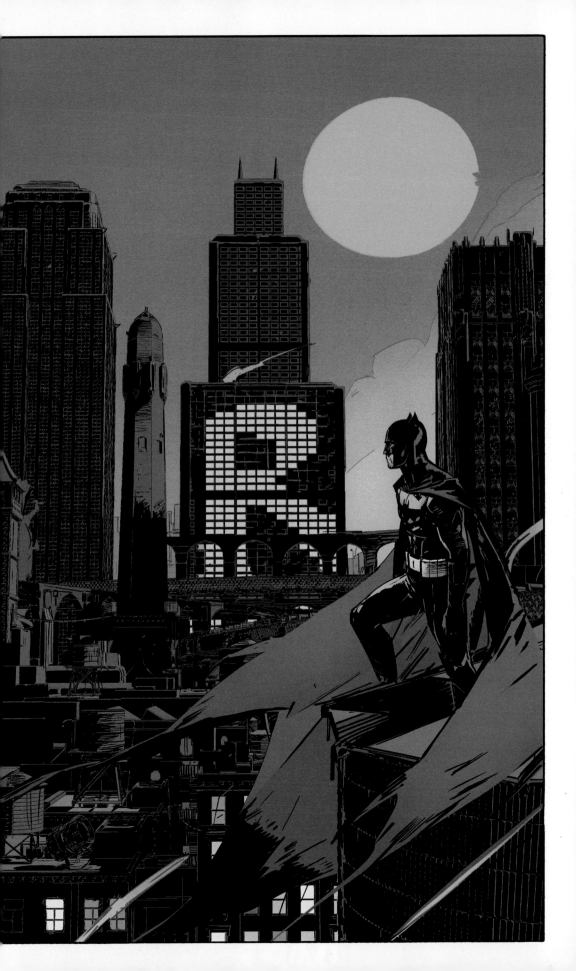

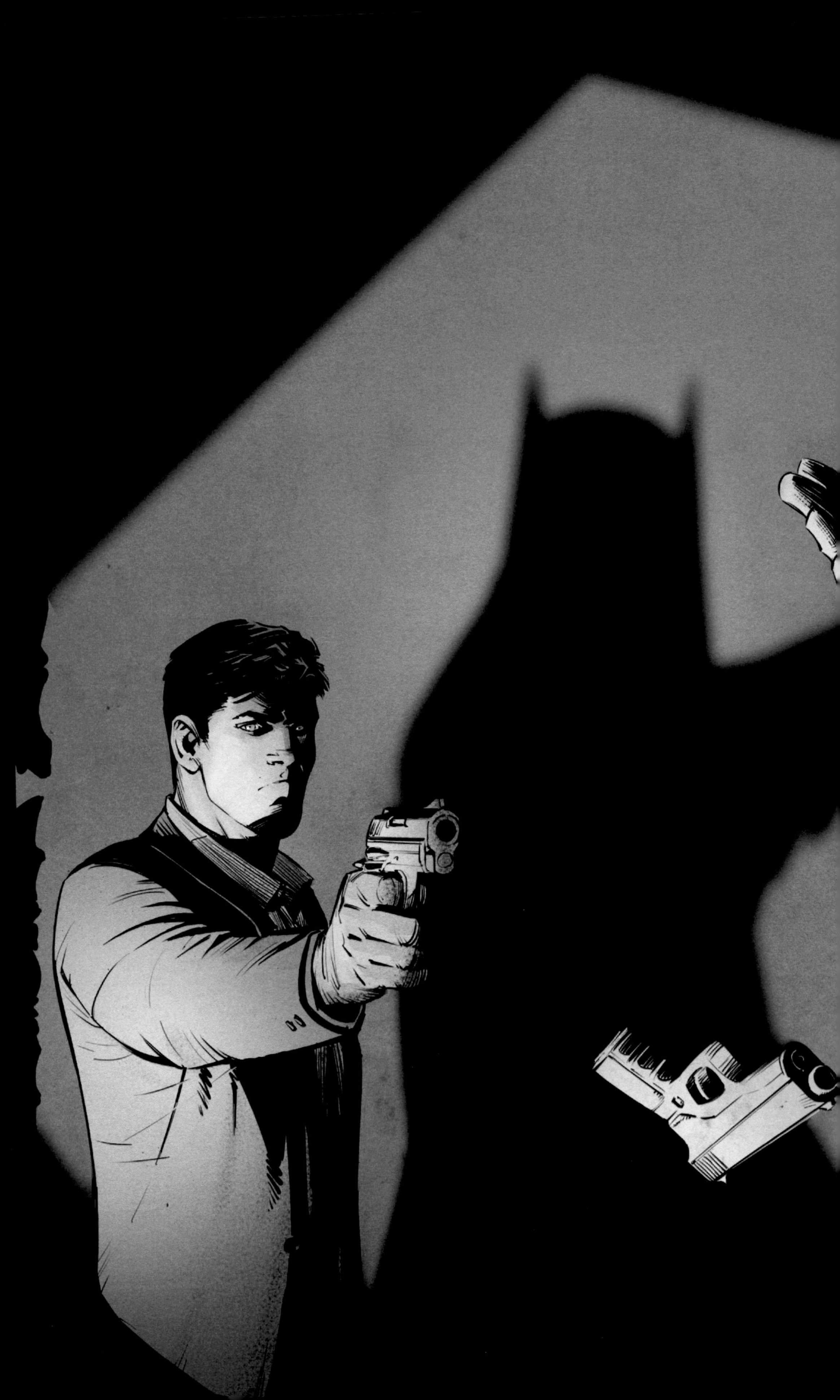

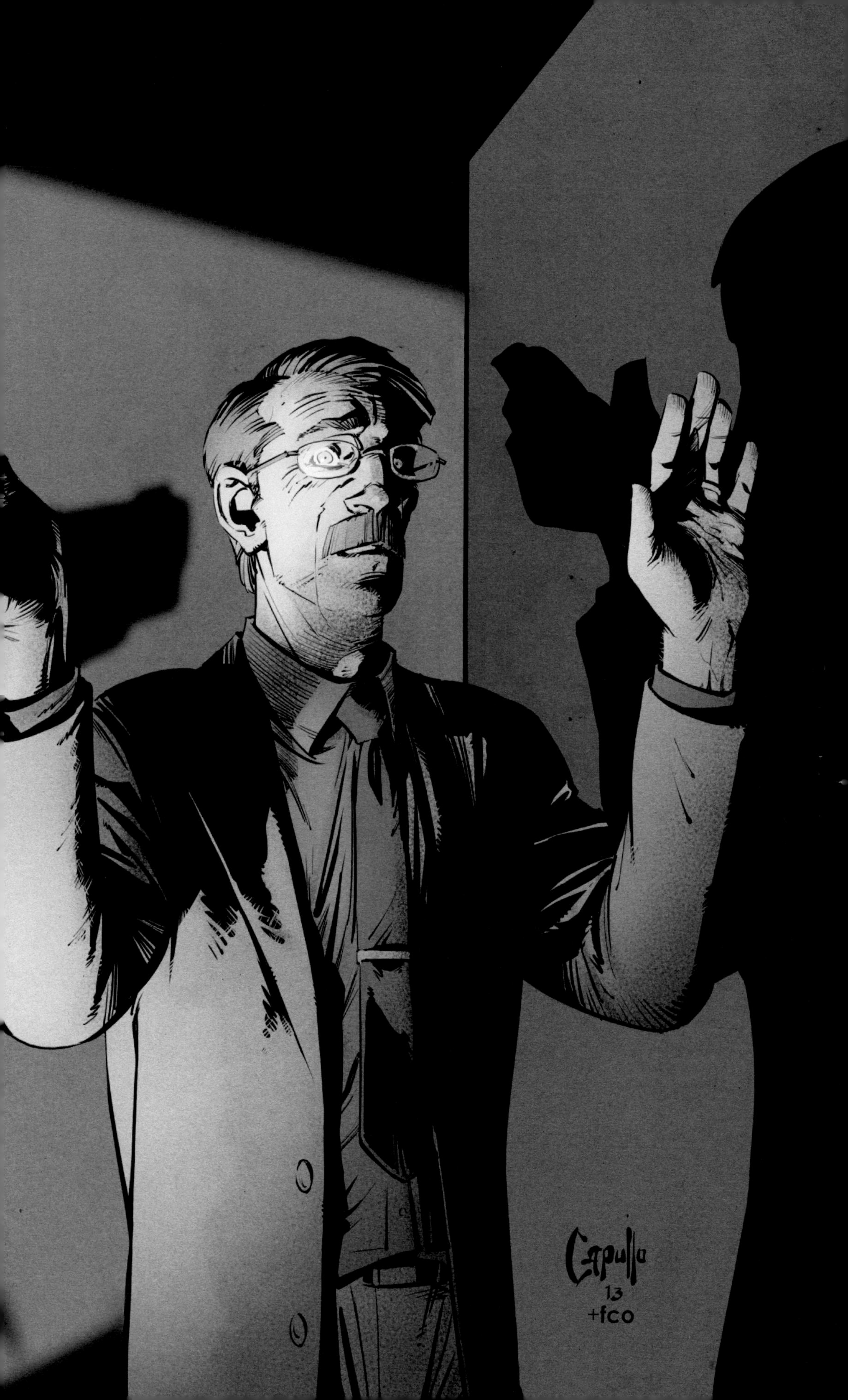
Capullo
13
+fco

NOWHERE MAN

SCOTT SNYDER writer **GREG CAPULLO** penciller **DANNY MIKI** inker **FCO PLASCENCIA** colorist cover by **GREG CAPULLO & FCO PLASCENCIA**

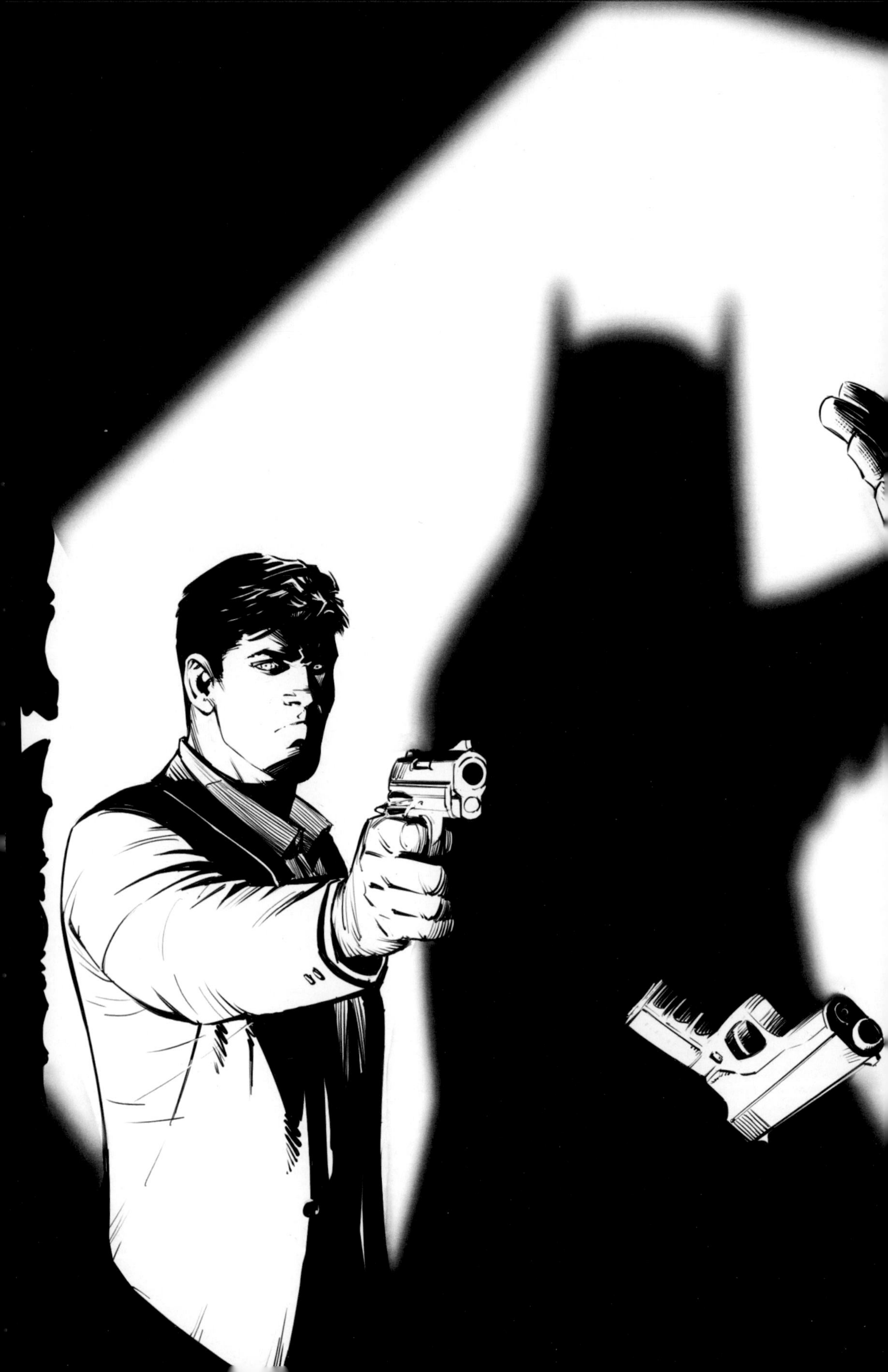

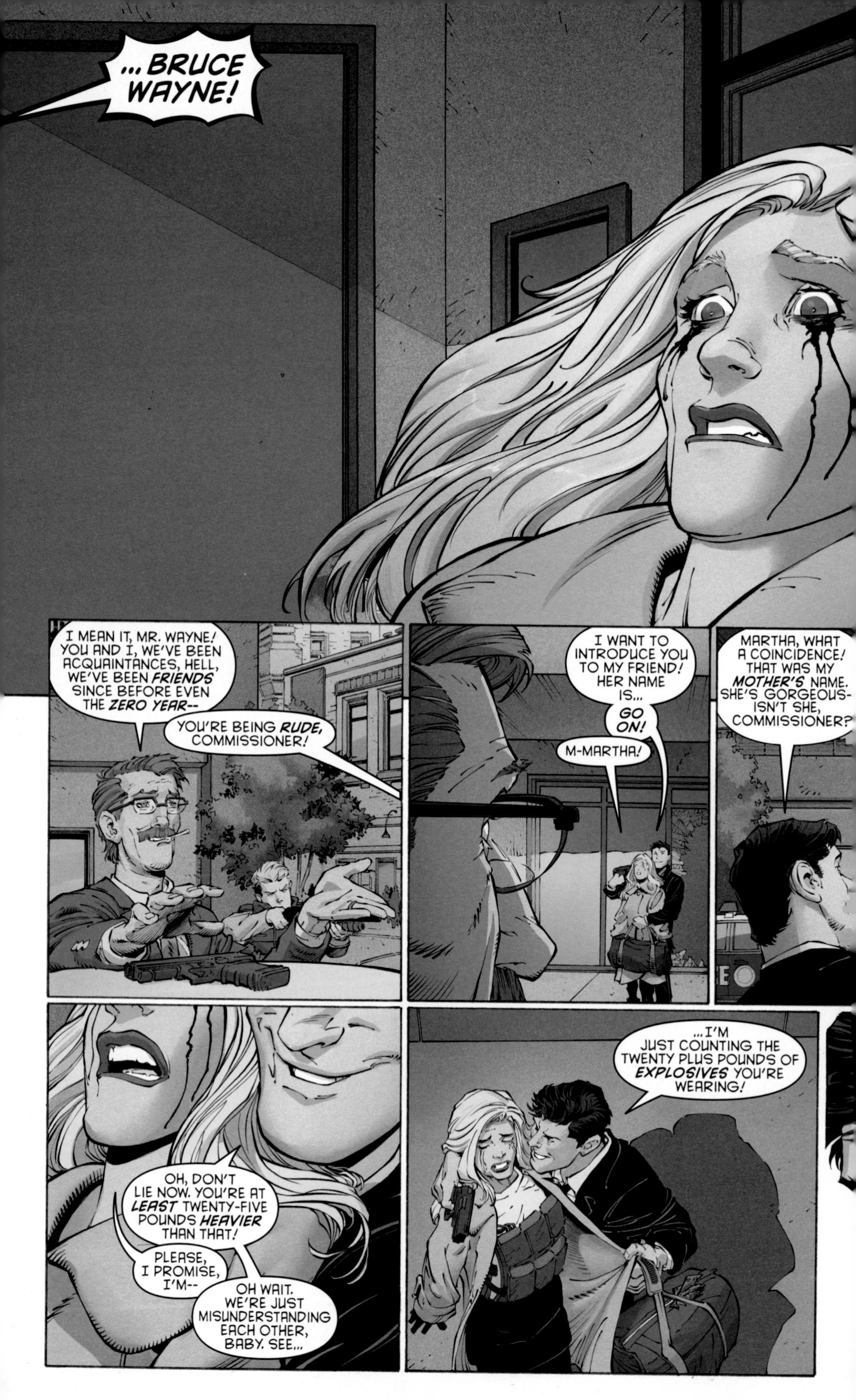
...BRUCE WAYNE!
I MEAN IT, MR. WAYNE! YOU AND I, WE'VE BEEN ACQUAINTANCES, HELL, WE'VE BEEN FRIENDS SINCE BEFORE EVEN THE ZERO YEAR--
YOU'RE BEING RUDE, COMMISSIONER!
I WANT TO INTRODUCE YOU TO MY FRIEND! HER NAME IS...
GO ON!
M-MARTHA!
MARTHA, WHAT A COINCIDENCE! THAT WAS MY MOTHER'S NAME. SHE'S GORGEOUS-ISN'T SHE, COMMISSIONER?
OH, DON'T LIE NOW. YOU'RE AT LEAST TWENTY-FIVE POUNDS HEAVIER THAN THAT!
PLEASE, I PROMISE, I'M--
OH WAIT. WE'RE JUST MISUNDERSTANDING EACH OTHER, BABY. SEE...
...I'M JUST COUNTING THE TWENTY PLUS POUNDS OF EXPLOSIVES YOU'RE WEARING!

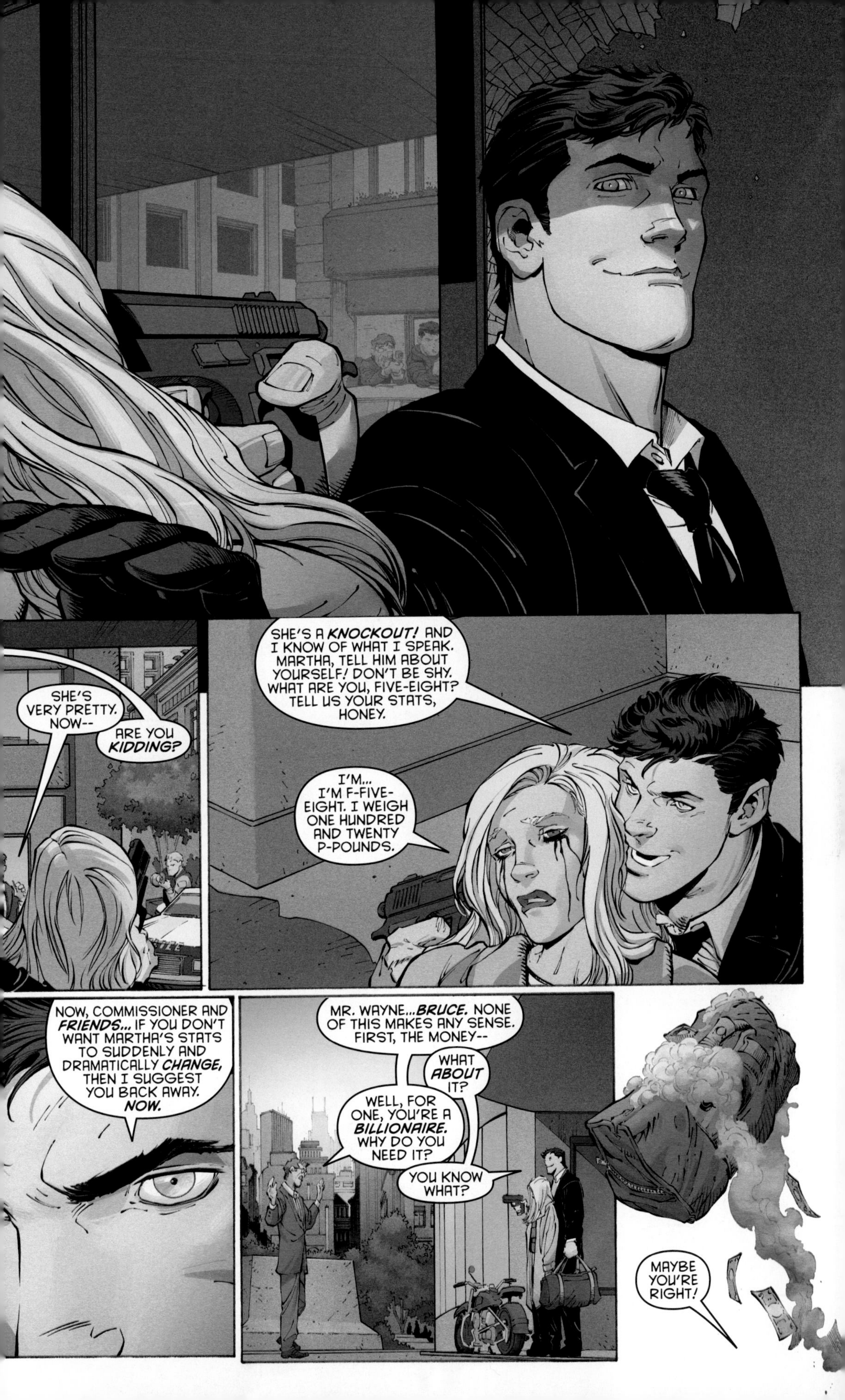
SHE'S VERY PRETTY. NOW--
ARE YOU KIDDING?
SHE'S A KNOCKOUT! AND I KNOW OF WHAT I SPEAK. MARTHA, TELL HIM ABOUT YOURSELF! DON'T BE SHY. WHAT ARE YOU, FIVE-EIGHT? TELL US YOUR STATS, HONEY.
I'M... I'M F-FIVE-EIGHT. I WEIGH ONE HUNDRED AND TWENTY P-POUNDS.
NOW, COMMISSIONER AND FRIENDS... IF YOU DON'T WANT MARTHA'S STATS TO SUDDENLY AND DRAMATICALLY CHANGE, THEN I SUGGEST YOU BACK AWAY. NOW.
MR. WAYNE...BRUCE. NONE OF THIS MAKES ANY SENSE. FIRST, THE MONEY--
WHAT ABOUT IT?
WELL, FOR ONE, YOU'RE A BILLIONAIRE. WHY DO YOU NEED IT?
YOU KNOW WHAT?
MAYBE YOU'RE RIGHT!

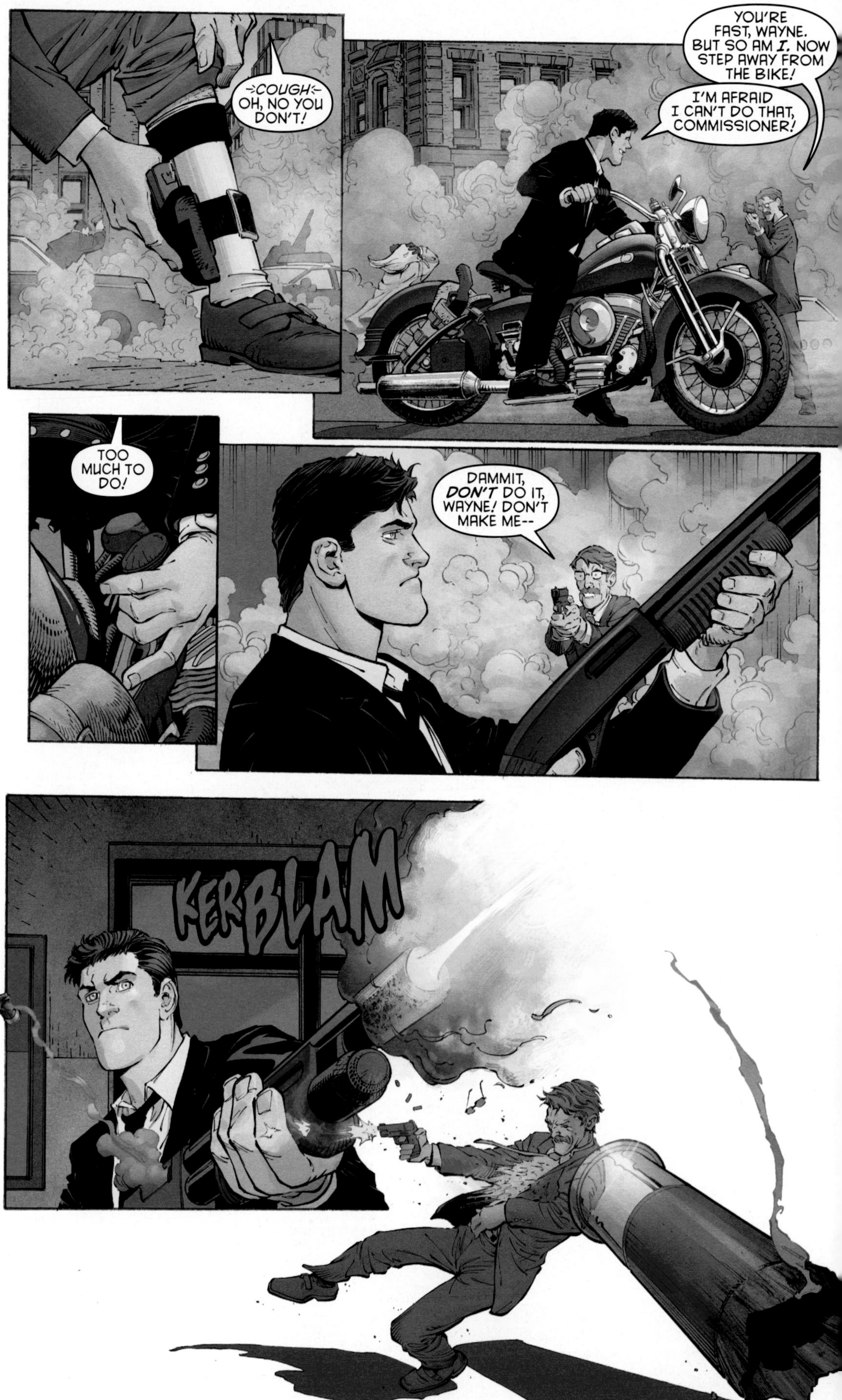

-COUGH- OH, NO YOU DON'T!
YOU'RE FAST, WAYNE. BUT SO AM I. NOW STEP AWAY FROM THE BIKE!
I'M AFRAID I CAN'T DO THAT, COMMISSIONER!
TOO MUCH TO DO!
DAMMIT, DON'T DO IT, WAYNE! DON'T MAKE ME--
KERBLAM

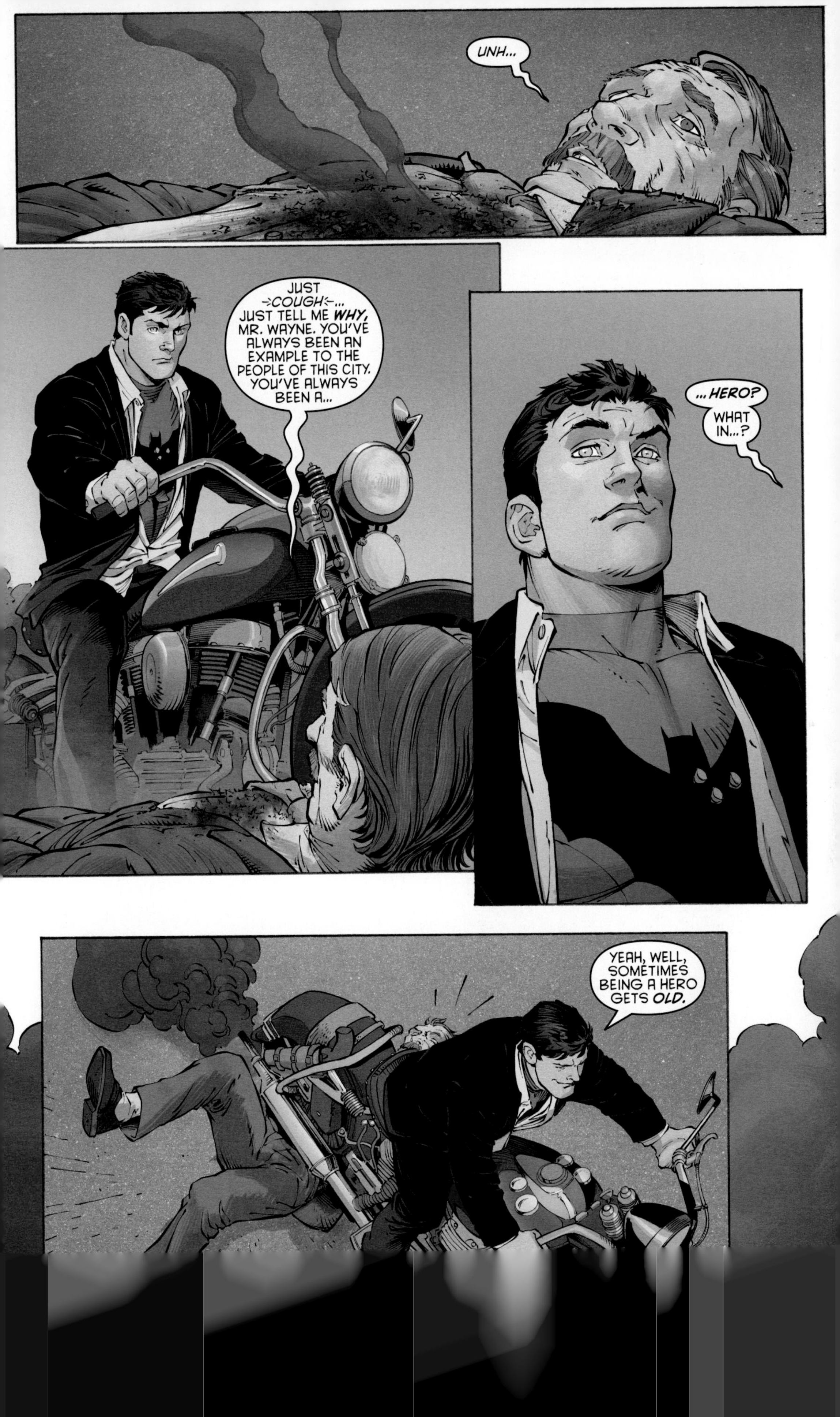
UNH...
JUST ⊰COUGH⊱... JUST TELL ME WHY, MR. WAYNE. YOU'VE ALWAYS BEEN AN EXAMPLE TO THE PEOPLE OF THIS CITY. YOU'VE ALWAYS BEEN A...
...HERO? WHAT IN...?
YEAH, WELL, SOMETIMES BEING A HERO GETS OLD.

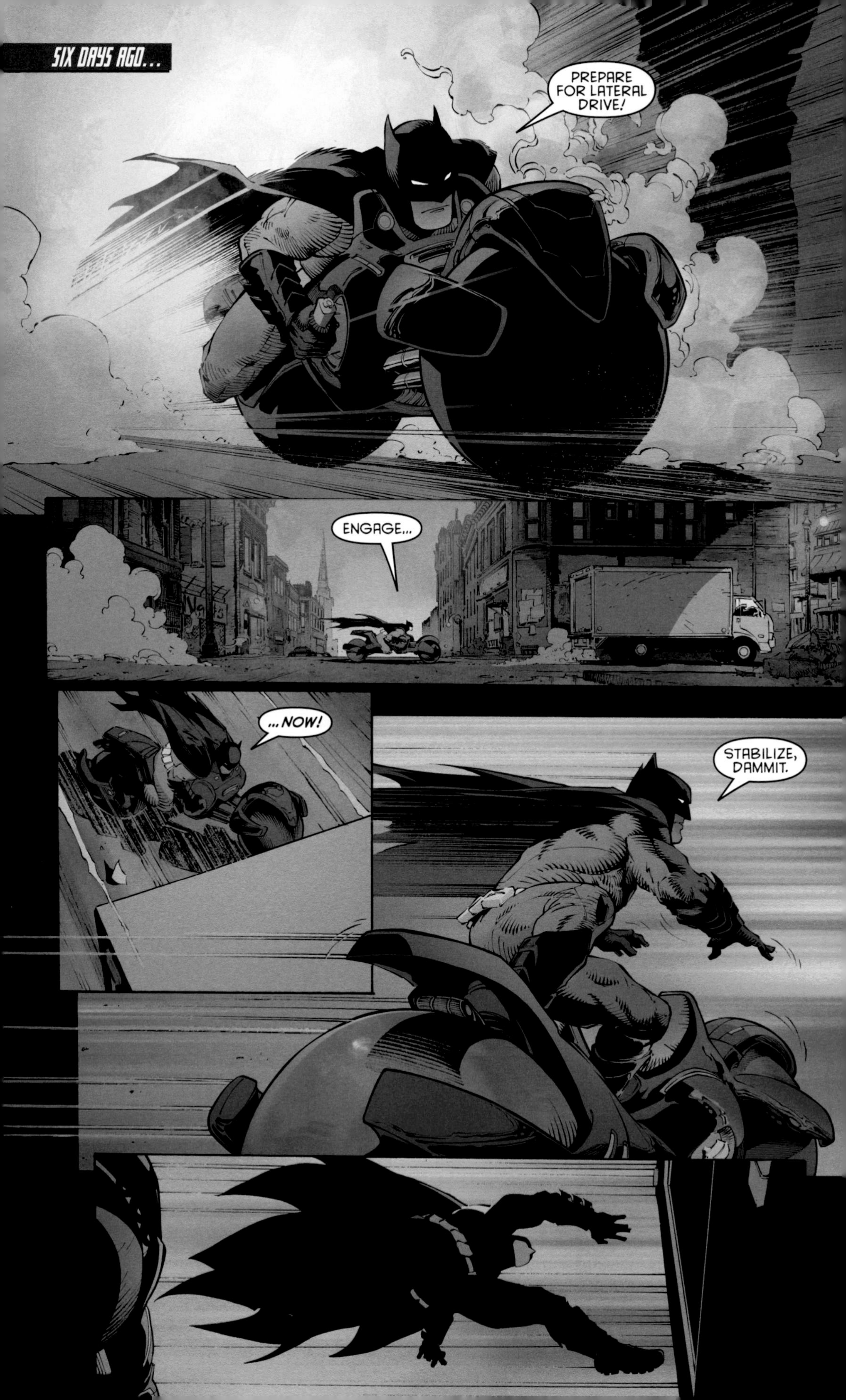
SIX DAYS AGO...
PREPARE FOR LATERAL DRIVE!
ENGAGE...
...NOW!
STABILIZE, DAMMIT.

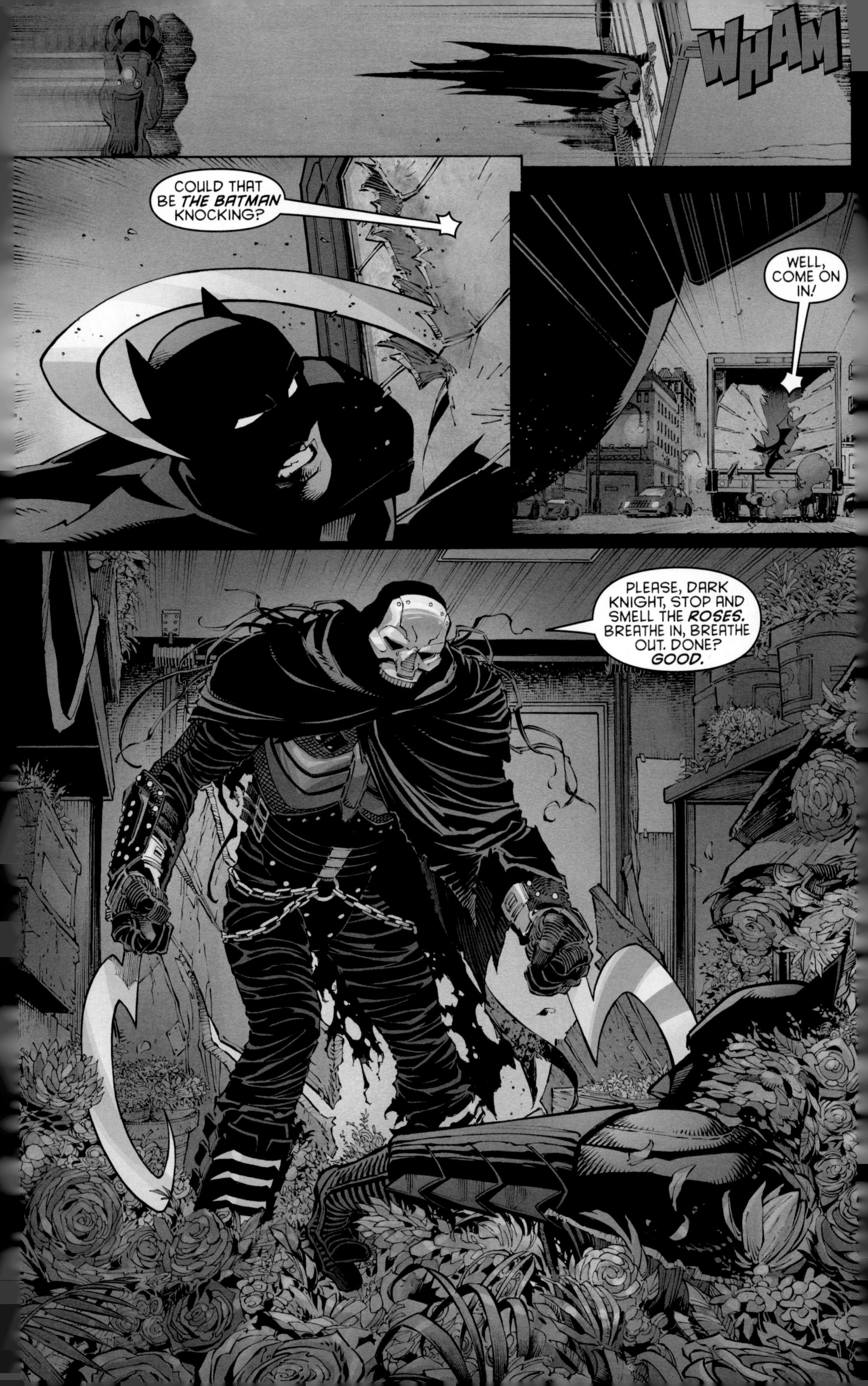
WHAM
COULD THAT BE THE BATMAN KNOCKING?
WELL, COME ON IN!
PLEASE, DARK KNIGHT, STOP AND SMELL THE ROSES. BREATHE IN, BREATHE OUT. DONE? GOOD.

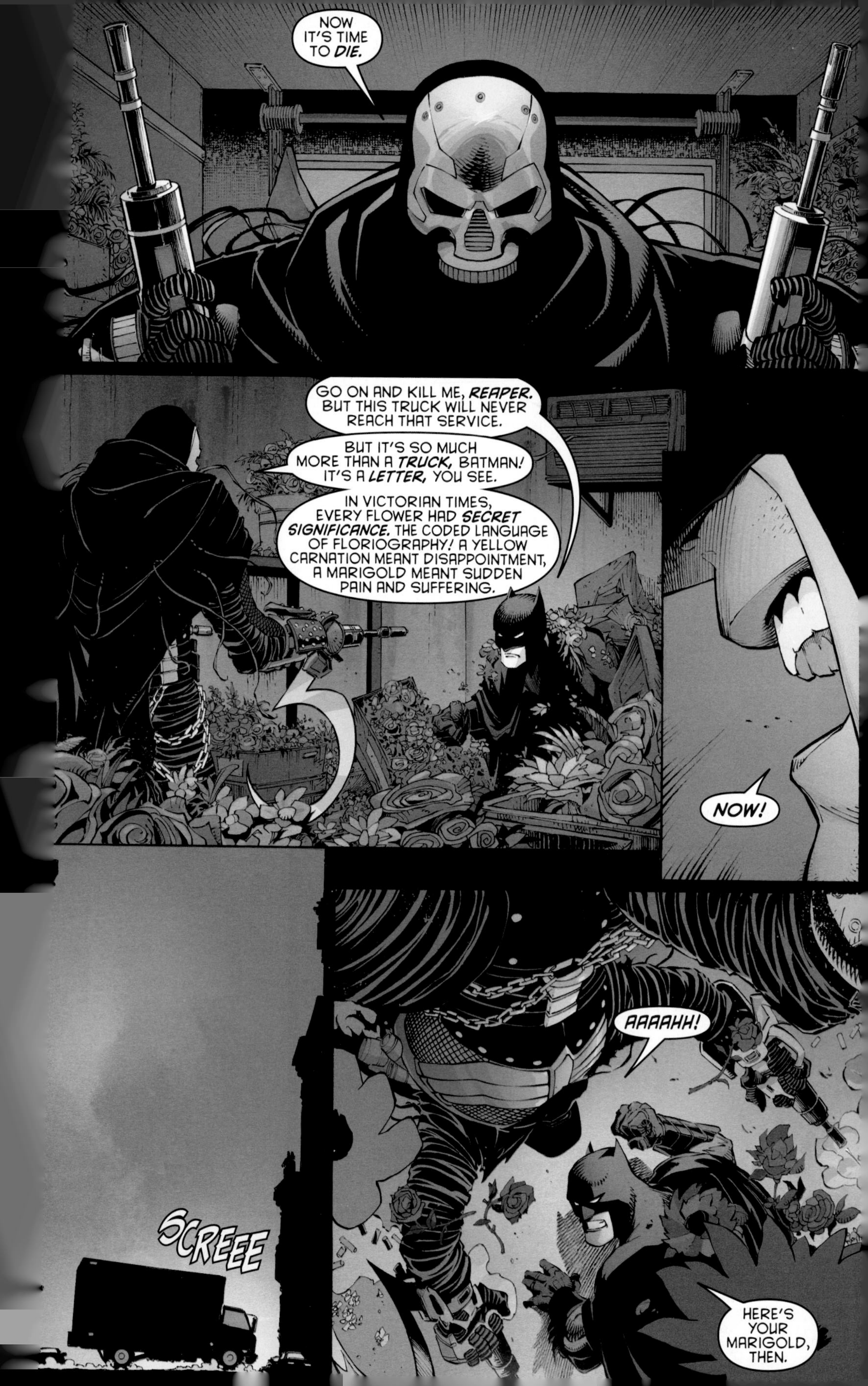
NOW IT'S TIME TO *DIE.*
GO ON AND KILL ME, *REAPER.* BUT THIS TRUCK WILL NEVER REACH THAT SERVICE.
BUT IT'S SO MUCH MORE THAN A *TRUCK,* BATMAN! IT'S A *LETTER,* YOU SEE.
IN VICTORIAN TIMES, EVERY FLOWER HAD *SECRET SIGNIFICANCE.* THE CODED LANGUAGE OF FLORIOGRAPHY! A YELLOW CARNATION MEANT DISAPPOINTMENT, A MARIGOLD MEANT SUDDEN PAIN AND SUFFERING.
NOW!
SCREEEE
AAAAHH!
HERE'S YOUR MARIGOLD, THEN.

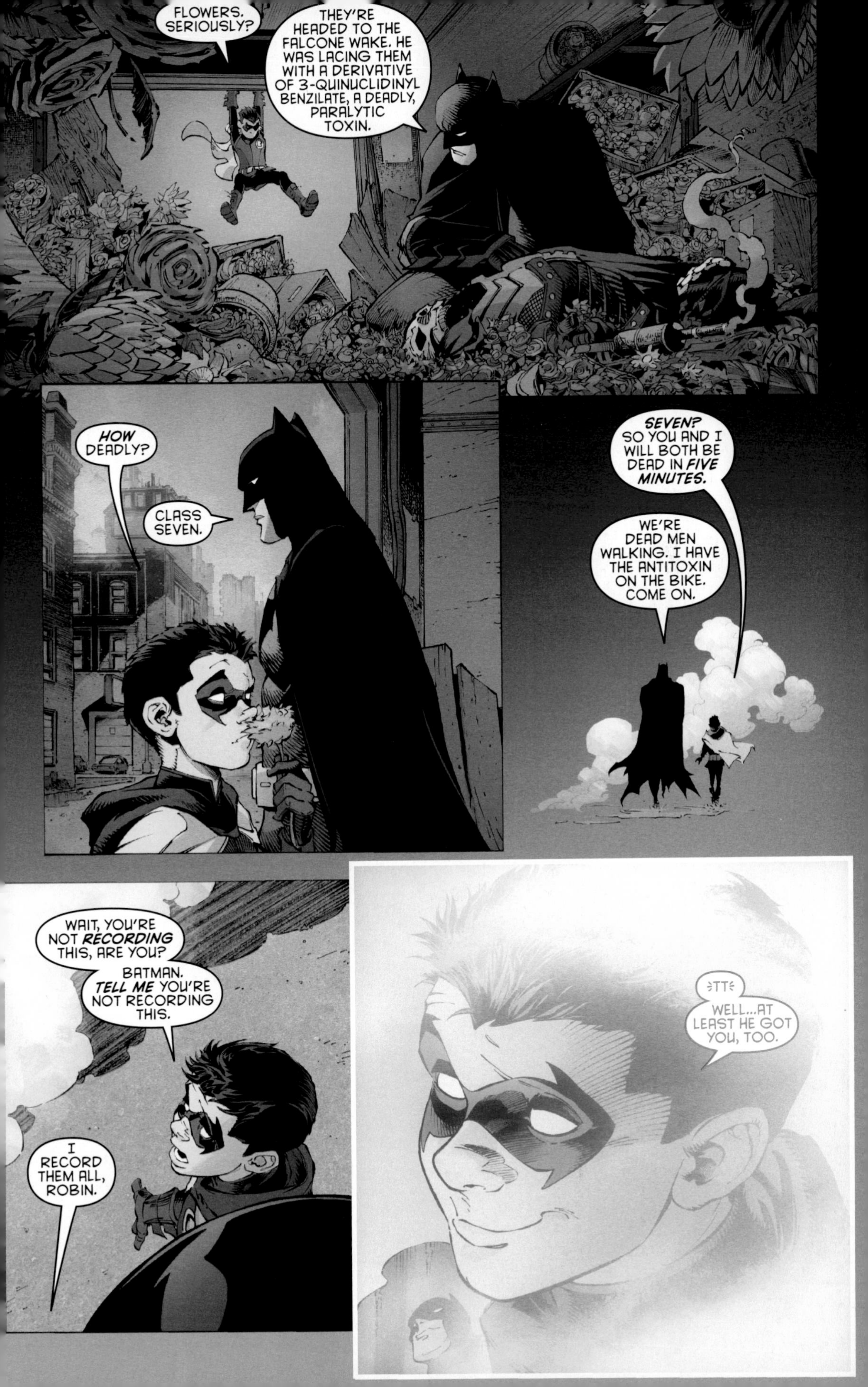
FLOWERS. SERIOUSLY?
THEY'RE HEADED TO THE FALCONE WAKE. HE WAS LACING THEM WITH A DERIVATIVE OF 3-QUINUCLIDINYL BENZILATE, A DEADLY, PARALYTIC TOXIN.
HOW DEADLY?
CLASS SEVEN.
SEVEN? SO YOU AND I WILL BOTH BE DEAD IN FIVE MINUTES.
WE'RE DEAD MEN WALKING. I HAVE THE ANTITOXIN ON THE BIKE. COME ON.
WAIT, YOU'RE NOT RECORDING THIS, ARE YOU?
BATMAN. TELL ME YOU'RE NOT RECORDING THIS.
I RECORD THEM ALL, ROBIN.
TT
WELL...AT LEAST HE GOT YOU, TOO.

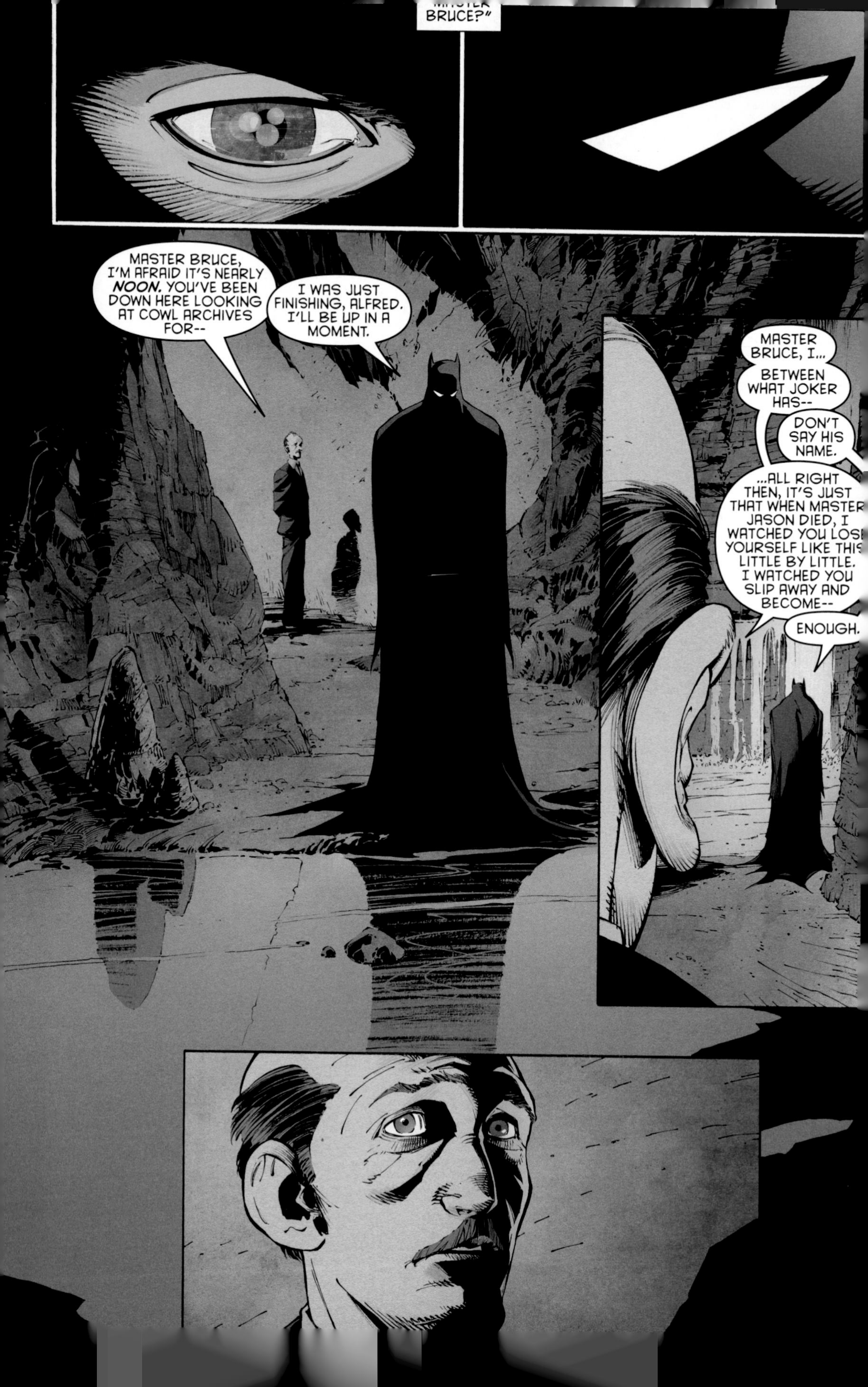
MASTER BRUCE?"
MASTER BRUCE, I'M AFRAID IT'S NEARLY *NOON.* YOU'VE BEEN DOWN HERE LOOKING AT COWL ARCHIVES FOR--
I WAS JUST FINISHING, ALFRED. I'LL BE UP IN A MOMENT.
MASTER BRUCE, I...
BETWEEN WHAT JOKER HAS--
DON'T SAY HIS NAME.
...ALL RIGHT THEN, IT'S JUST THAT WHEN MASTER JASON DIED, I WATCHED YOU LOSE YOURSELF LIKE THIS LITTLE BY LITTLE. I WATCHED YOU SLIP AWAY AND BECOME--
ENOUGH.

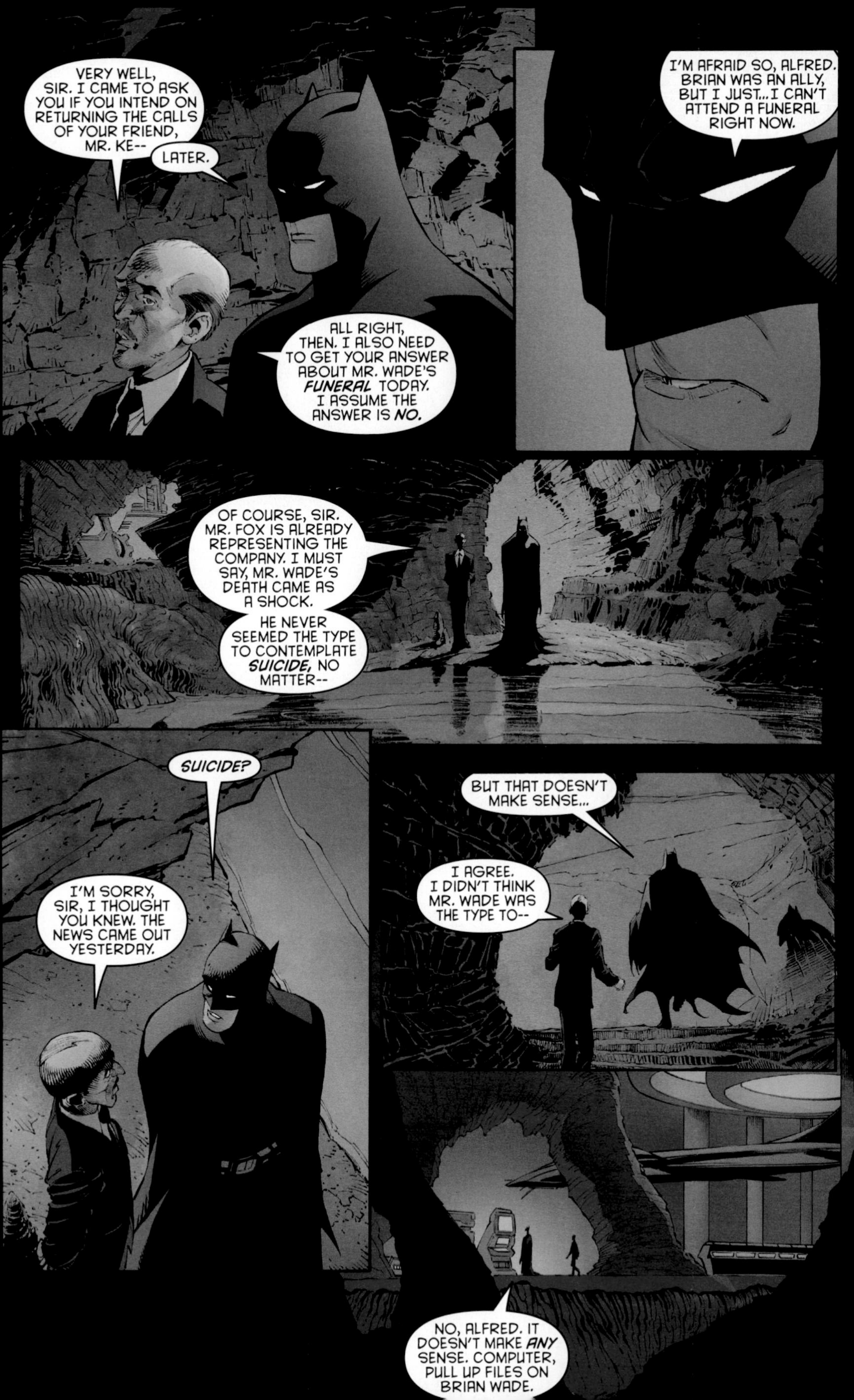
VERY WELL, SIR. I CAME TO ASK YOU IF YOU INTEND ON RETURNING THE CALLS OF YOUR FRIEND, MR. KE--
LATER.
ALL RIGHT, THEN. I ALSO NEED TO GET YOUR ANSWER ABOUT MR. WADE'S FUNERAL TODAY. I ASSUME THE ANSWER IS NO.
I'M AFRAID SO, ALFRED. BRIAN WAS AN ALLY, BUT I JUST...I CAN'T ATTEND A FUNERAL RIGHT NOW.
OF COURSE, SIR. MR. FOX IS ALREADY REPRESENTING THE COMPANY. I MUST SAY, MR. WADE'S DEATH CAME AS A SHOCK.
HE NEVER SEEMED THE TYPE TO CONTEMPLATE SUICIDE, NO MATTER--
SUICIDE?
I'M SORRY, SIR, I THOUGHT YOU KNEW. THE NEWS CAME OUT YESTERDAY.
BUT THAT DOESN'T MAKE SENSE...
I AGREE. I DIDN'T THINK MR. WADE WAS THE TYPE TO--
NO, ALFRED. IT DOESN'T MAKE ANY SENSE. COMPUTER, PULL UP FILES ON BRIAN WADE.

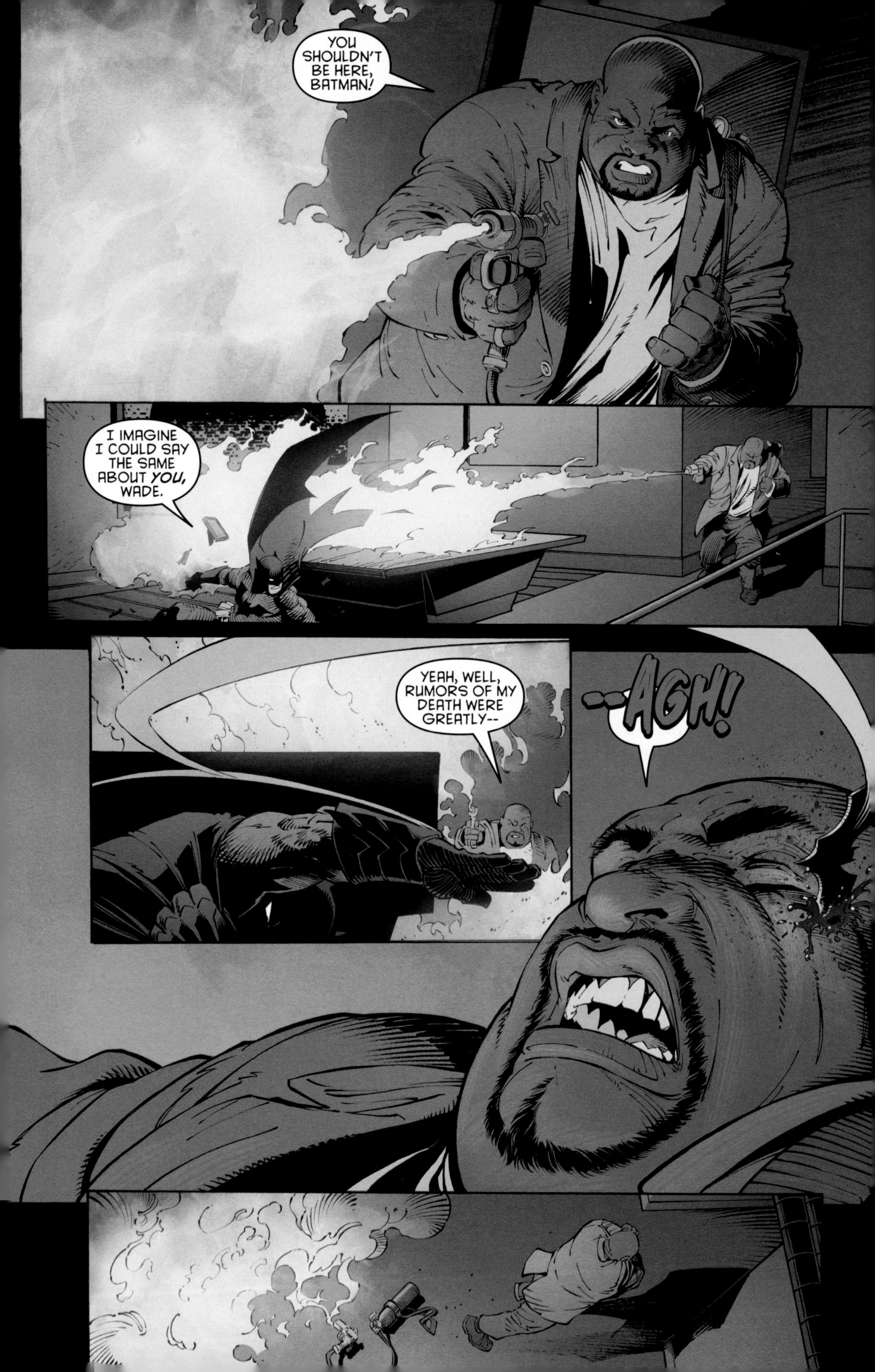
YOU SHOULDN'T BE HERE, BATMAN!
I IMAGINE I COULD SAY THE SAME ABOUT YOU, WADE.
YEAH, WELL, RUMORS OF MY DEATH WERE GREATLY--
--AGH!

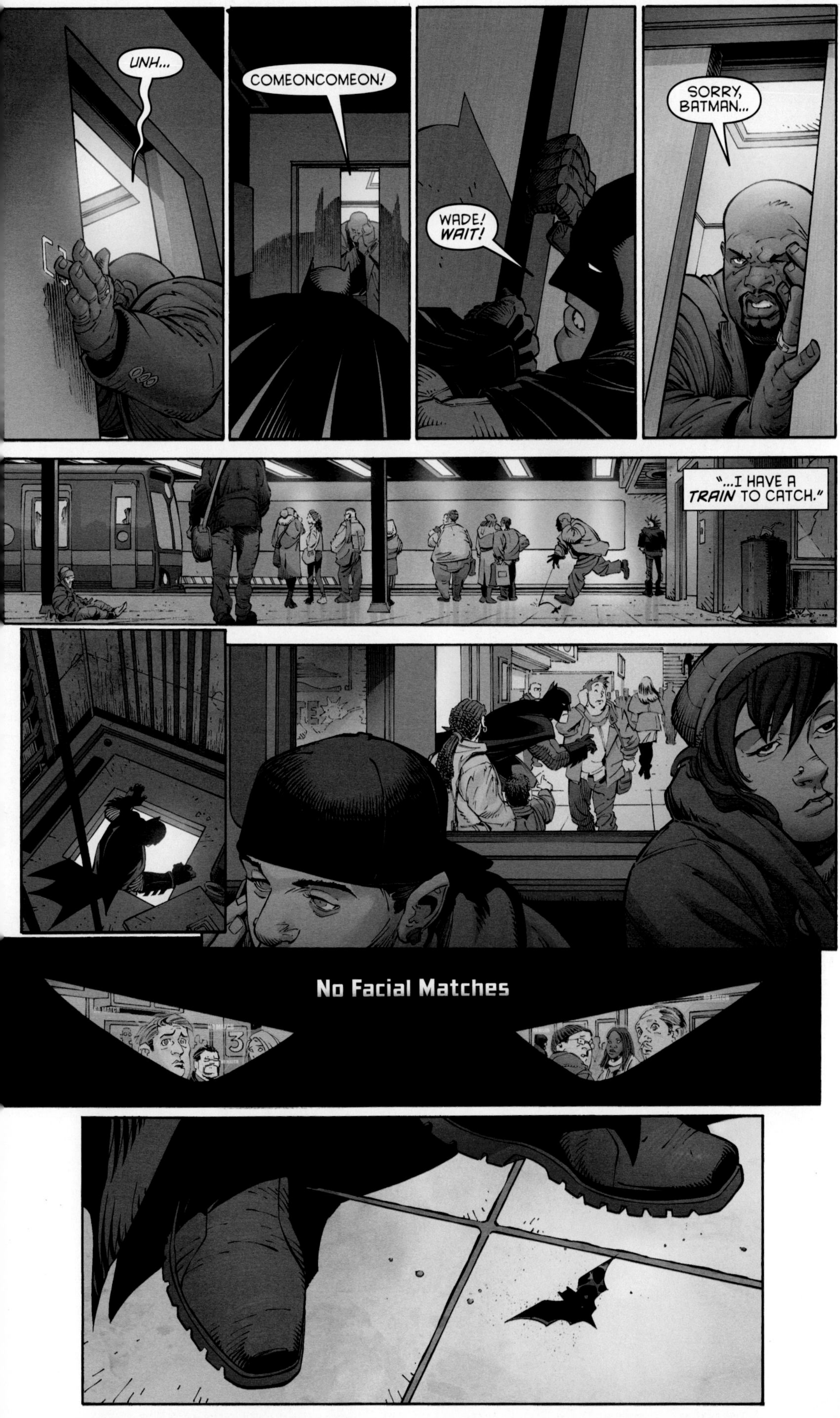
UNH...
COMEONCOMEON!
WADE! WAIT!
SORRY, BATMAN...
"...I HAVE A TRAIN TO CATCH."
No Facial Matches

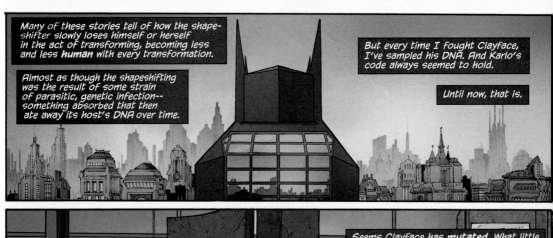

Many of these stories tell of how the shape-shifter slowly loses himself or herself in the act of transforming, becoming less and less **human** with every transformation.

Almost as though the shapeshifting was the result of some strain of parasitic, genetic infection-- something absorbed that then ate away its host's DNA over time.

But every time I fought Clayface, I've sampled his DNA. And Karlo's code always seemed to hold.

Until now, that is.

Seems Clayface has **mutated.** What little left there is of Basil Karlo's DNA is disappearing fast. Meaning, Clayface is no longer an actor. No longer a mimic.

If he samples a person's DNA, brushes their skin, finds a single hair, he can absorb it and fully **become** them.

Which means, he's truly a clay man now. Everyone and no one. The only question is...

...who will he become **next?**

MR. WAYNE...

...I RECEIVED YOUR MESSAGE ABOUT THE NEW SUIT FOR BATMAN.

THANK YOU FOR COMING IN SO QUICKLY, LUCIUS.

BATMAN CALLED ME LAST NIGHT. THIS SUIT IS OF THE HIGHEST PRIORITY. HE SAID ANYTHING YOU HAVE WITH HEAVY *EPIDERMAL PROTECTION...*

...IT'S CLAYFACE. SEEMS HE'S... *EVOLVED.*

EVOLVED?

IT'S A TROUBLING TURN OF EVENTS TO SAY THE LEAST.

VERY TROUBLING. WELL THEN,... I'LL GET RIGHT ON THAT SUIT, MR. WAYNE.

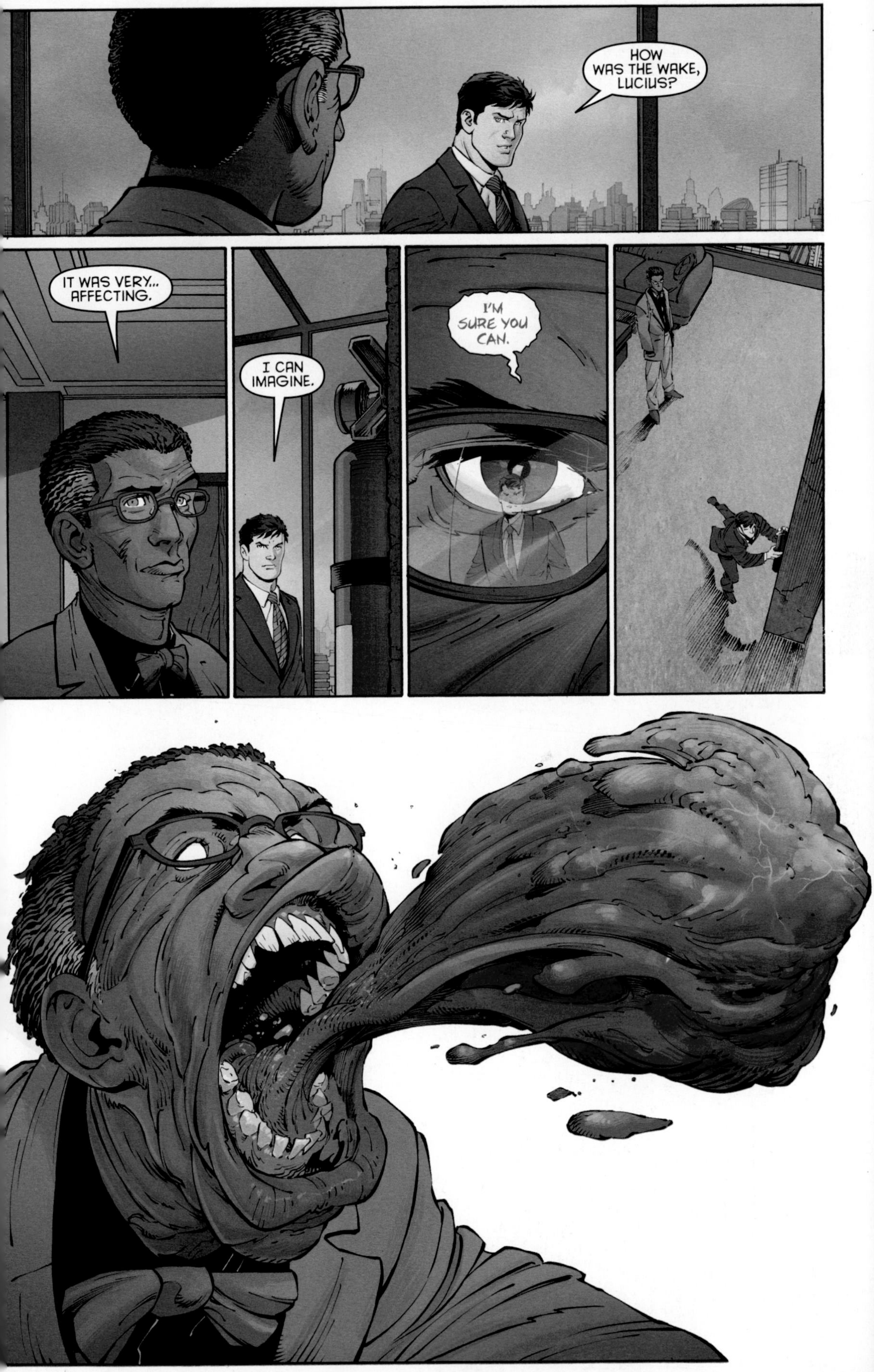
HOW WAS THE WAKE, LUCIUS?
IT WAS VERY... AFFECTING.
I CAN IMAGINE.
I'M SURE YOU CAN.

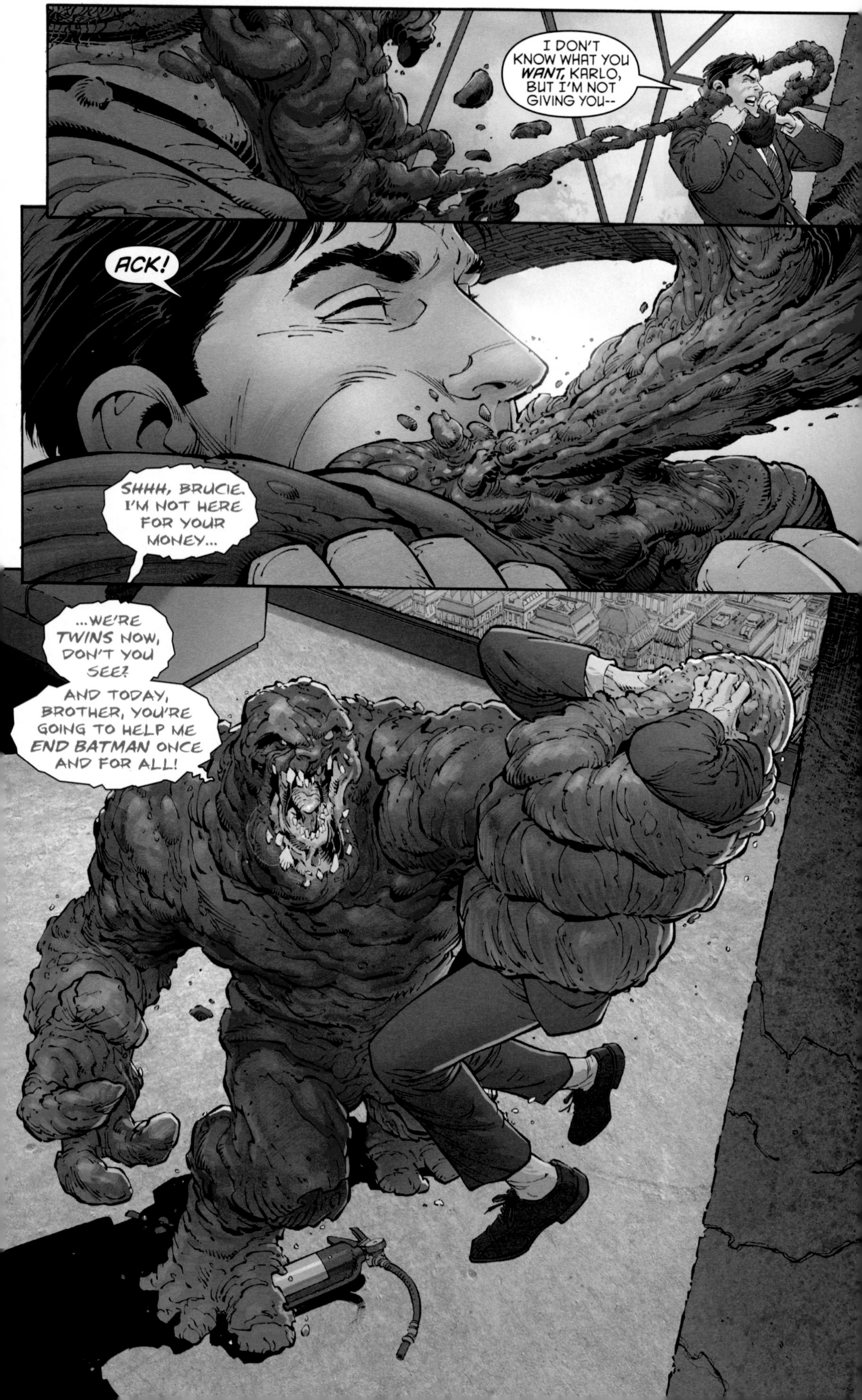
I DON'T KNOW WHAT YOU WANT, KARLO, BUT I'M NOT GIVING YOU--
ACK!
SHHH, BRUCIE. I'M NOT HERE FOR YOUR MONEY...
...WE'RE TWINS NOW, DON'T YOU SEE?
AND TODAY, BROTHER, YOU'RE GOING TO HELP ME END BATMAN ONCE AND FOR ALL!

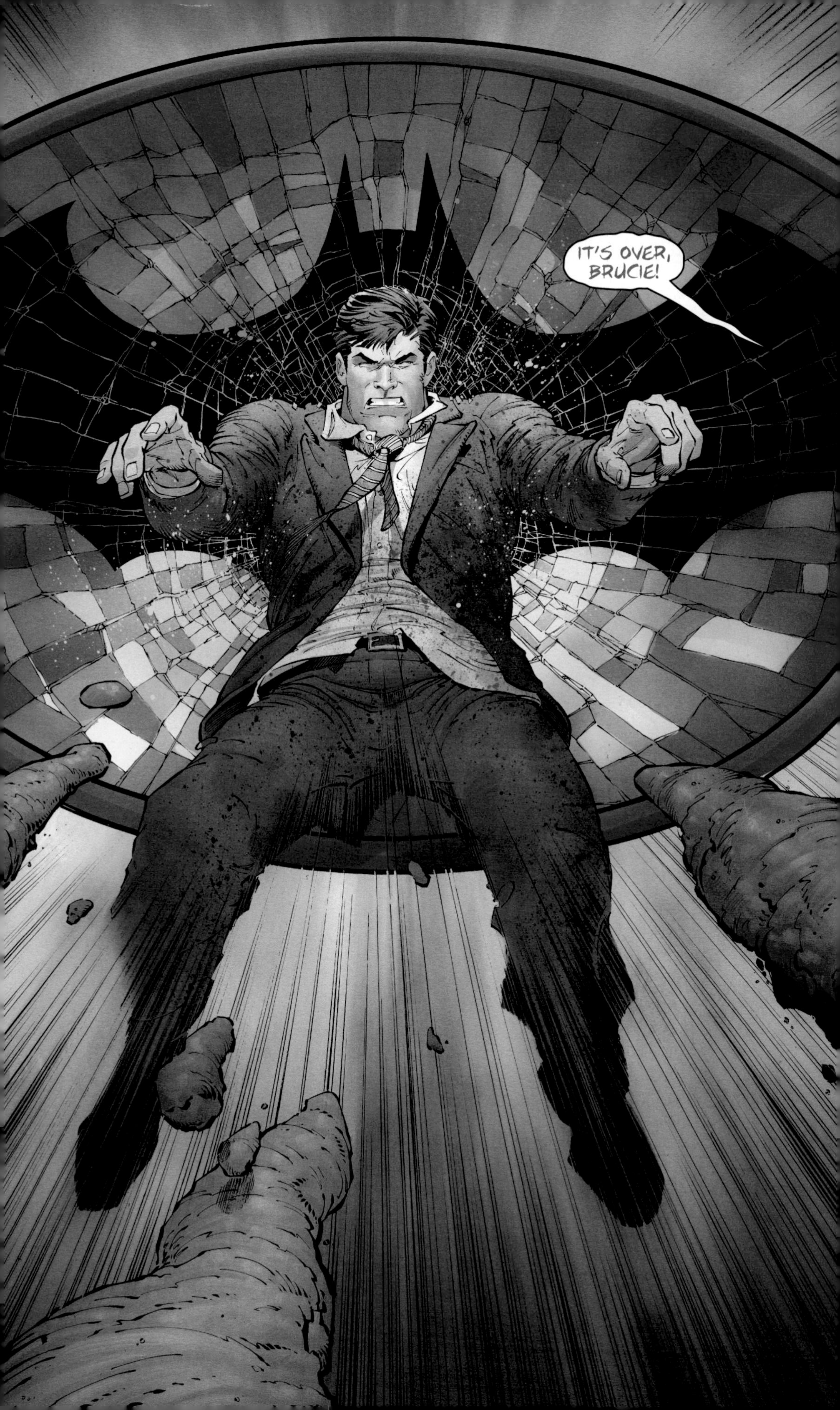
IT'S OVER, BRUCIE!

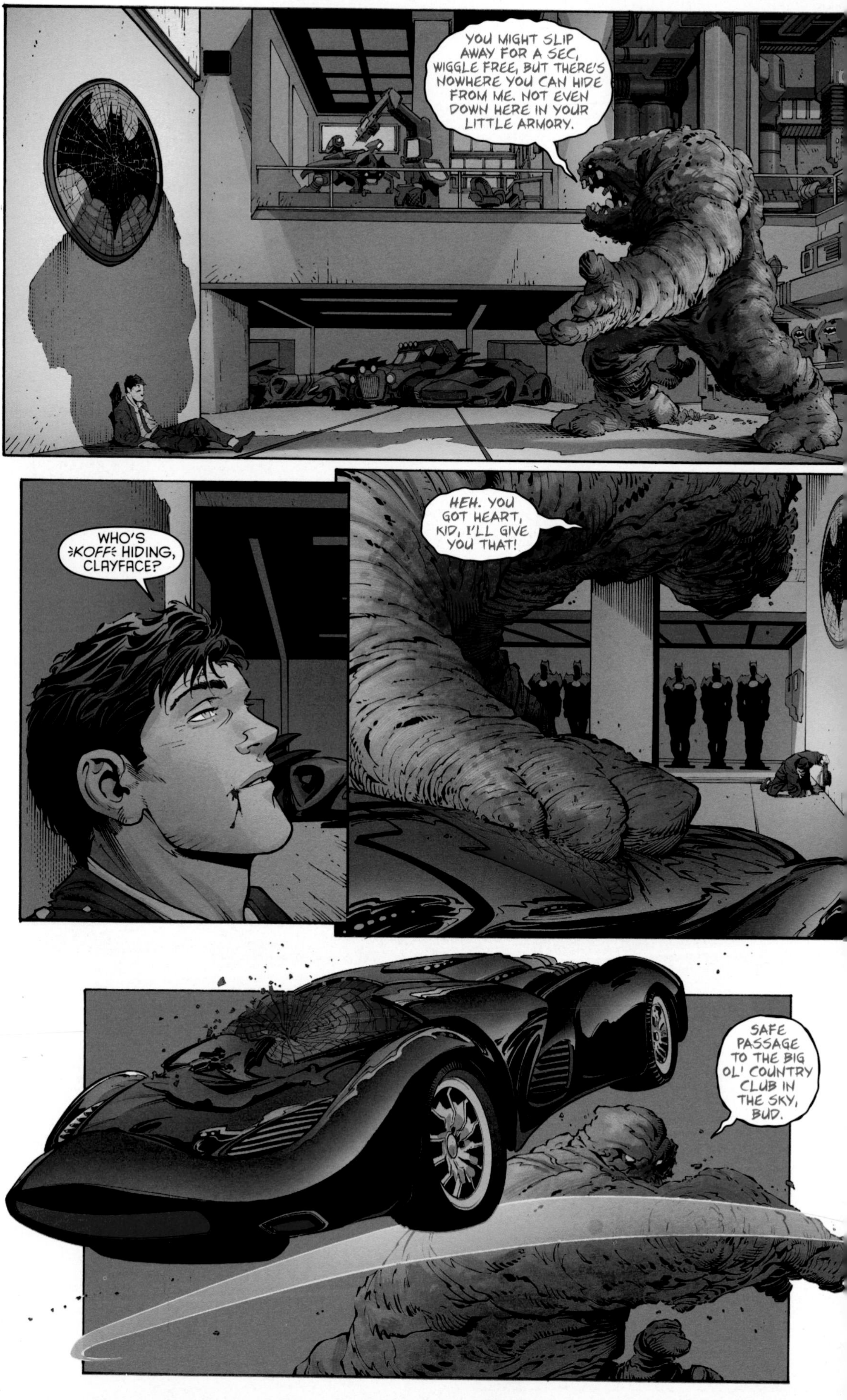
YOU MIGHT SLIP AWAY FOR A SEC, WIGGLE FREE, BUT THERE'S NOWHERE YOU CAN HIDE FROM ME. NOT EVEN DOWN HERE IN YOUR LITTLE ARMORY.
WHO'S *KOFF* HIDING, CLAYFACE?
HEH. YOU GOT HEART, KID, I'LL GIVE YOU THAT!
SAFE PASSAGE TO THE BIG OL' COUNTRY CLUB IN THE SKY, BUD.

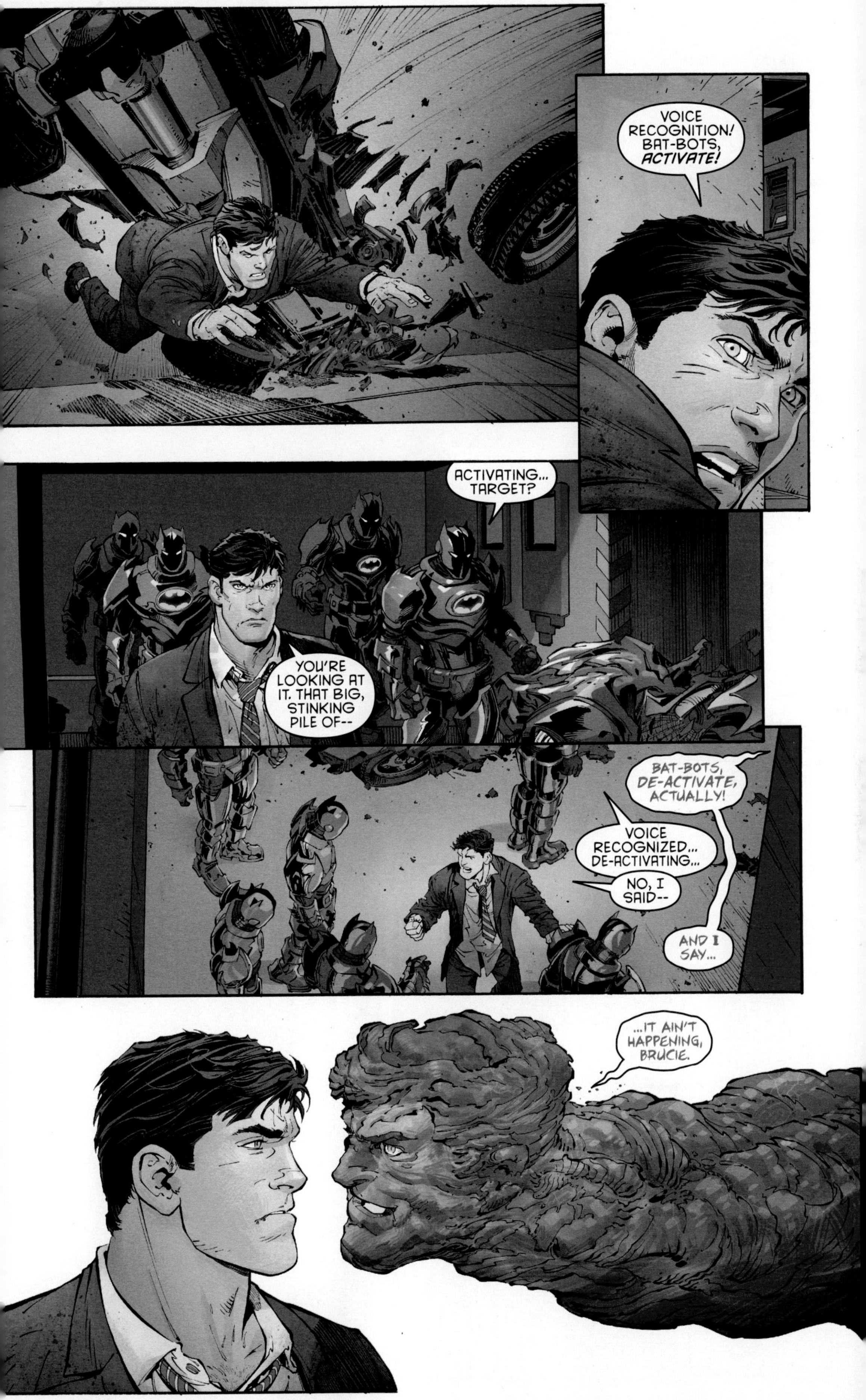
VOICE RECOGNITION! BAT-BOTS, *ACTIVATE!*
ACTIVATING... TARGET?
YOU'RE LOOKING AT IT. THAT BIG, STINKING PILE OF--
BAT-BOTS, *DE-ACTIVATE,* ACTUALLY!
VOICE RECOGNIZED... DE-ACTIVATING...
NO, I SAID--
AND **I** SAY...
...IT AIN'T HAPPENING, BRUCIE.

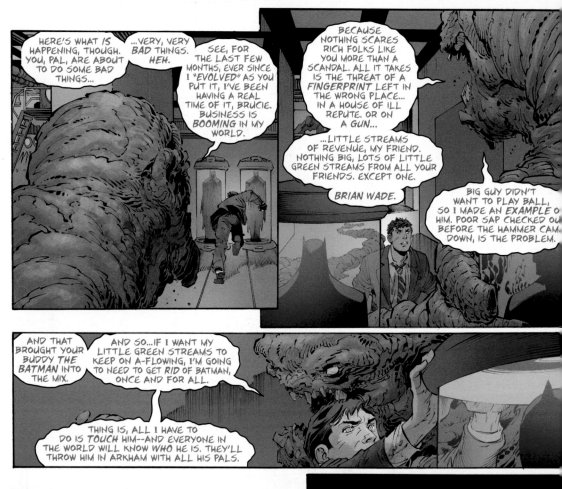

HERE'S WHAT *IS* HAPPENING, THOUGH. YOU, PAL, ARE ABOUT TO DO SOME BAD THINGS...

...VERY, VERY *BAD* THINGS. HEH.

SEE, FOR THE LAST FEW MONTHS, EVER SINCE I *"EVOLVED"* AS YOU PUT IT, I'VE BEEN HAVING A REAL TIME OF IT, BRUCIE. BUSINESS IS *BOOMING* IN MY WORLD.

BECAUSE NOTHING SCARES RICH FOLKS LIKE YOU MORE THAN A *SCANDAL.* ALL IT TAKES IS THE THREAT OF A *FINGERPRINT* LEFT IN THE WRONG PLACE... IN A HOUSE OF ILL REPUTE. OR ON A *GUN*...

...LITTLE STREAMS OF REVENUE, MY FRIEND. NOTHING BIG, LOTS OF LITTLE GREEN STREAMS FROM ALL YOUR FRIENDS. EXCEPT ONE.

BRIAN WADE.

BIG GUY DIDN'T WANT TO PLAY BALL, SO I MADE AN *EXAMPLE* OF HIM. POOR SAP CHECKED OUT BEFORE THE HAMMER CAME DOWN, IS THE PROBLEM.

AND THAT BROUGHT YOUR BUDDY *THE BATMAN* INTO THE MIX.

AND SO...IF I WANT MY LITTLE GREEN STREAMS TO KEEP ON A-FLOWING, I'M GOING TO NEED TO GET *RID* OF BATMAN, ONCE AND FOR ALL.

THING IS, ALL I HAVE TO DO IS *TOUCH* HIM--AND EVERYONE IN THE WORLD WILL KNOW *WHO* HE IS. THEY'LL THROW HIM IN ARKHAM WITH ALL HIS PALS.

AND WHAT BETTER WAY TO LURE HIM OUT THAN BY USING HIS FAVORITE GOTHAMITE, HIS OWN BENEFACTOR, MR. BRUCE WAYNE?! *YOU* GO BAD, USING HIS GEAR TO WREAK HAVOC, *HE* SHOWS UP, I TOUCH HIM AND PUT AN END TO HIS ANTICS. BEST PART IS, NO ONE KNOWS I WAS EVER HERE.

SO, I'M SORRY, BRUCIE, BUT IT'S OVER. NOWHERE LEFT FOR YOU TO GO BUT...

...*DOWN THE HATCH!*

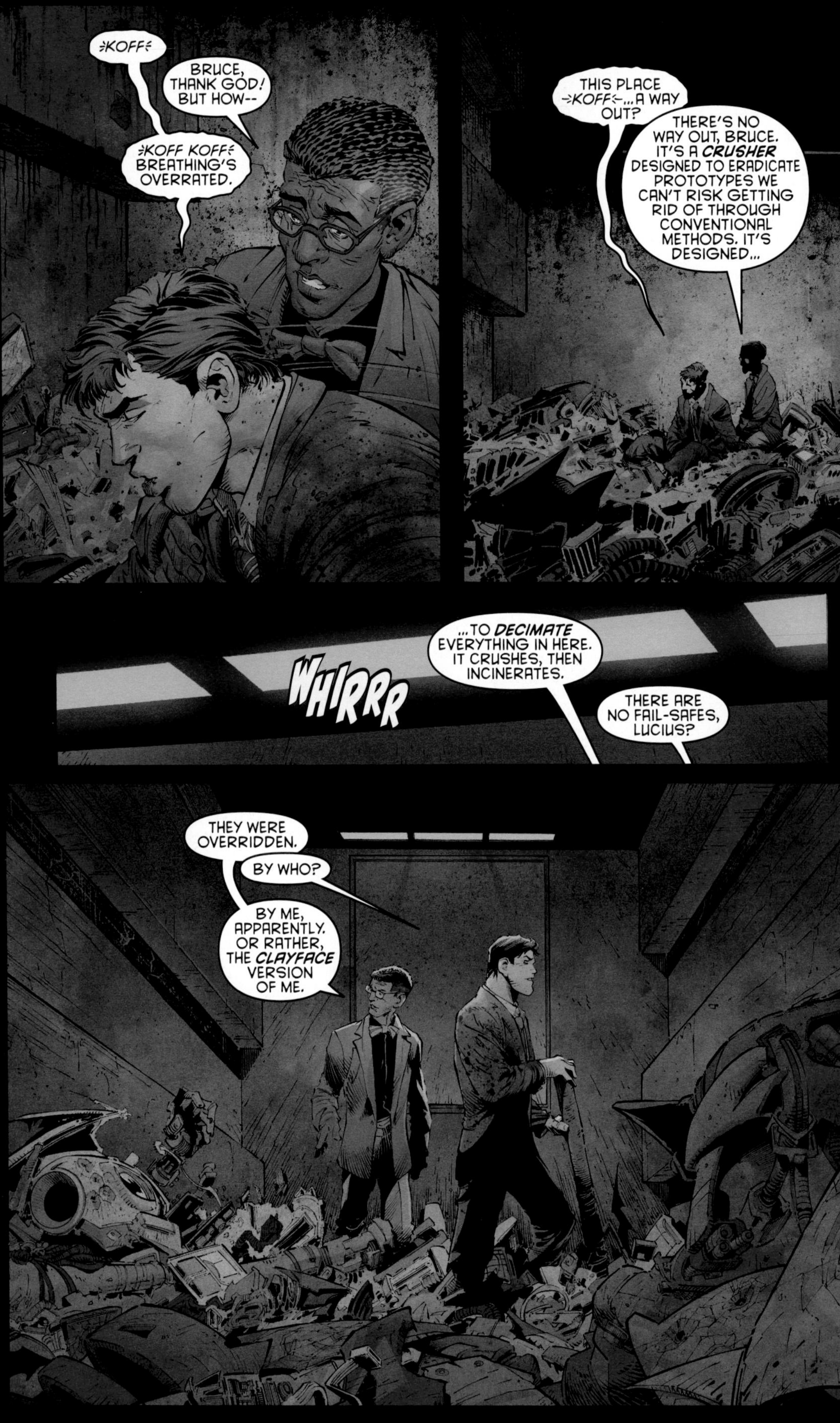
KOFF
BRUCE, THANK GOD! BUT HOW--
KOFF KOFF BREATHING'S OVERRATED.
THIS PLACE *KOFF*...A WAY OUT?
THERE'S NO WAY OUT, BRUCE. IT'S A CRUSHER DESIGNED TO ERADICATE PROTOTYPES WE CAN'T RISK GETTING RID OF THROUGH CONVENTIONAL METHODS. IT'S DESIGNED...
WHIRRR
...TO DECIMATE EVERYTHING IN HERE. IT CRUSHES, THEN INCINERATES.
THERE ARE NO FAIL-SAFES, LUCIUS?
THEY WERE OVERRIDDEN.
BY WHO?
BY ME, APPARENTLY. OR RATHER, THE CLAYFACE VERSION OF ME.

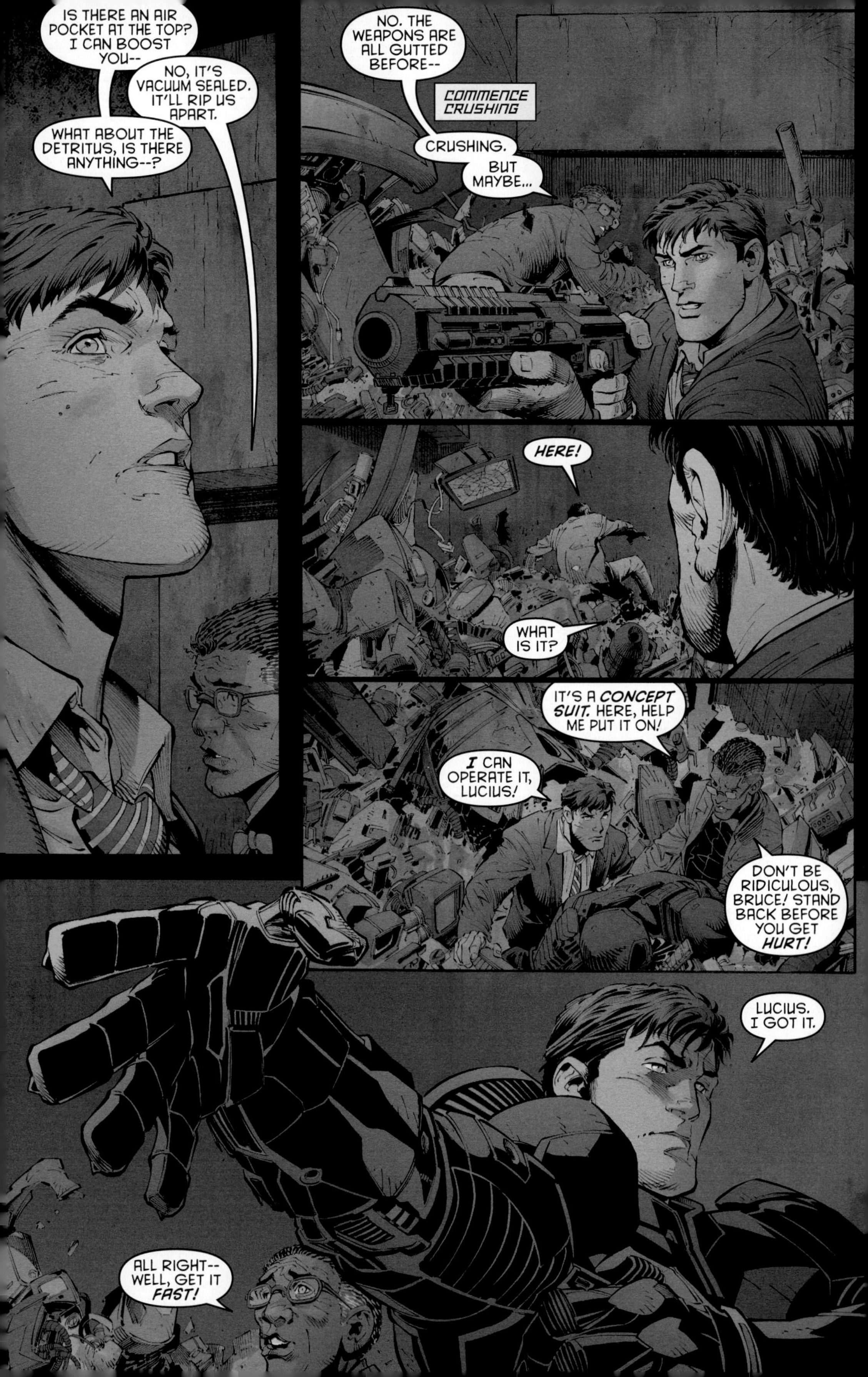
IS THERE AN AIR POCKET AT THE TOP? I CAN BOOST YOU--
NO, IT'S VACUUM SEALED. IT'LL RIP US APART.
WHAT ABOUT THE DETRITUS, IS THERE ANYTHING--?
NO. THE WEAPONS ARE ALL GUTTED BEFORE--
COMMENCE CRUSHING
CRUSHING.
BUT MAYBE...
HERE!
WHAT IS IT?
IT'S A CONCEPT SUIT. HERE, HELP ME PUT IT ON!
I CAN OPERATE IT, LUCIUS!
DON'T BE RIDICULOUS, BRUCE! STAND BACK BEFORE YOU GET HURT!
LUCIUS. I GOT IT.
ALL RIGHT-- WELL, GET IT FAST!

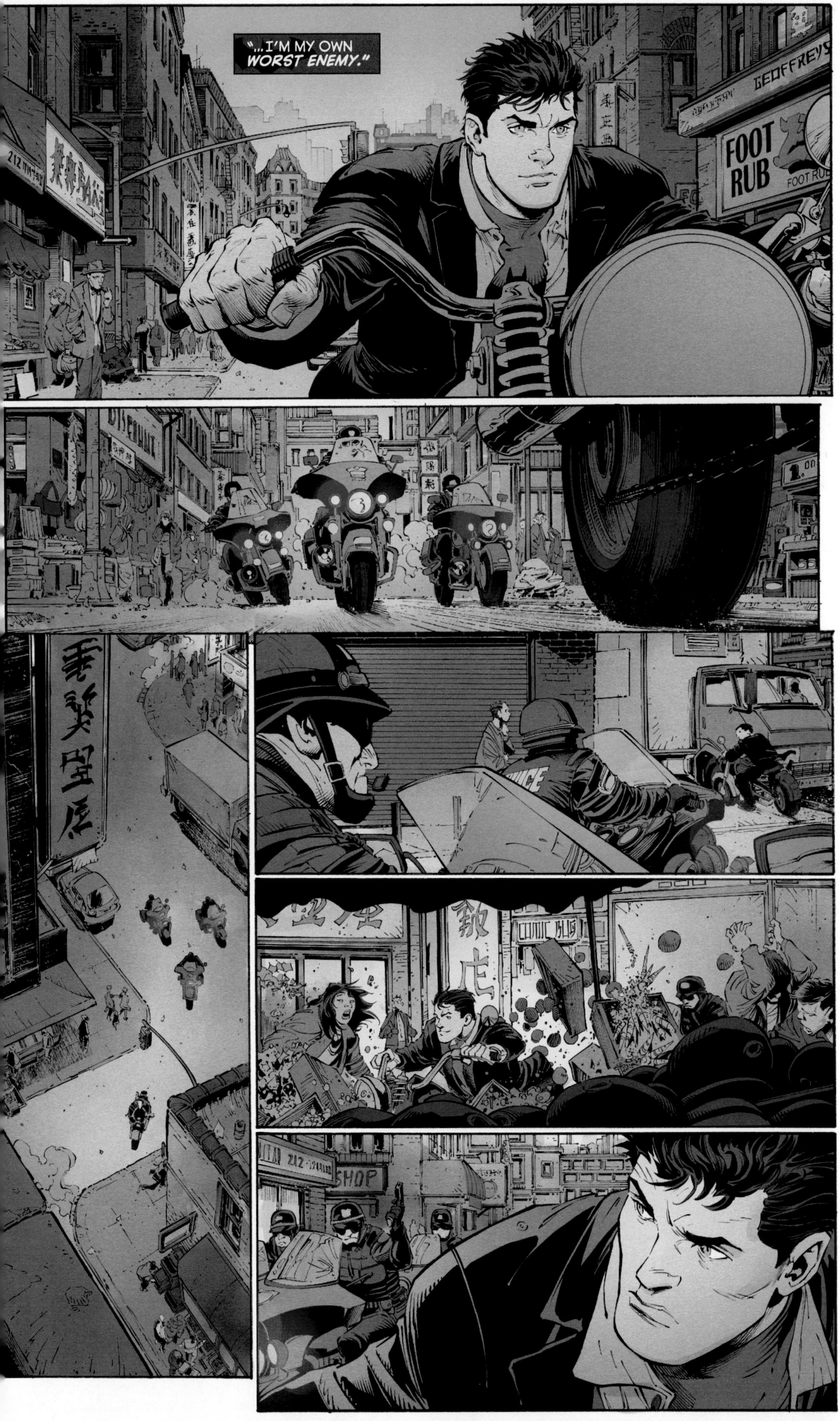
"...I'M MY OWN WORST ENEMY."
GEOFFREYS
FOOT RUB
SHOP

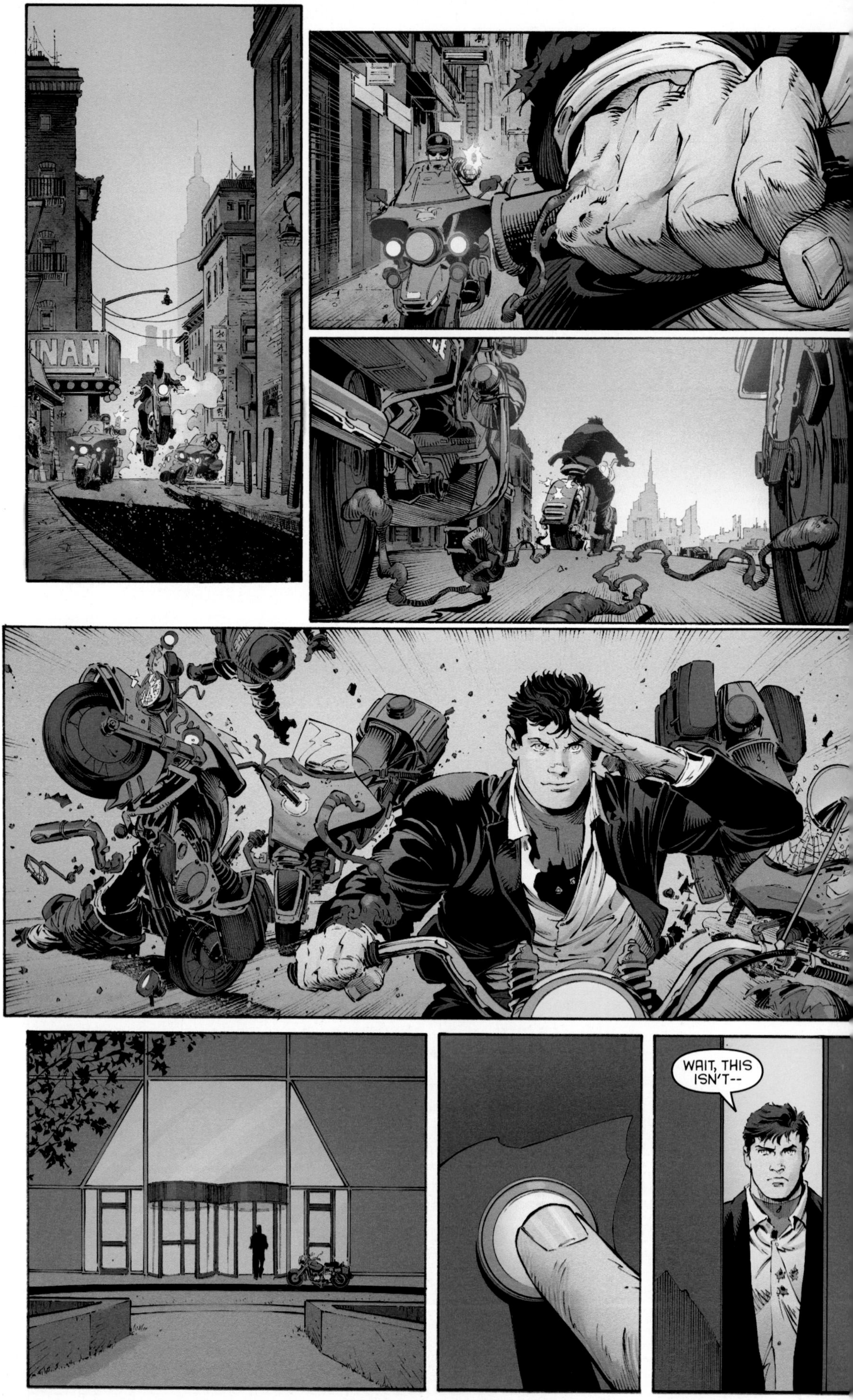
INAN
WAIT, THIS ISN'T--

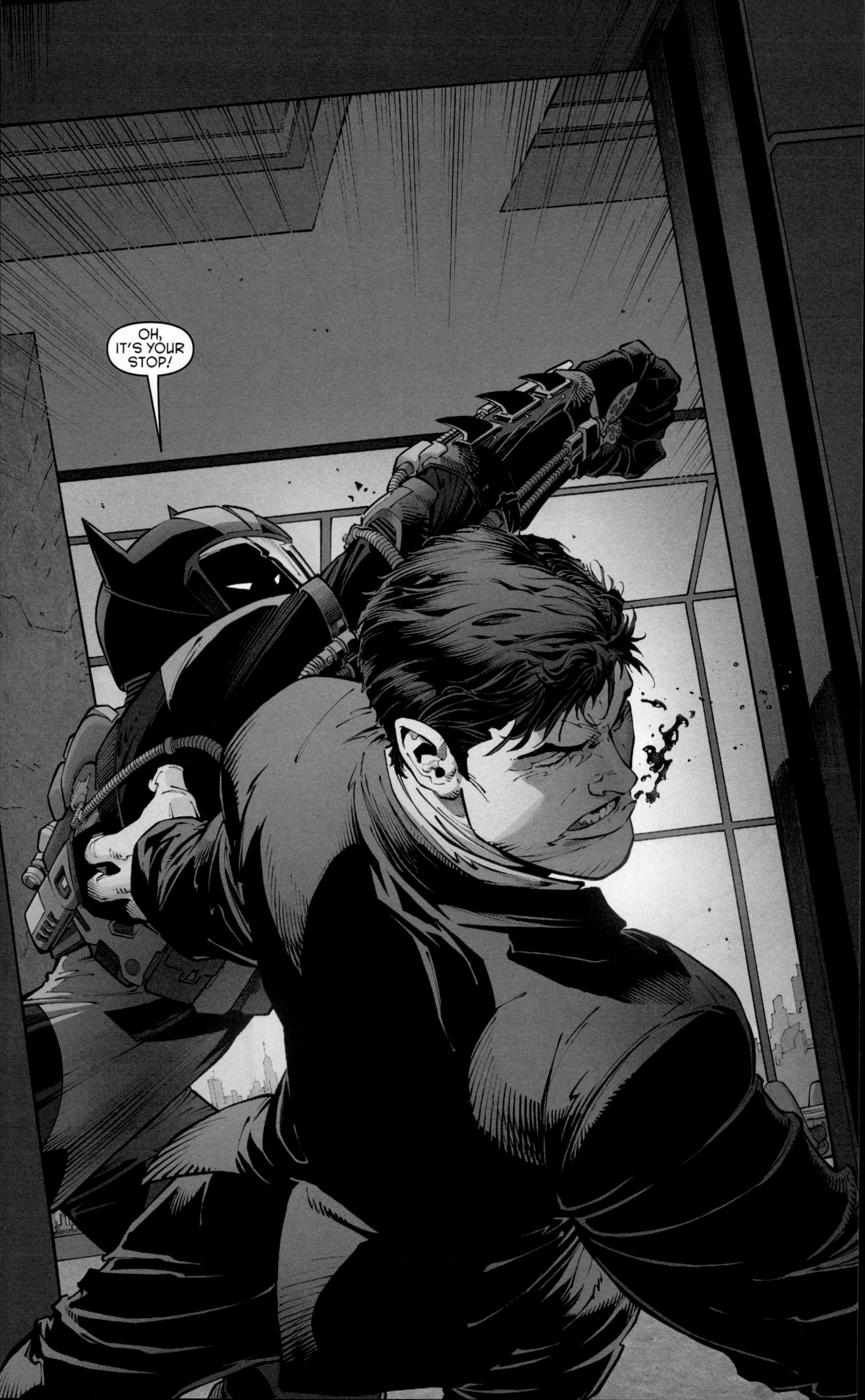
OH, IT'S YOUR STOP!

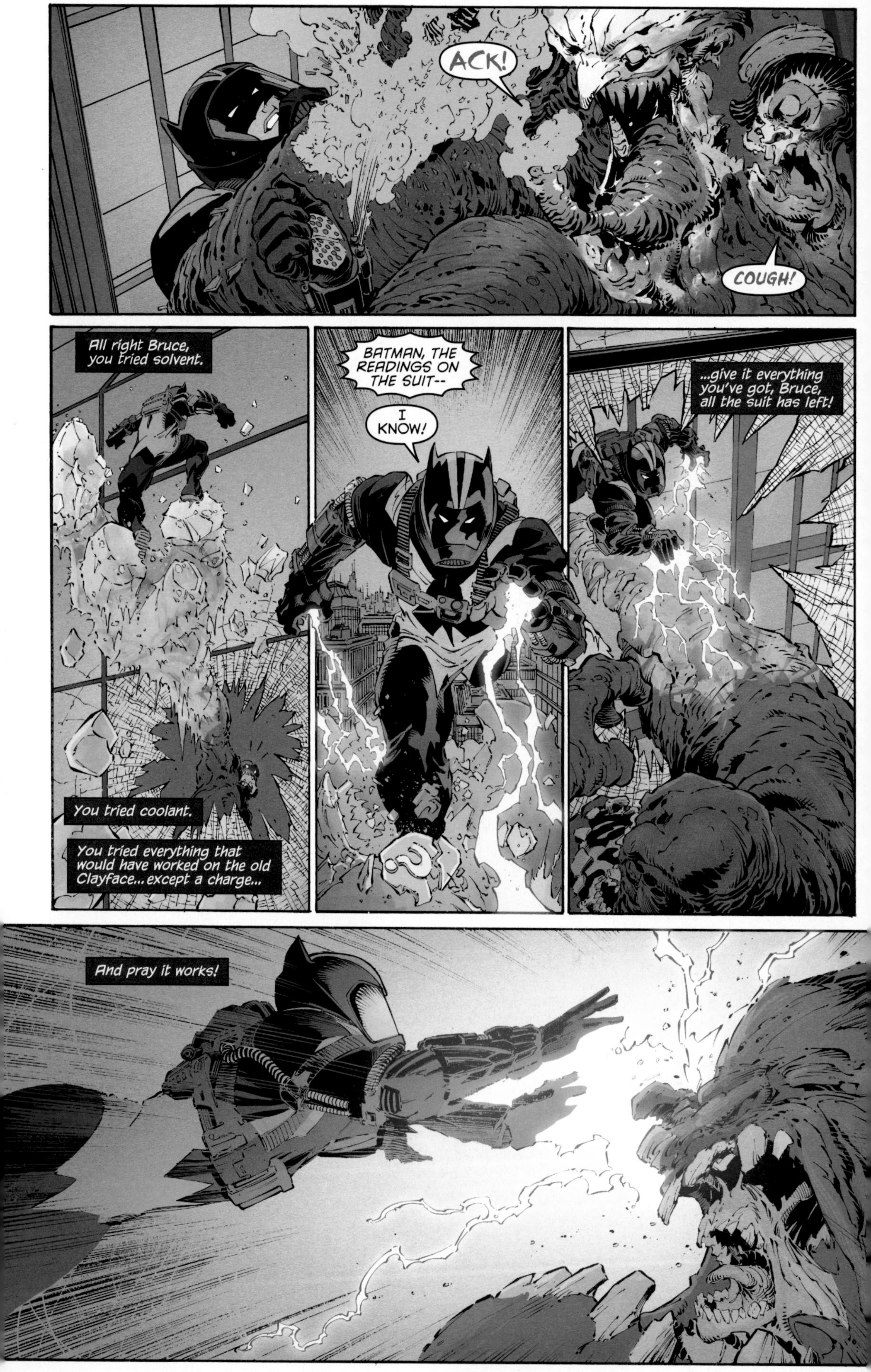

ACK!
COUGH!
All right Bruce, you tried solvent.
You tried coolant.
You tried everything that would have worked on the old Clayface...except a charge...
BATMAN, THE READINGS ON THE SUIT--
I KNOW!
...give it everything you've got, Bruce, all the suit has left!
And pray it works!

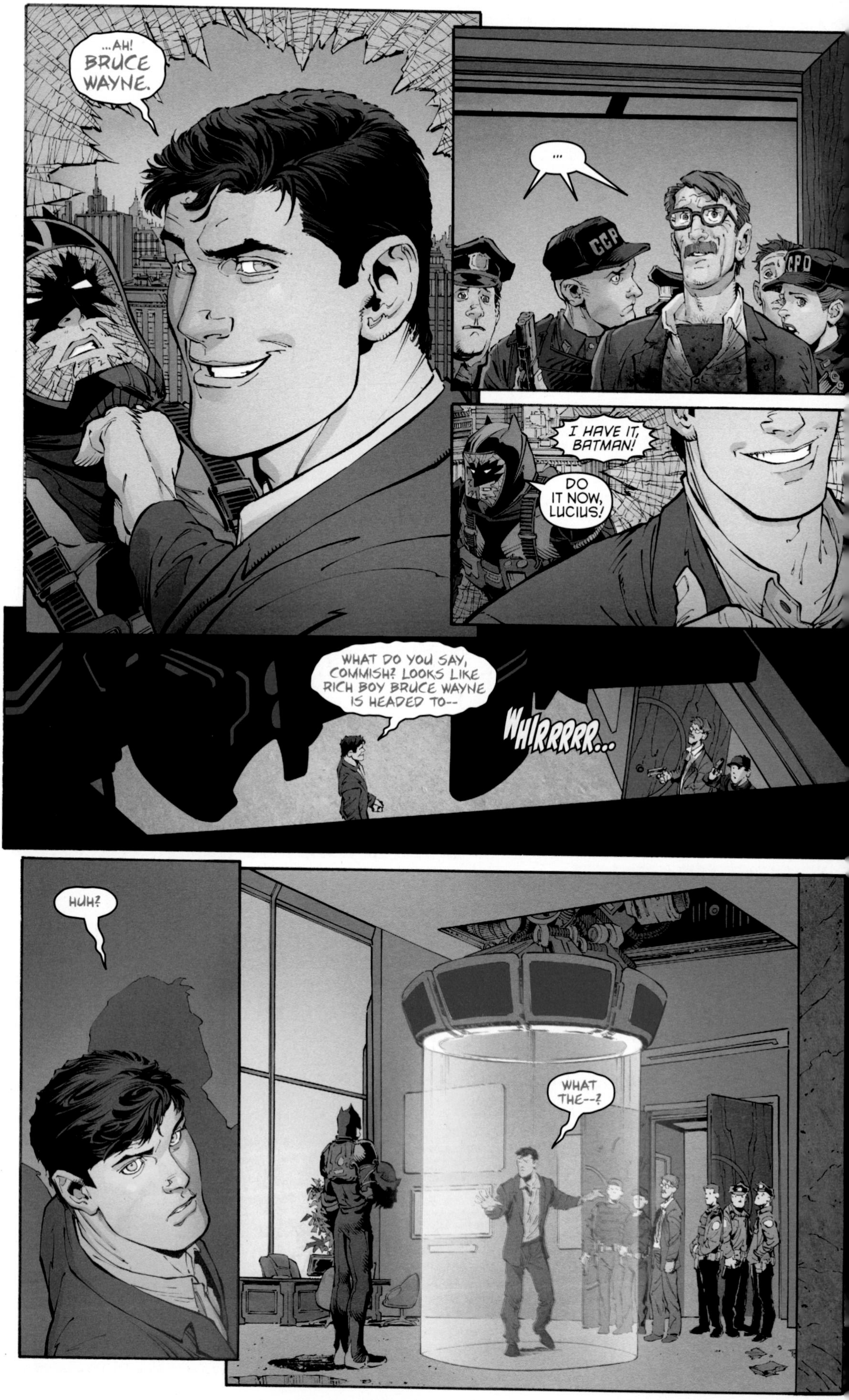

...AH! BRUCE WAYNE.
...
I HAVE IT, BATMAN!
DO IT NOW, LUCIUS!
WHAT DO YOU SAY, COMMISH? LOOKS LIKE RICH BOY BRUCE WAYNE IS HEADED TO--
WHIRRRRR...
HUH?
WHAT THE--?

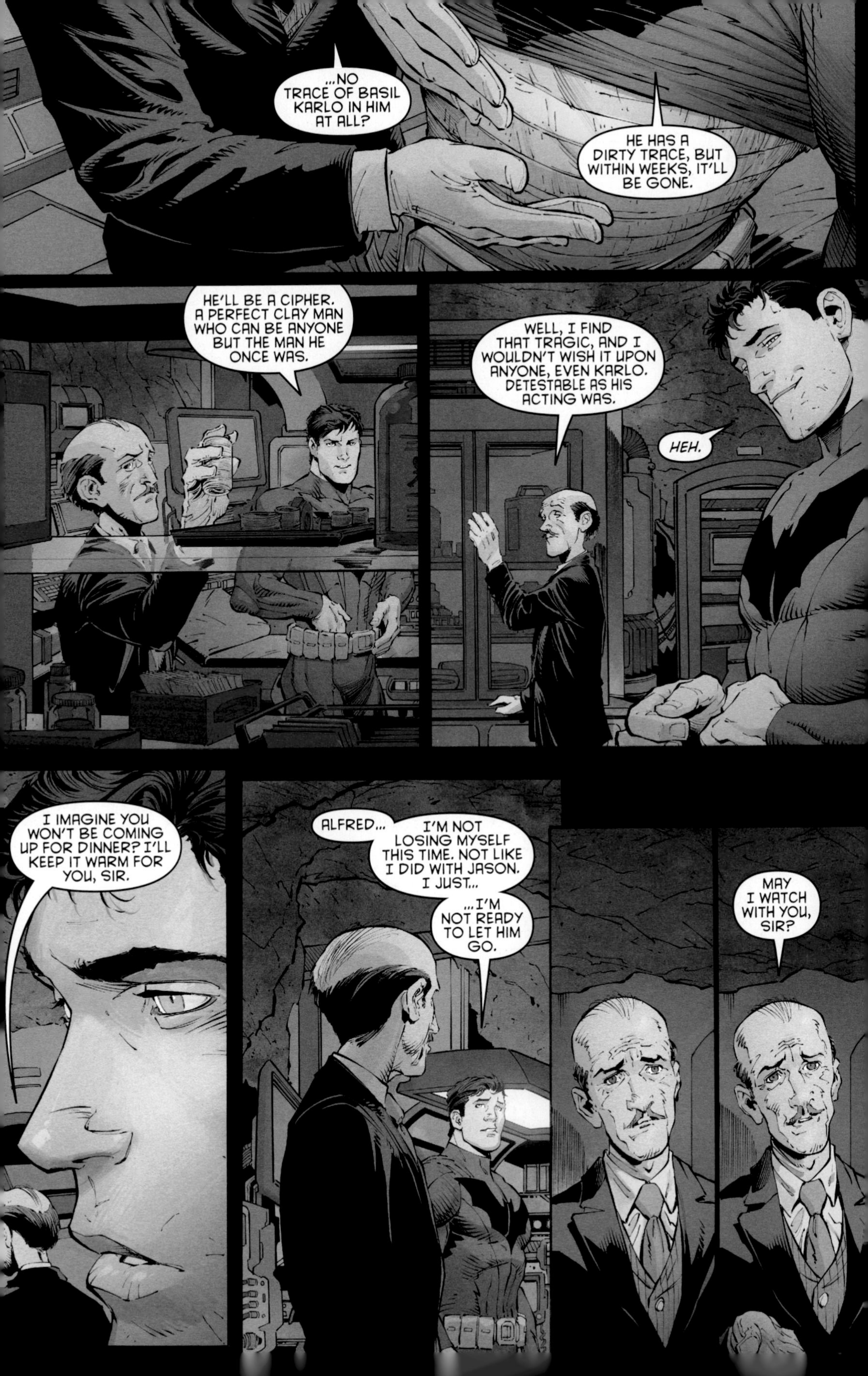
...NO TRACE OF BASIL KARLO IN HIM AT ALL?
HE HAS A DIRTY TRACE, BUT WITHIN WEEKS, IT'LL BE GONE.
HE'LL BE A CIPHER. A PERFECT CLAY MAN WHO CAN BE ANYONE BUT THE MAN HE ONCE WAS.
WELL, I FIND THAT TRAGIC, AND I WOULDN'T WISH IT UPON ANYONE, EVEN KARLO. DETESTABLE AS HIS ACTING WAS.
HEH.
I IMAGINE YOU WON'T BE COMING UP FOR DINNER? I'LL KEEP IT WARM FOR YOU, SIR.
ALFRED...
I'M NOT LOSING MYSELF THIS TIME. NOT LIKE I DID WITH JASON. I JUST...
...I'M NOT READY TO LET HIM GO.
MAY I WATCH WITH YOU, SIR?

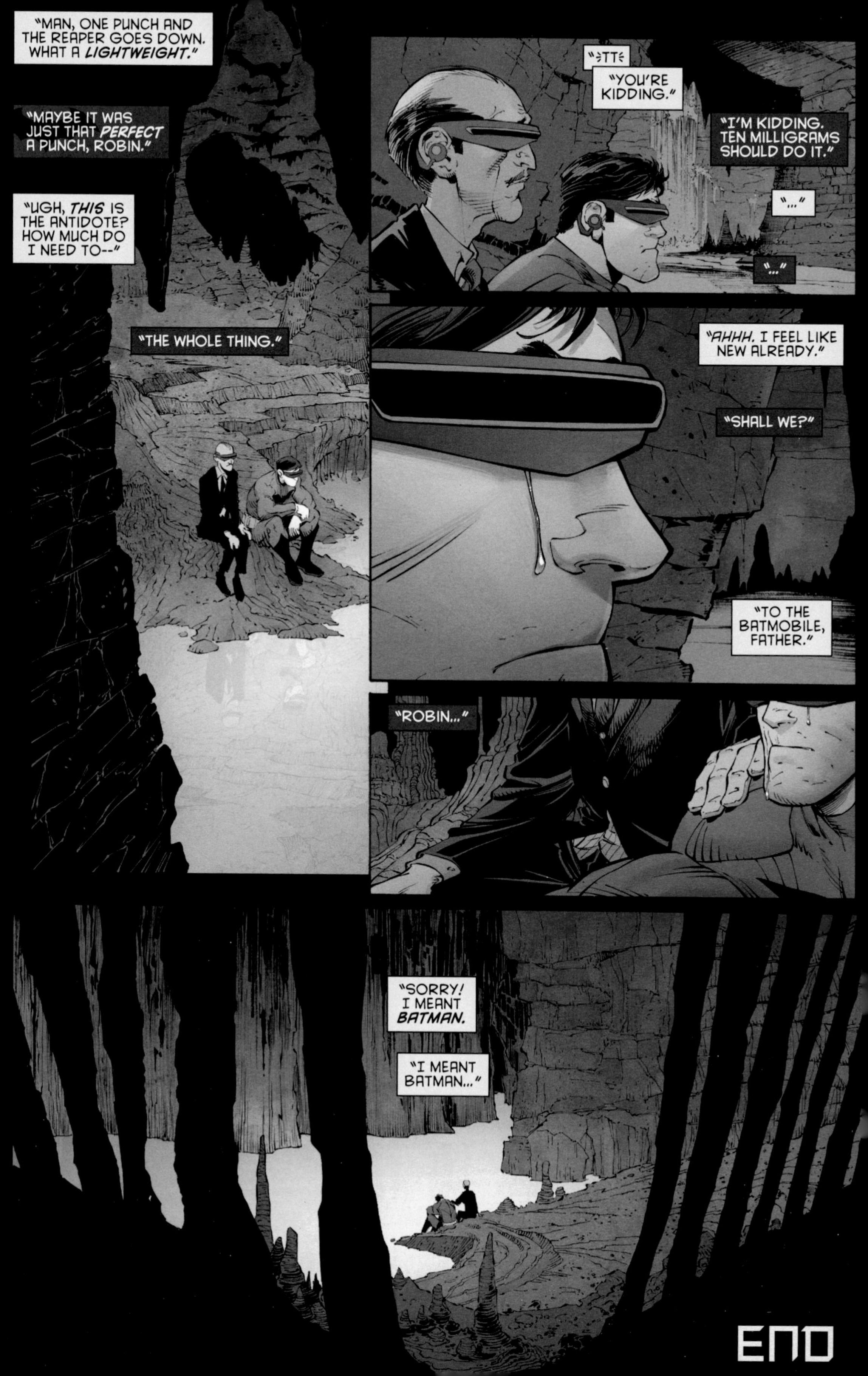
"MAN, ONE PUNCH AND THE REAPER GOES DOWN. WHAT A LIGHTWEIGHT."
"MAYBE IT WAS JUST THAT PERFECT A PUNCH, ROBIN."
"UGH, THIS IS THE ANTIDOTE? HOW MUCH DO I NEED TO--"
"THE WHOLE THING."
"TT
"YOU'RE KIDDING."
"I'M KIDDING. TEN MILLIGRAMS SHOULD DO IT."
"..."
"..."
"AHHH. I FEEL LIKE NEW ALREADY."
"SHALL WE?"
"TO THE BATMOBILE, FATHER."
"ROBIN..."
"SORRY! I MEANT BATMAN.
"I MEANT BATMAN..."
END

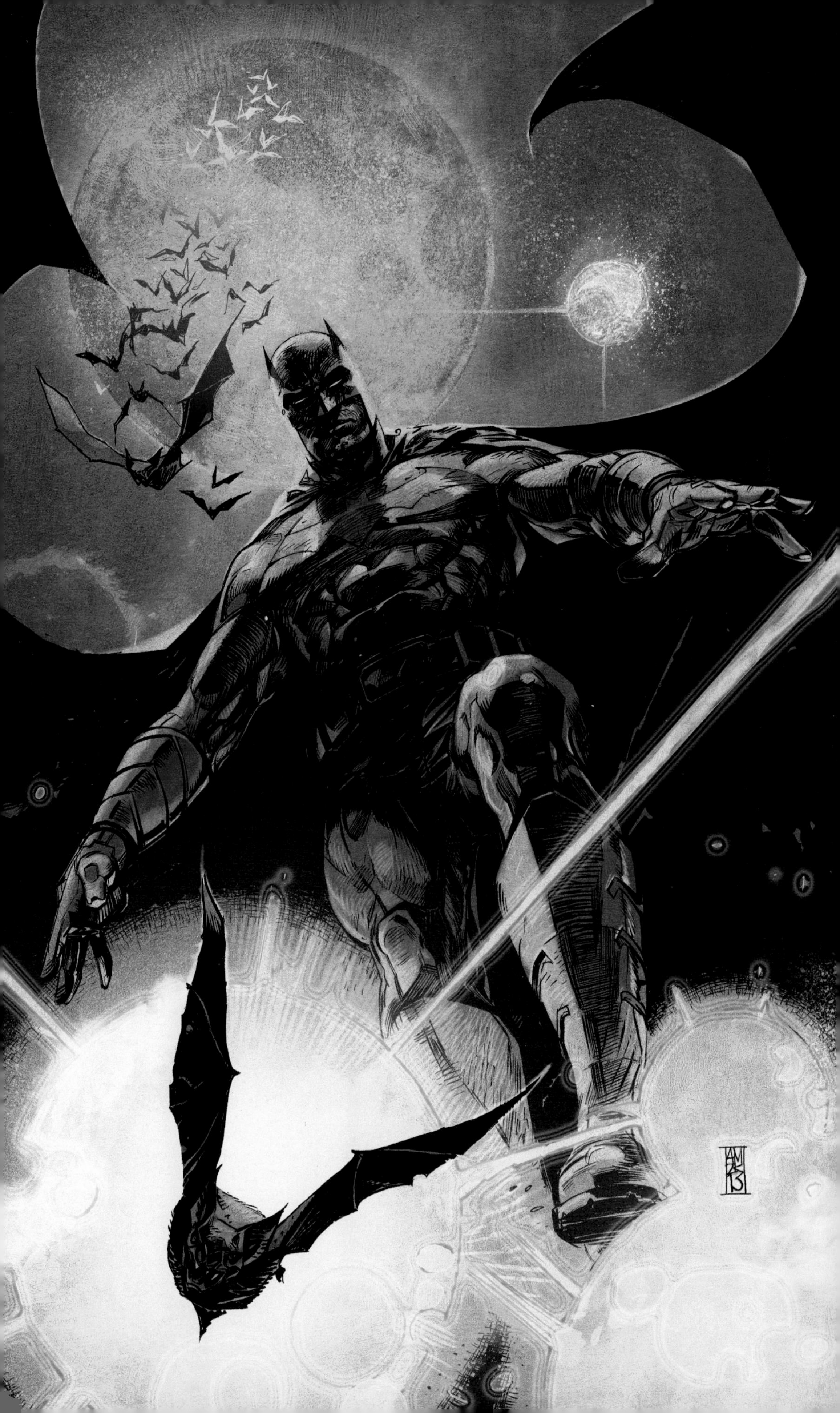

JAMES TYNION IV writer ALEX MALEEV artist BRAD ANDERSON NATHAN FAIRBAIRN colorists variant cover by ALEX MALEEV
SUPERMAN created by JERRY SIEGEL & JOE SHUSTER By special arrangement with the JERRY SIEGEL family

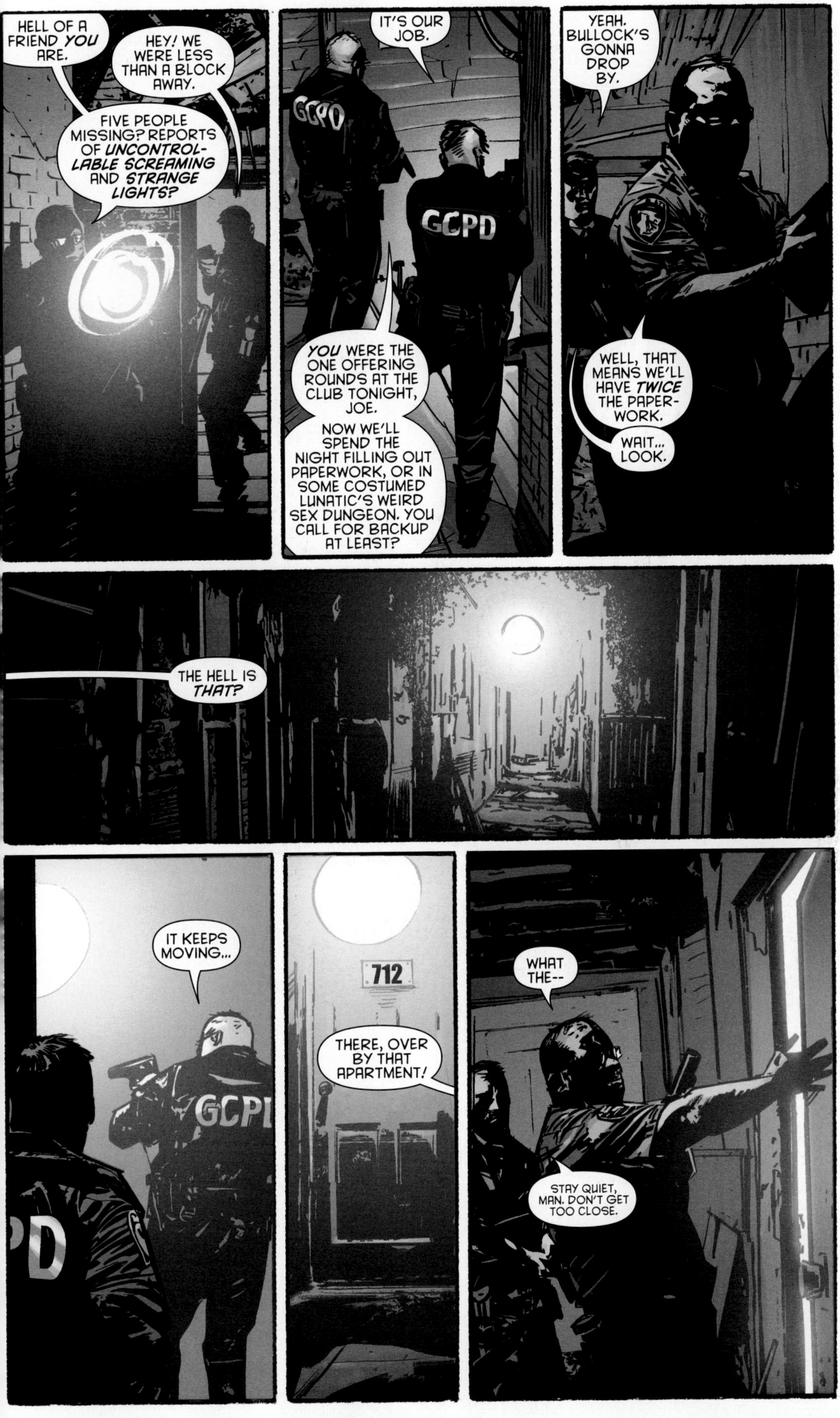

HELL OF A FRIEND *YOU* ARE.
HEY! WE WERE LESS THAN A BLOCK AWAY.
FIVE PEOPLE MISSING? REPORTS OF *UNCONTROL-LABLE SCREAMING* AND *STRANGE LIGHTS?*
IT'S OUR JOB.
GCPD
GCPD
YOU WERE THE ONE OFFERING ROUNDS AT THE CLUB TONIGHT, JOE.
NOW WE'LL SPEND THE NIGHT FILLING OUT PAPERWORK, OR IN SOME COSTUMED LUNATIC'S WEIRD SEX DUNGEON. YOU CALL FOR BACKUP AT LEAST?
YEAH. BULLOCK'S GONNA DROP BY.
WELL, THAT MEANS WE'LL HAVE *TWICE* THE PAPER-WORK.
WAIT... LOOK.
THE HELL IS *THAT?*
IT KEEPS MOVING...
GCPD
PD
712
THERE, OVER BY THAT APARTMENT!
WHAT THE--
STAY QUIET, MAN. DON'T GET TOO CLOSE.

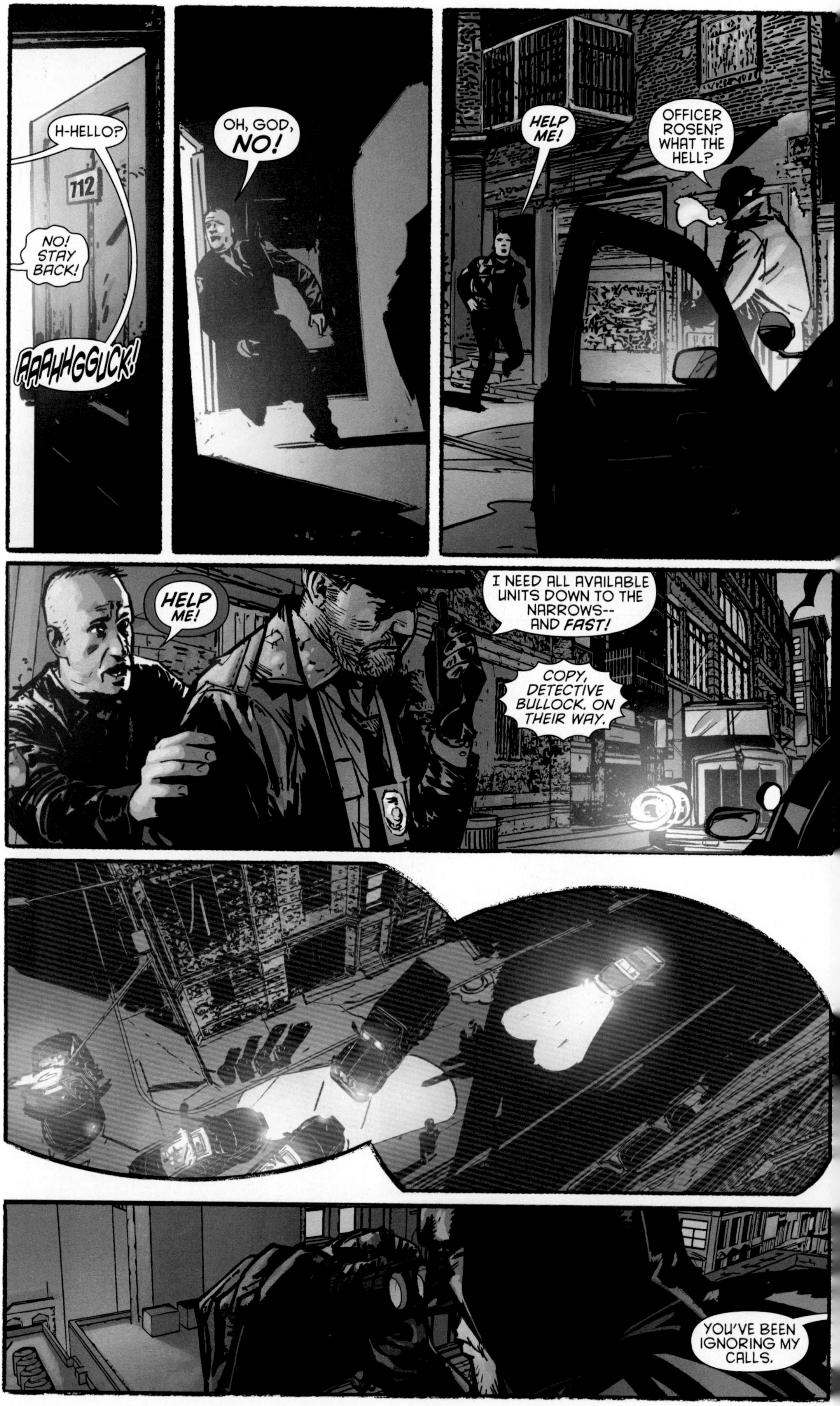
H-HELLO?
NO! STAY BACK!
AAAHHGGUCK!
OH, GOD, NO!
HELP ME!
OFFICER ROSEN? WHAT THE HELL?
HELP ME!
I NEED ALL AVAILABLE UNITS DOWN TO THE NARROWS-- AND FAST!
COPY, DETECTIVE BULLOCK. ON THEIR WAY.
YOU'VE BEEN IGNORING MY CALLS.

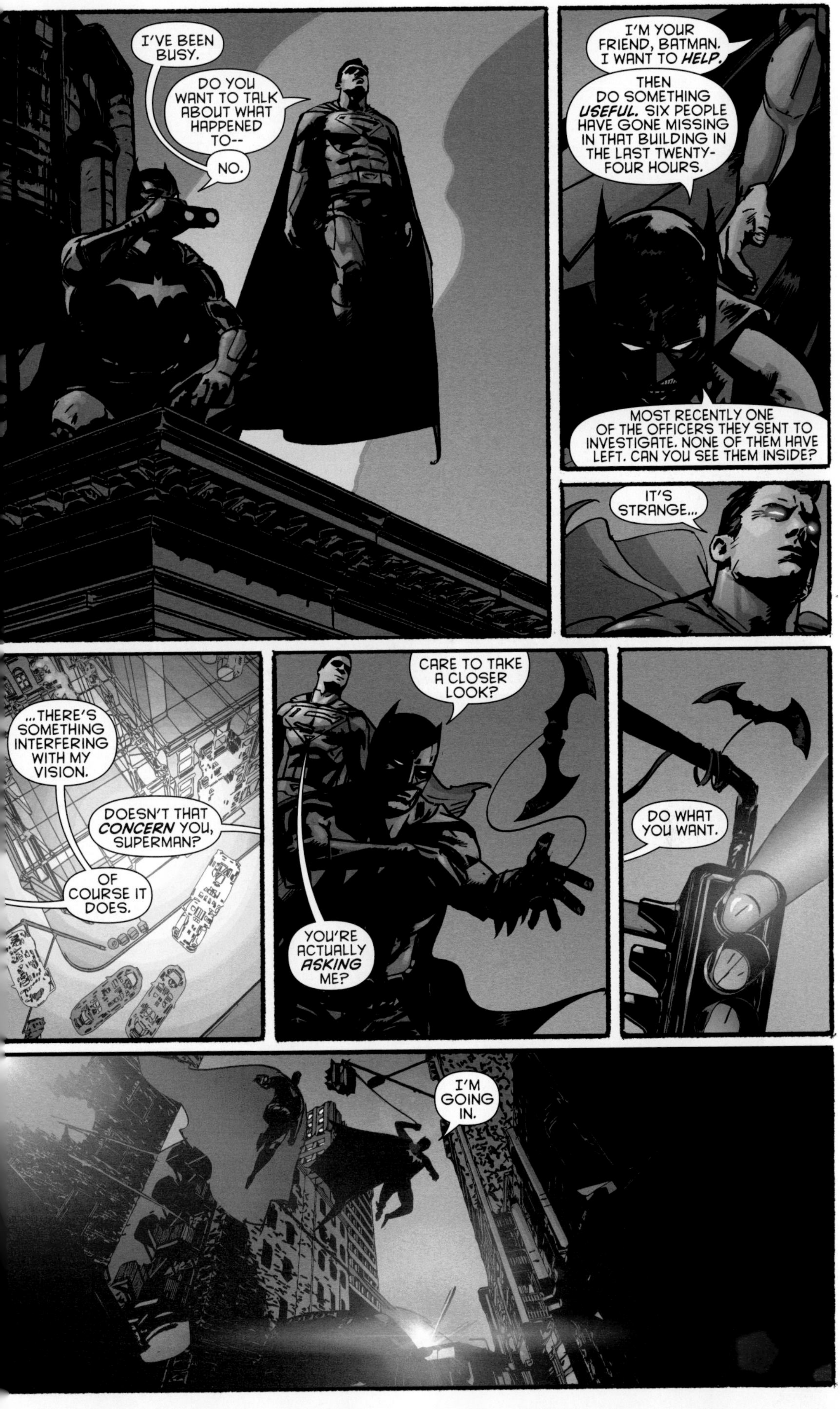
I'VE BEEN BUSY.
DO YOU WANT TO TALK ABOUT WHAT HAPPENED TO--
NO.
I'M YOUR FRIEND, BATMAN. I WANT TO *HELP.*
THEN DO SOMETHING *USEFUL.* SIX PEOPLE HAVE GONE MISSING IN THAT BUILDING IN THE LAST TWENTY-FOUR HOURS.
MOST RECENTLY ONE OF THE OFFICERS THEY SENT TO INVESTIGATE. NONE OF THEM HAVE LEFT. CAN YOU SEE THEM INSIDE?
IT'S STRANGE...
...THERE'S SOMETHING INTERFERING WITH MY VISION.
DOESN'T THAT *CONCERN* YOU, SUPERMAN?
OF COURSE IT DOES.
CARE TO TAKE A CLOSER LOOK?
YOU'RE ACTUALLY *ASKING* ME?
DO WHAT YOU WANT.
I'M GOING IN.

YOU DO REALIZE YOU CAN TALK TO ME, RIGHT? I'M *LITERALLY* ALWAYS JUST A FEW MINUTES AWAY IF YOU NEED TO *TALK.*

STAY FOCUSED.

THERE'S SOMETHING OFF ABOUT THIS PLACE. LIGHT ISN'T TRAVELING CORRECTLY...IT'S DIFFICULT TO DESCRIBE TO SOMEONE WHO CAN'T SEE LIKE I CAN.

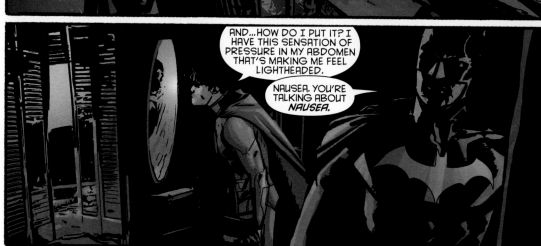

AND...HOW DO I PUT IT? I HAVE THIS SENSATION OF PRESSURE IN MY ABDOMEN THAT'S MAKING ME FEEL LIGHTHEADED.

NAUSEA. YOU'RE TALKING ABOUT *NAUSEA.*

THERE. THAT'S WHAT WE'RE LOOKING FOR.

A *GHOST LIGHT?*

WILL O' THE WISP, HOBBY LANTERN... THEY CALL IT DIFFERENT THINGS IN DIFFERENT PLACES. THE OFFICER WHO WAS TAKEN FROM THE BUILDING SAID IT LED THEM TO WHATEVER TOOK HIS PARTNER.

IN KANSAS WE CALLED THEM *GHOST LIGHTS.* YOU WEREN'T SUPPOSED TO FOLLOW THEM INTO THE FIELDS AT NIGHT. YOU'D NEVER BE SEEN AGAIN.

MY FRIENDS AND I WOULD GO LOOKING, BUT WE NEVER ACTUALLY *SAW* ONE. IT'S LIKE STARING AT A STROBE LIGHT. IT *HURTS* TO LOOK DIRECTLY AT IT.

I CAN HANDLE IT JUST FINE.

712

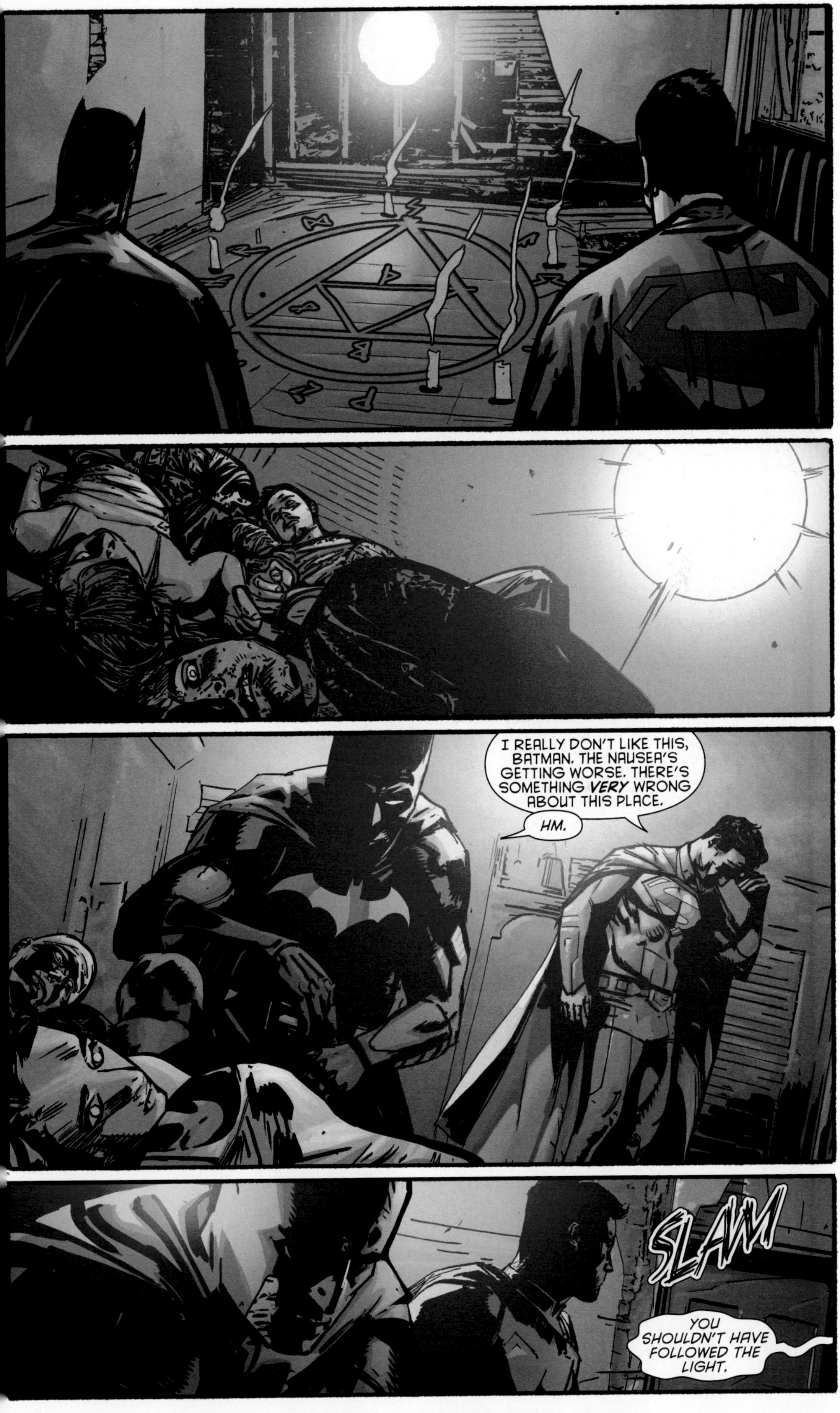
I REALLY DON'T LIKE THIS, BATMAN. THE NAUSEA'S GETTING WORSE. THERE'S SOMETHING *VERY* WRONG ABOUT THIS PLACE.
HM.
SLAM
YOU SHOULDN'T HAVE FOLLOWED THE LIGHT.

WHY DO THEY *ALL* HAVE TO FOLLOW THE LIGHT?

SHE'S ABOUT A HUNDRED TIMES *WORSE* THAN THE ORB. MY VISION CAN'T MAKE SENSE OF IT.

STICK WITH IT. TELL ME WHAT SHE IS.

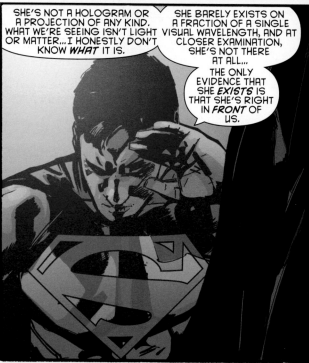

SHE'S NOT A HOLOGRAM OR A PROJECTION OF ANY KIND. WHAT WE'RE SEEING ISN'T LIGHT OR MATTER... I HONESTLY DON'T KNOW *WHAT* IT IS.

SHE BARELY EXISTS ON A FRACTION OF A SINGLE VISUAL WAVELENGTH, AND AT CLOSER EXAMINATION, SHE'S NOT THERE AT ALL...

THE ONLY EVIDENCE THAT SHE *EXISTS* IS THAT SHE'S RIGHT IN *FRONT* OF US.

NO WONDER THIS PLACE IS AFFECTING ME SO MUCH... THIS IS REAL *SUPERNATURAL* PHENOMENA. YOU KNOW THIS ISN'T MY STRONG SUIT.

FASCINATING...

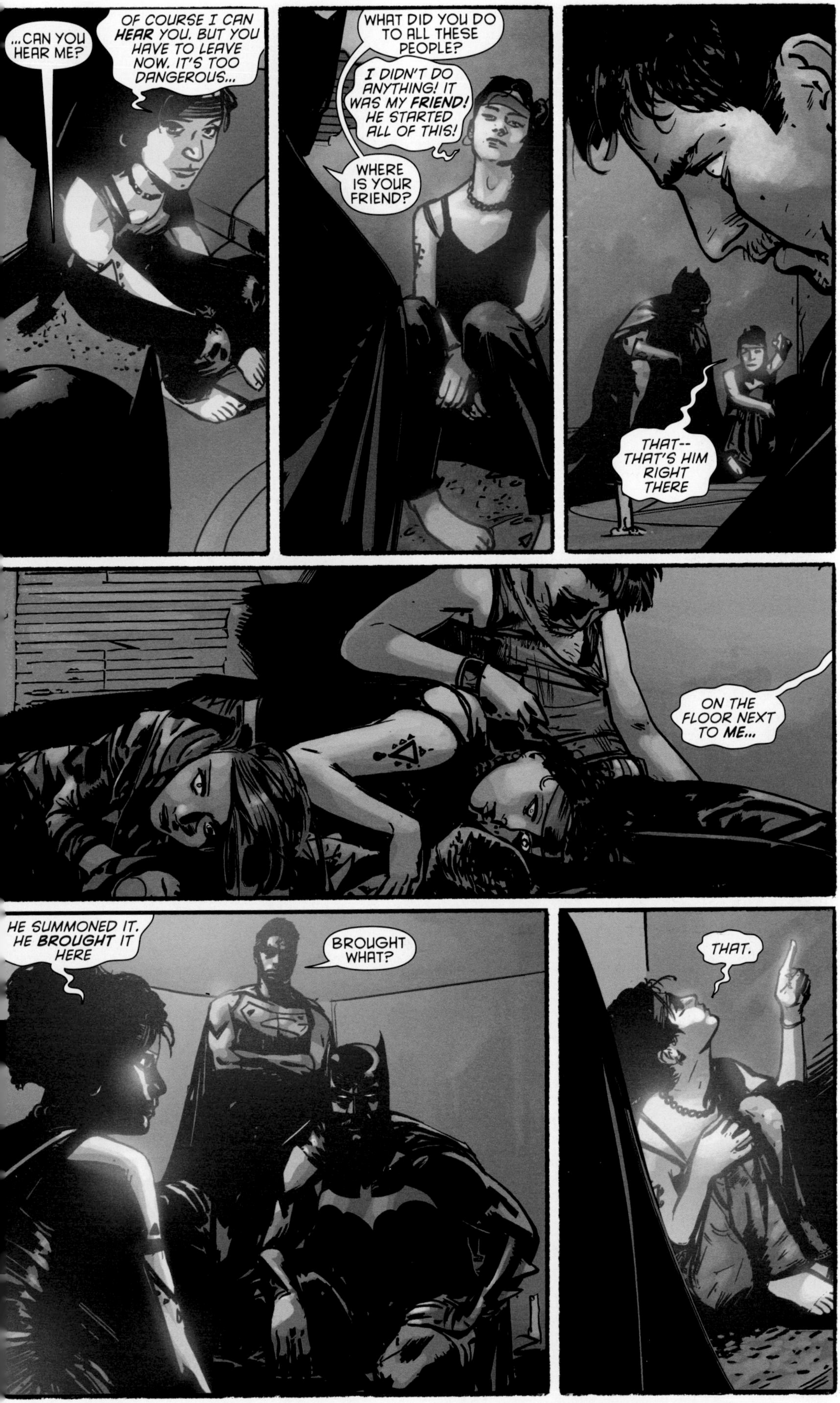
...CAN YOU HEAR ME?
OF COURSE I CAN HEAR YOU. BUT YOU HAVE TO LEAVE NOW. IT'S TOO DANGEROUS...
WHAT DID YOU DO TO ALL THESE PEOPLE?
I DIDN'T DO ANYTHING! IT WAS MY FRIEND! HE STARTED ALL OF THIS!
WHERE IS YOUR FRIEND?
THAT-- THAT'S HIM RIGHT THERE
ON THE FLOOR NEXT TO ME...
HE SUMMONED IT. HE BROUGHT IT HERE
BROUGHT WHAT?
THAT.

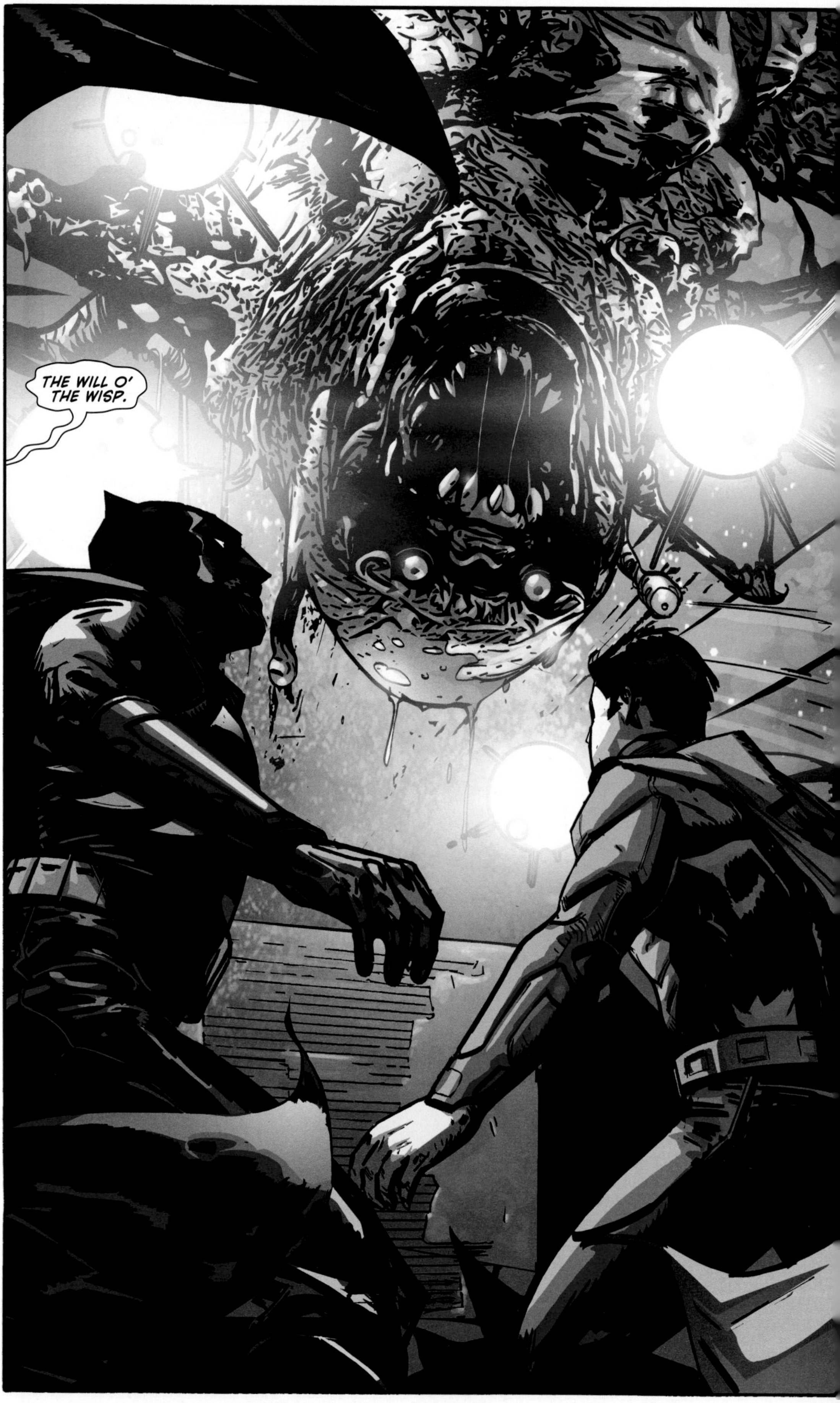
THE WILL O' THE WISP.

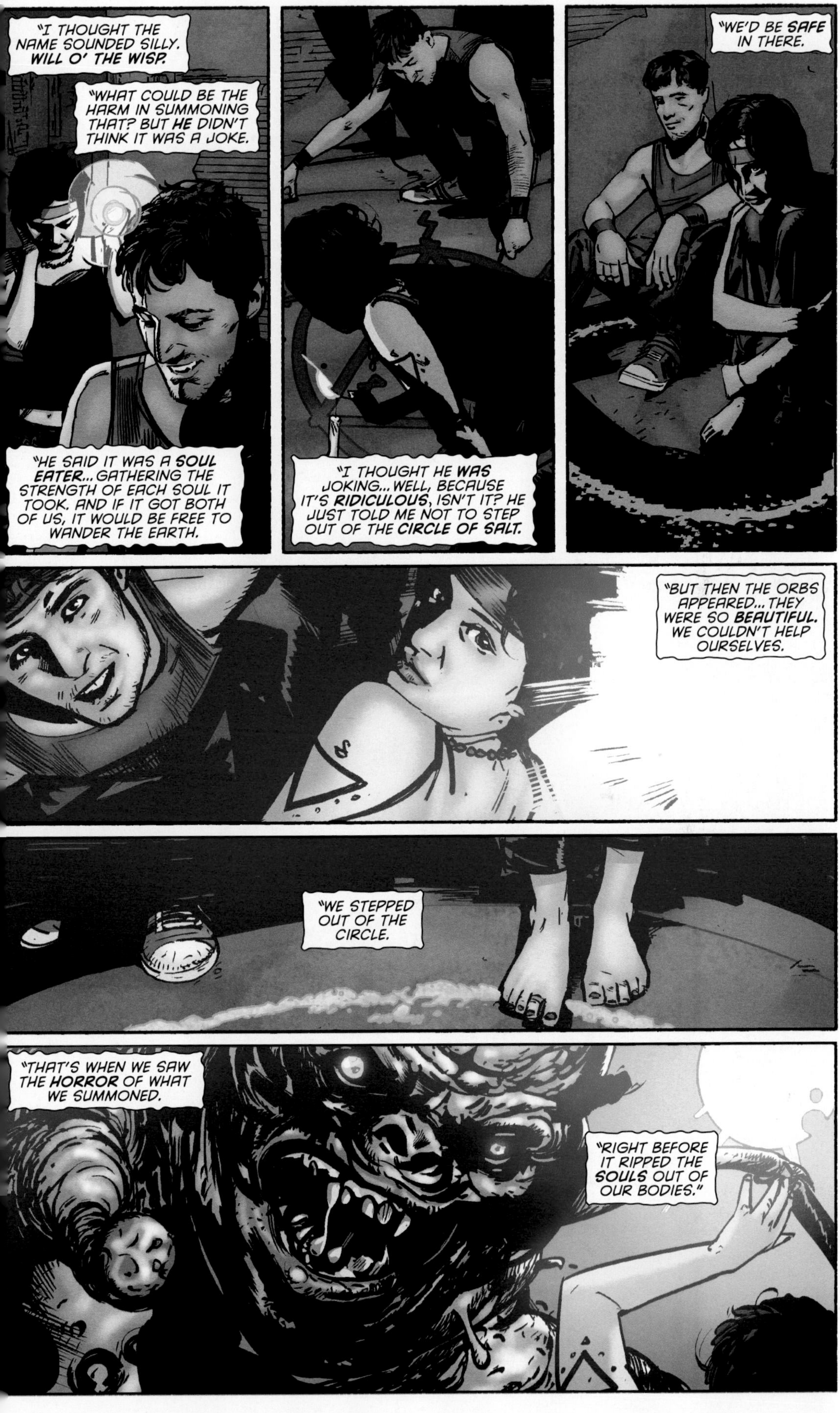

"I THOUGHT THE NAME SOUNDED SILLY. **WILL O' THE WISP.**
"WHAT COULD BE THE HARM IN SUMMONING THAT? BUT **HE** DIDN'T THINK IT WAS A JOKE.
"HE SAID IT WAS A **SOUL EATER**... GATHERING THE STRENGTH OF EACH SOUL IT TOOK. AND IF IT GOT BOTH OF US, IT WOULD BE FREE TO WANDER THE EARTH.
"I THOUGHT HE **WAS** JOKING... WELL, BECAUSE IT'S **RIDICULOUS**, ISN'T IT? HE JUST TOLD ME NOT TO STEP OUT OF THE **CIRCLE OF SALT.**
"WE'D BE **SAFE** IN THERE.
"BUT THEN THE ORBS APPEARED... THEY WERE SO **BEAUTIFUL.** WE COULDN'T HELP OURSELVES.
"WE STEPPED OUT OF THE CIRCLE.
"THAT'S WHEN WE SAW THE **HORROR** OF WHAT WE SUMMONED.
"RIGHT BEFORE IT RIPPED THE **SOULS** OUT OF OUR BODIES."

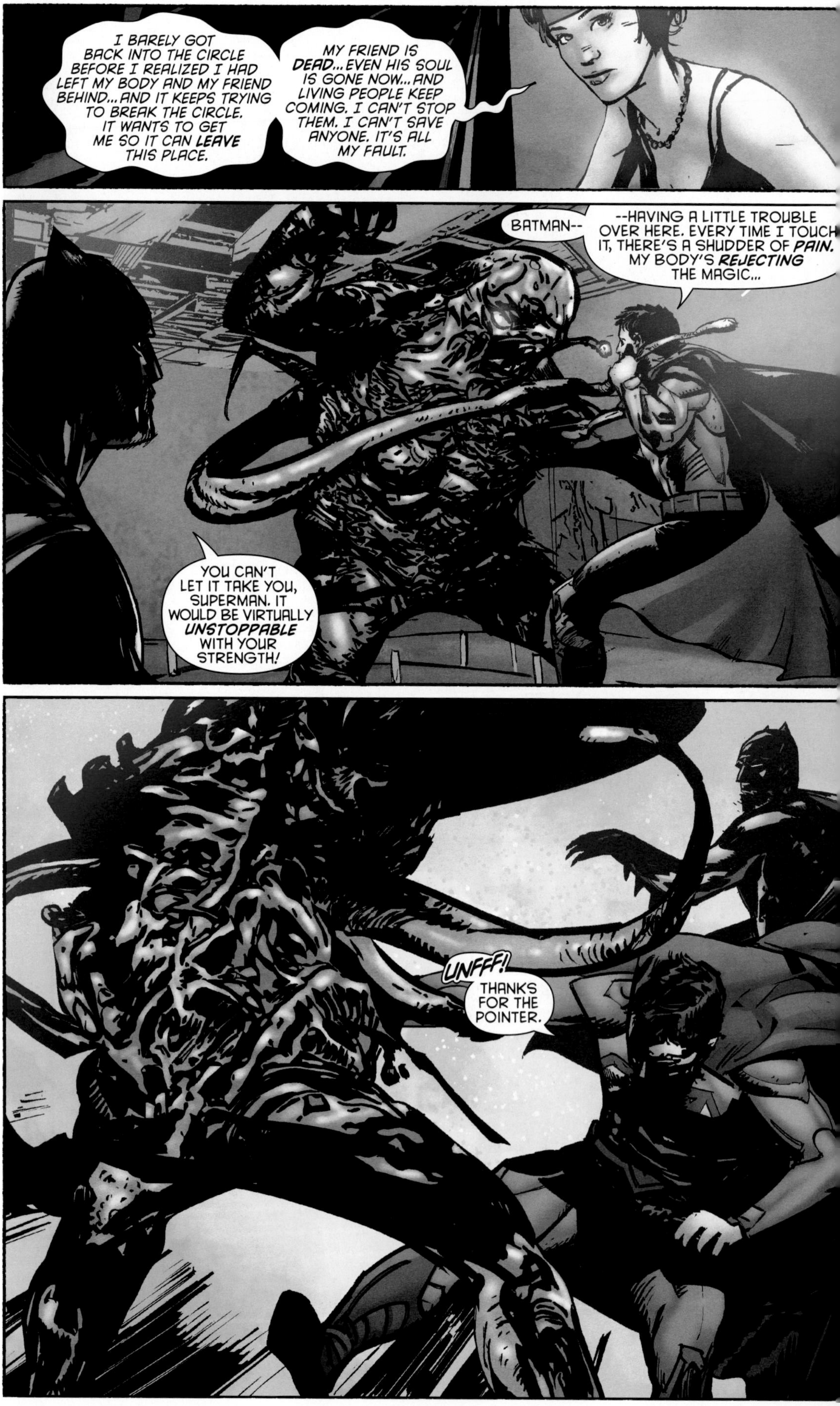

I BARELY GOT BACK INTO THE CIRCLE BEFORE I REALIZED I HAD LEFT MY BODY AND MY FRIEND BEHIND... AND IT KEEPS TRYING TO BREAK THE CIRCLE. IT WANTS TO GET ME SO IT CAN LEAVE THIS PLACE.
MY FRIEND IS DEAD... EVEN HIS SOUL IS GONE NOW... AND LIVING PEOPLE KEEP COMING. I CAN'T STOP THEM. I CAN'T SAVE ANYONE. IT'S ALL MY FAULT.
BATMAN--
--HAVING A LITTLE TROUBLE OVER HERE. EVERY TIME I TOUCH IT, THERE'S A SHUDDER OF PAIN. MY BODY'S REJECTING THE MAGIC...
YOU CAN'T LET IT TAKE YOU, SUPERMAN. IT WOULD BE VIRTUALLY UNSTOPPABLE WITH YOUR STRENGTH!
UNFFF!
THANKS FOR THE POINTER.

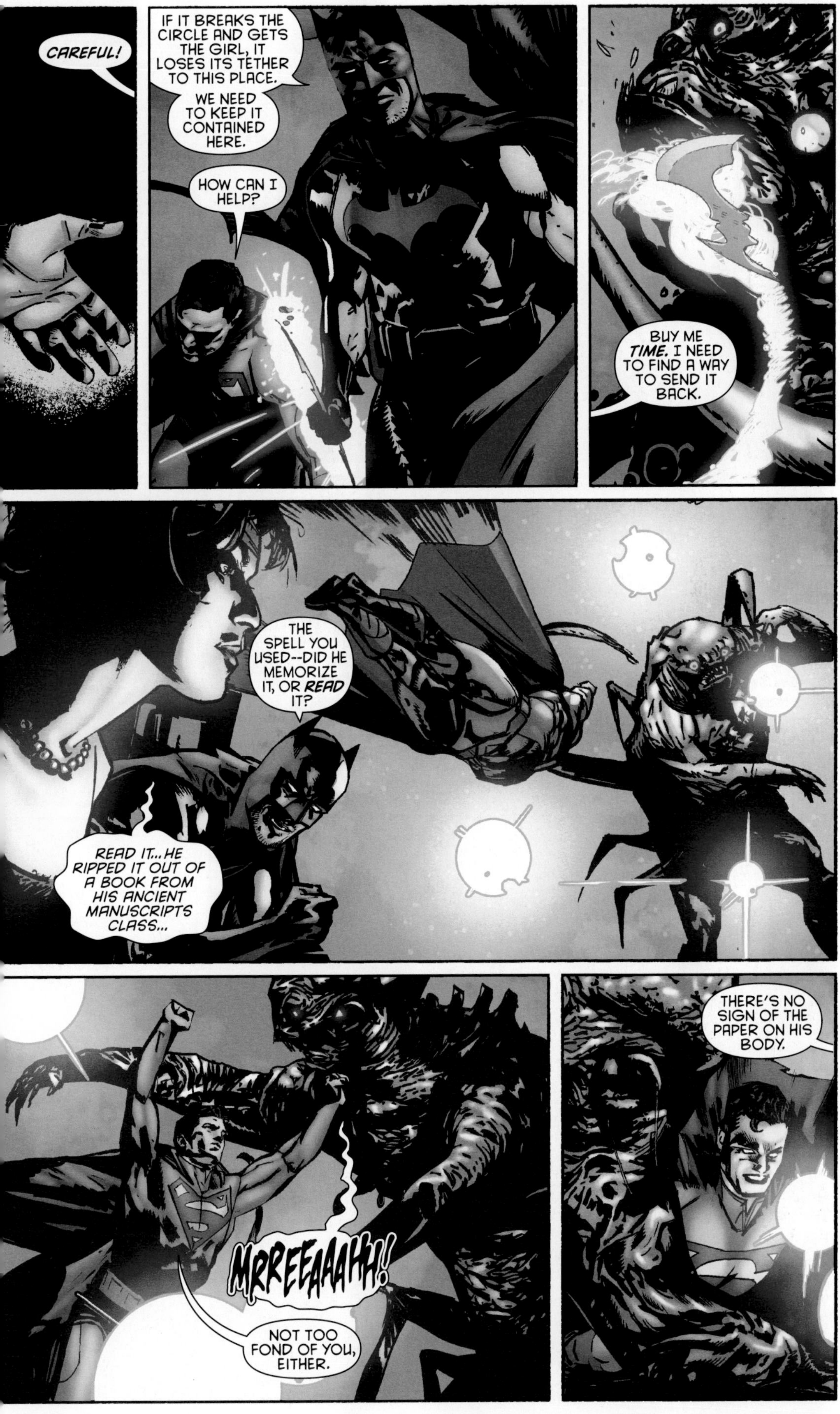
CAREFUL!
IF IT BREAKS THE CIRCLE AND GETS THE GIRL, IT LOSES ITS TETHER TO THIS PLACE.
WE NEED TO KEEP IT CONTAINED HERE.
HOW CAN I HELP?
BUY ME TIME. I NEED TO FIND A WAY TO SEND IT BACK.
THE SPELL YOU USED--DID HE MEMORIZE IT, OR READ IT?
READ IT... HE RIPPED IT OUT OF A BOOK FROM HIS ANCIENT MANUSCRIPTS CLASS...
MRREEAAAHH!
NOT TOO FOND OF YOU, EITHER.
THERE'S NO SIGN OF THE PAPER ON HIS BODY.

THE THING KNOCKED IT AWAY...DRAGGED OUR BODIES TO THE CORNER.

WHERE WAS YOUR FRIEND *STANDING* WHEN HE DIED?!

I... I DON'T *REMEMBER*...

I NEED YOU TO *THINK*.

IT'S ALL MY FAULT! I *KILLED* HIM...TONY IS DEAD BECAUSE--

SHH. WHAT'S YOUR NAME?

...BECCA.

BECCA...

...THAT MAN RIGHT THERE...HE'S ONE OF THE CLOSEST FRIENDS I HAVE. HE'S HERE TONIGHT BECAUSE HE WANTED TO HELP ME GET THROUGH... SOMETHING.

HE'S HERE BECAUSE HE *CARES*.

JUST STANDING IN THIS PLACE IS *KILLING* HIM. HIS BODY REJECTS MAGIC.

HE COULD RUN, BUT INSTEAD, HE'S FIGHTING JUST TO KEEP OUR BODIES AND YOUR SOUL SAFE.

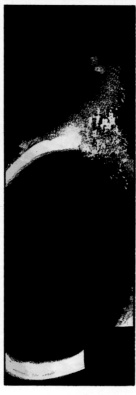

I NEED YOU TO *HELP* ME SAVE HIS LIFE. WILL YOU HELP ME, BECCA?

WILL YOU HELP ME SAVE MY FRIEND?

TONY DIED... OVER IN THAT CORNER.

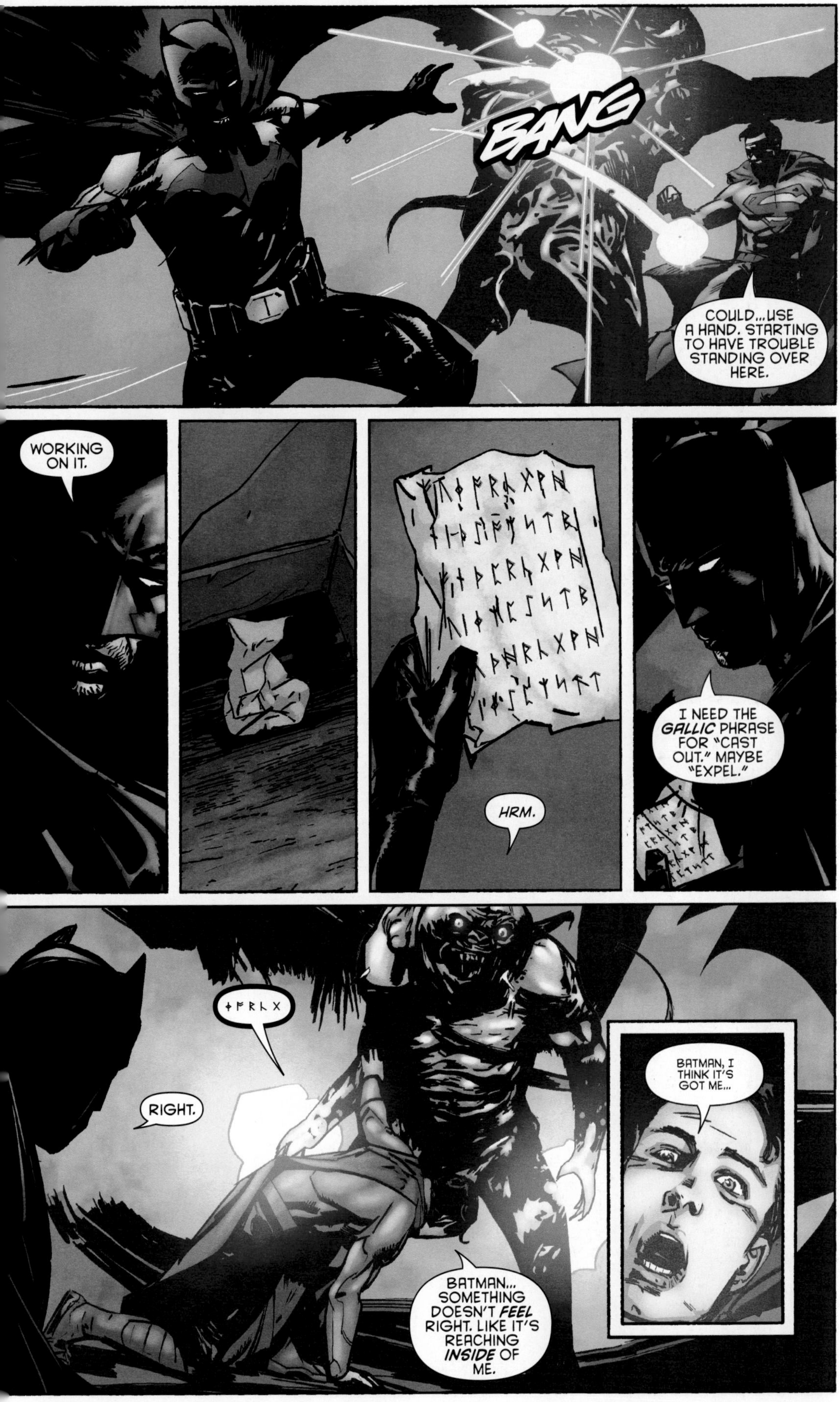
BANG
COULD...USE A HAND. STARTING TO HAVE TROUBLE STANDING OVER HERE.
WORKING ON IT.
HRM.
I NEED THE GALLIC PHRASE FOR "CAST OUT." MAYBE "EXPEL."
RIGHT.
BATMAN... SOMETHING DOESN'T FEEL RIGHT. LIKE IT'S REACHING INSIDE OF ME.
BATMAN, I THINK IT'S GOT ME...

NO!

HEAT ON.

ᛏᚠᚱᛚᚷ
ᛒᛋᚠᛏᛉᛋ
ᛏᚠᛒᚱᛚᚷᚠᚢ
ᛏᛉᛖᛋᚾ
ᛒᚾᚾᛋ

MREH?

ᛋᚠᚱ
ᛒᛏᛏᛋ
ᛏᚠᛏᚠᚱᚱ
ᛏᛖᛖᛋ
ᚾᚾᛋ

MREAAGHH!!

HARUMMMGHP...*

THE MAGIC IN THIS PLACE...IT'S *GONE.*

AND ME NEXT, I'M GUESSING...I CAN FEEL SOMETHING PULLING ME AWAY.

THANK YOU, BECCA.

I'M JUST THE DUMB GIRL WHO GOT US ALL INTO THIS MESS.

YOU HAD NO WAY OF KNOWING WHAT WOULD HAPPEN.

STILL...

HEY, SUPERMAN... TAKE CARE OF THIS ONE, OKAY?

HE MIGHT LOOK SCARY AND ALL, BUT HE'S MUCH SWEETER THAN HE LOOKS.

I'LL TAKE THAT INTO CONSIDERATION.

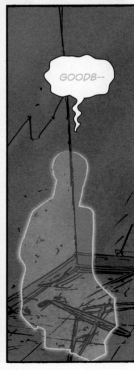

GOODB--

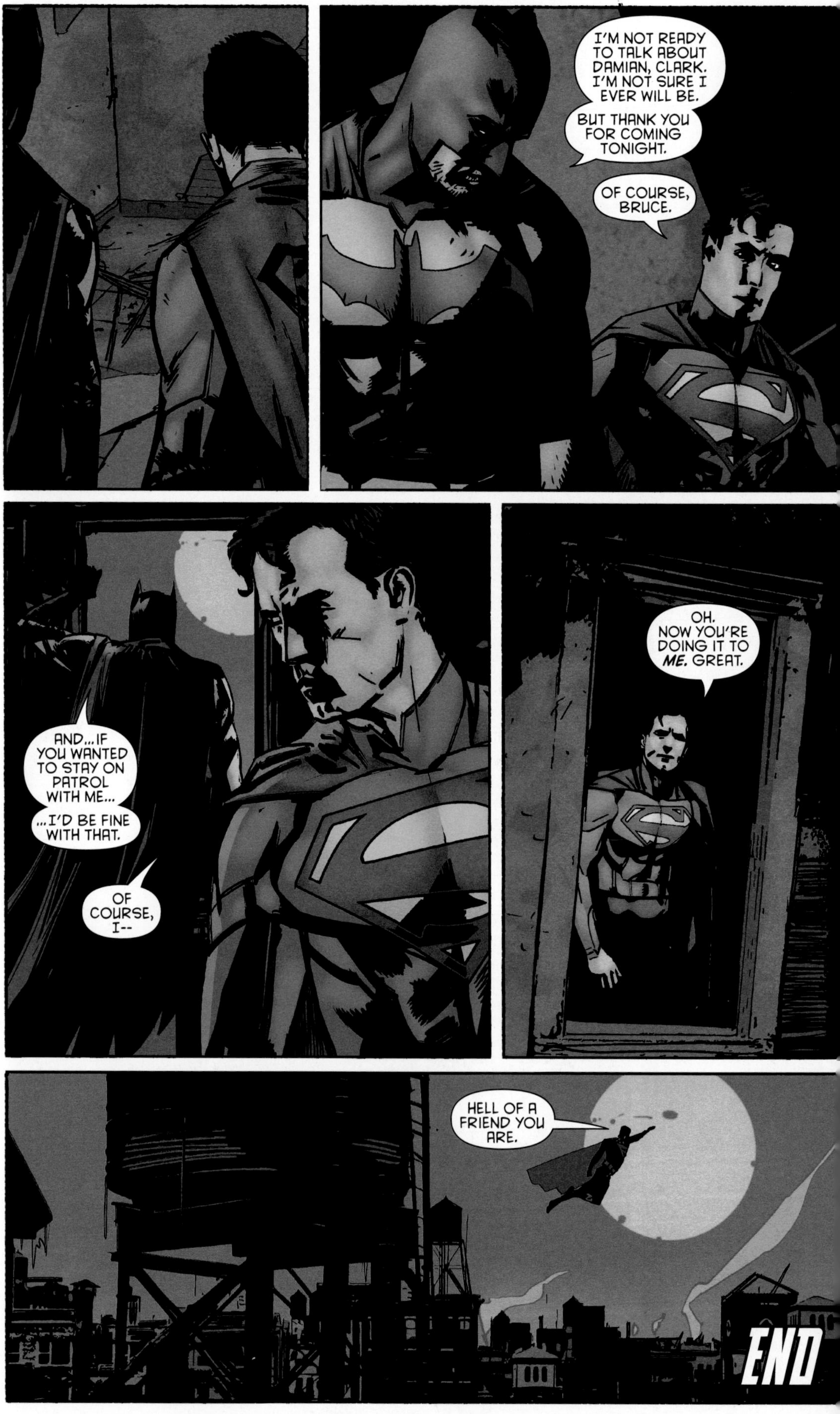

I'M NOT READY TO TALK ABOUT DAMIAN, CLARK. I'M NOT SURE I EVER WILL BE.
BUT THANK YOU FOR COMING TONIGHT.
OF COURSE, BRUCE.
AND...IF YOU WANTED TO STAY ON PATROL WITH ME...
...I'D BE FINE WITH THAT.
OF COURSE, I--
OH. NOW YOU'RE DOING IT TO ME. GREAT.
HELL OF A FRIEND YOU ARE.
END

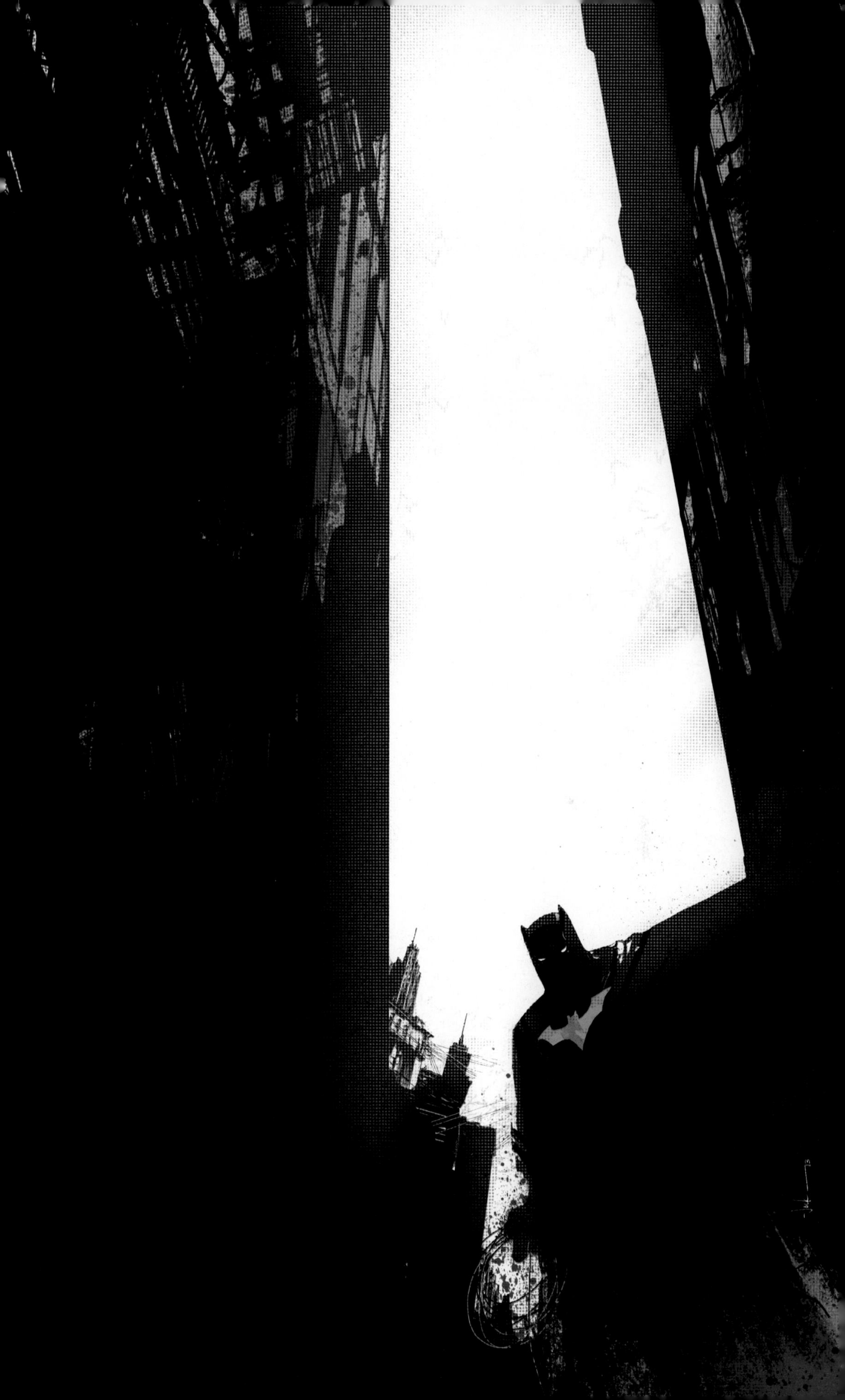

AGES

SCOTT SNYDER MARGUERITE BENNETT plotters **MARGUERITE BENNETT** writer **WES CRAIG** penciller **CRAIG YEUNG DREW GERACI WES CRAIG JACK PURCELL SANDU FLOREA MARC DEERING** inkers **IAN HANNIN** colorist cover by **JOCK**

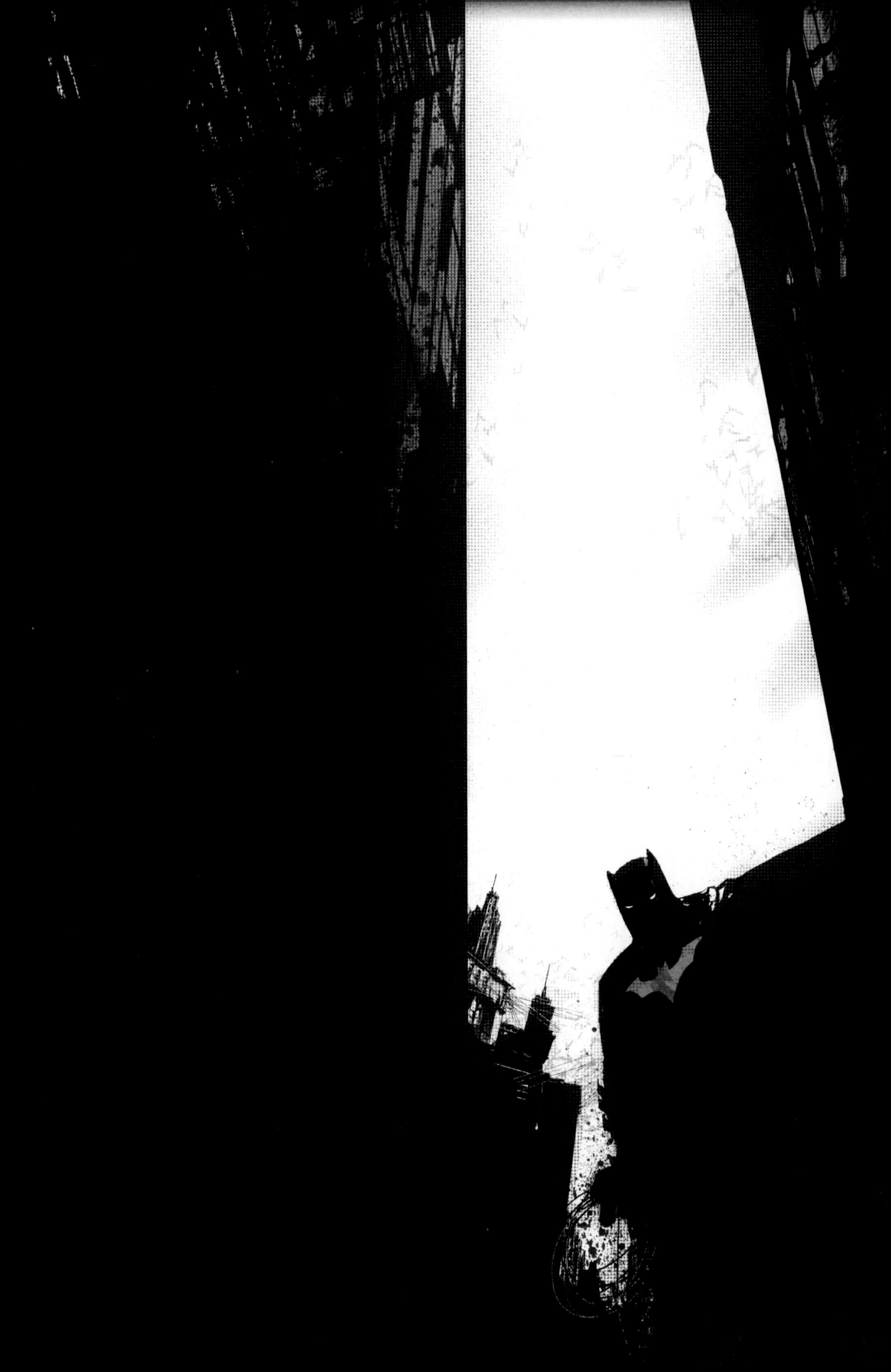

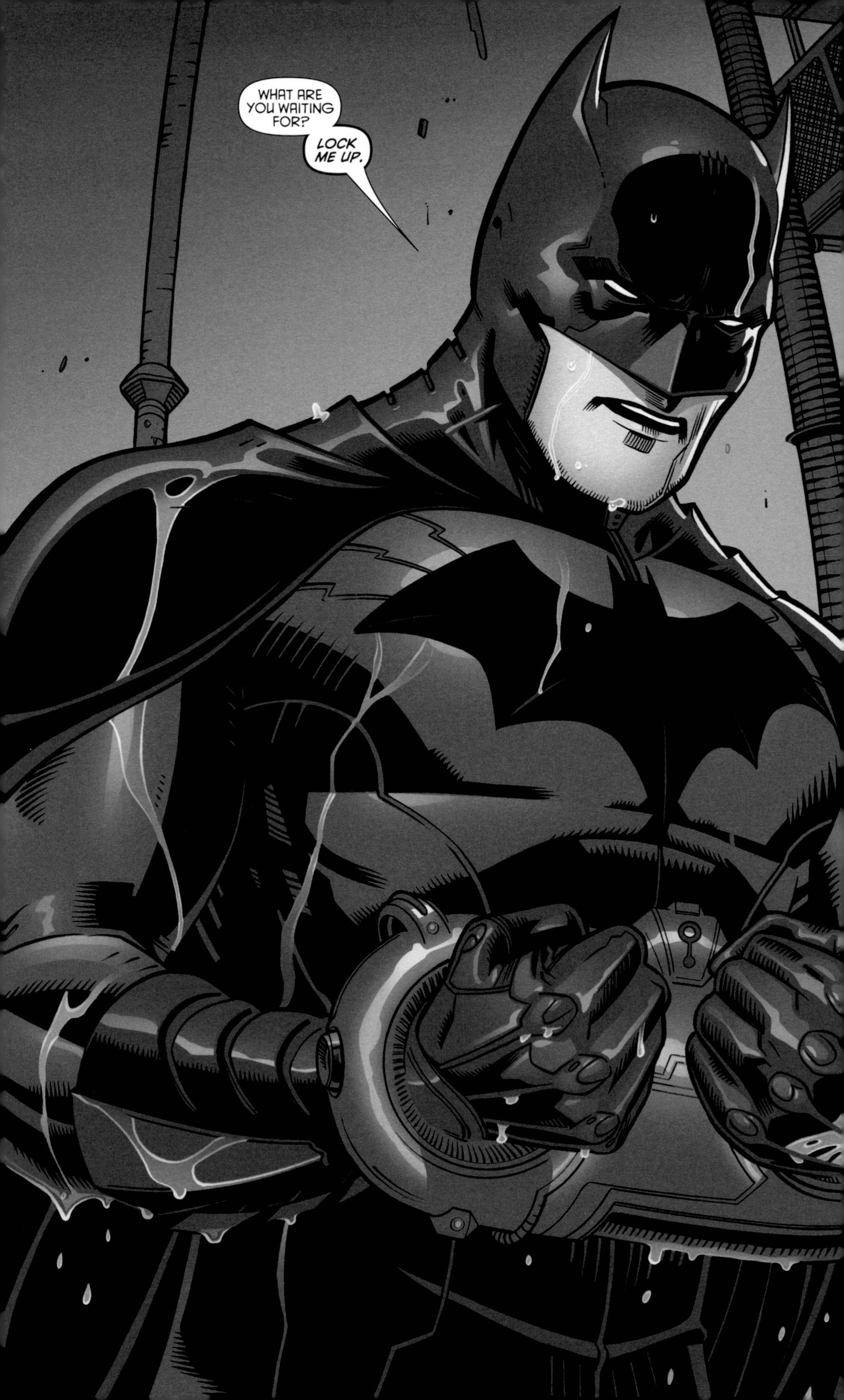
WHAT ARE YOU WAITING FOR?
LOCK ME UP.

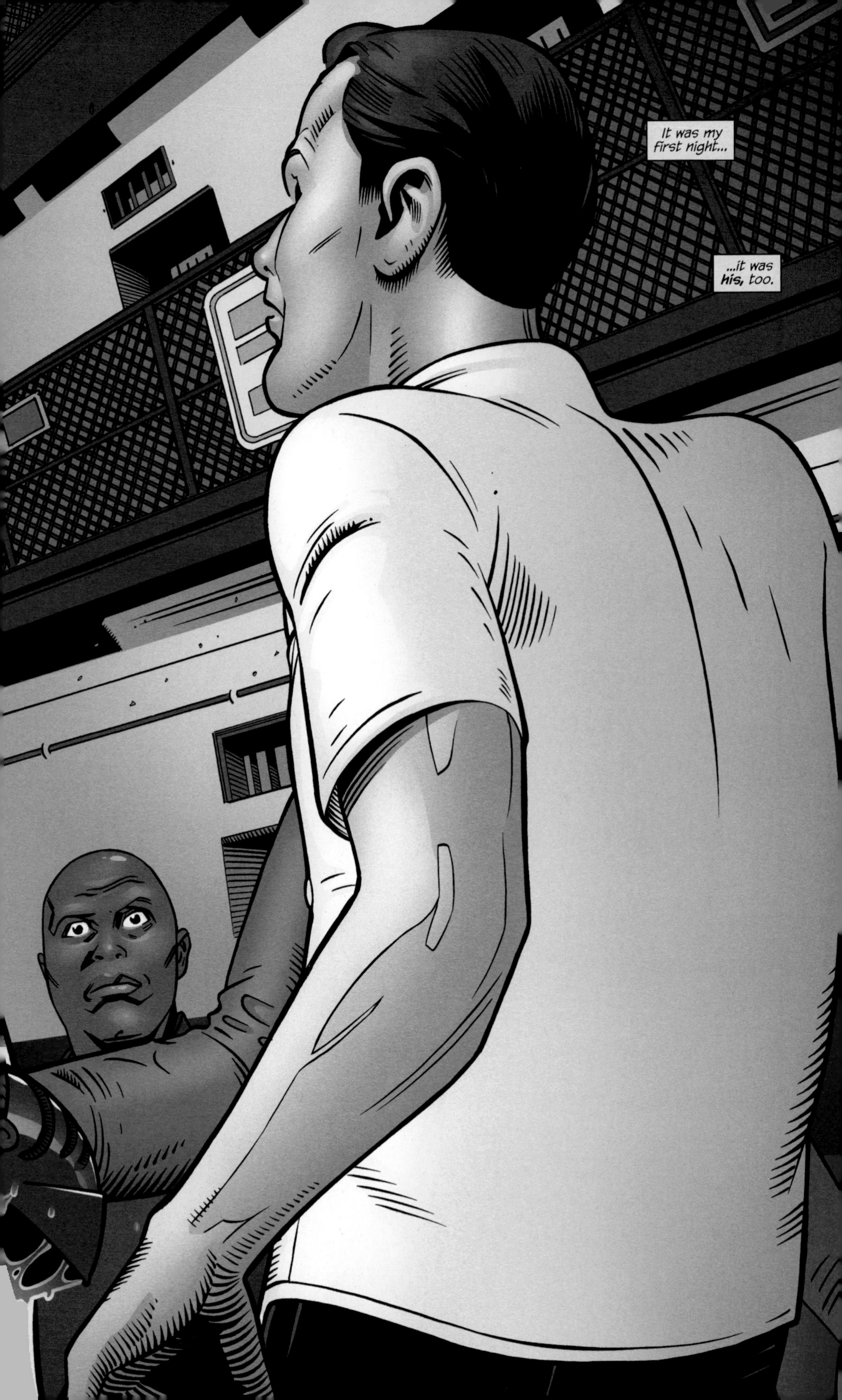
It was my first night...
...it was his, too.

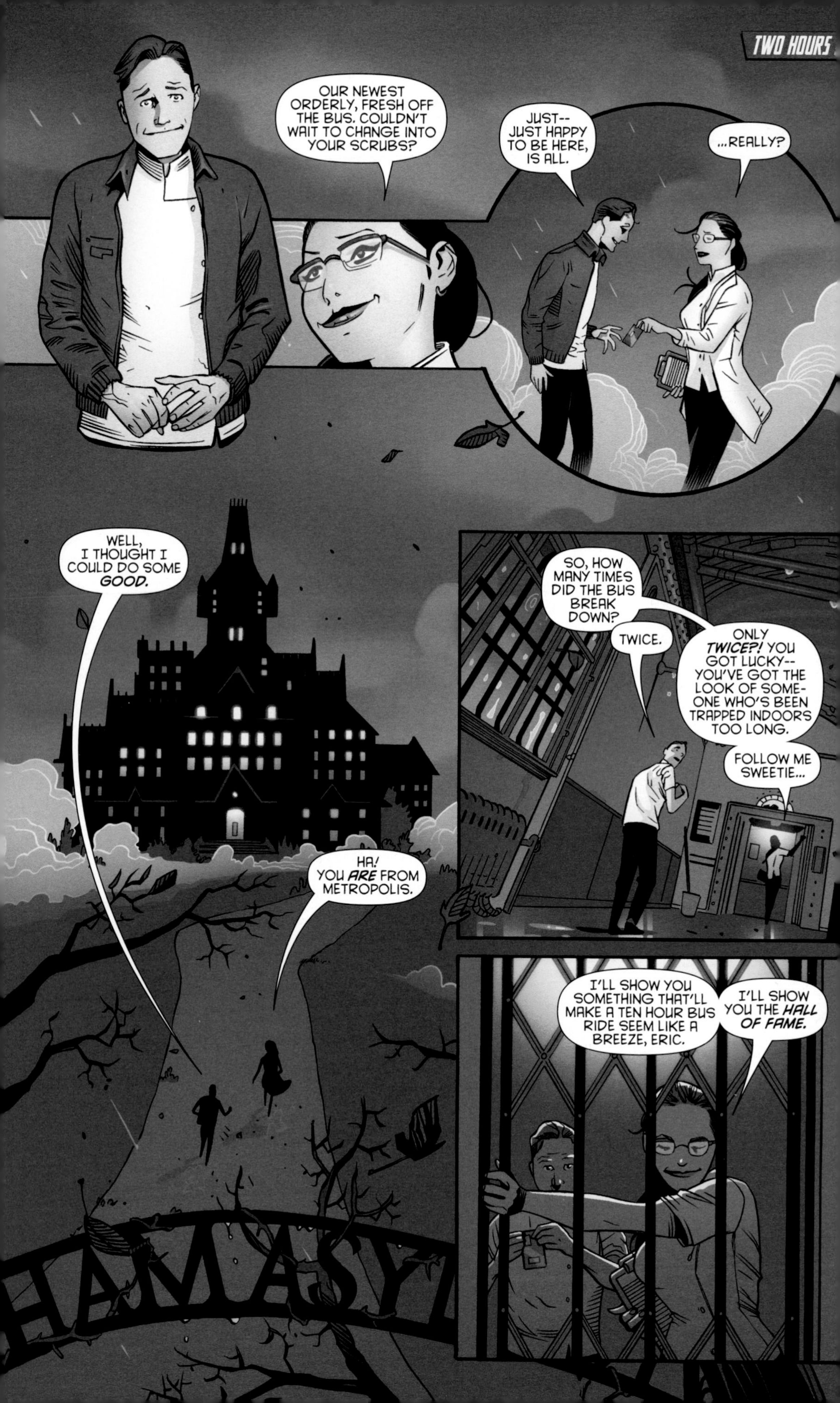

TWO HOURS
OUR NEWEST ORDERLY, FRESH OFF THE BUS. COULDN'T WAIT TO CHANGE INTO YOUR SCRUBS?
JUST-- JUST HAPPY TO BE HERE, IS ALL.
...REALLY?
WELL, I THOUGHT I COULD DO SOME GOOD.
HA! YOU ARE FROM METROPOLIS.
SO, HOW MANY TIMES DID THE BUS BREAK DOWN?
TWICE.
ONLY TWICE?! YOU GOT LUCKY-- YOU'VE GOT THE LOOK OF SOME-ONE WHO'S BEEN TRAPPED INDOORS TOO LONG.
FOLLOW ME SWEETIE...
I'LL SHOW YOU SOMETHING THAT'LL MAKE A TEN HOUR BUS RIDE SEEM LIKE A BREEZE, ERIC.
I'LL SHOW YOU THE HALL OF FAME.

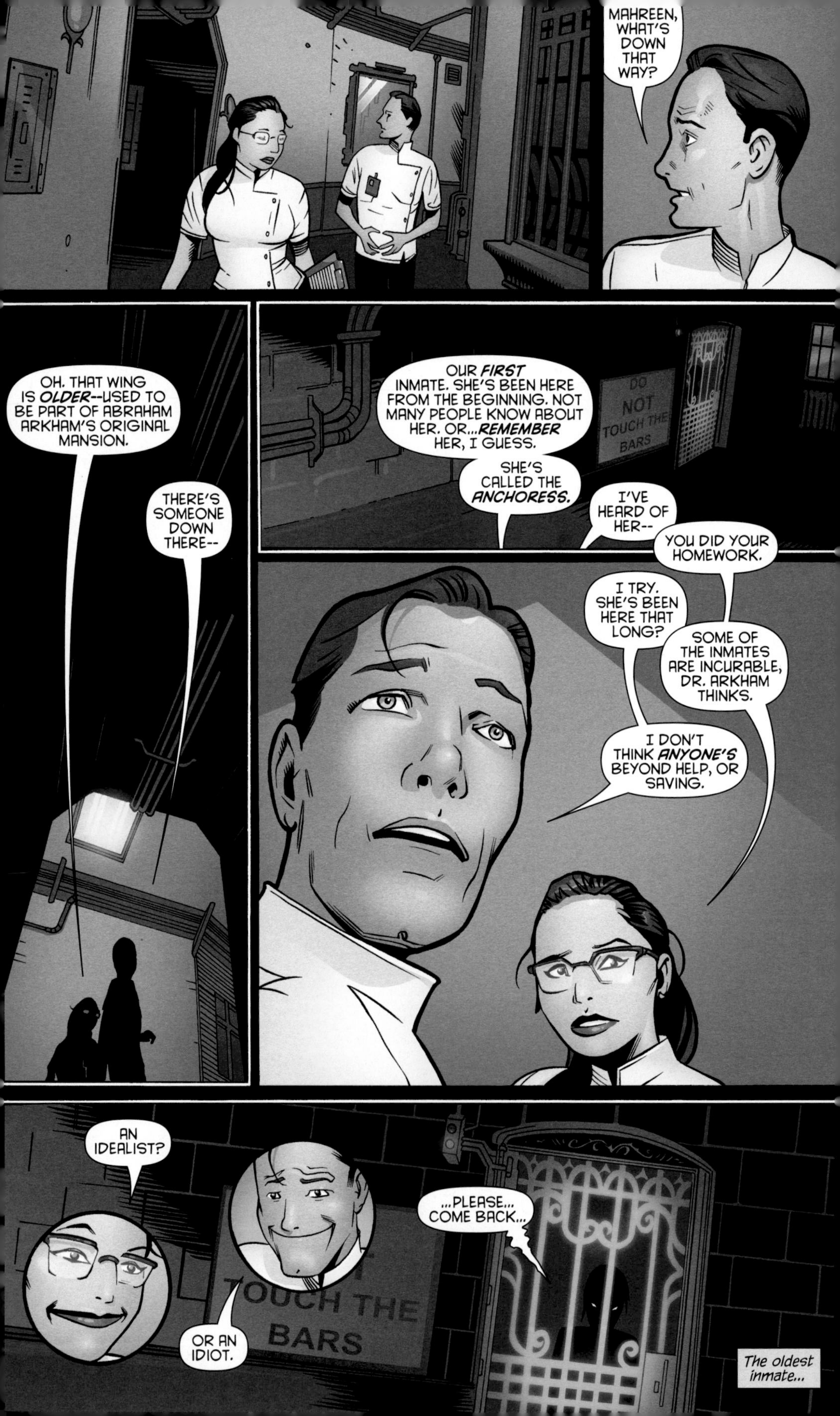
MAHREEN, WHAT'S DOWN THAT WAY?
OH. THAT WING IS OLDER--USED TO BE PART OF ABRAHAM ARKHAM'S ORIGINAL MANSION.
THERE'S SOMEONE DOWN THERE--
OUR FIRST INMATE. SHE'S BEEN HERE FROM THE BEGINNING. NOT MANY PEOPLE KNOW ABOUT HER. OR...REMEMBER HER, I GUESS.
DO NOT TOUCH THE BARS
SHE'S CALLED THE ANCHORESS.
I'VE HEARD OF HER--
YOU DID YOUR HOMEWORK.
I TRY. SHE'S BEEN HERE THAT LONG?
SOME OF THE INMATES ARE INCURABLE, DR. ARKHAM THINKS.
I DON'T THINK ANYONE'S BEYOND HELP, OR SAVING.
AN IDEALIST?
OR AN IDIOT.
TOUCH THE BARS
...PLEASE... COME BACK...
The oldest inmate...

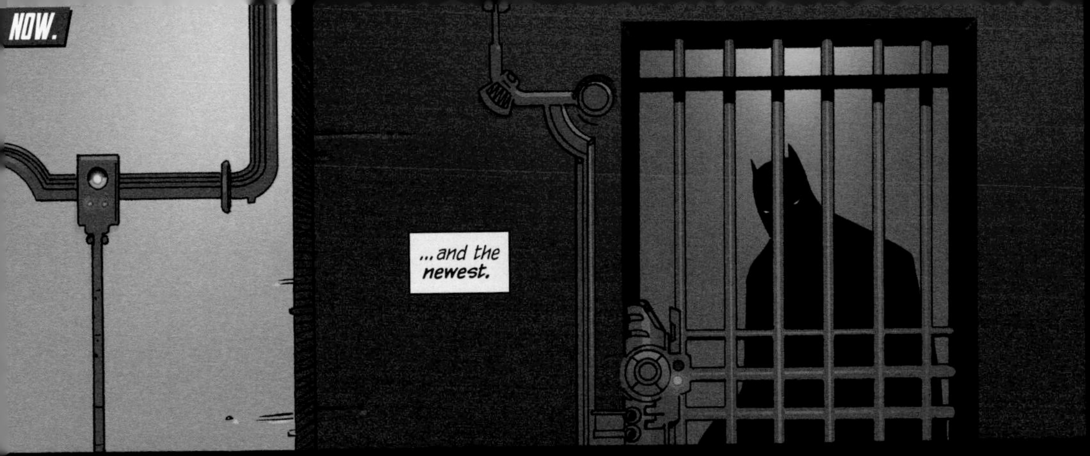
NOW.
...and the
newest.

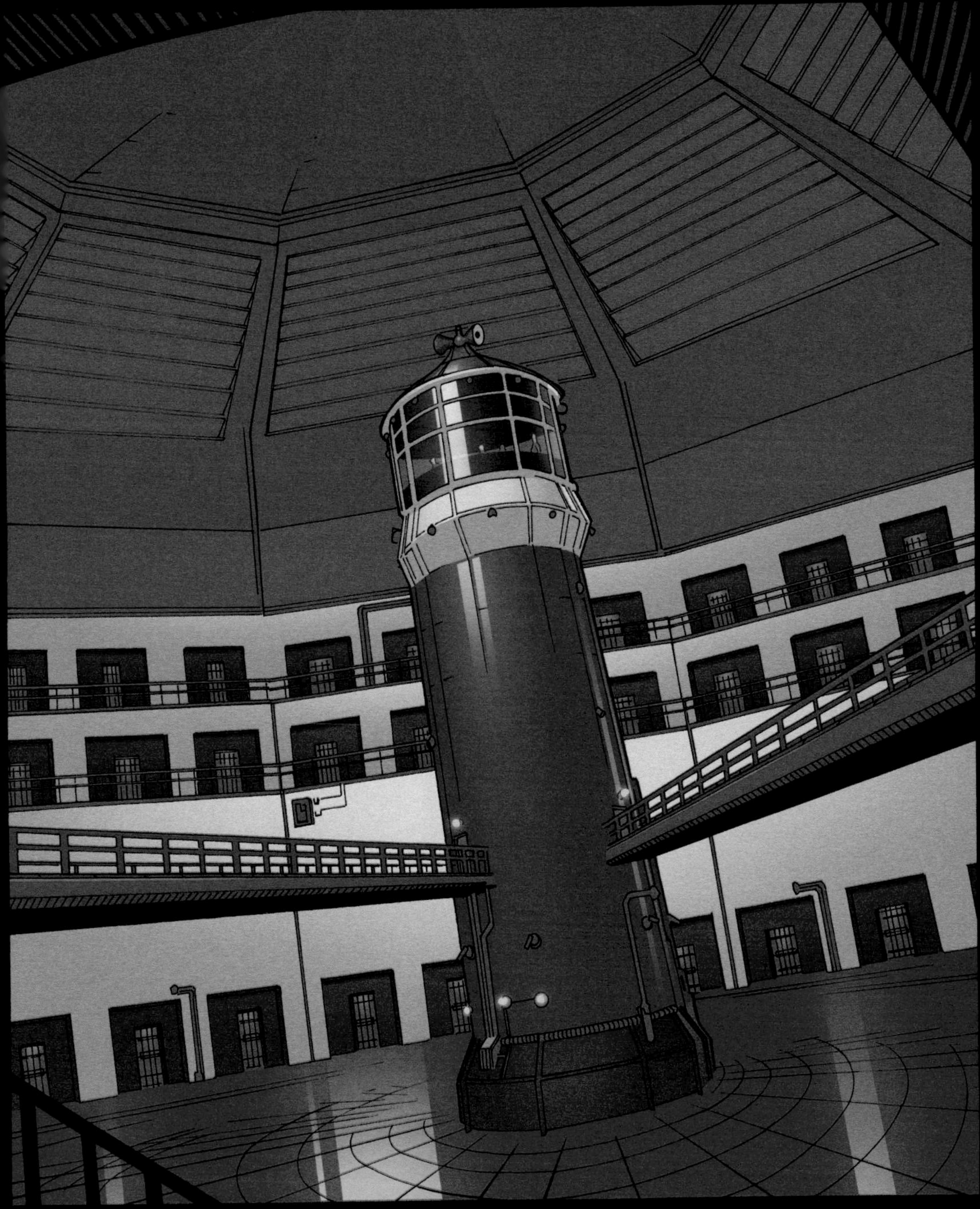

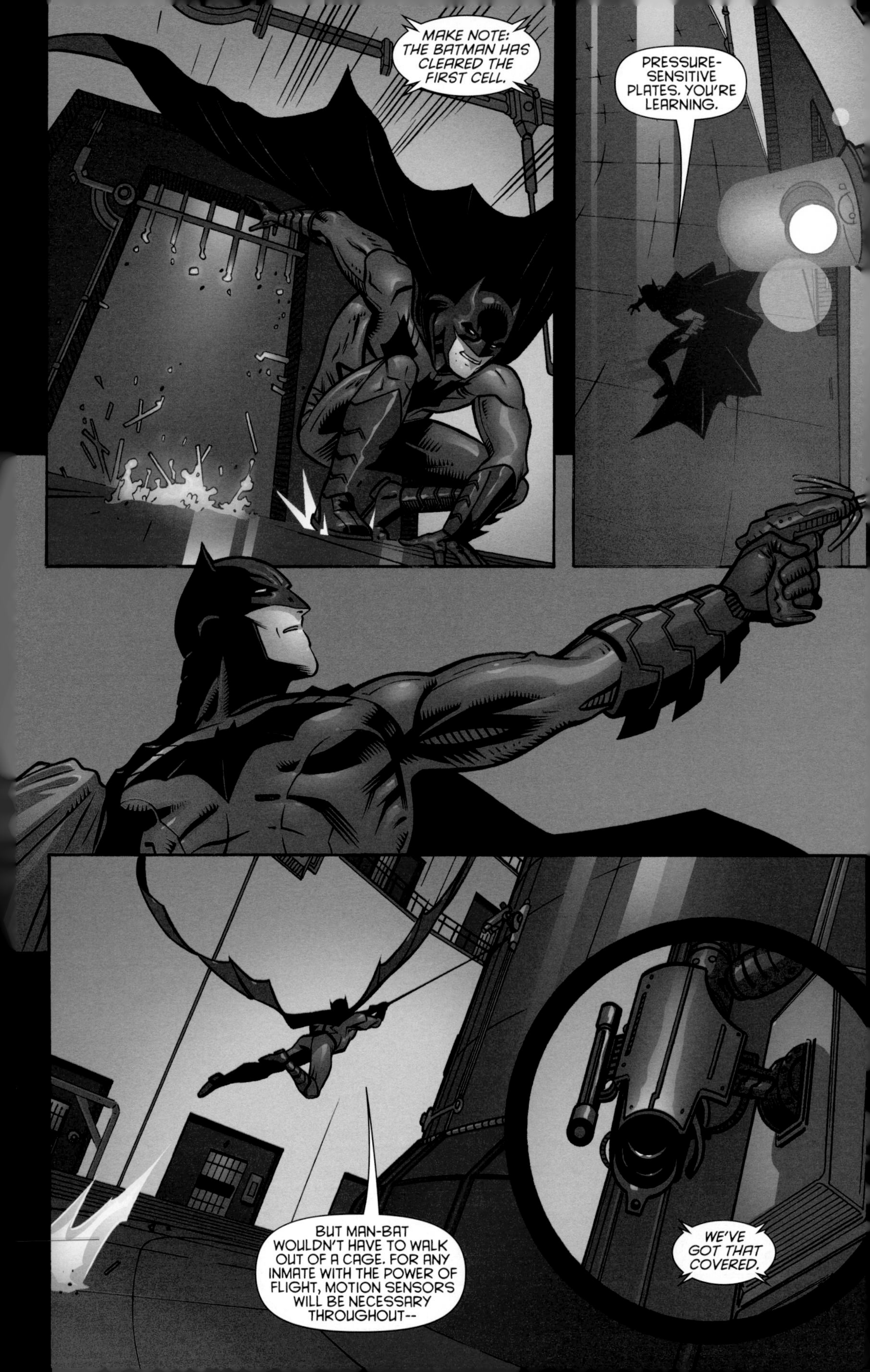
MAKE NOTE: THE BATMAN HAS CLEARED THE FIRST CELL.
PRESSURE-SENSITIVE PLATES. YOU'RE LEARNING.
BUT MAN-BAT WOULDN'T HAVE TO WALK OUT OF A CAGE. FOR ANY INMATE WITH THE POWER OF FLIGHT, MOTION SENSORS WILL BE NECESSARY THROUGHOUT--
WE'VE GOT THAT COVERED.

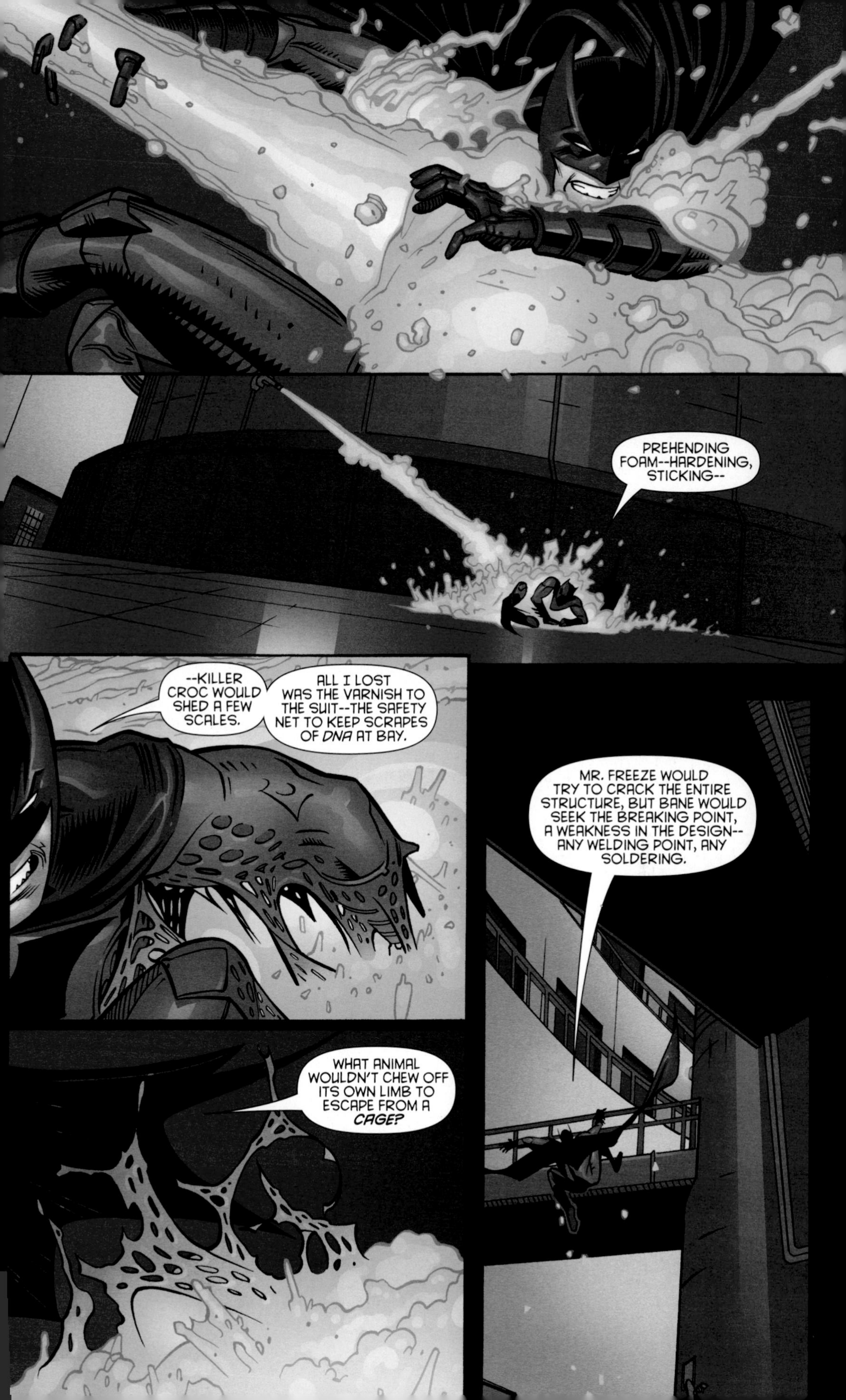
PREHENDING FOAM--HARDENING, STICKING--
--KILLER CROC WOULD SHED A FEW SCALES.
ALL I LOST WAS THE VARNISH TO THE SUIT--THE SAFETY NET TO KEEP SCRAPES OF *DNA* AT BAY.
MR. FREEZE WOULD TRY TO CRACK THE ENTIRE STRUCTURE, BUT BANE WOULD SEEK THE BREAKING POINT, A WEAKNESS IN THE DESIGN--ANY WELDING POINT, ANY SOLDERING.
WHAT ANIMAL WOULDN'T CHEW OFF ITS OWN LIMB TO ESCAPE FROM A *CAGE?*

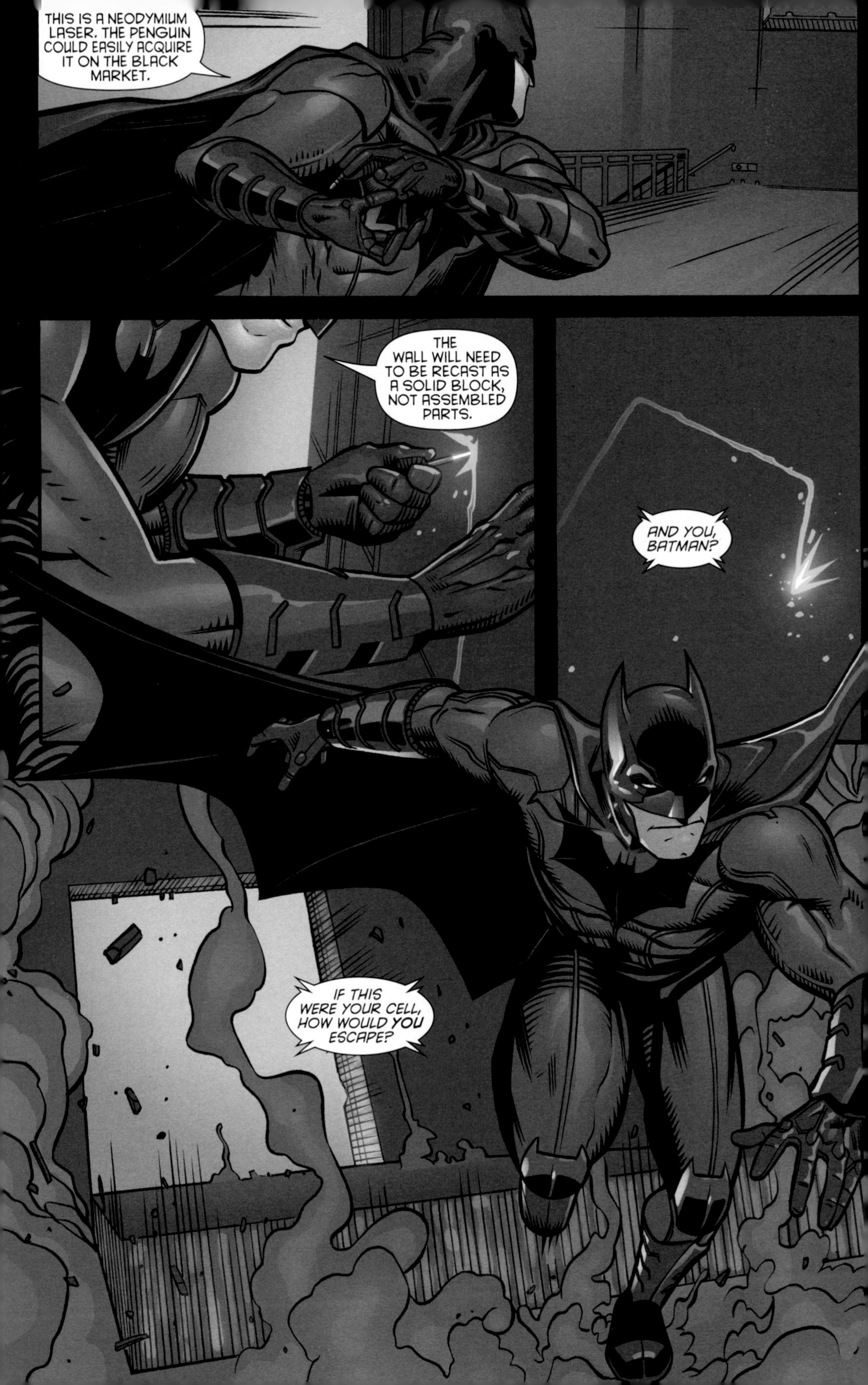
THIS IS A NEODYMIUM LASER. THE PENGUIN COULD EASILY ACQUIRE IT ON THE BLACK MARKET.
THE WALL WILL NEED TO BE RECAST AS A SOLID BLOCK, NOT ASSEMBLED PARTS.
AND YOU, BATMAN?
IF THIS WERE YOUR CELL, HOW WOULD YOU ESCAPE?

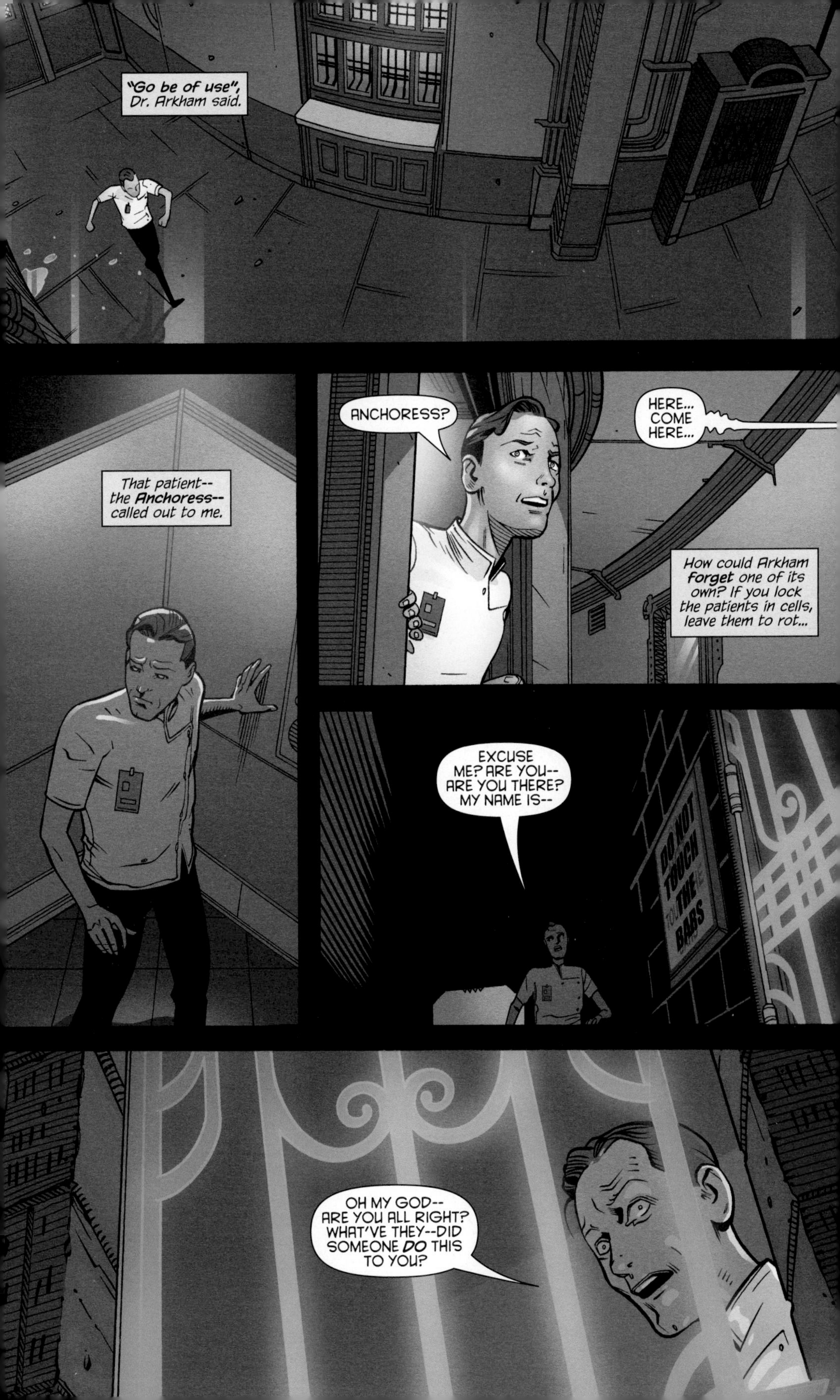
"Go be of use", Dr. Arkham said.
That patient-- the Anchoress-- called out to me.
ANCHORESS?
HERE... COME HERE...
How could Arkham forget one of its own? If you lock the patients in cells, leave them to rot...
EXCUSE ME? ARE YOU-- ARE YOU THERE? MY NAME IS--
DO NOT TOUCH THE BARS
OH MY GOD-- ARE YOU ALL RIGHT? WHAT'VE THEY--DID SOMEONE DO THIS TO YOU?

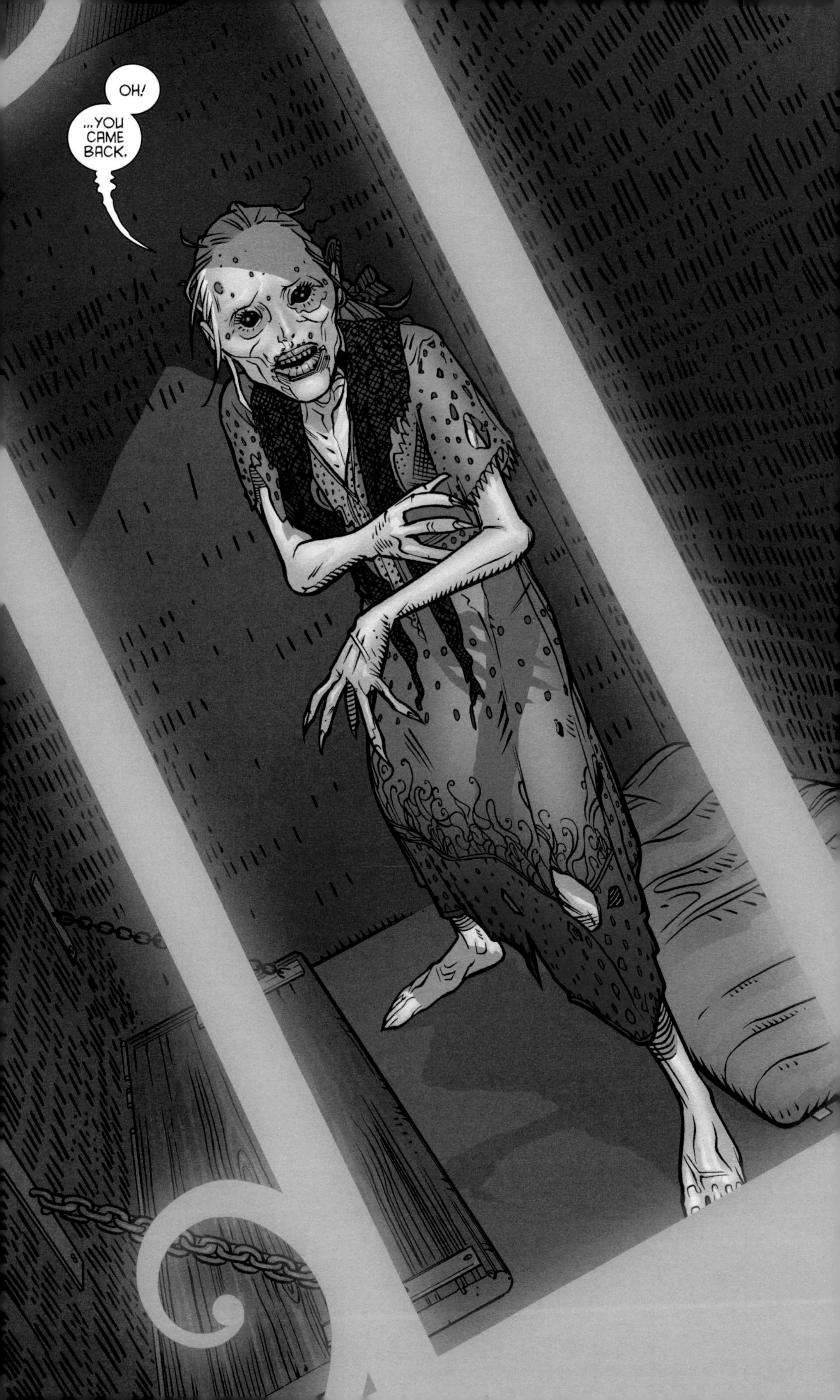
OH!
...YOU CAME BACK.

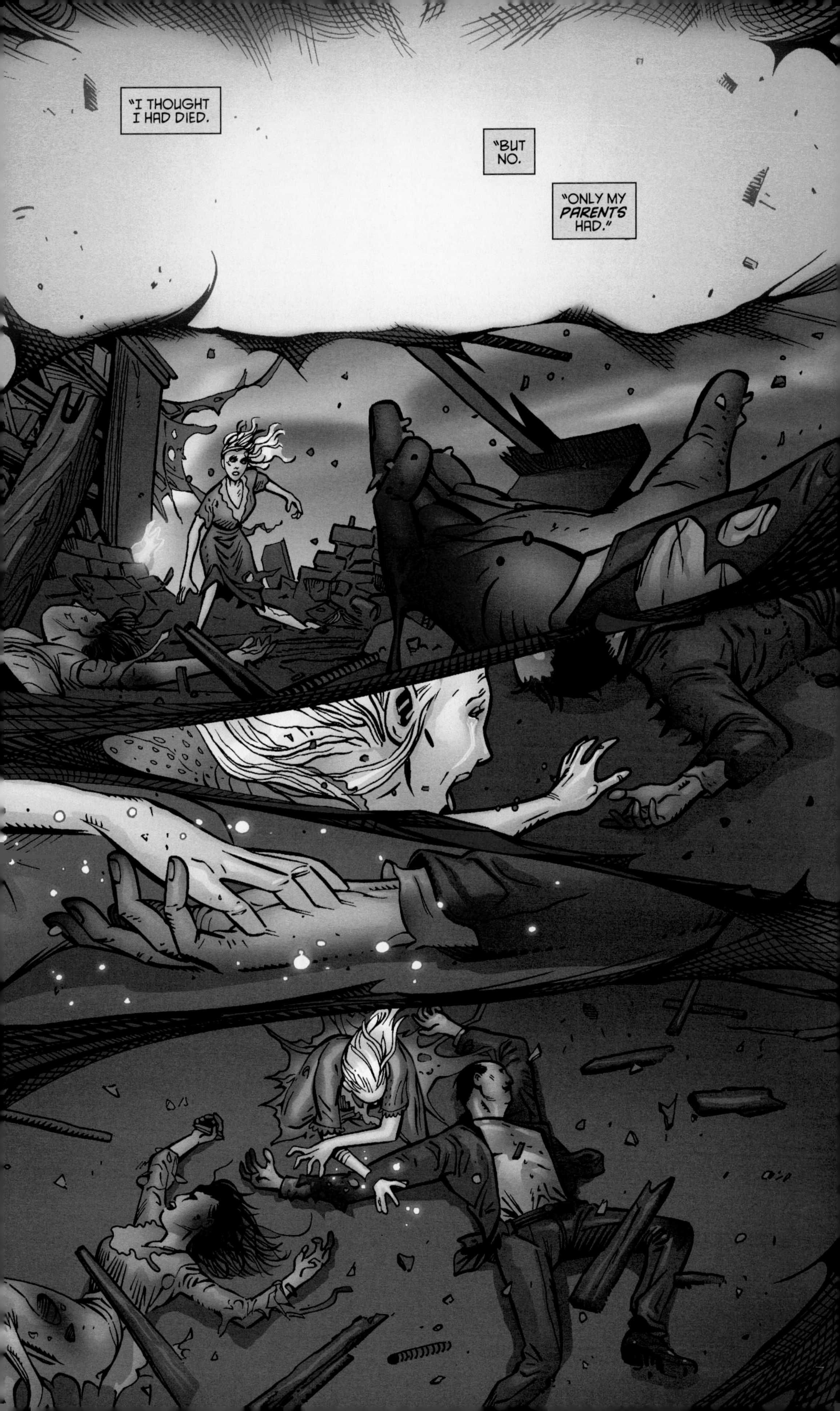
"I THOUGHT I HAD DIED.
"BUT NO.
"ONLY MY *PARENTS* HAD."

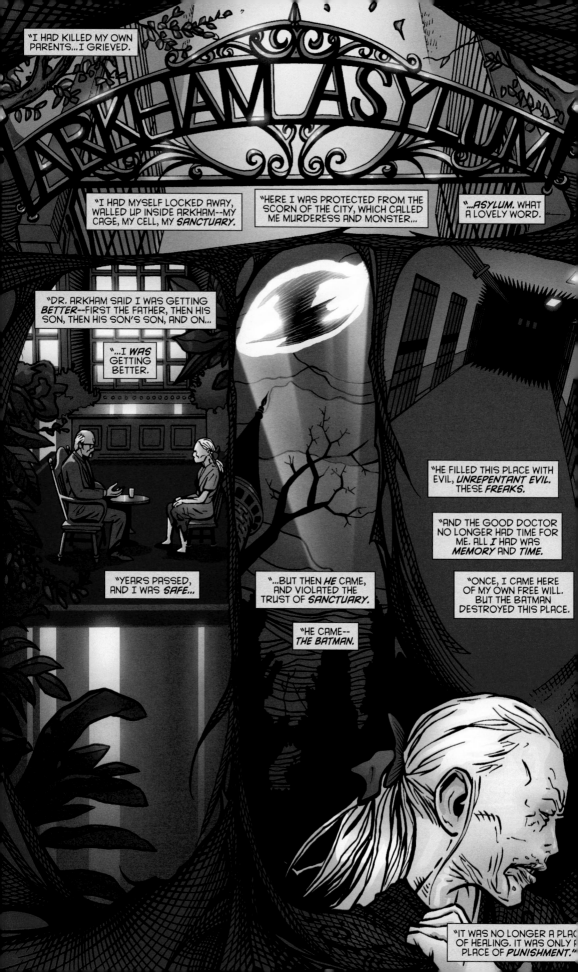

"I HAD KILLED MY OWN PARENTS...I GRIEVED.

ARKHAM ASYLUM

"I HAD MYSELF LOCKED AWAY, WALLED UP INSIDE ARKHAM--MY CAGE, MY CELL, MY *SANCTUARY.*

"HERE I WAS PROTECTED FROM THE SCORN OF THE CITY, WHICH CALLED ME MURDERESS AND MONSTER...

"...*ASYLUM.* WHAT A LOVELY WORD.

"DR. ARKHAM SAID I WAS GETTING *BETTER*--FIRST THE FATHER, THEN HIS SON, THEN HIS SON'S SON, AND ON...

"...*I WAS* GETTING BETTER.

"HE FILLED THIS PLACE WITH EVIL, *UNREPENTANT EVIL.* THESE *FREAKS.*

"AND THE GOOD DOCTOR NO LONGER HAD TIME FOR ME. ALL *I* HAD WAS *MEMORY* AND *TIME.*

"YEARS PASSED, AND I WAS *SAFE*...

"...BUT THEN *HE* CAME, AND VIOLATED THE TRUST OF *SANCTUARY.*

"ONCE, I CAME HERE OF MY OWN FREE WILL. BUT THE BATMAN DESTROYED THIS PLACE.

"HE CAME-- *THE BATMAN.*

"IT WAS NO LONGER A PLAC[E] OF HEALING. IT WAS ONLY [A] PLACE OF *PUNISHMENT.*"

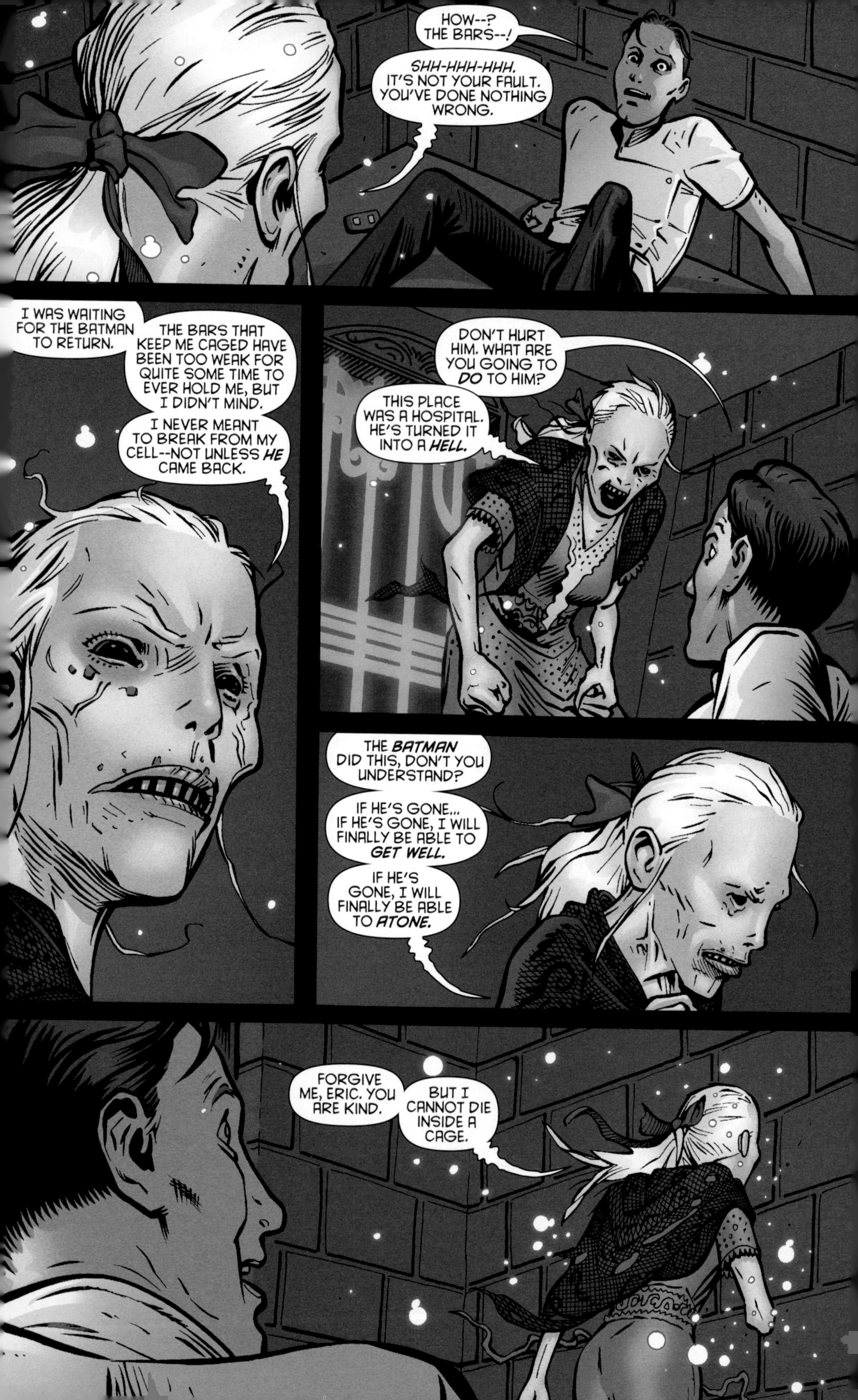
HOW--? THE BARS--!
SHH-HHH-HHH. IT'S NOT YOUR FAULT. YOU'VE DONE NOTHING WRONG.
I WAS WAITING FOR THE BATMAN TO RETURN.
THE BARS THAT KEEP ME CAGED HAVE BEEN TOO WEAK FOR QUITE SOME TIME TO EVER HOLD ME, BUT I DIDN'T MIND.
I NEVER MEANT TO BREAK FROM MY CELL--NOT UNLESS HE CAME BACK.
DON'T HURT HIM. WHAT ARE YOU GOING TO DO TO HIM?
THIS PLACE WAS A HOSPITAL. HE'S TURNED IT INTO A HELL.
THE BATMAN DID THIS, DON'T YOU UNDERSTAND?
IF HE'S GONE... IF HE'S GONE, I WILL FINALLY BE ABLE TO GET WELL.
IF HE'S GONE, I WILL FINALLY BE ABLE TO ATONE.
FORGIVE ME, ERIC. YOU ARE KIND.
BUT I CANNOT DIE INSIDE A CAGE.

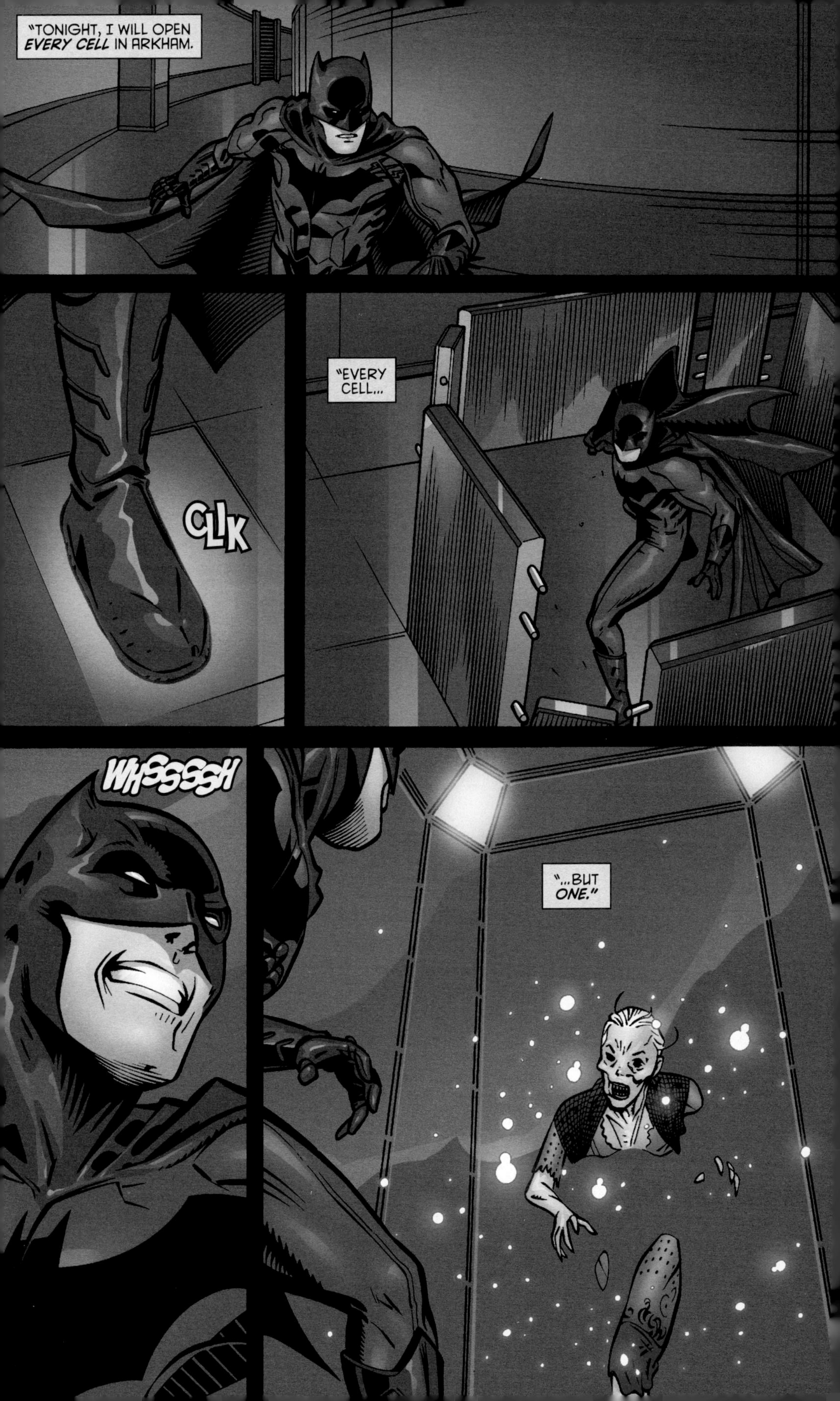
"TONIGHT, I WILL OPEN EVERY CELL IN ARKHAM.
CLIK
"EVERY CELL...
WHSSSSH
"...BUT ONE."

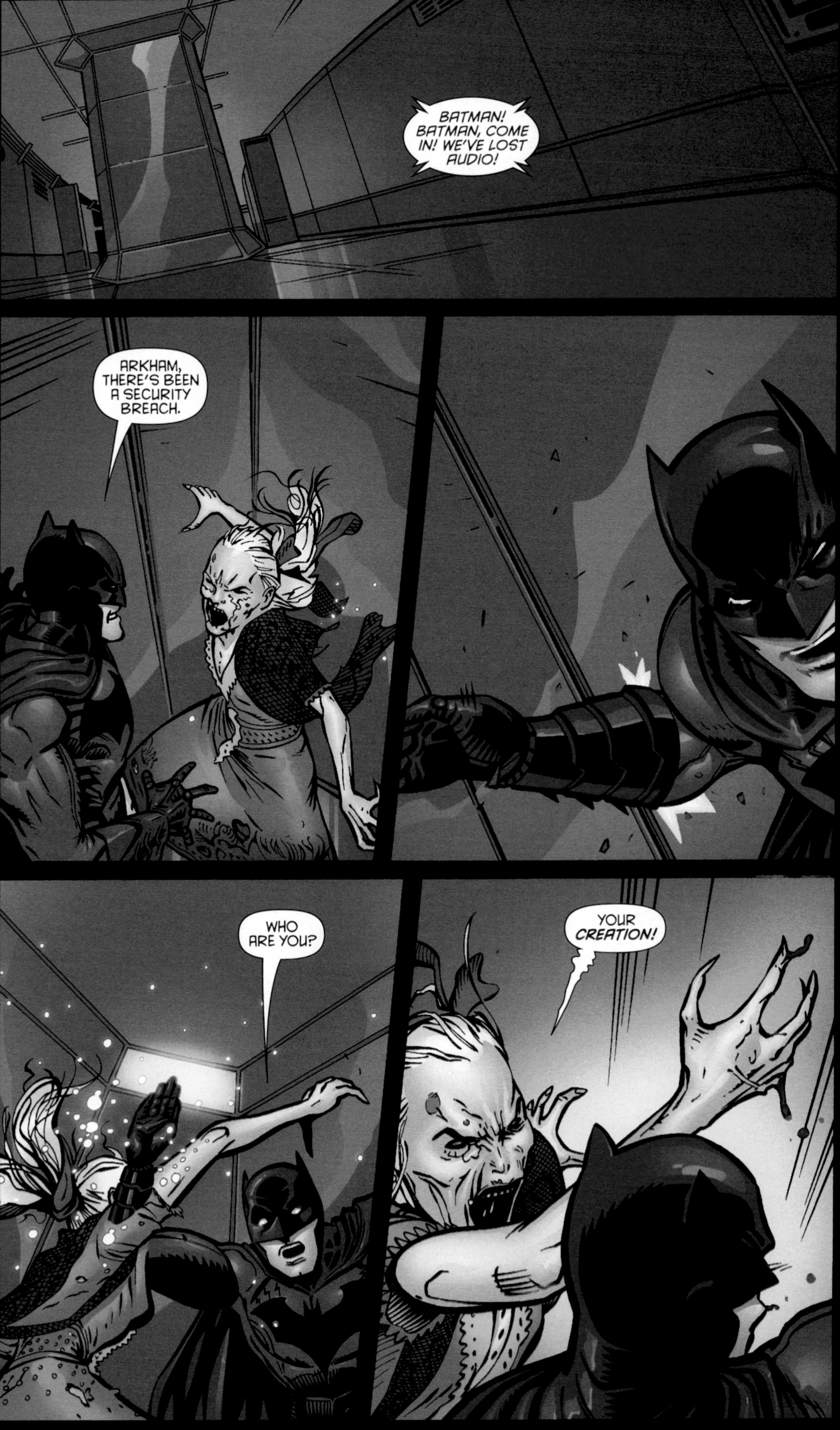
BATMAN! BATMAN, COME IN! WE'VE LOST AUDIO!
ARKHAM, THERE'S BEEN A SECURITY BREACH.
WHO ARE YOU?
YOUR *CREATION!*

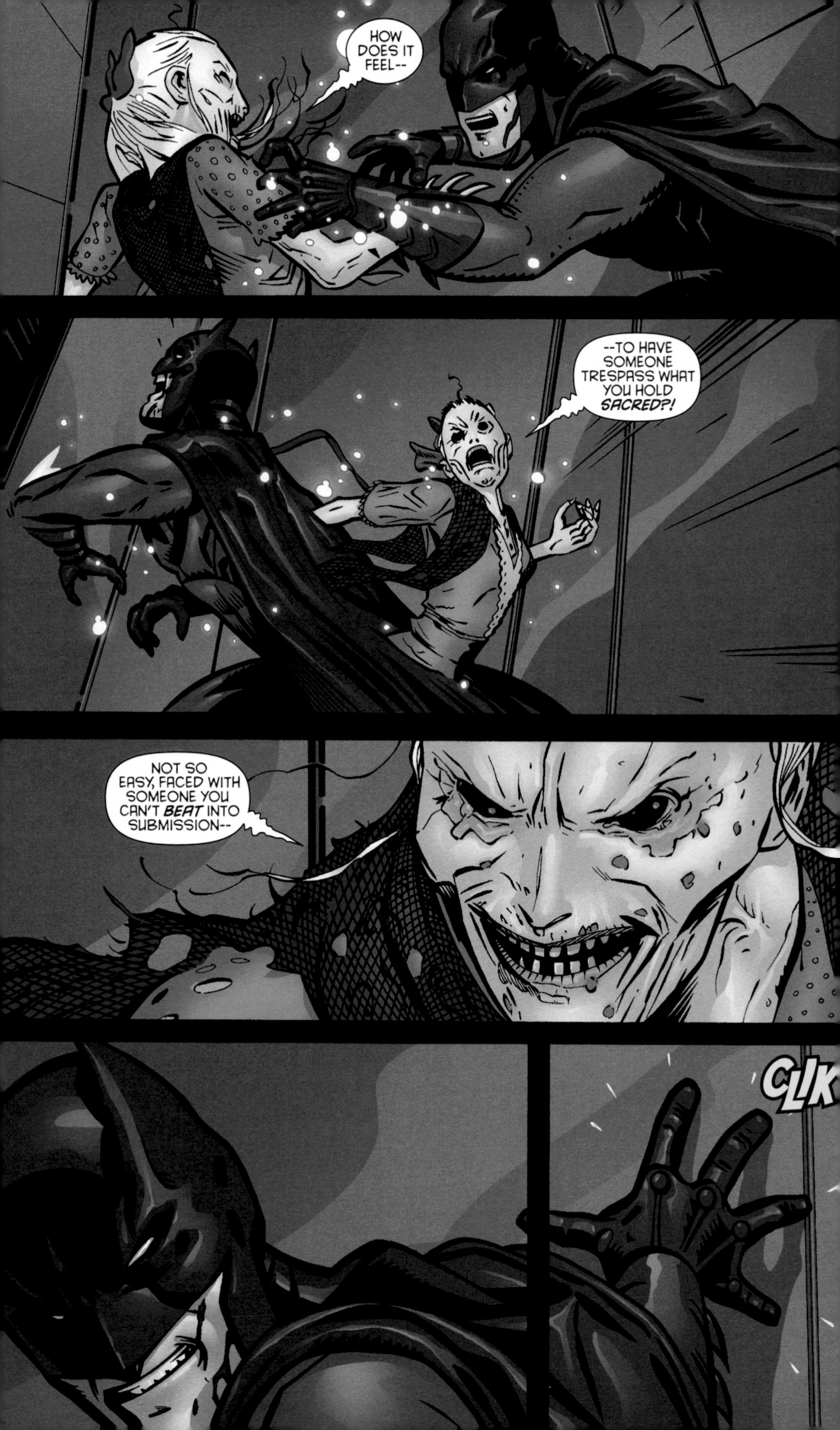
HOW DOES IT FEEL--
--TO HAVE SOMEONE TRESPASS WHAT YOU HOLD *SACRED?!*
NOT SO EASY, FACED WITH SOMEONE YOU CAN'T *BEAT* INTO SUBMISSION--
CLIK

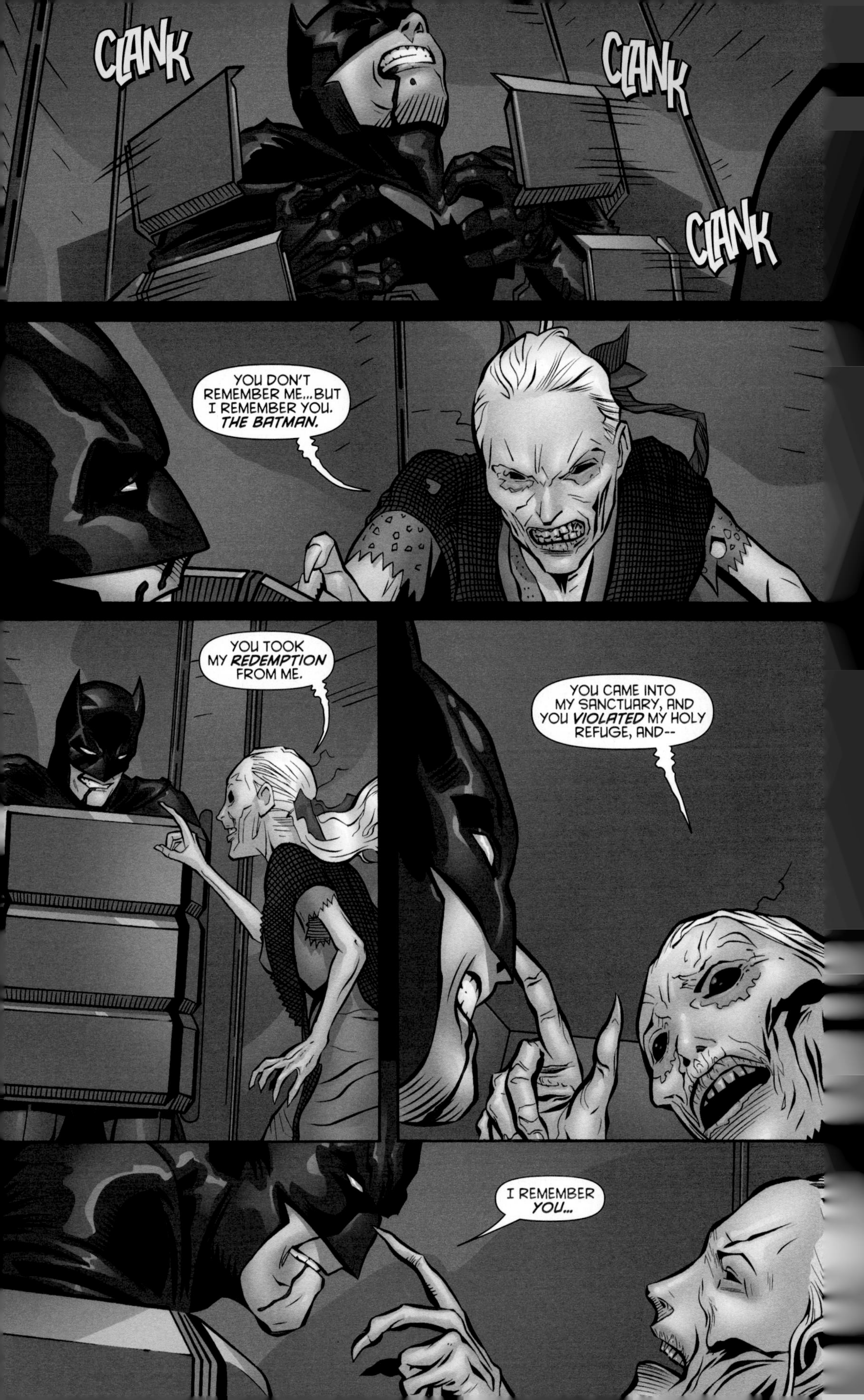
CLANK
CLANK
CLANK
YOU DON'T REMEMBER ME...BUT I REMEMBER YOU. THE BATMAN.
YOU TOOK MY REDEMPTION FROM ME.
YOU CAME INTO MY SANCTUARY, AND YOU VIOLATED MY HOLY REFUGE, AND--
I REMEMBER YOU...

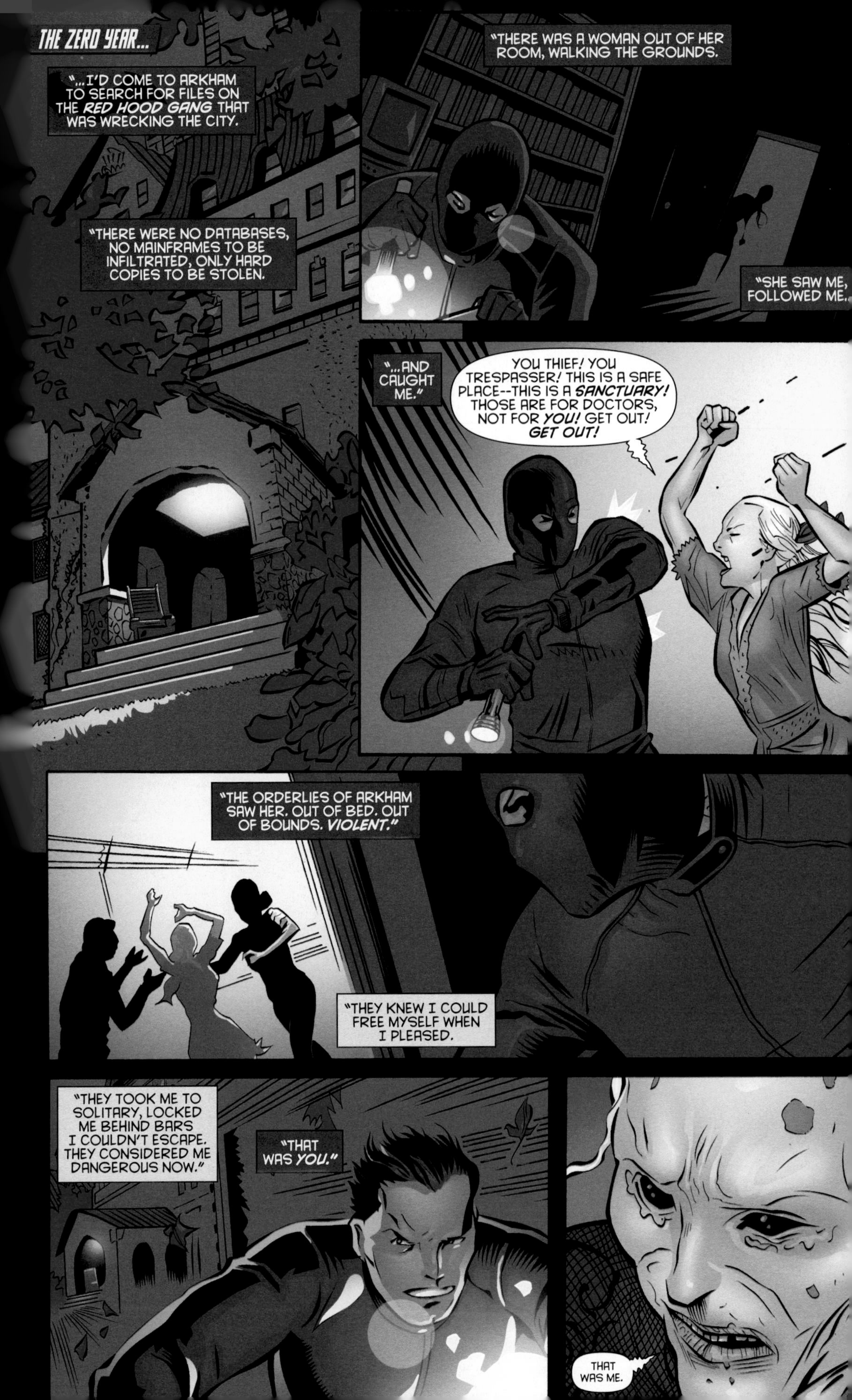
THE ZERO YEAR...
"...I'D COME TO ARKHAM TO SEARCH FOR FILES ON THE RED HOOD GANG THAT WAS WRECKING THE CITY.
"THERE WERE NO DATABASES, NO MAINFRAMES TO BE INFILTRATED, ONLY HARD COPIES TO BE STOLEN.
"THERE WAS A WOMAN OUT OF HER ROOM, WALKING THE GROUNDS.
"SHE SAW ME, FOLLOWED ME...
"...AND CAUGHT ME."
YOU THIEF! YOU TRESPASSER! THIS IS A SAFE PLACE--THIS IS A SANCTUARY! THOSE ARE FOR DOCTORS, NOT FOR YOU! GET OUT! GET OUT!
"THE ORDERLIES OF ARKHAM SAW HER. OUT OF BED. OUT OF BOUNDS. VIOLENT."
"THEY KNEW I COULD FREE MYSELF WHEN I PLEASED.
"THEY TOOK ME TO SOLITARY, LOCKED ME BEHIND BARS I COULDN'T ESCAPE. THEY CONSIDERED ME DANGEROUS NOW."
"THAT WAS YOU."
THAT WAS ME.

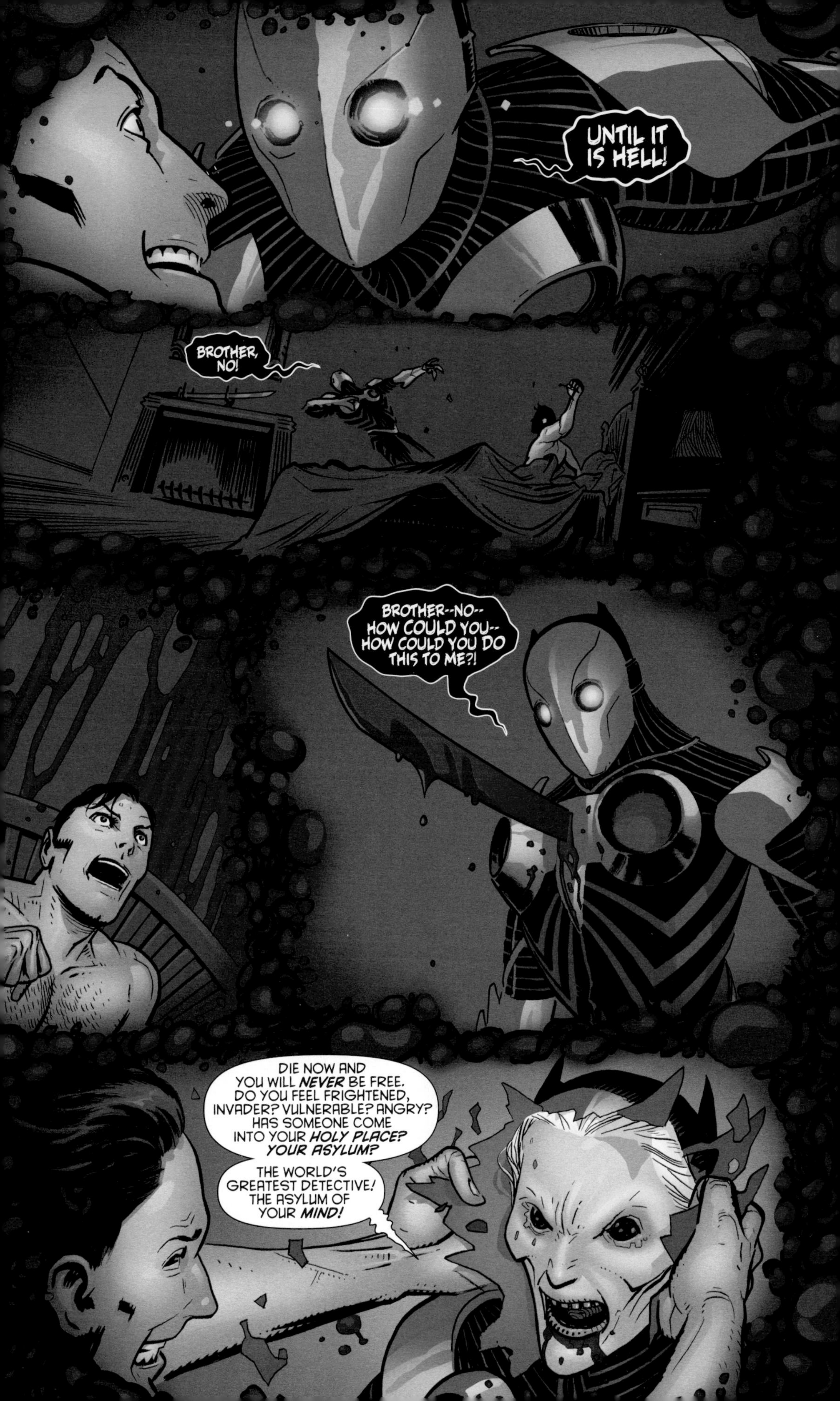
UNTIL IT IS HELL!
BROTHER, NO!
BROTHER--NO-- HOW COULD YOU-- HOW COULD YOU DO THIS TO ME?!
DIE NOW AND YOU WILL *NEVER* BE FREE. DO YOU FEEL FRIGHTENED, INVADER? VULNERABLE? ANGRY? HAS SOMEONE COME INTO YOUR *HOLY PLACE? YOUR ASYLUM?*
THE WORLD'S GREATEST DETECTIVE! THE ASYLUM OF YOUR *MIND!*

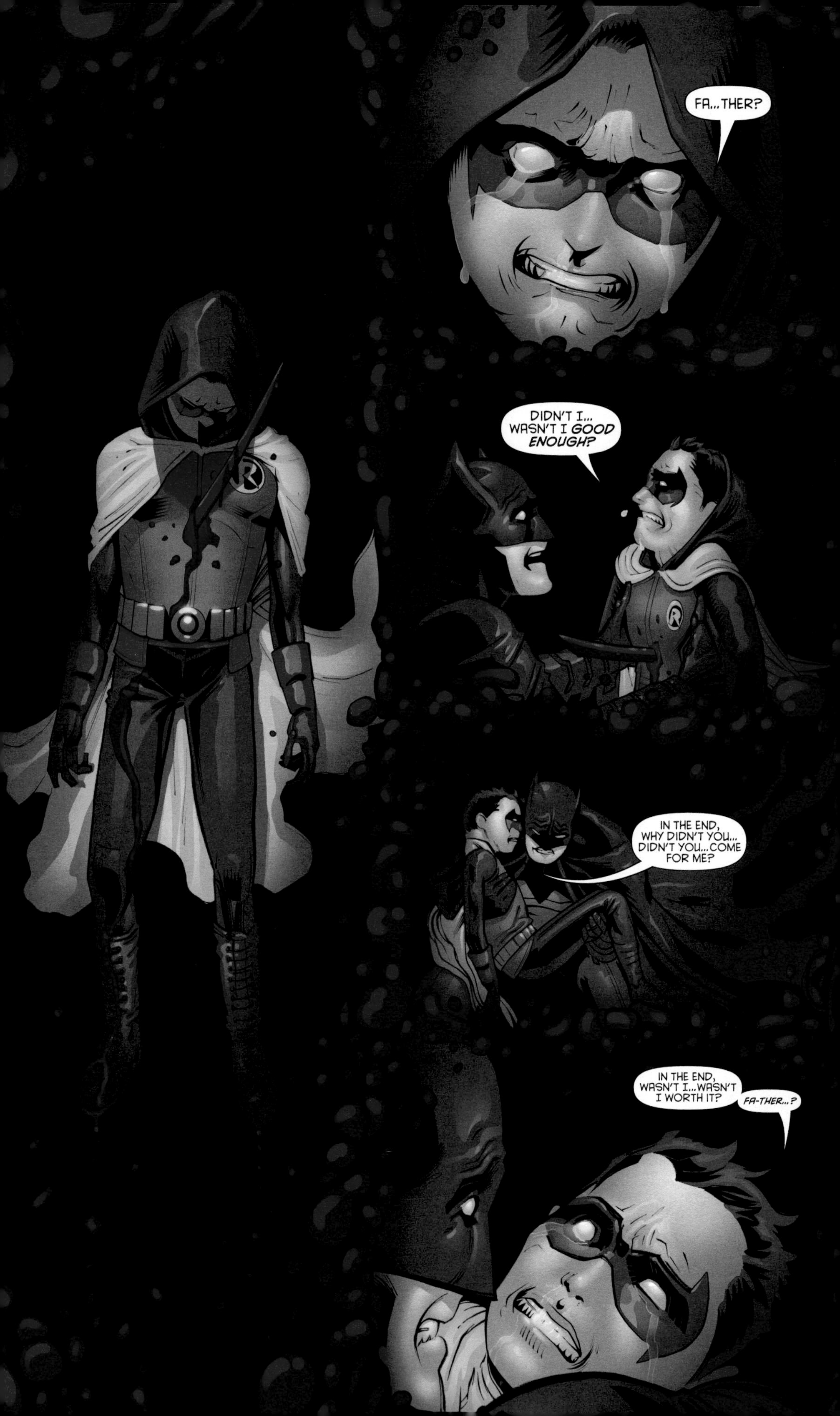
FA...THER?
DIDN'T I... WASN'T I *GOOD ENOUGH?*
IN THE END, WHY DIDN'T YOU... DIDN'T YOU...COME FOR ME?
IN THE END, WASN'T I...WASN'T I WORTH IT?
FA-THER...?

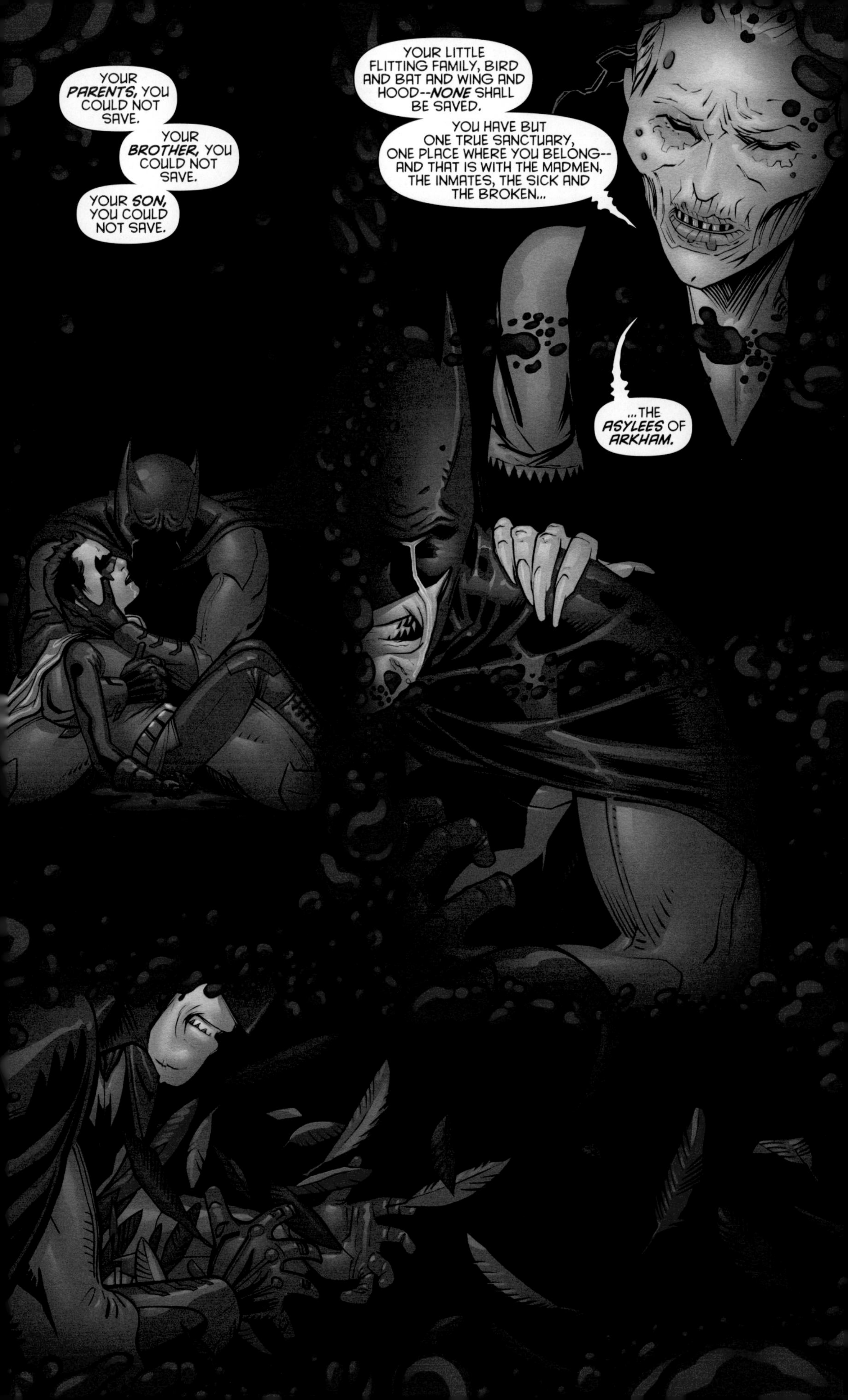
YOUR PARENTS, YOU COULD NOT SAVE.
YOUR BROTHER, YOU COULD NOT SAVE.
YOUR SON, YOU COULD NOT SAVE.
YOUR LITTLE FLITTING FAMILY, BIRD AND BAT AND WING AND HOOD--NONE SHALL BE SAVED.
YOU HAVE BUT ONE TRUE SANCTUARY, ONE PLACE WHERE YOU BELONG--AND THAT IS WITH THE MADMEN, THE INMATES, THE SICK AND THE BROKEN...
...THE ASYLEES OF ARKHAM.

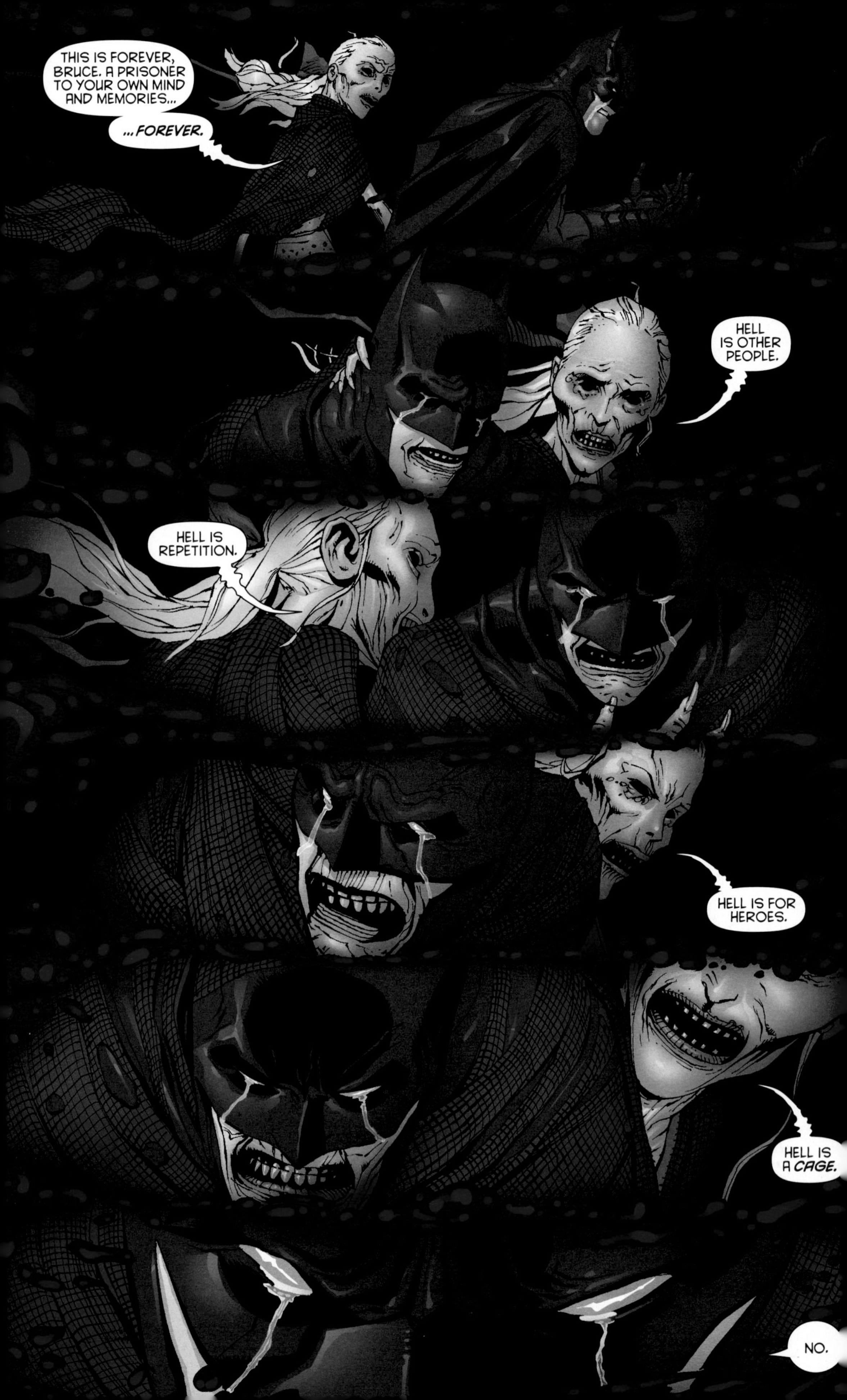
THIS IS FOREVER, BRUCE. A PRISONER TO YOUR OWN MIND AND MEMORIES...
...FOREVER.
HELL IS OTHER PEOPLE.
HELL IS REPETITION.
HELL IS FOR HEROES.
HELL IS A CAGE.
NO.

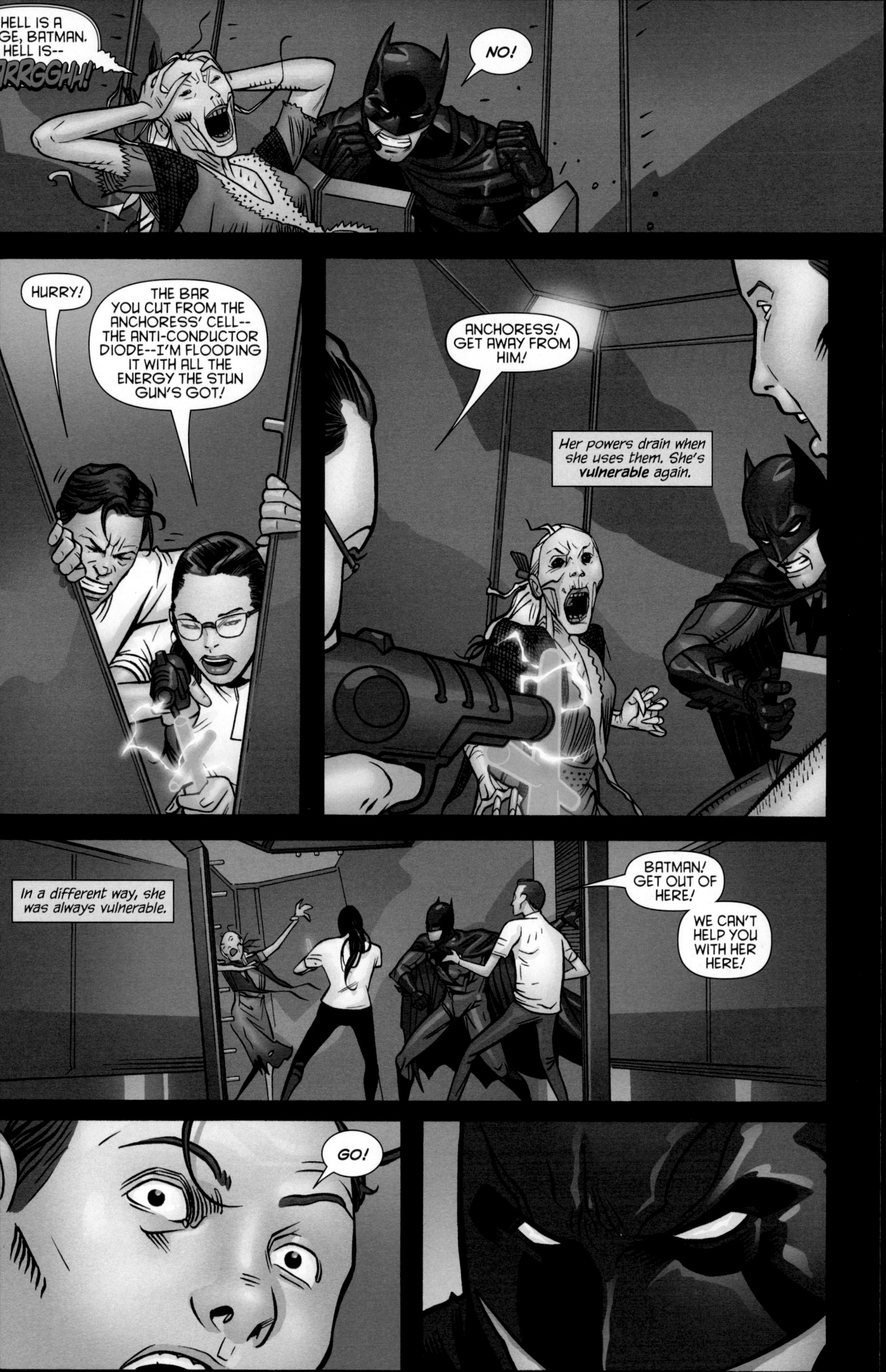
HELL IS A
GE, BATMAN.
HELL IS--
RRGGHH!
NO!
HURRY!
THE BAR YOU CUT FROM THE ANCHORESS' CELL--THE ANTI-CONDUCTOR DIODE--I'M FLOODING IT WITH ALL THE ENERGY THE STUN GUN'S GOT!
ANCHORESS! GET AWAY FROM HIM!
Her powers drain when she uses them. She's **vulnerable** again.
In a different way, she was always vulnerable.
BATMAN! GET OUT OF HERE!
WE CAN'T HELP YOU WITH HER HERE!
GO!

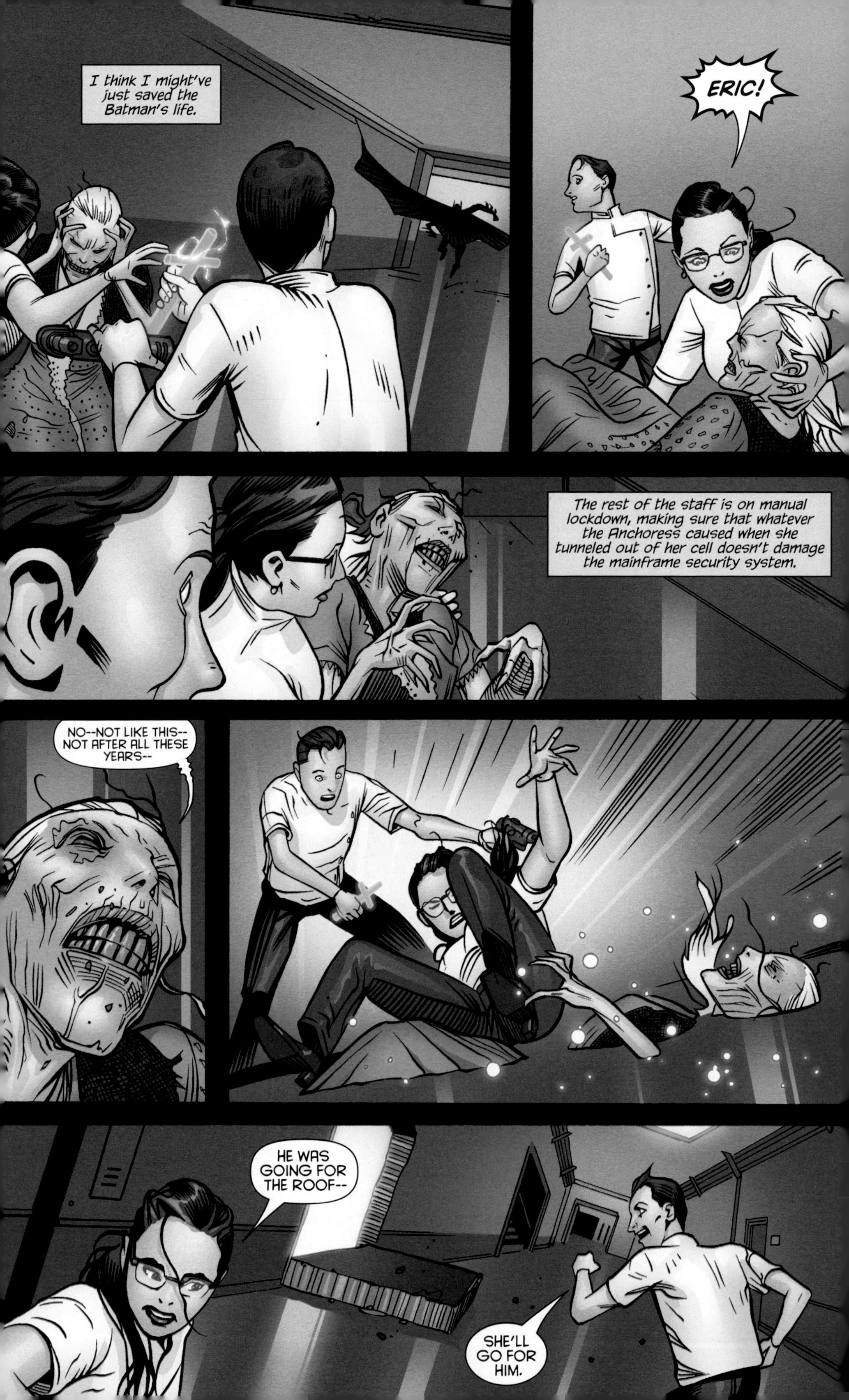
I think I might've just saved the Batman's life.
ERIC!
The rest of the staff is on manual lockdown, making sure that whatever the Anchoress caused when she tunneled out of her cell doesn't damage the mainframe security system.
NO--NOT LIKE THIS--NOT AFTER ALL THESE YEARS--
HE WAS GOING FOR THE ROOF--
SHE'LL GO FOR HIM.

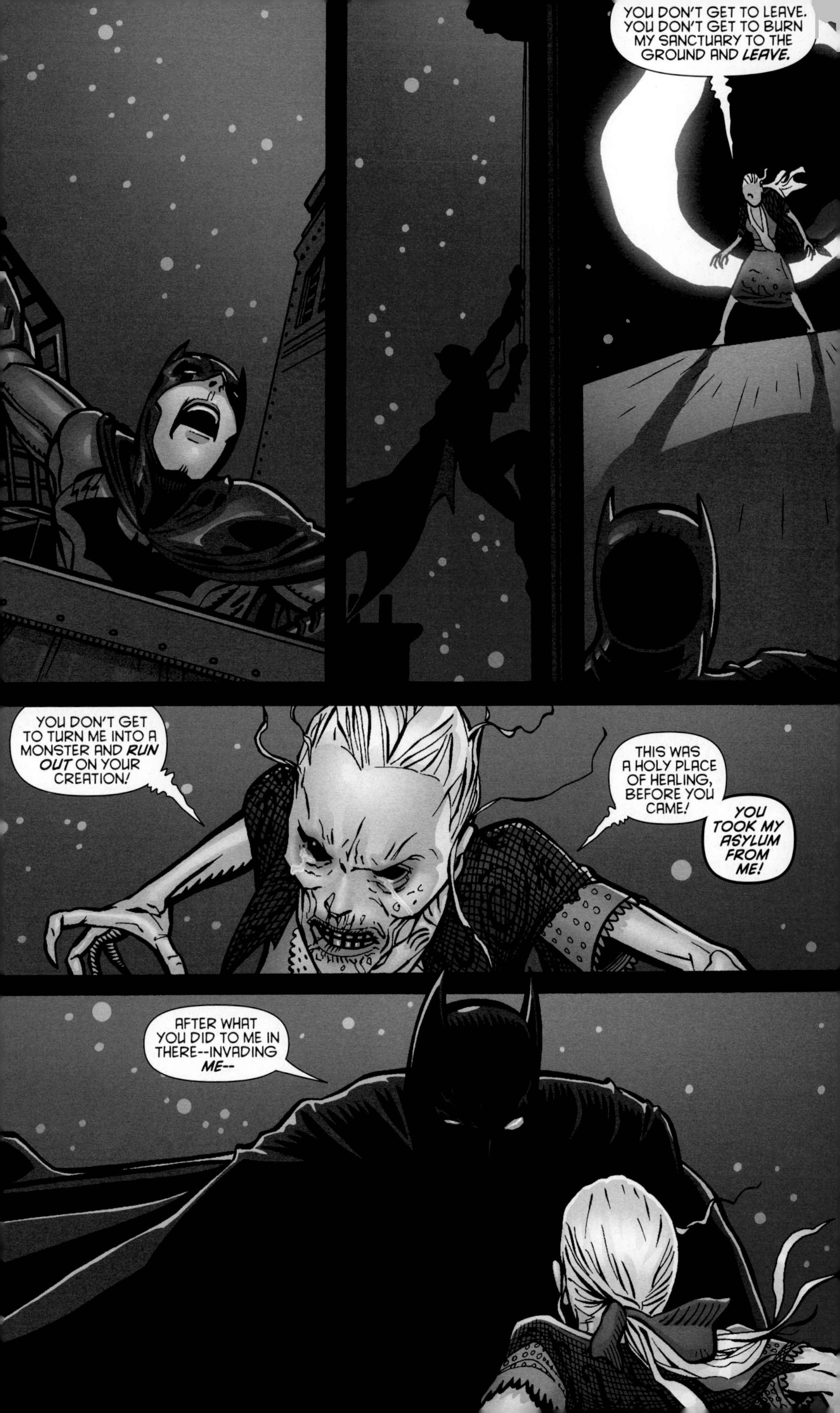
YOU DON'T GET TO LEAVE. YOU DON'T GET TO BURN MY SANCTUARY TO THE GROUND AND *LEAVE.*
YOU DON'T GET TO TURN ME INTO A MONSTER AND *RUN OUT* ON YOUR CREATION!
THIS WAS A HOLY PLACE OF HEALING, BEFORE YOU CAME!
YOU TOOK MY ASYLUM FROM ME!
AFTER WHAT YOU DID TO ME IN THERE--INVADING *ME--*

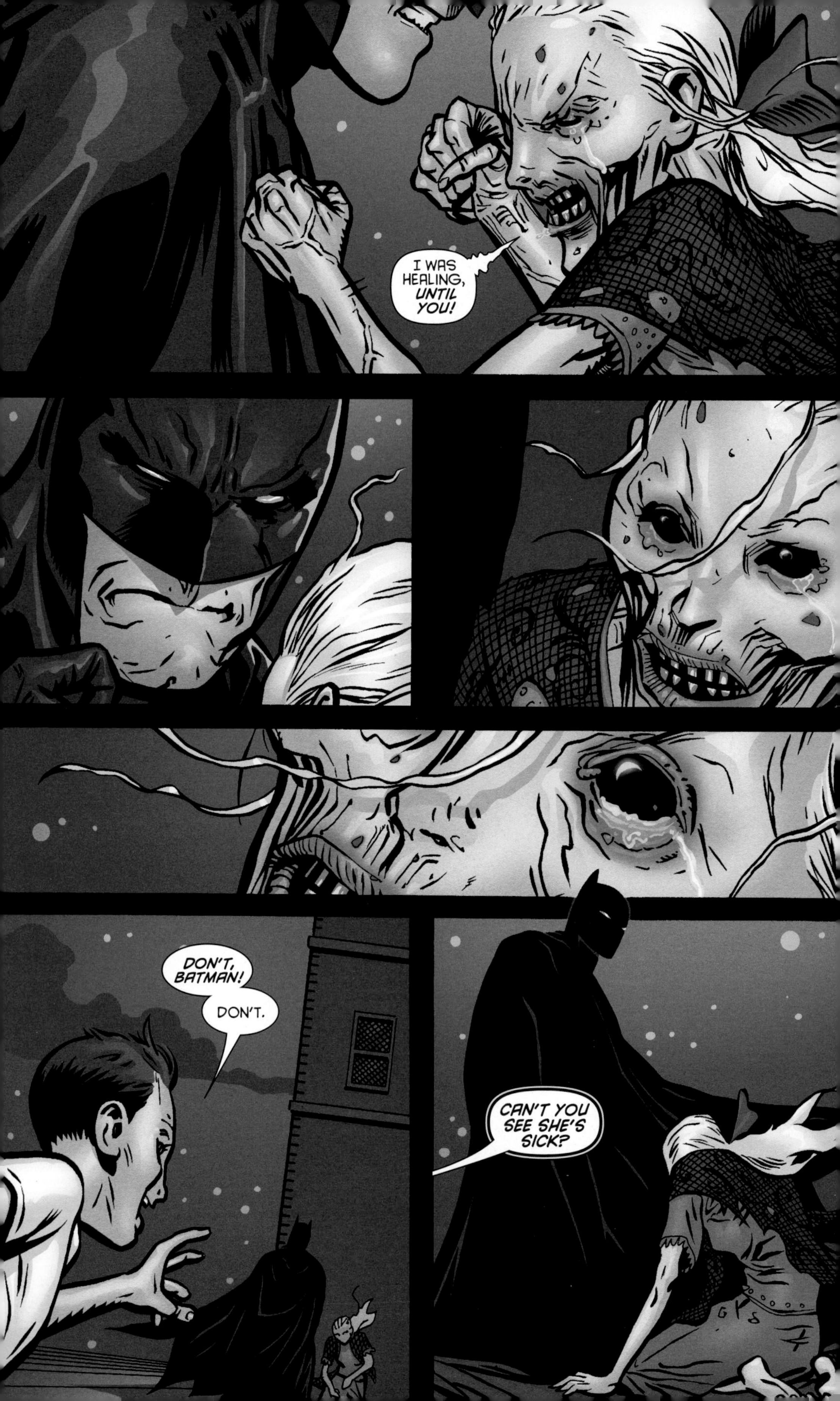
I WAS HEALING, UNTIL YOU!
DON'T, BATMAN!
DON'T.
CAN'T YOU SEE SHE'S SICK?

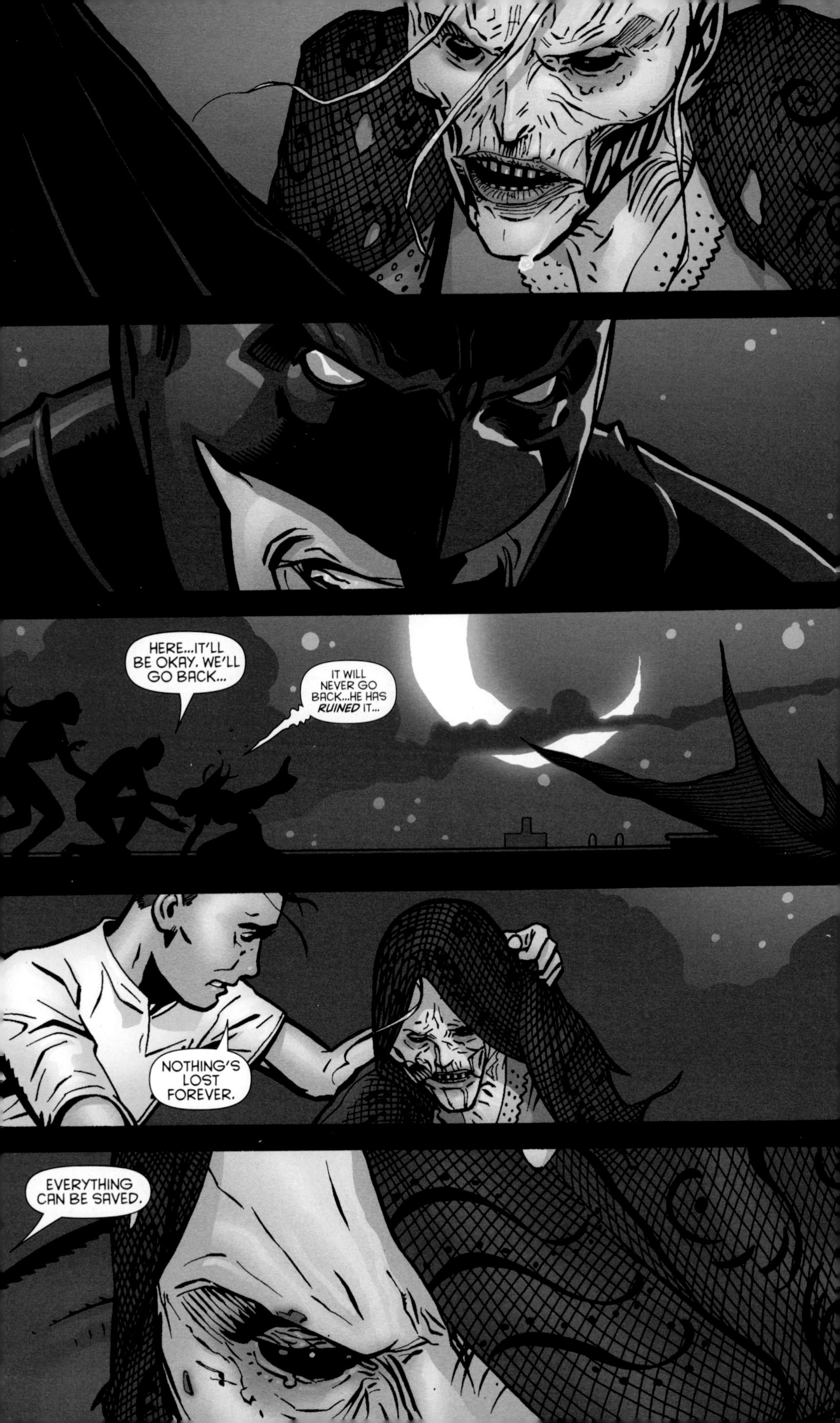
HERE...IT'LL BE OKAY. WE'LL GO BACK...
IT WILL NEVER GO BACK...HE HAS *RUINED* IT...
NOTHING'S LOST FOREVER.
EVERYTHING CAN BE SAVED.

END

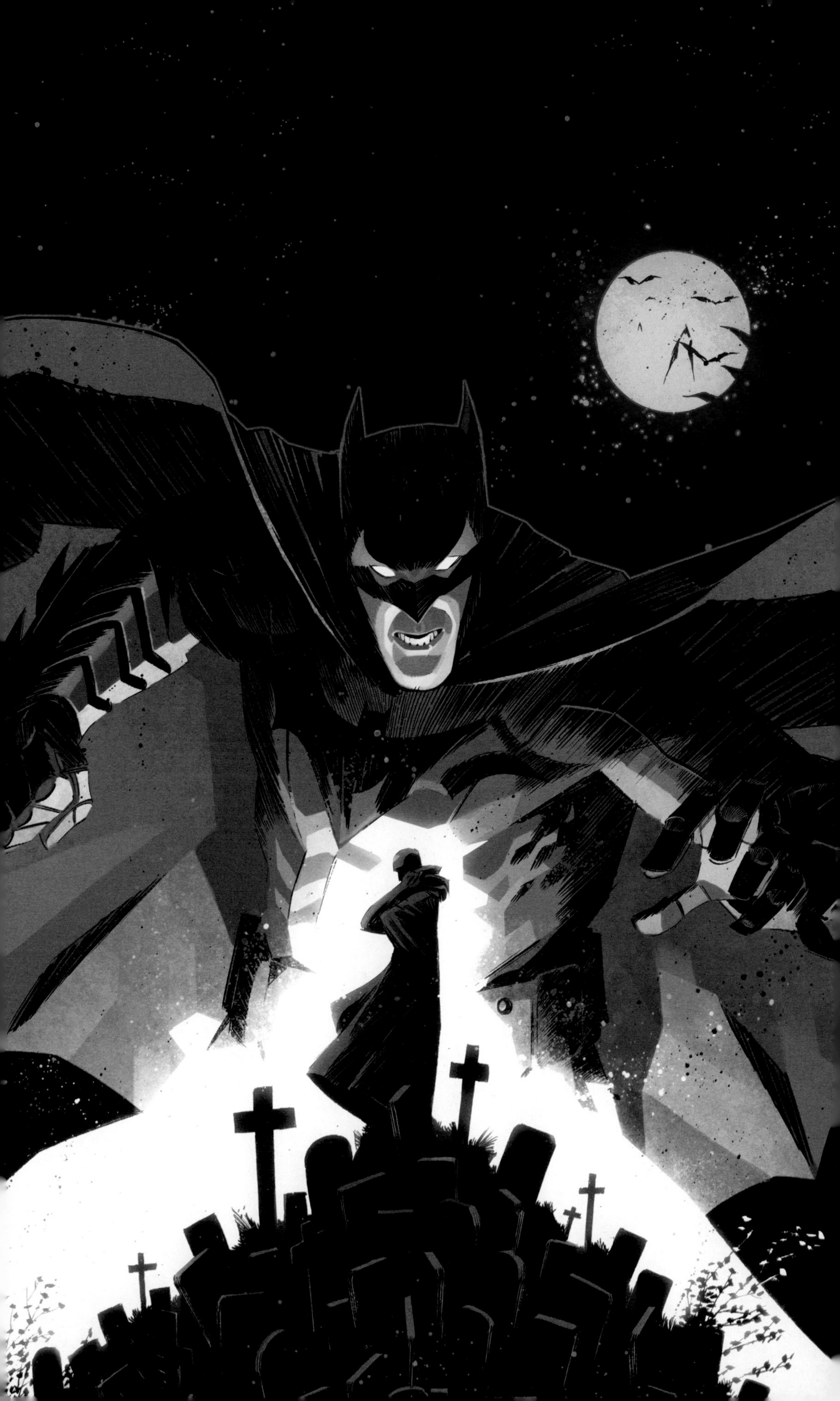

THE MEEK

SCOTT SNYDER GERRY DUGGAN plotters **GERRY DUGGAN** writer **MATTEO SCALERA** artist **LEE LOUGHRIDGE** colorist
cover by **MATTEO SCALERA** and **MORENO DINISIO**

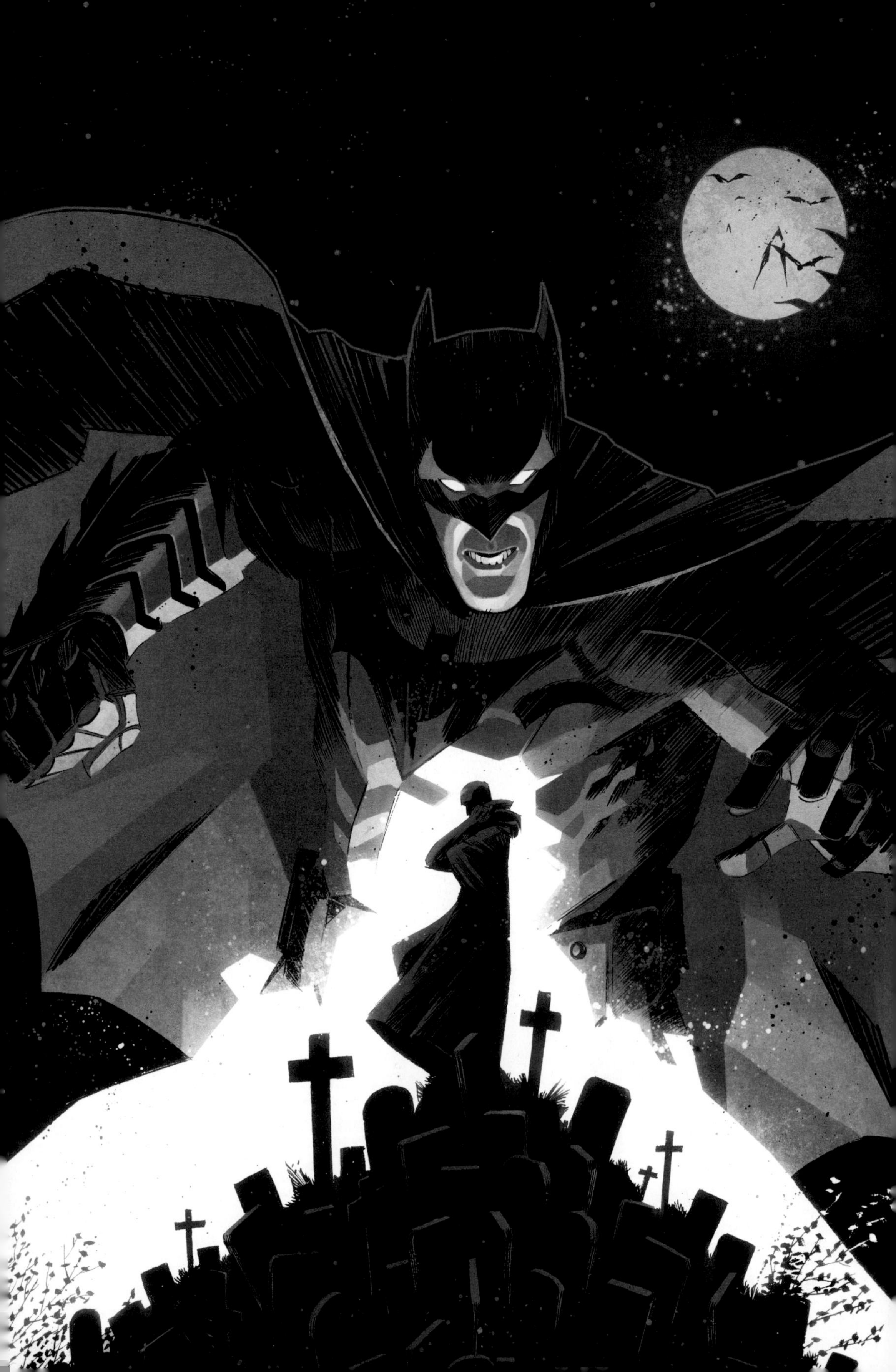

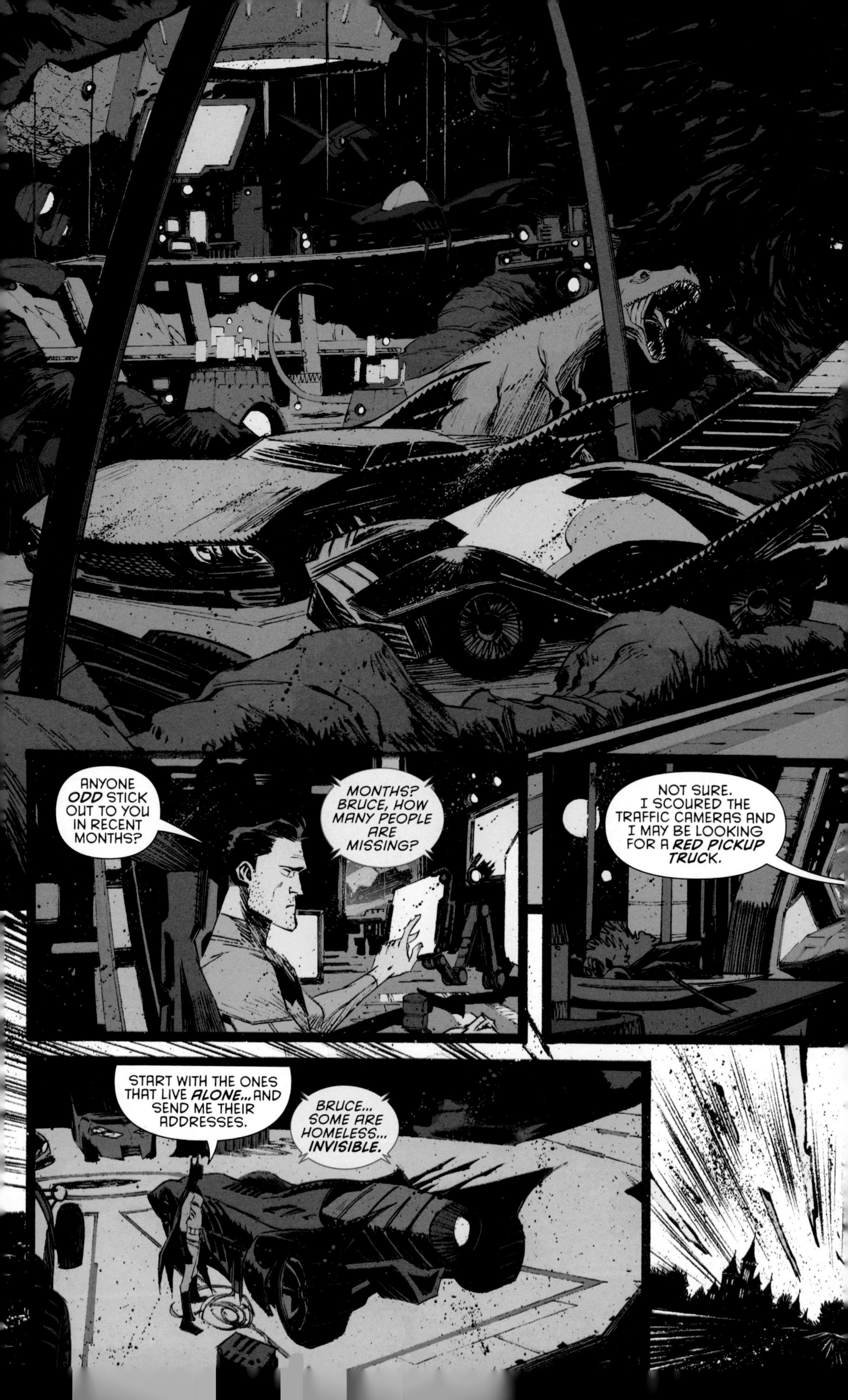

ANYONE ODD STICK OUT TO YOU IN RECENT MONTHS?
MONTHS? BRUCE, HOW MANY PEOPLE ARE MISSING?
NOT SURE. I SCOURED THE TRAFFIC CAMERAS AND I MAY BE LOOKING FOR A RED PICKUP TRUCK.
START WITH THE ONES THAT LIVE ALONE... AND SEND ME THEIR ADDRESSES.
BRUCE... SOME ARE HOMELESS... INVISIBLE.

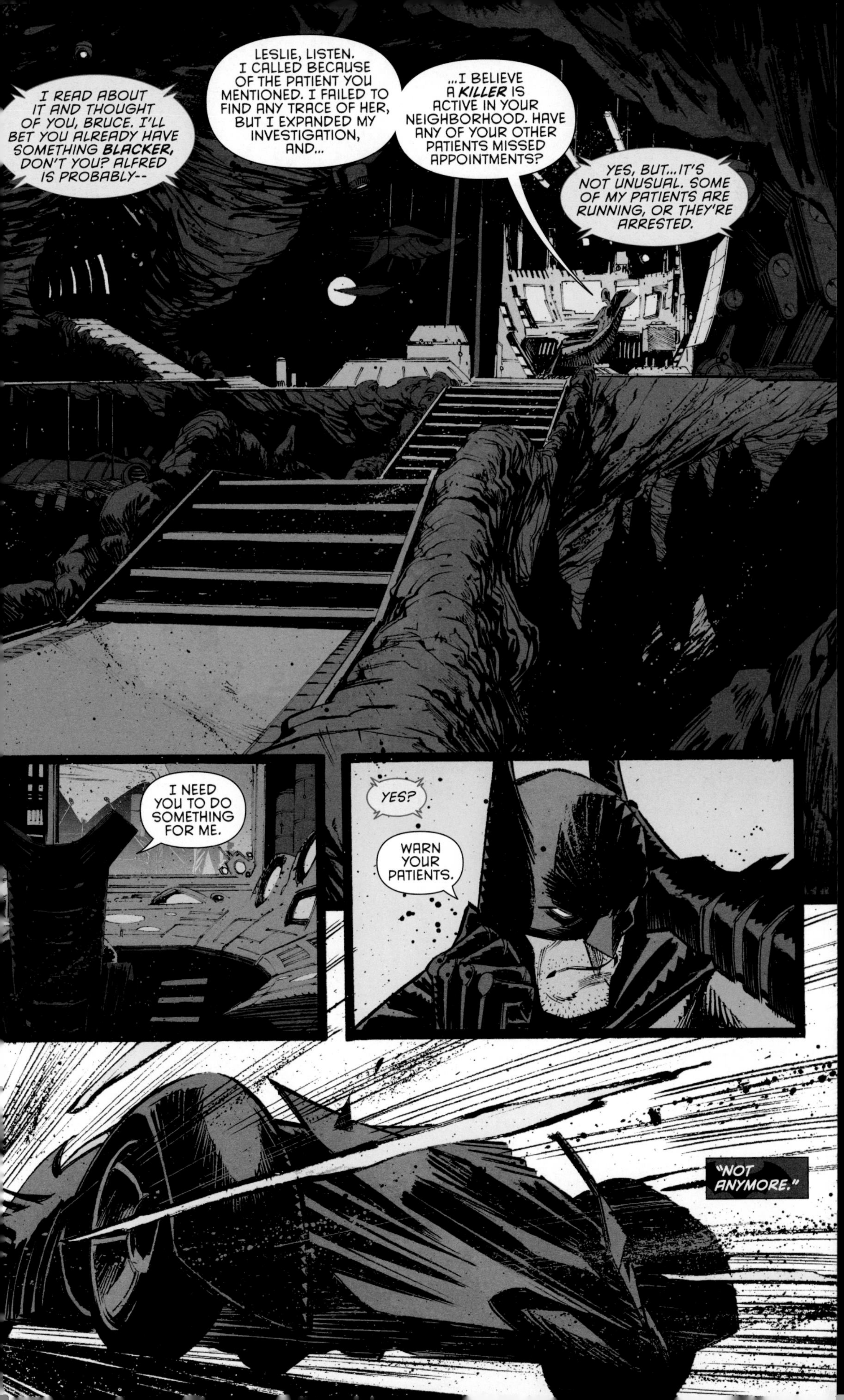
I READ ABOUT IT AND THOUGHT OF YOU, BRUCE. I'LL BET YOU ALREADY HAVE SOMETHING BLACKER, DON'T YOU? ALFRED IS PROBABLY--
LESLIE, LISTEN. I CALLED BECAUSE OF THE PATIENT YOU MENTIONED. I FAILED TO FIND ANY TRACE OF HER, BUT I EXPANDED MY INVESTIGATION, AND...
...I BELIEVE A KILLER IS ACTIVE IN YOUR NEIGHBORHOOD. HAVE ANY OF YOUR OTHER PATIENTS MISSED APPOINTMENTS?
YES, BUT...IT'S NOT UNUSUAL. SOME OF MY PATIENTS ARE RUNNING, OR THEY'RE ARRESTED.
I NEED YOU TO DO SOMETHING FOR ME.
YES?
WARN YOUR PATIENTS.
"NOT ANYMORE."

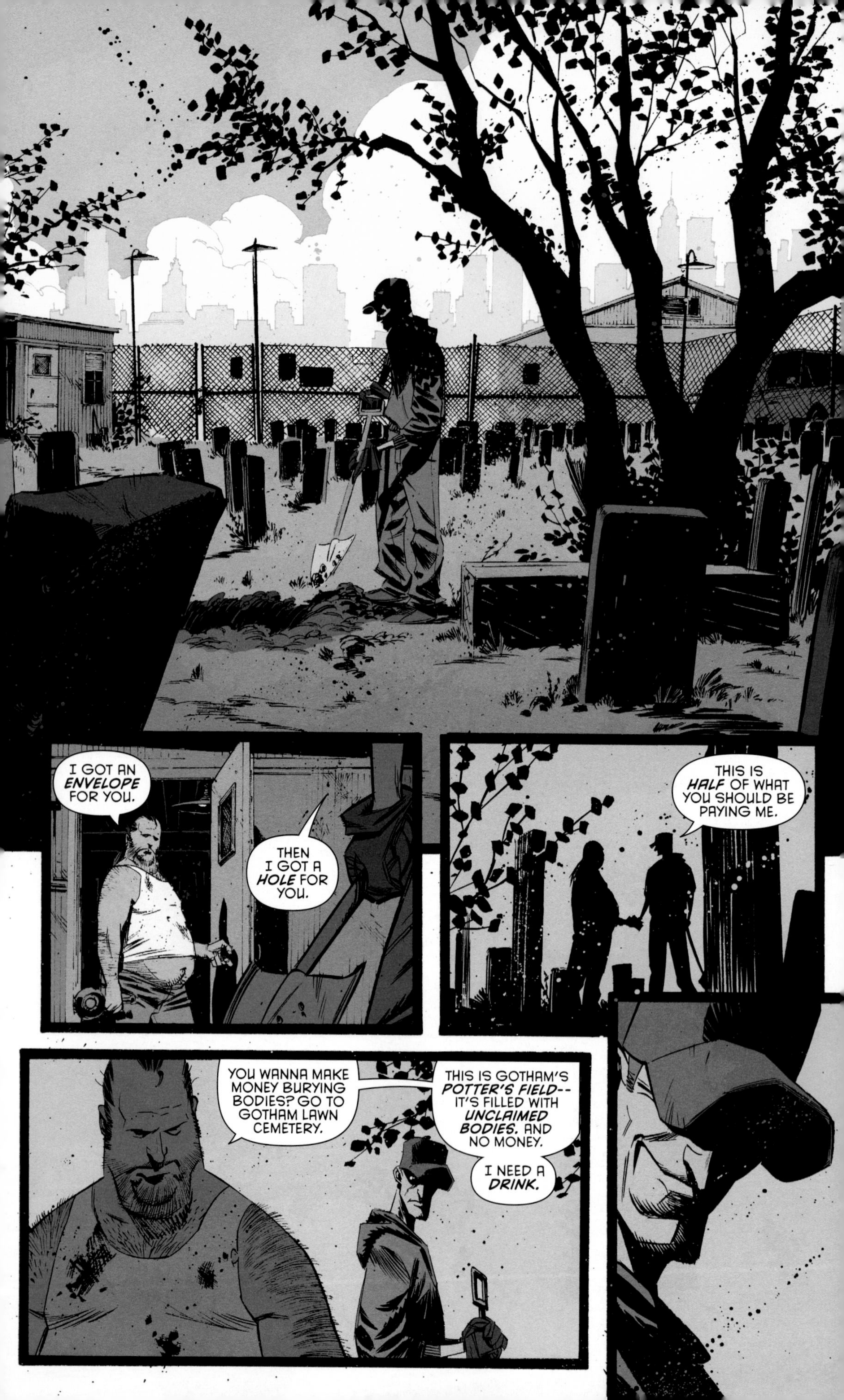
I GOT AN *ENVELOPE* FOR YOU.
THEN I GOT A *HOLE* FOR YOU.
THIS IS *HALF* OF WHAT YOU SHOULD BE PAYING ME.
YOU WANNA MAKE MONEY BURYING BODIES? GO TO GOTHAM LAWN CEMETERY.
THIS IS GOTHAM'S *POTTER'S FIELD*-- IT'S FILLED WITH *UNCLAIMED BODIES.* AND NO MONEY.
I NEED A *DRINK.*

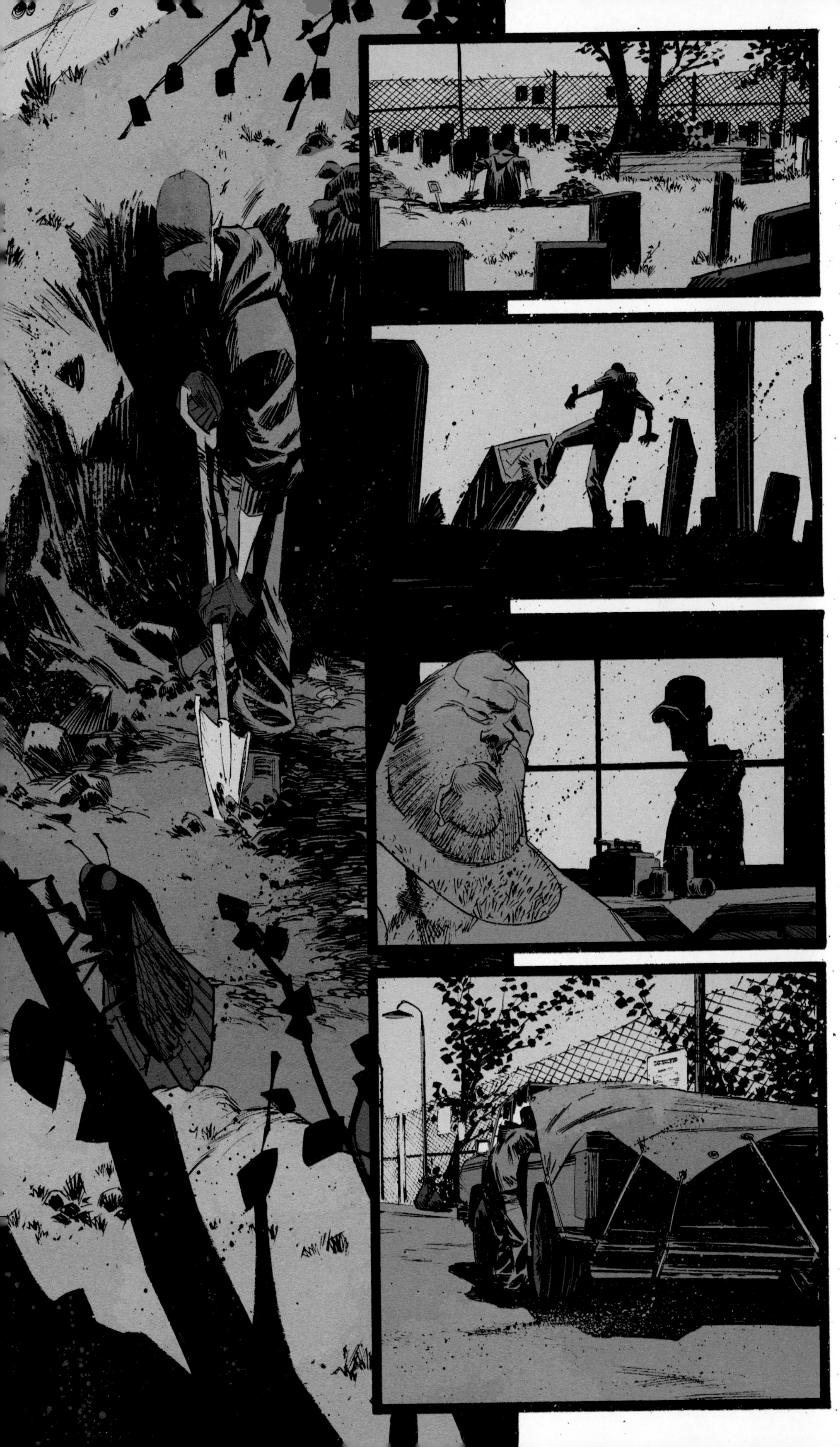

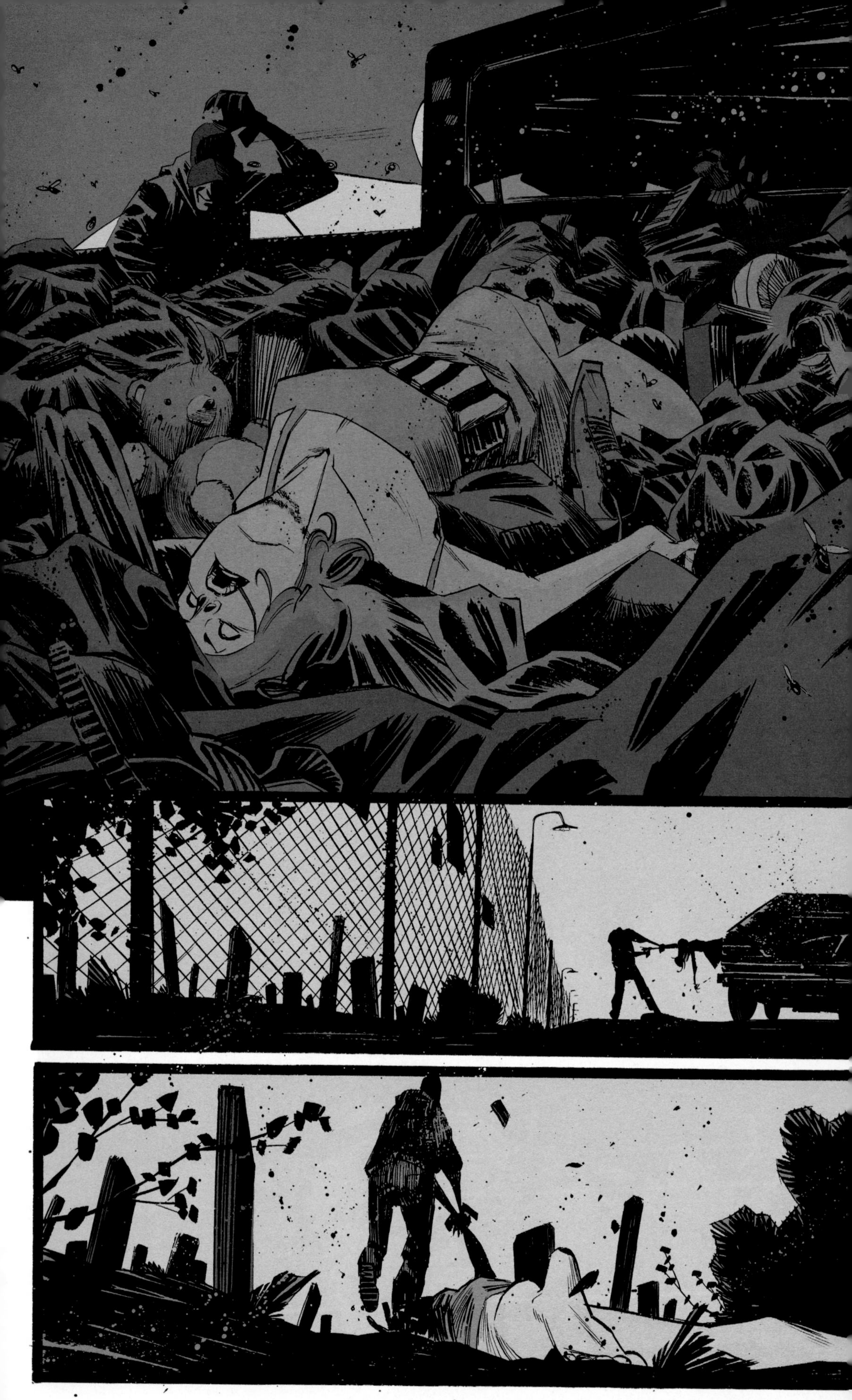

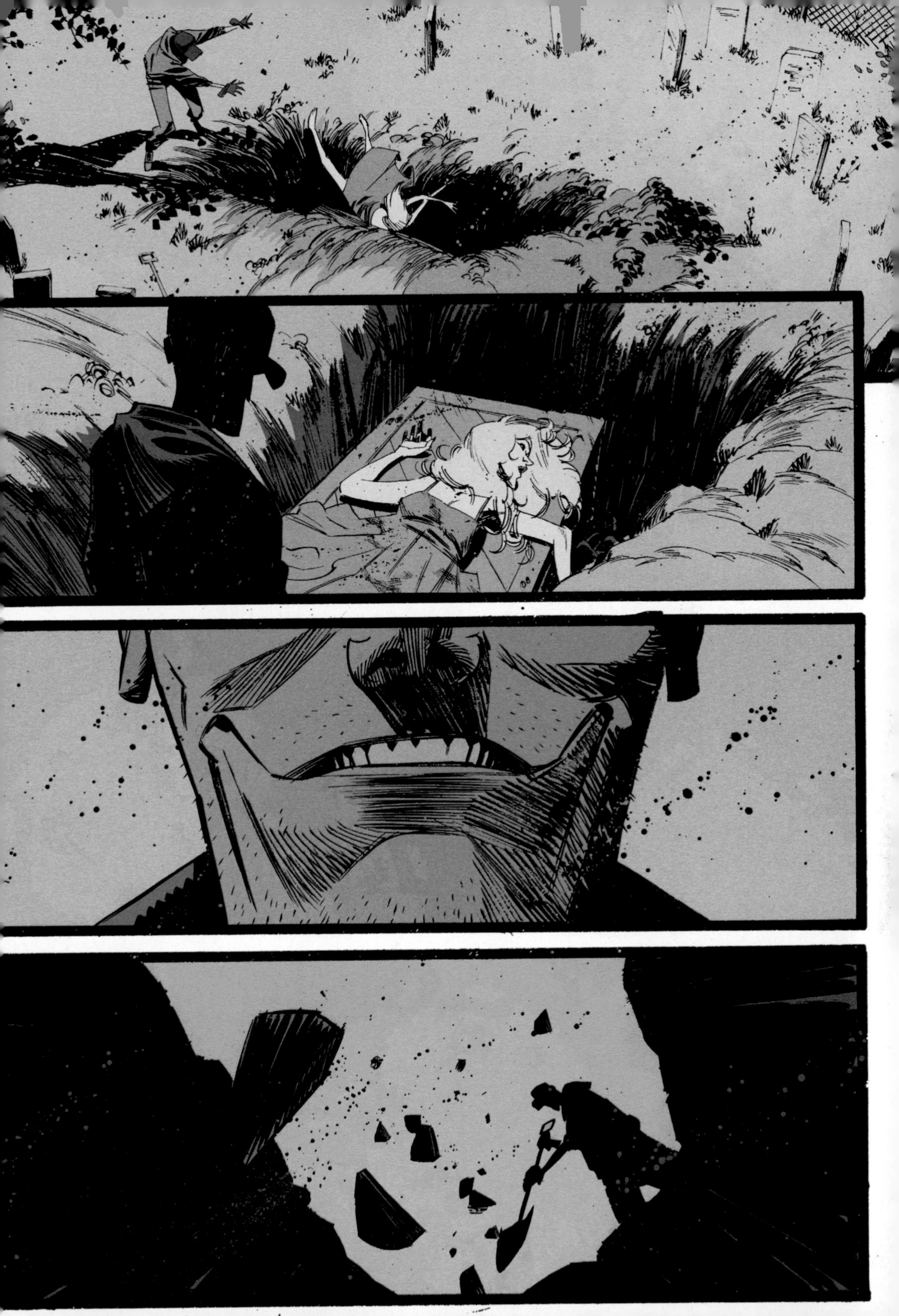

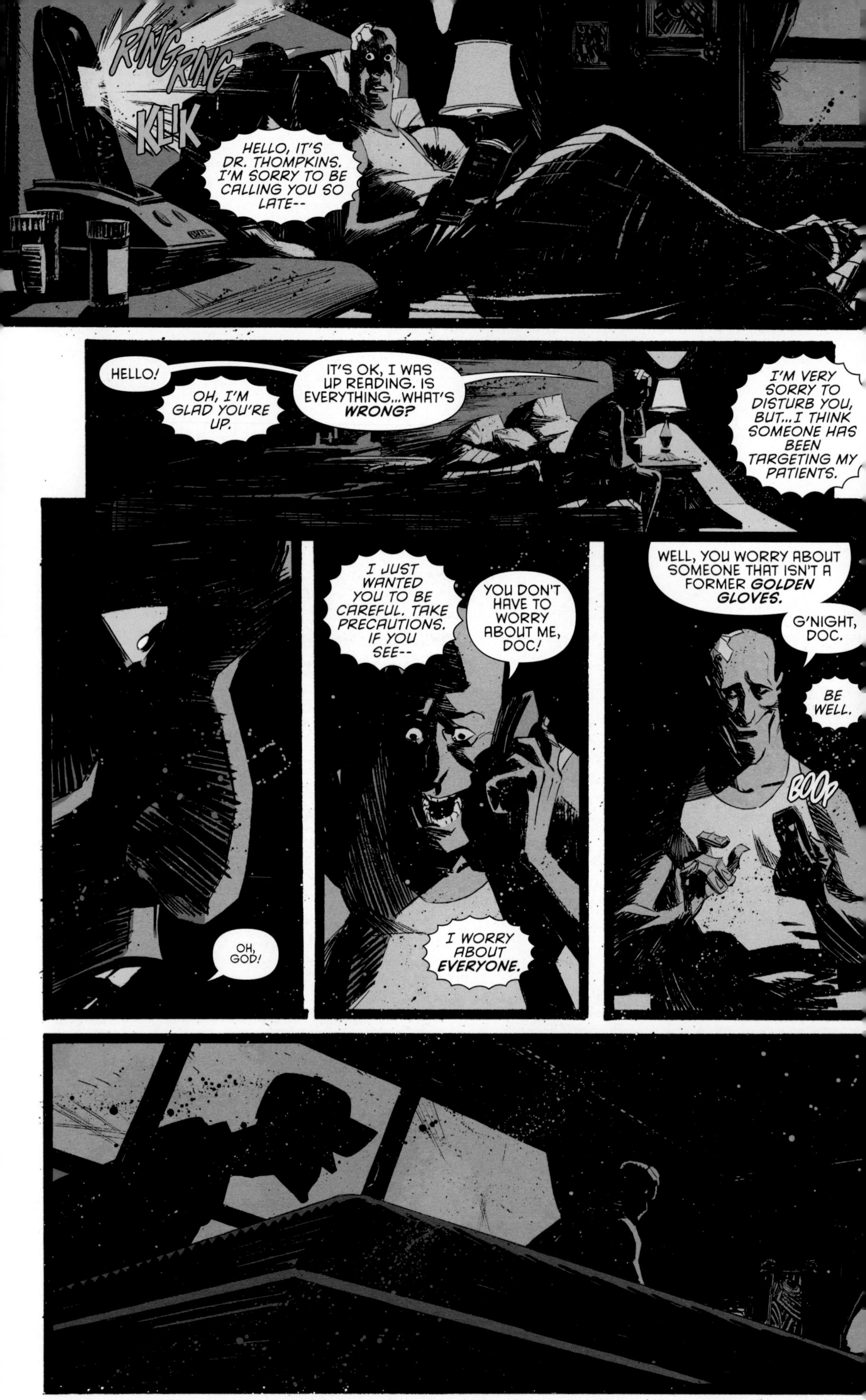

RINGRING
KLIK
HELLO, IT'S DR. THOMPKINS. I'M SORRY TO BE CALLING YOU SO LATE--
HELLO!
OH, I'M GLAD YOU'RE UP.
IT'S OK, I WAS UP READING. IS EVERYTHING...WHAT'S WRONG?
I'M VERY SORRY TO DISTURB YOU, BUT...I THINK SOMEONE HAS BEEN TARGETING MY PATIENTS.
OH, GOD!
I JUST WANTED YOU TO BE CAREFUL. TAKE PRECAUTIONS. IF YOU SEE--
YOU DON'T HAVE TO WORRY ABOUT ME, DOC!
I WORRY ABOUT EVERYONE.
WELL, YOU WORRY ABOUT SOMEONE THAT ISN'T A FORMER GOLDEN GLOVES.
G'NIGHT, DOC.
BE WELL.
BOOP

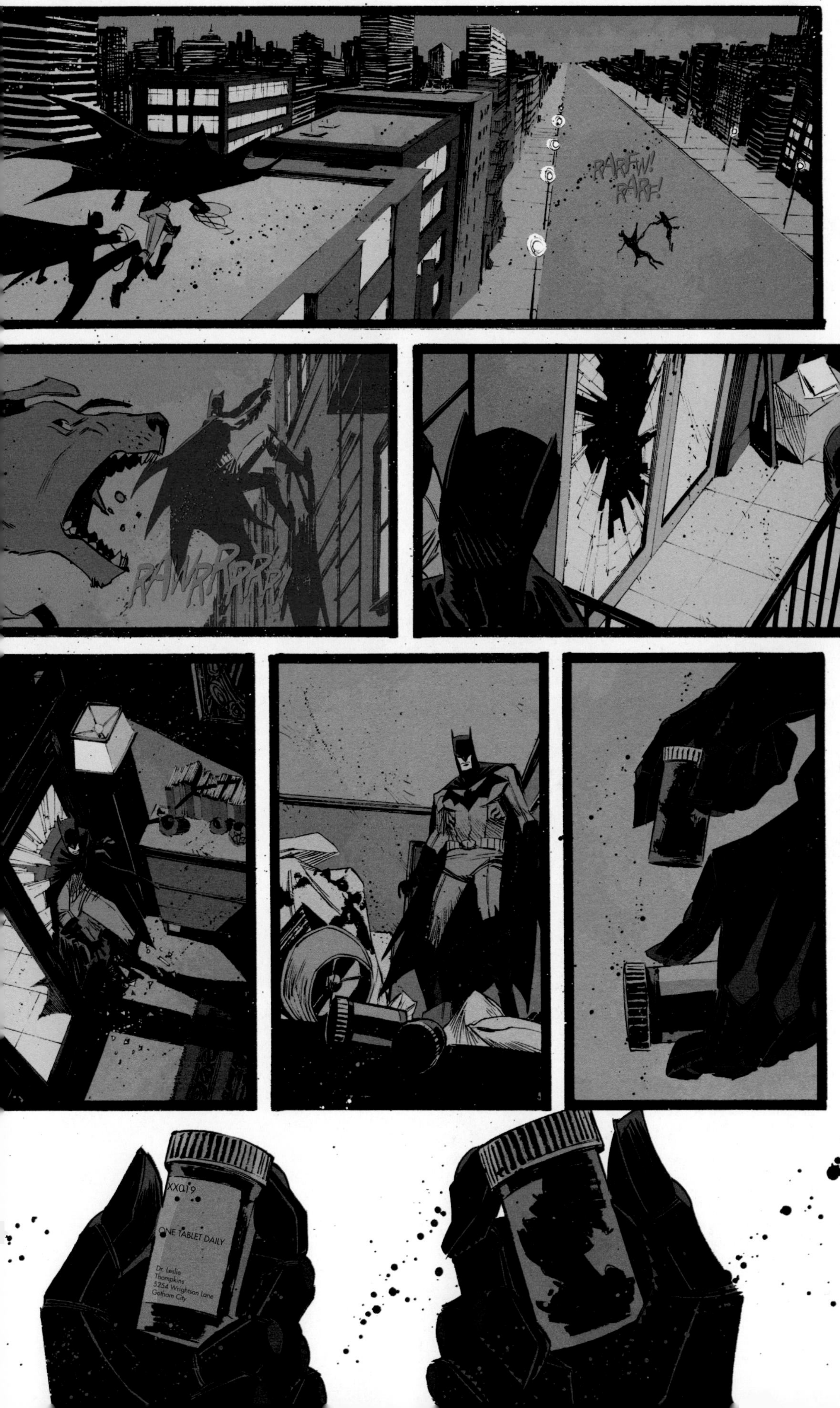
RARFW! RARF!
RAWRRRRR!
XXQ19
ONE TABLET DAILY
Dr. Leslie Thompkins
5254 Wrightson Lane
Gotham City

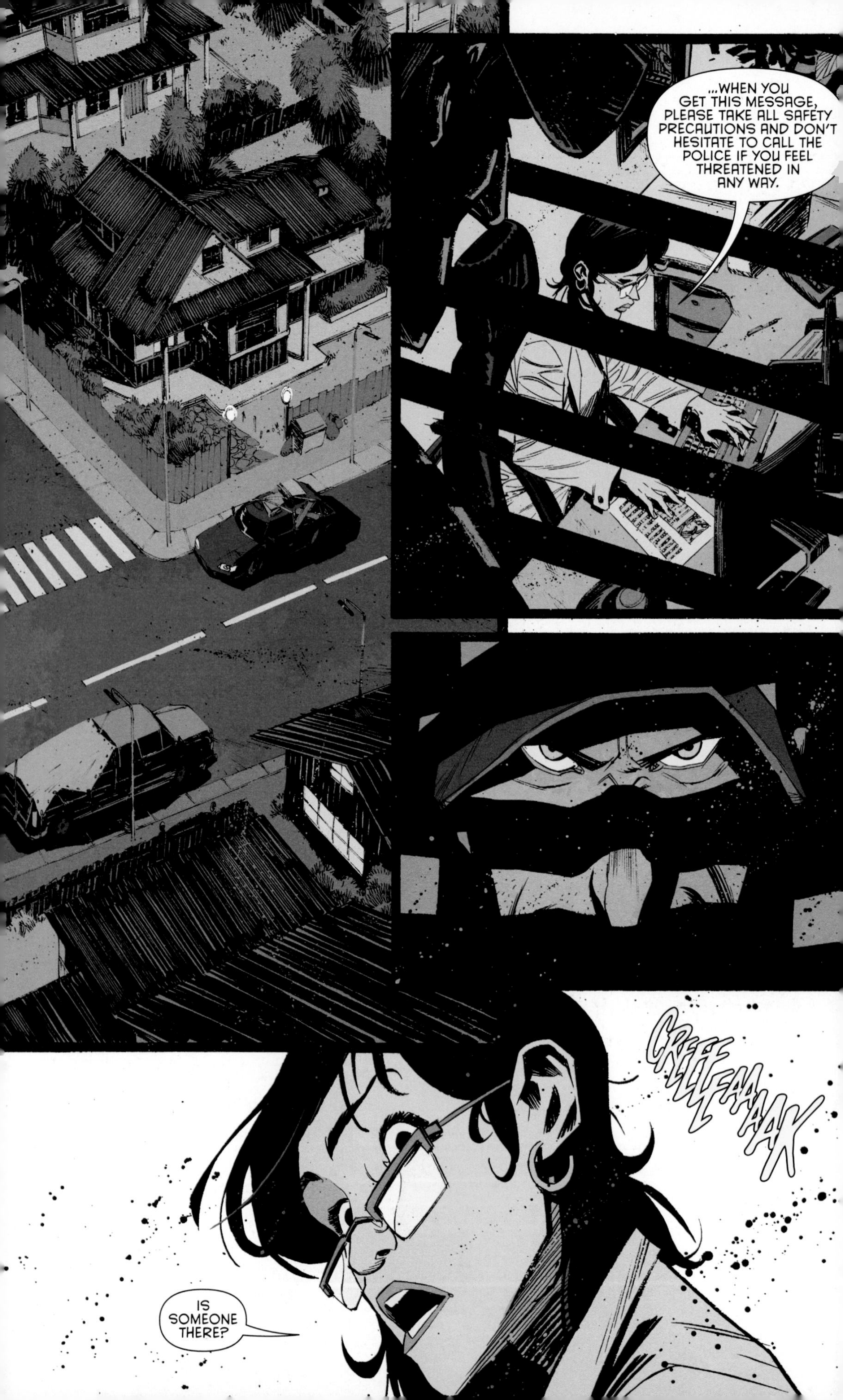
...WHEN YOU GET THIS MESSAGE, PLEASE TAKE ALL SAFETY PRECAUTIONS AND DON'T HESITATE TO CALL THE POLICE IF YOU FEEL THREATENED IN ANY WAY.
CREEEAAAAK
IS SOMEONE THERE?

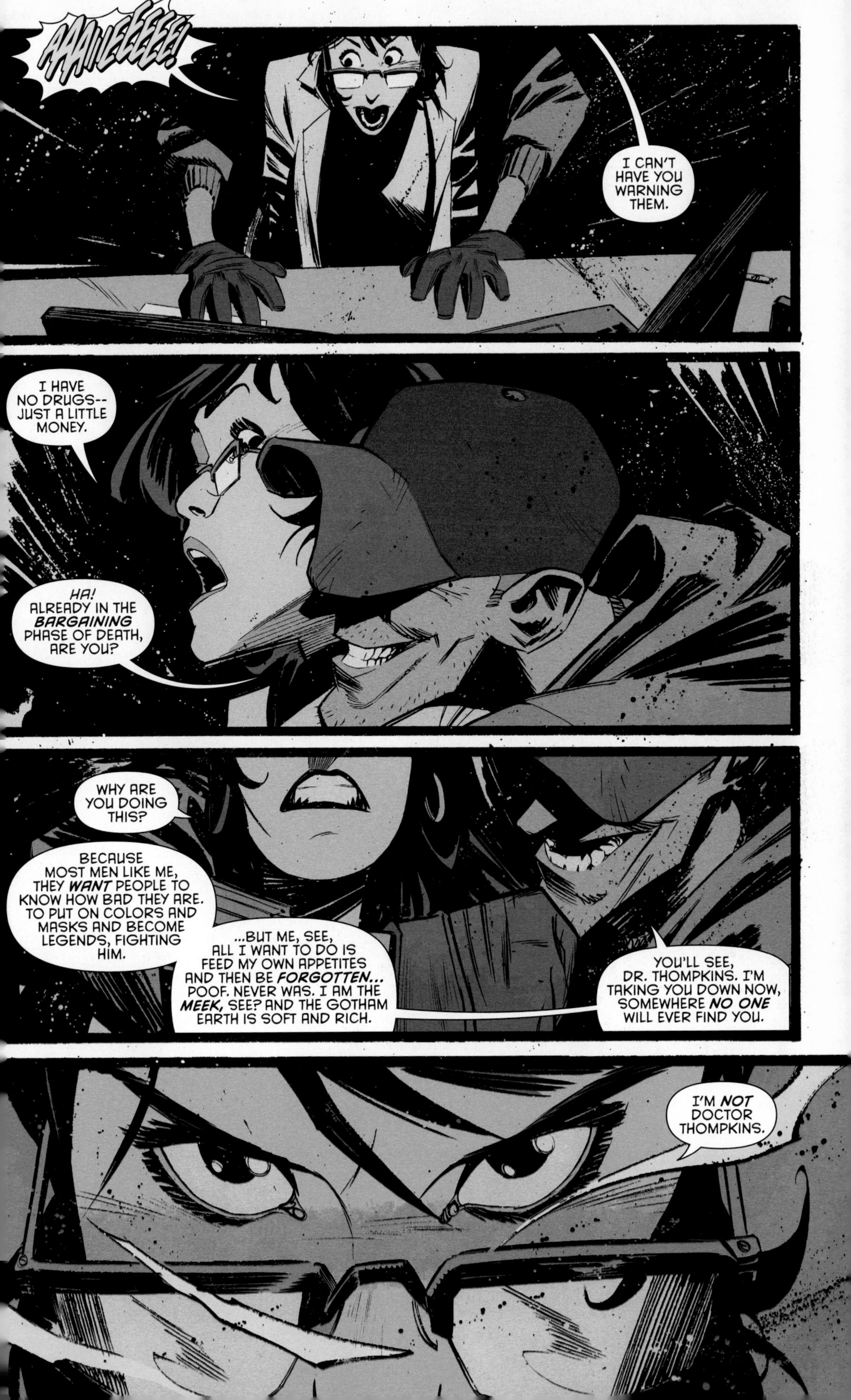
AAAIIIEEEEEE!
I CAN'T HAVE YOU WARNING THEM.
I HAVE NO DRUGS-- JUST A LITTLE MONEY.
HA! ALREADY IN THE *BARGAINING* PHASE OF DEATH, ARE YOU?
WHY ARE YOU DOING THIS?
BECAUSE MOST MEN LIKE ME, THEY *WANT* PEOPLE TO KNOW HOW BAD THEY ARE. TO PUT ON COLORS AND MASKS AND BECOME LEGENDS, FIGHTING HIM.
...BUT ME, SEE, ALL I WANT TO DO IS FEED MY OWN APPETITES AND THEN BE *FORGOTTEN...* POOF. NEVER WAS. I AM THE *MEEK,* SEE? AND THE GOTHAM EARTH IS SOFT AND RICH.
YOU'LL SEE, DR. THOMPKINS. I'M TAKING YOU DOWN NOW, SOMEWHERE *NO ONE* WILL EVER FIND YOU.
I'M *NOT* DOCTOR THOMPKINS.

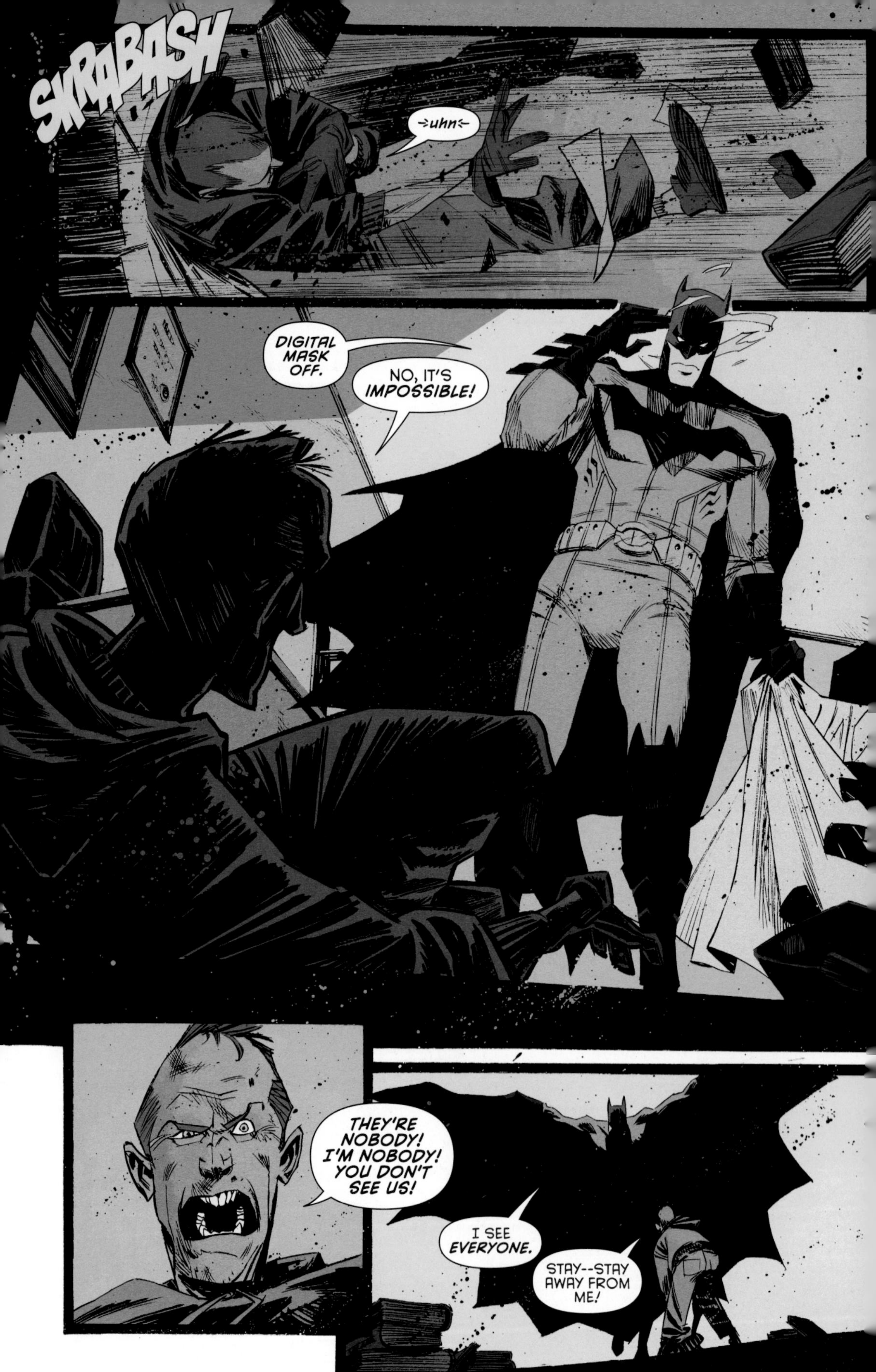
SKRABASH
~uhn~
DIGITAL MASK OFF.
NO, IT'S IMPOSSIBLE!
THEY'RE NOBODY! I'M NOBODY! YOU DON'T SEE US!
I SEE EVERYONE.
STAY--STAY AWAY FROM ME!

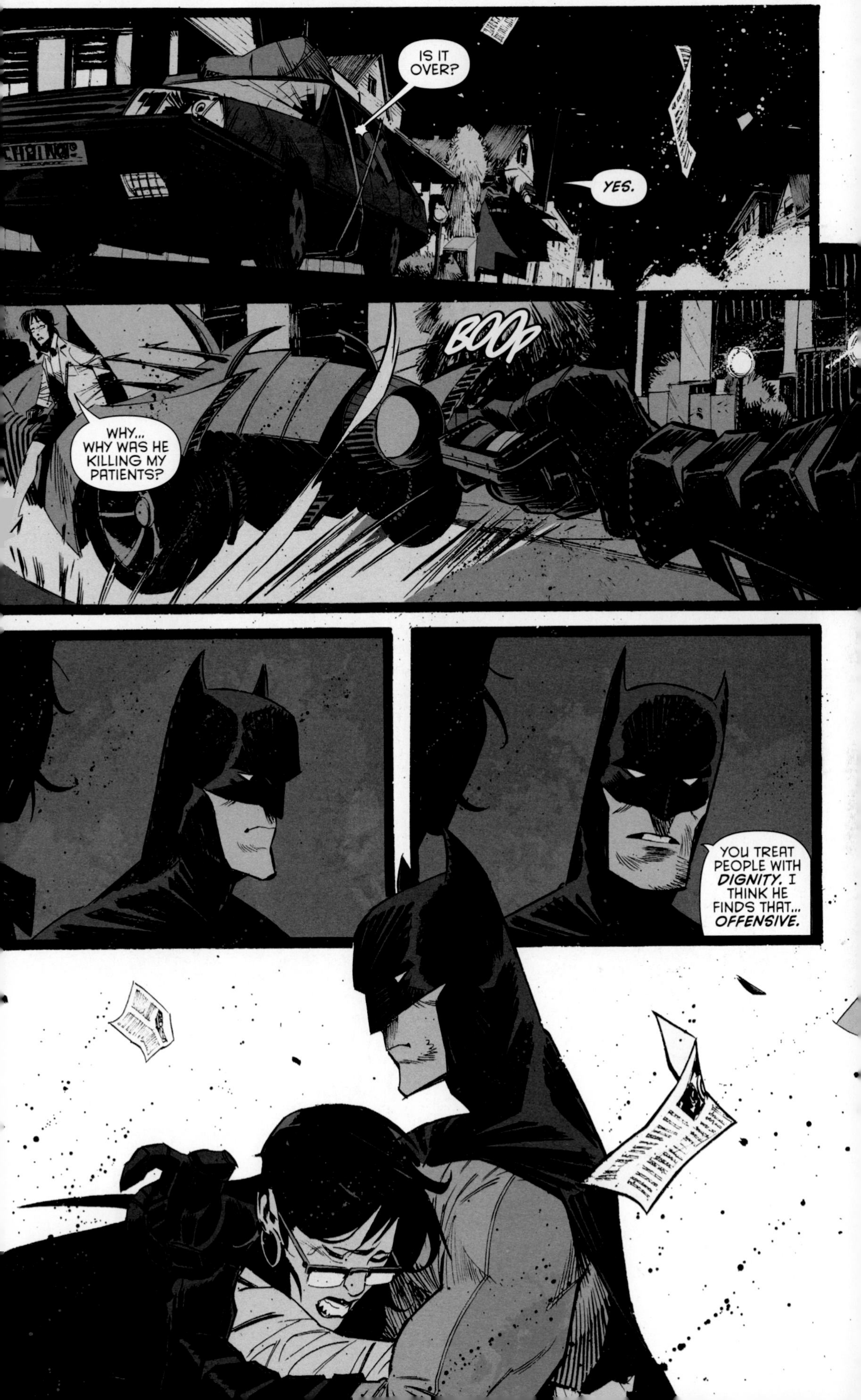
IS IT OVER?
YES.
BOOM
WHY... WHY WAS HE KILLING MY PATIENTS?
YOU TREAT PEOPLE WITH DIGNITY. I THINK HE FINDS THAT... OFFENSIVE.

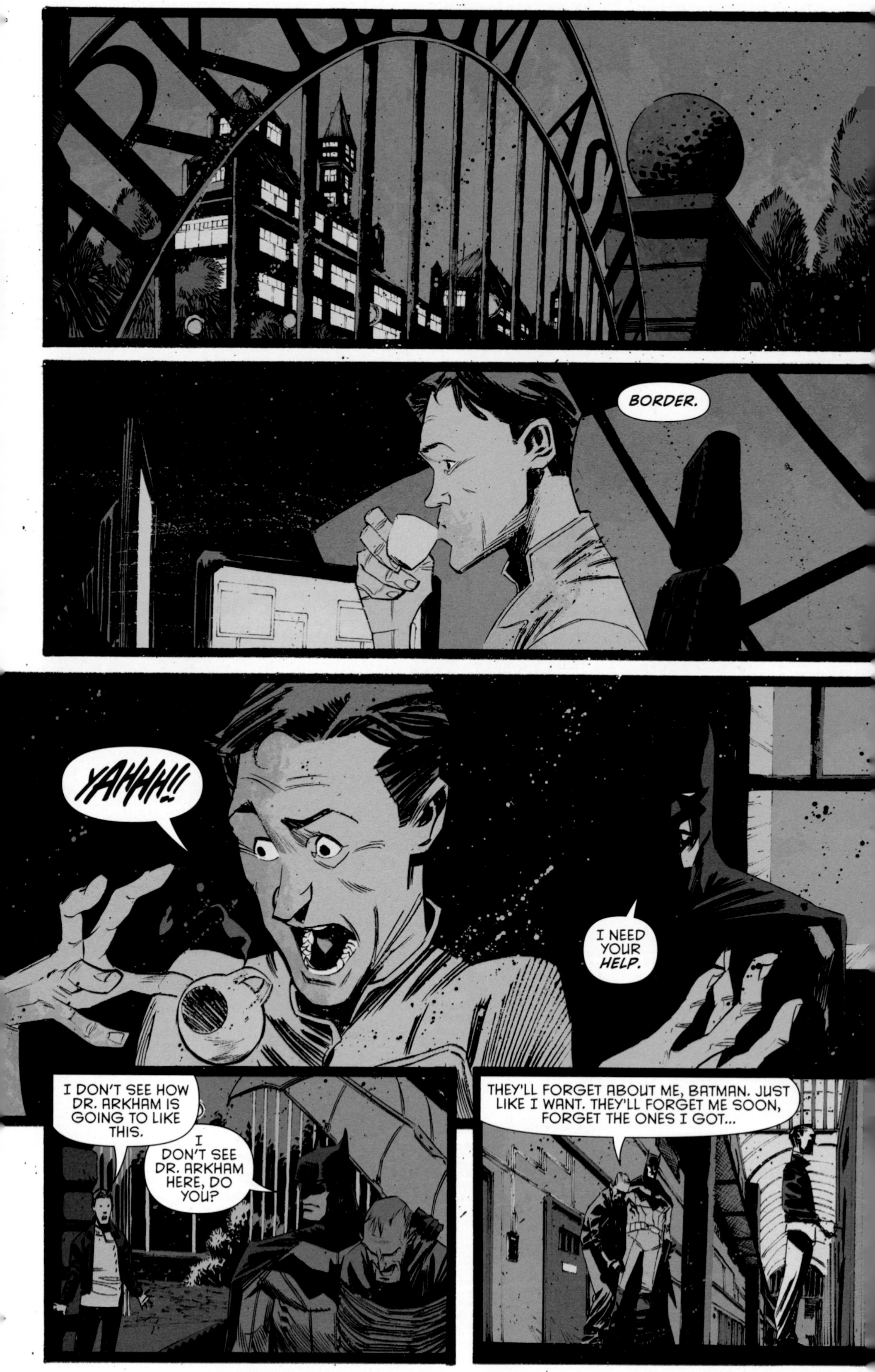
BORDER.
YAHHH!!
I NEED YOUR *HELP*.
I DON'T SEE HOW DR. ARKHAM IS GOING TO LIKE THIS.
I DON'T SEE DR. ARKHAM HERE, DO YOU?
THEY'LL FORGET ABOUT ME, BATMAN. JUST LIKE I WANT. THEY'LL FORGET ME SOON, FORGET THE ONES I GOT...

YOU SURE LOCKING HIM THIS ROOM IS A GOOD IDEA?

IT'S THE *JOKER'S* CELL.

I *uh*, GUESS YOU KNOW THAT ALREADY.

WHAT?!

GET ME OUT OF HERE!

UNKNOWN SUBJECT

0801

YOUR VICTIMS HAD *NAMES.* THEY WERE *HUMANS* DESERVING OF DIGNITY.

IN THE MORNING THE PAPERS WILL WONDER... WHAT IS SO *SPECIAL* ABOUT THE *MANIAC* LOCKED IN THE *JOKER'S CELL?* NO ONE'S FORGETTING YOU THAT QUICKLY.

LET ME OUT OF HERE AND I'LL TELL YOU WHERE THEY *ARE!*

ALREADY IN THE *BARGAINING* PHASE, ARE YOU?

I'M HEADED TO THE *POTTER'S FIELD...* COURTESY OF THE *MUD* ON YOUR TRUCK.

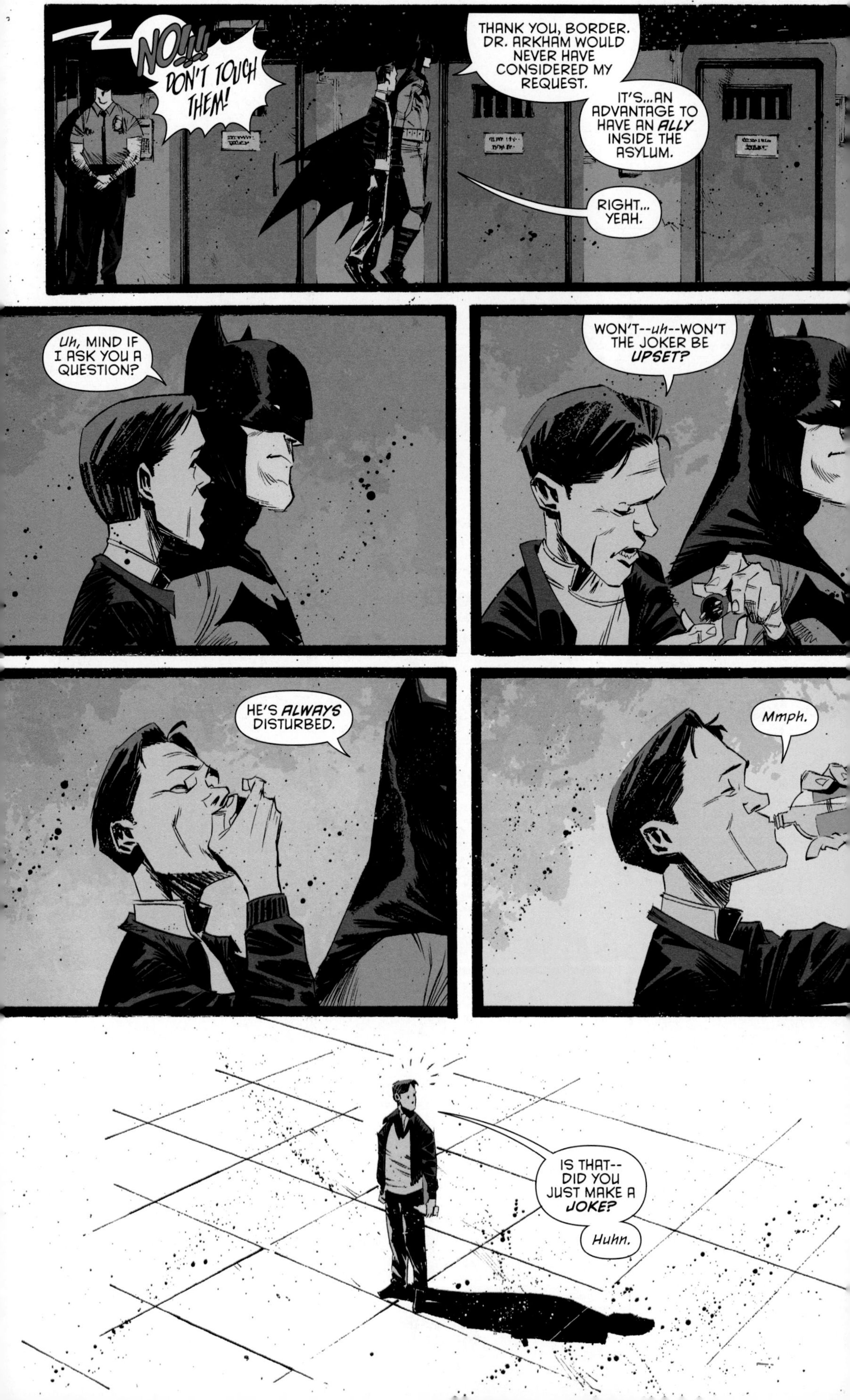
NO!!!
DON'T TOUCH THEM!
THANK YOU, BORDER. DR. ARKHAM WOULD NEVER HAVE CONSIDERED MY REQUEST.
IT'S...AN ADVANTAGE TO HAVE AN ALLY INSIDE THE ASYLUM.
RIGHT... YEAH.
Uh, MIND IF I ASK YOU A QUESTION?
WON'T--uh--WON'T THE JOKER BE UPSET?
HE'S ALWAYS DISTURBED.
Mmph.
IS THAT-- DID YOU JUST MAKE A JOKE?
Huhn.

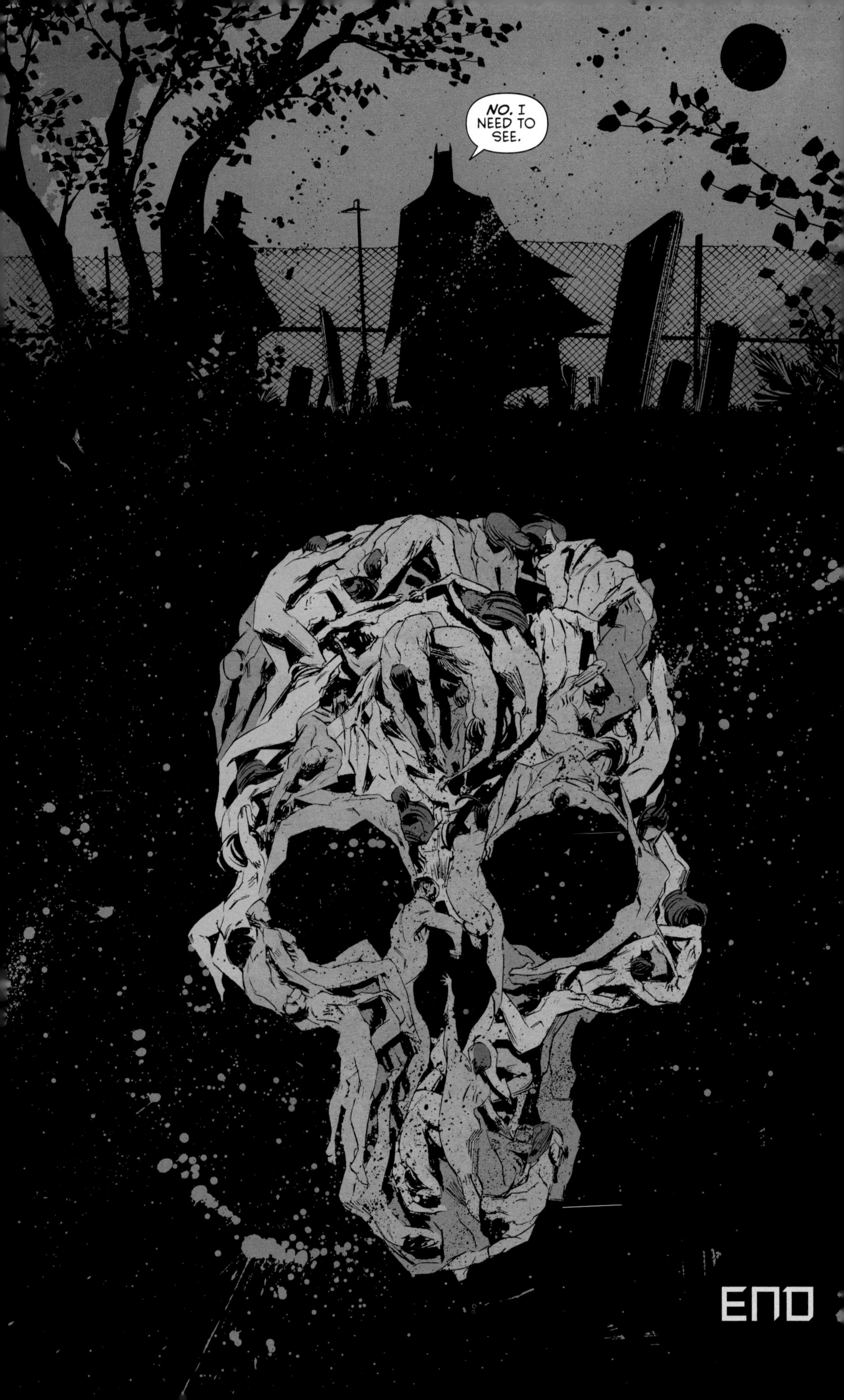
NO. I NEED TO SEE.
END

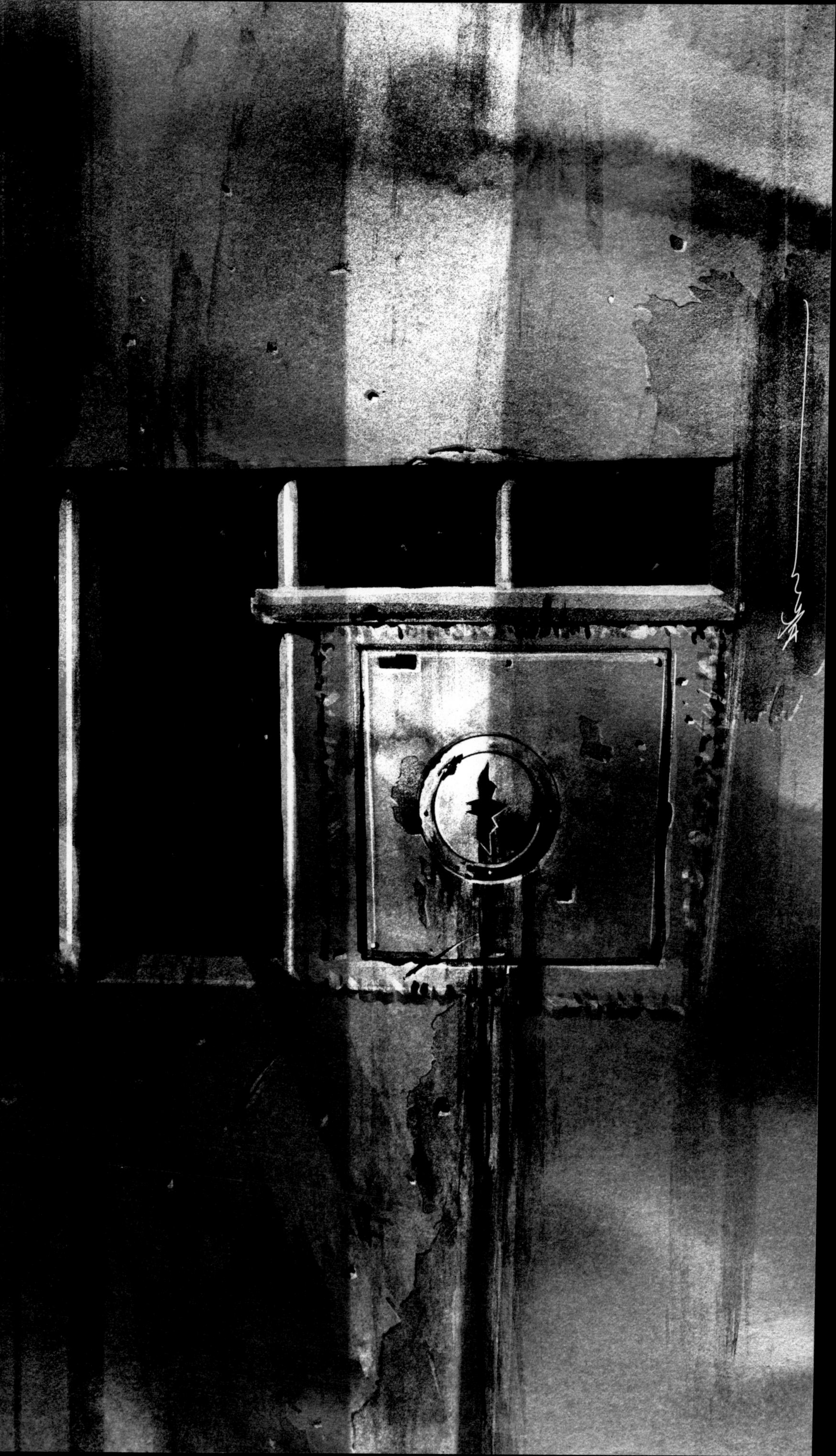

GOTHAM ETERNAL

SCOTT SNYDER JAMES TYNION IV writers DUSTIN NGUYEN penciller DEREK FRIDOLFS inker JOHN KALISZ colorist cover by DUSTIN NGUYEN

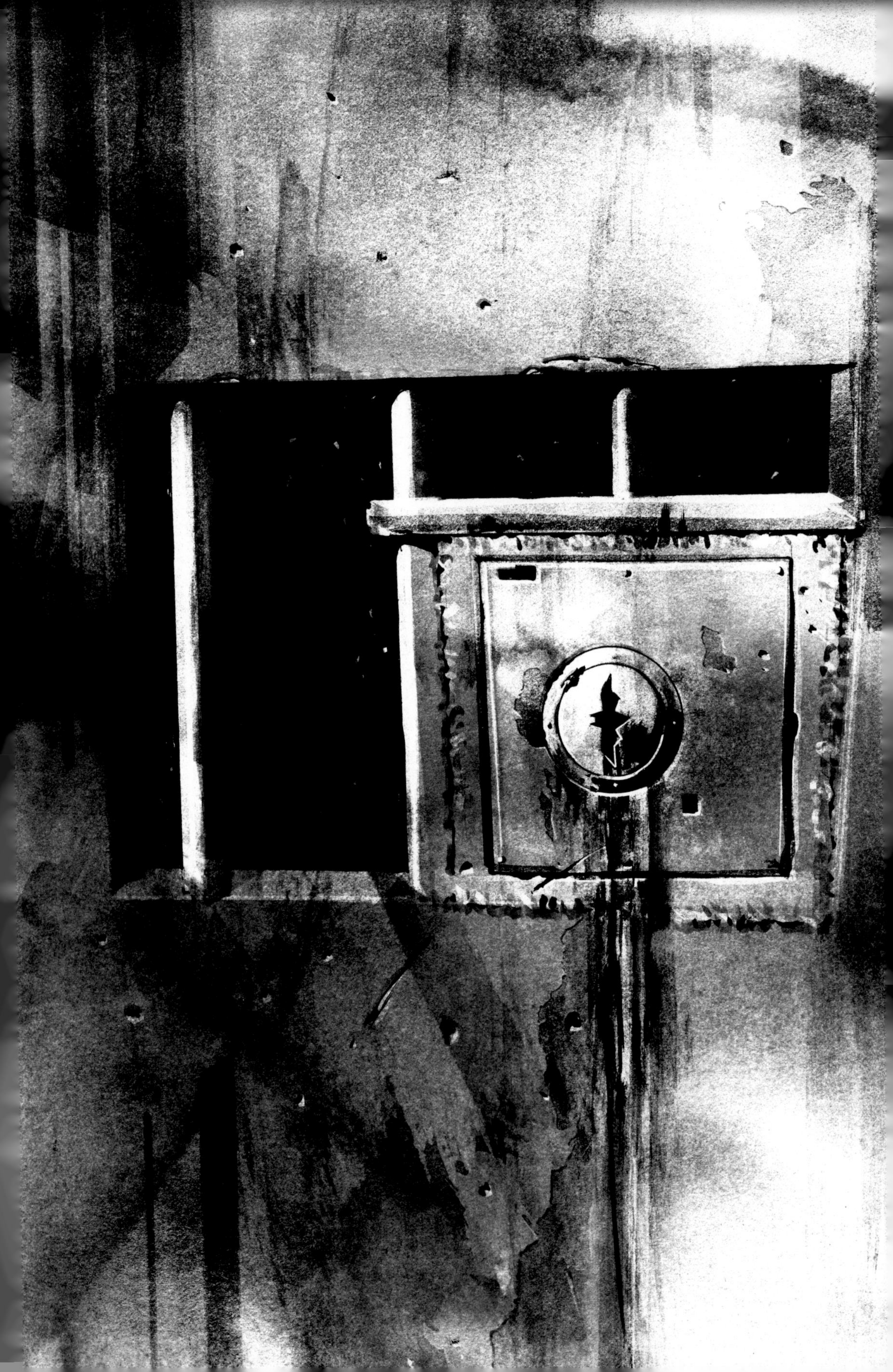

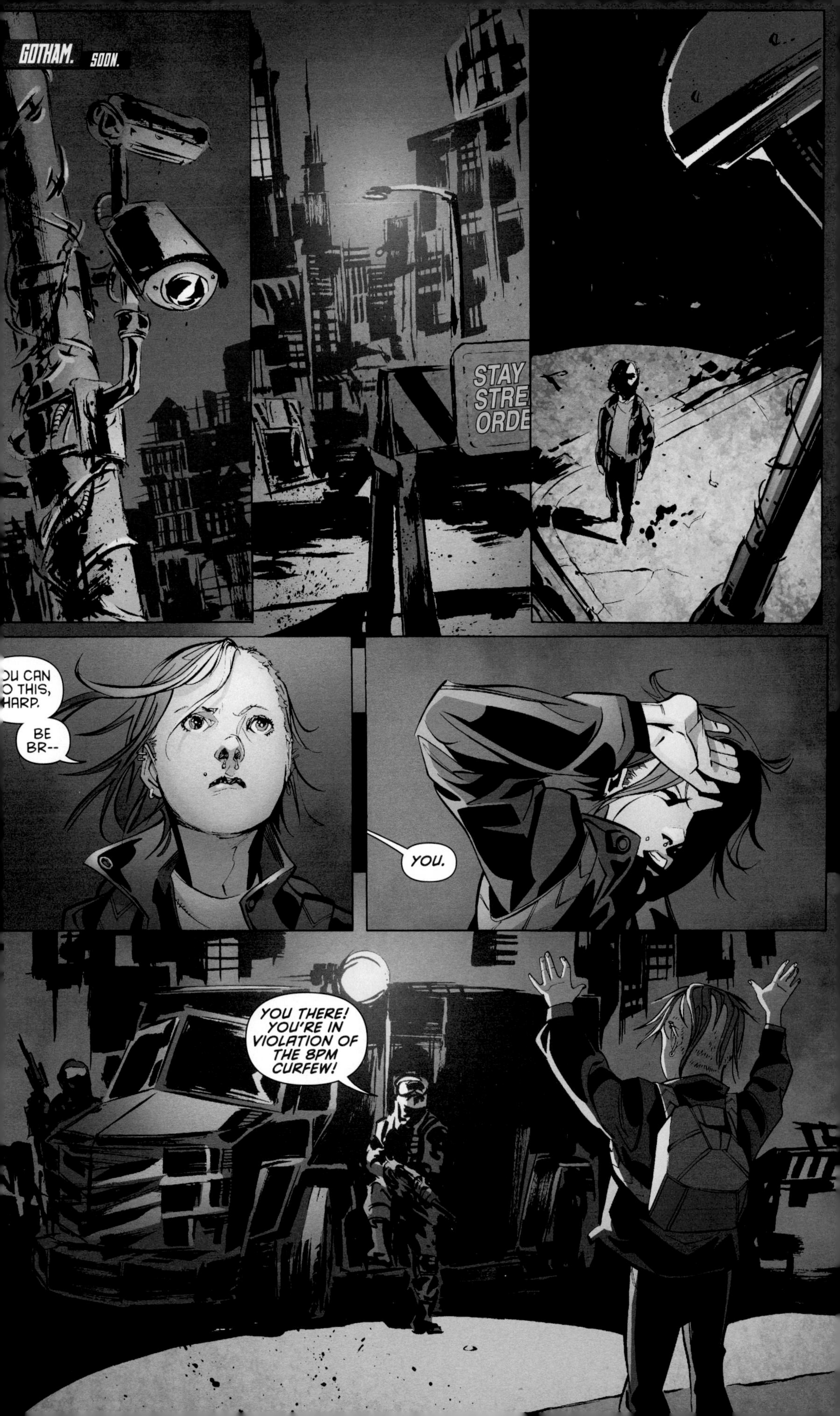
GOTHAM. SOON.
STAY
STRE
ORDE
OU CAN O THIS, HARP.
BE BR--
YOU.
YOU THERE! YOU'RE IN VIOLATION OF THE 8PM CURFEW!

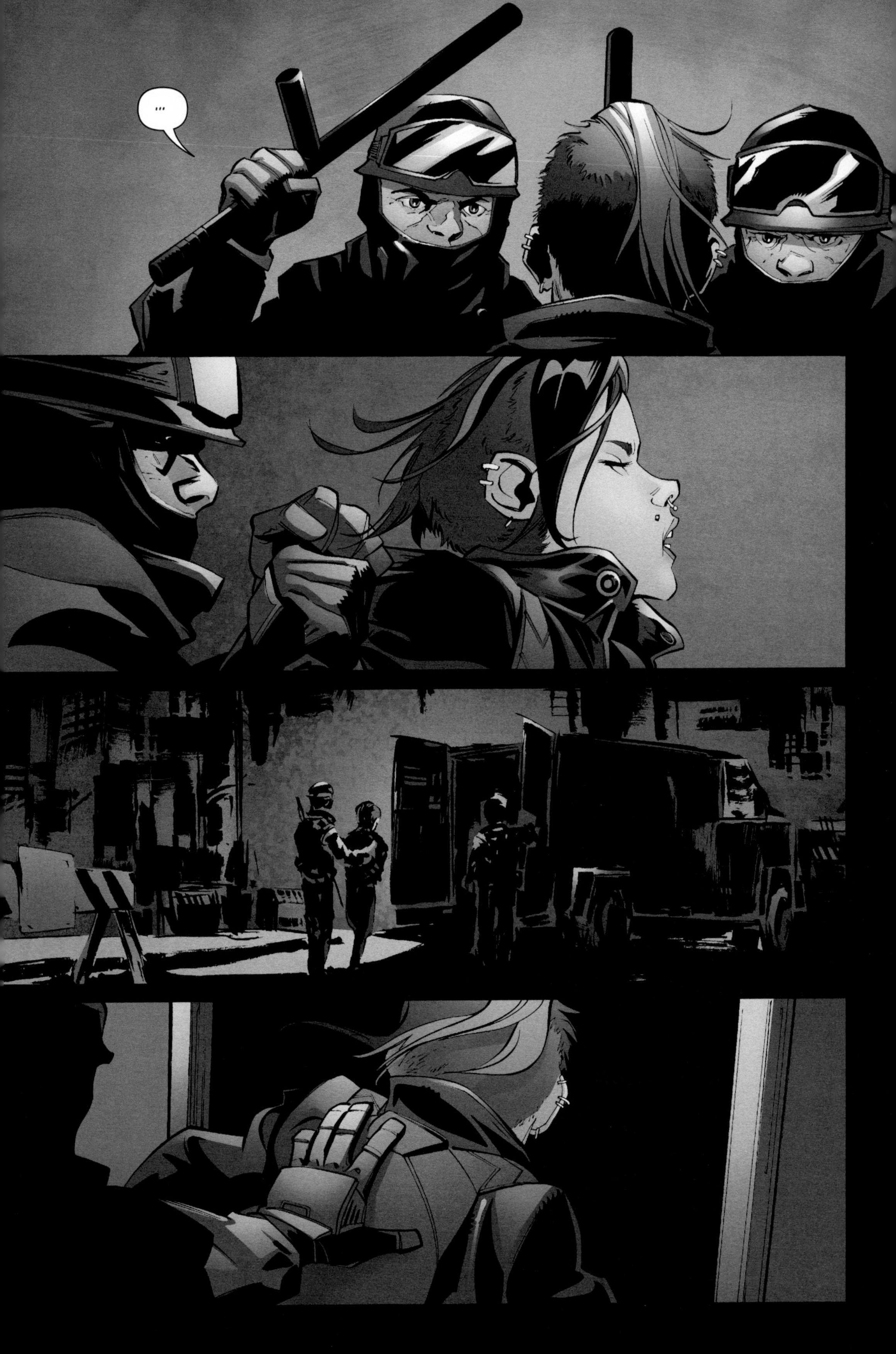
...

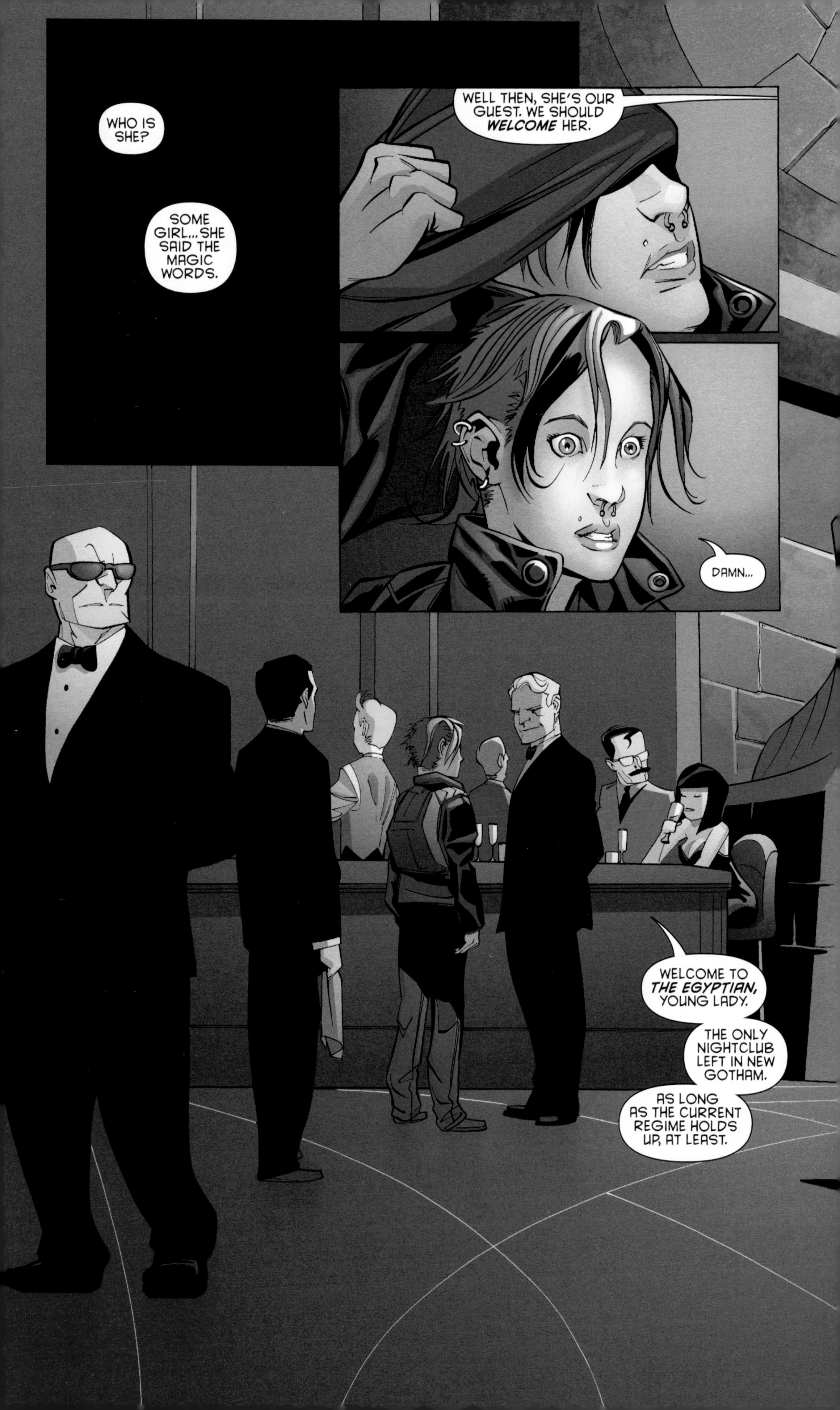
WHO IS SHE?
SOME GIRL... SHE SAID THE MAGIC WORDS.
WELL THEN, SHE'S OUR GUEST. WE SHOULD *WELCOME* HER.
DAMN...
WELCOME TO *THE EGYPTIAN,* YOUNG LADY.
THE ONLY NIGHTCLUB LEFT IN NEW GOTHAM.
AS LONG AS THE CURRENT REGIME HOLDS UP, AT LEAST.

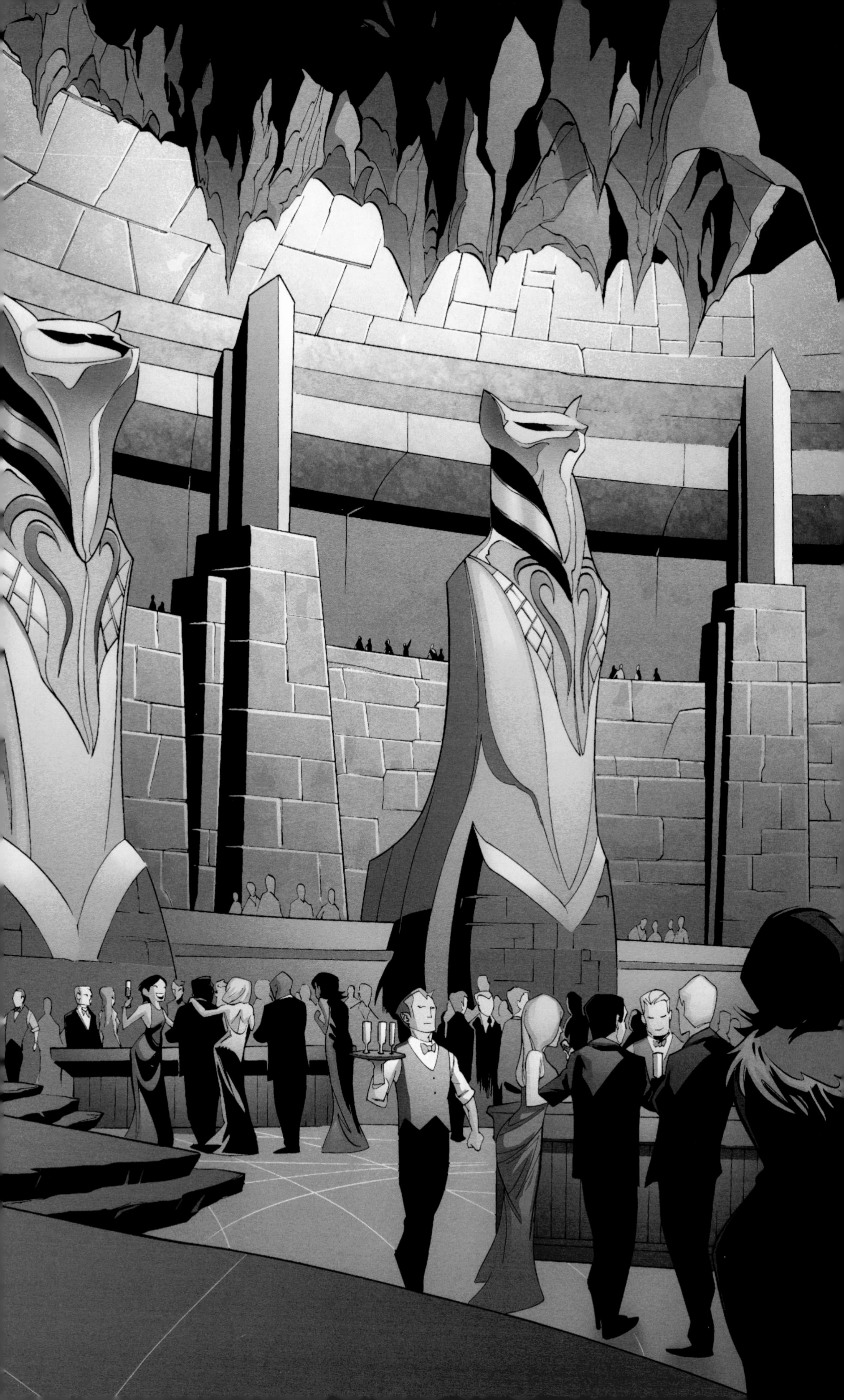

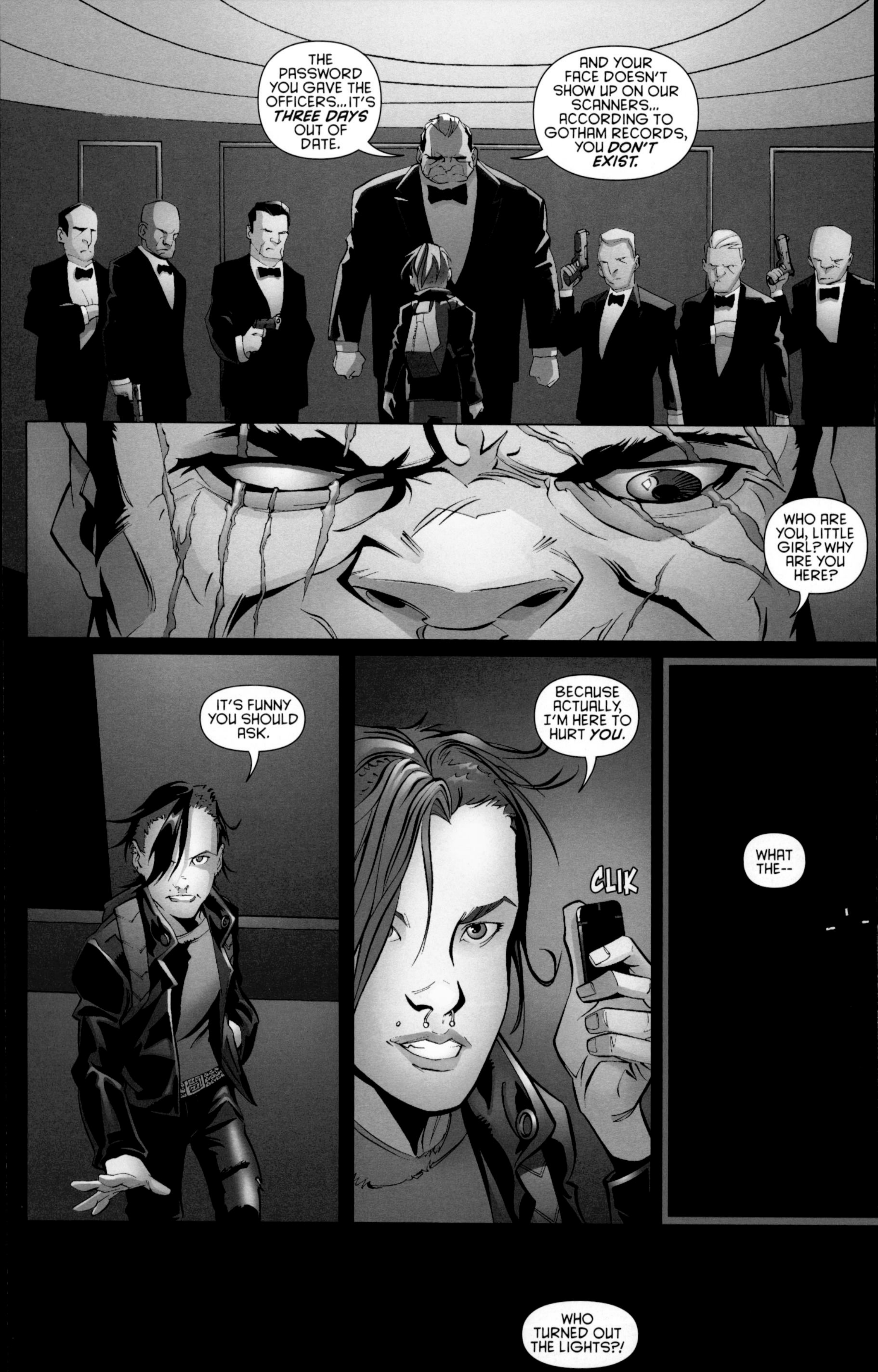
THE PASSWORD YOU GAVE THE OFFICERS...IT'S *THREE DAYS* OUT OF DATE.
AND YOUR FACE DOESN'T SHOW UP ON OUR SCANNERS... ACCORDING TO GOTHAM RECORDS, YOU *DON'T EXIST.*
WHO ARE YOU, LITTLE GIRL? WHY ARE YOU HERE?
IT'S FUNNY YOU SHOULD ASK.
BECAUSE ACTUALLY, I'M HERE TO HURT *YOU*.
CLIK
WHAT THE--
WHO TURNED OUT THE LIGHTS?!

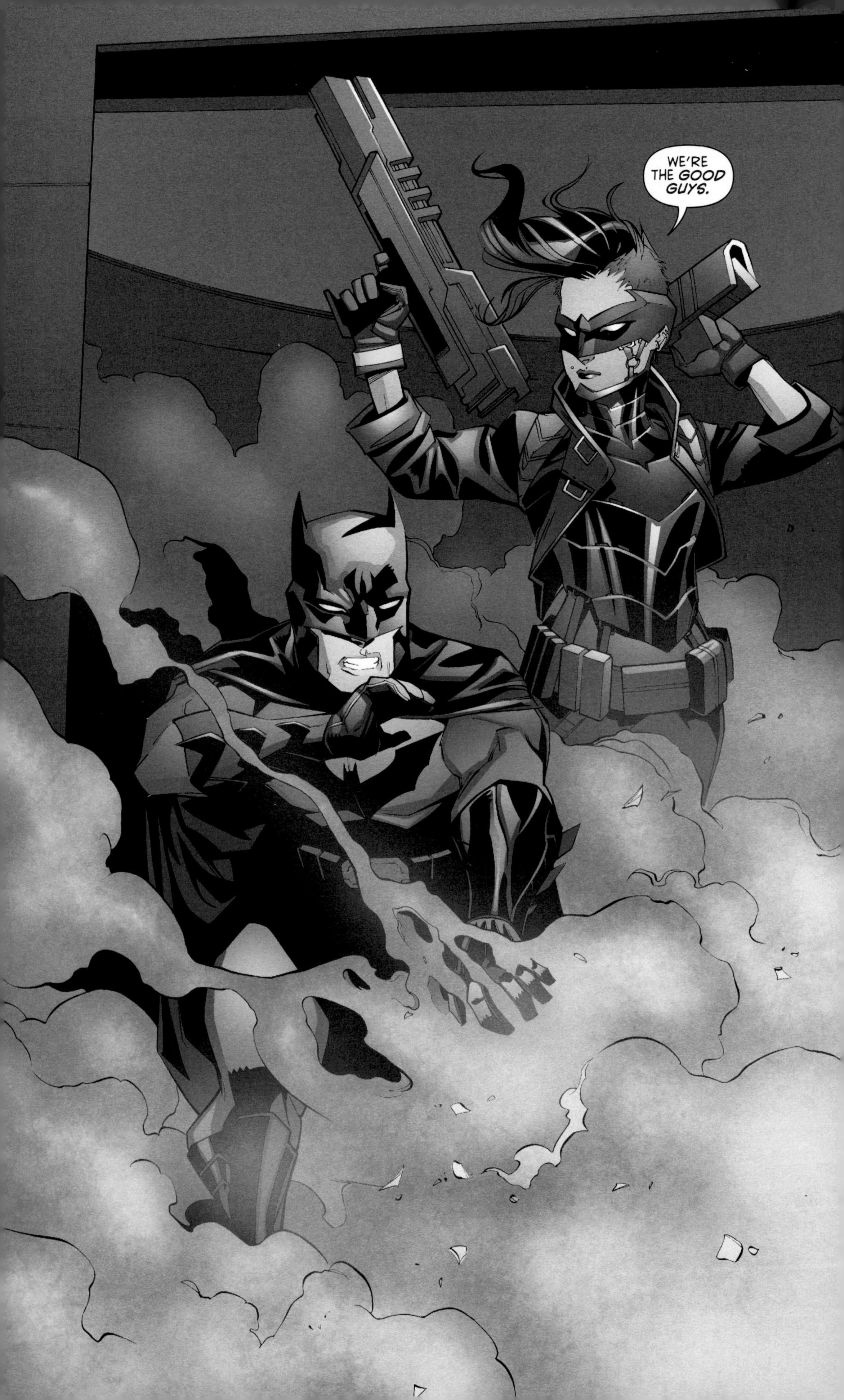
WE'RE THE GOOD GUYS.

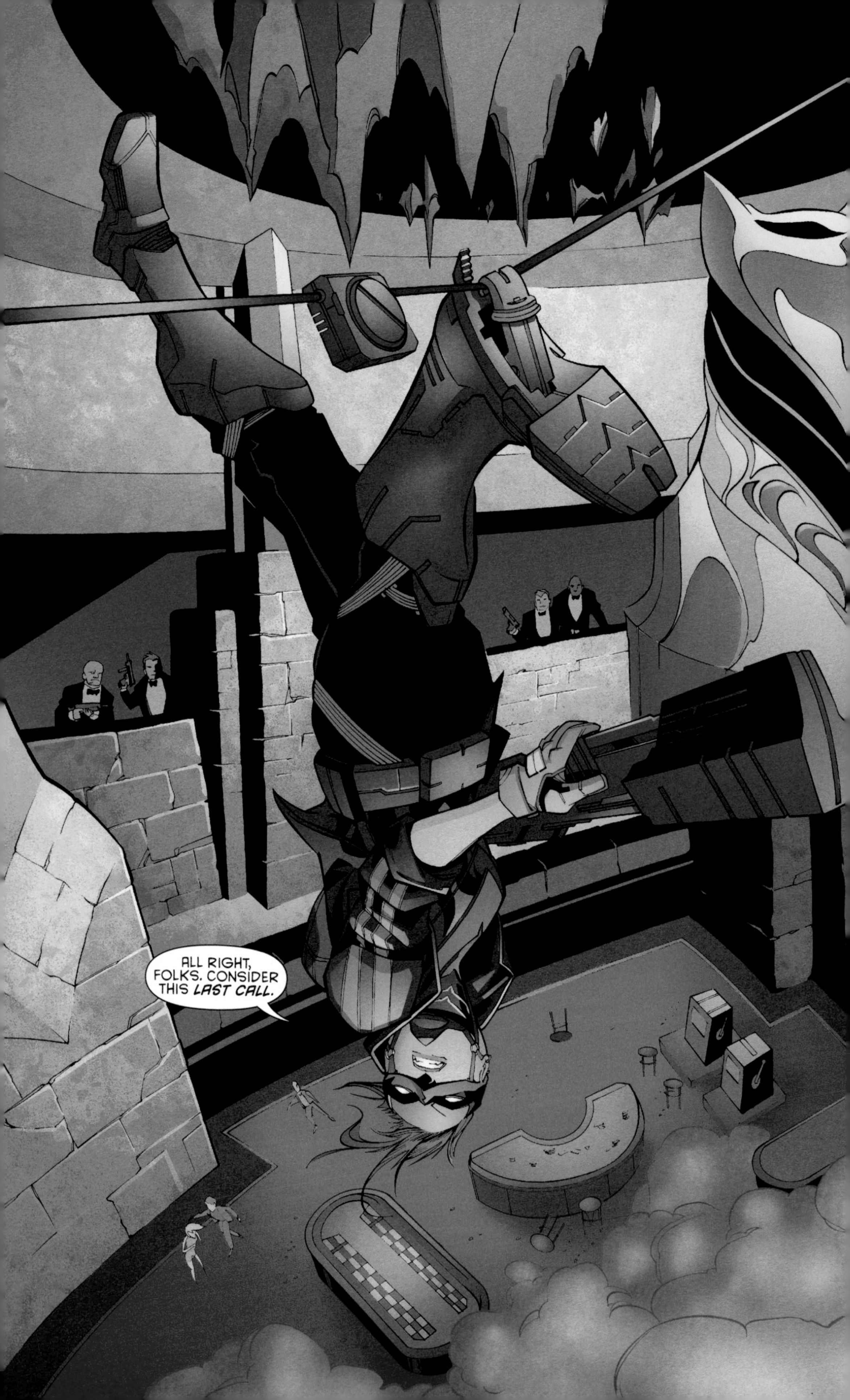
ALL RIGHT, FOLKS. CONSIDER THIS LAST CALL.

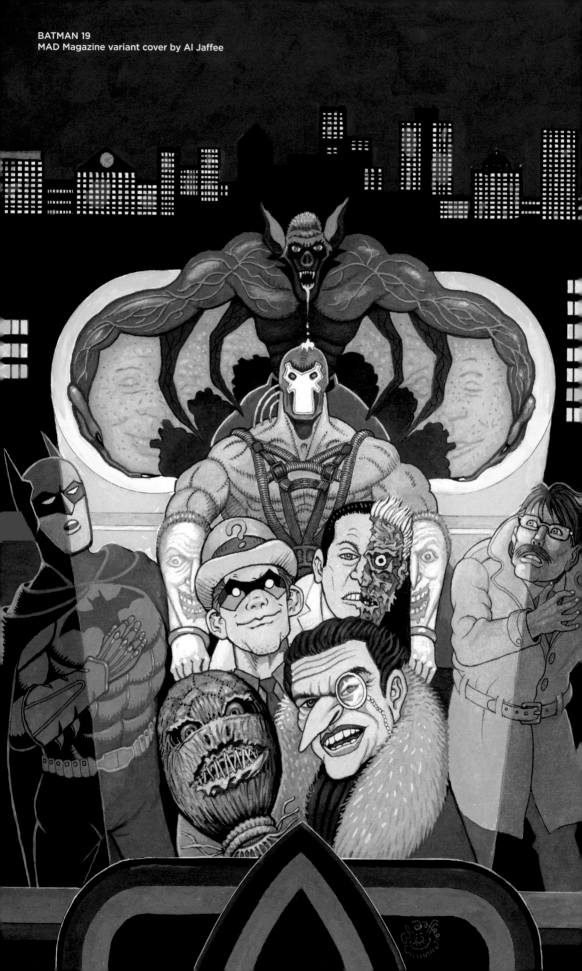

BATMAN 20
Cover by Greg Capullo & FCO Plascencia

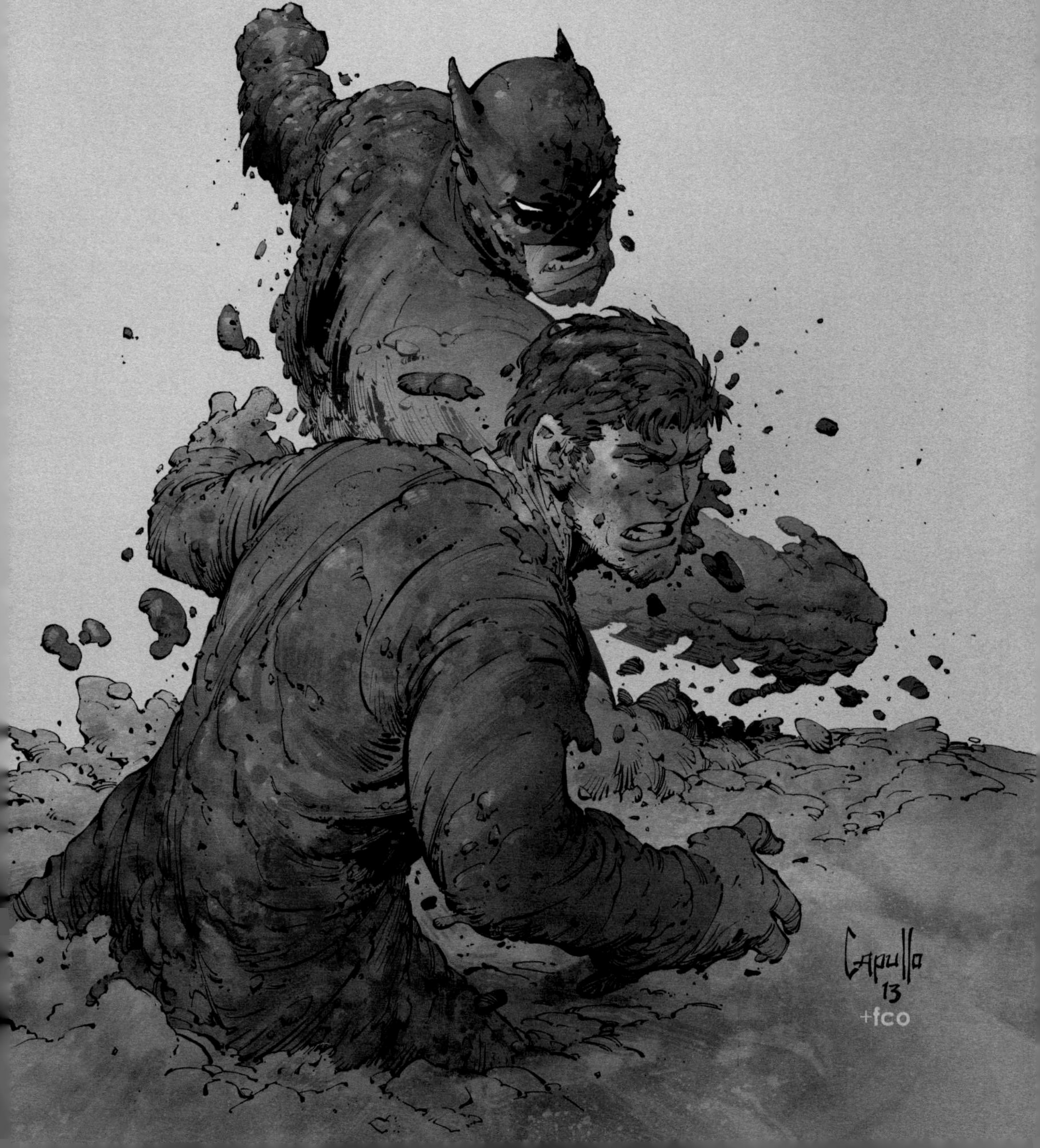
Capullo
13
+fco

BATMAN 34
Variant cover by Rafael Albuquerque

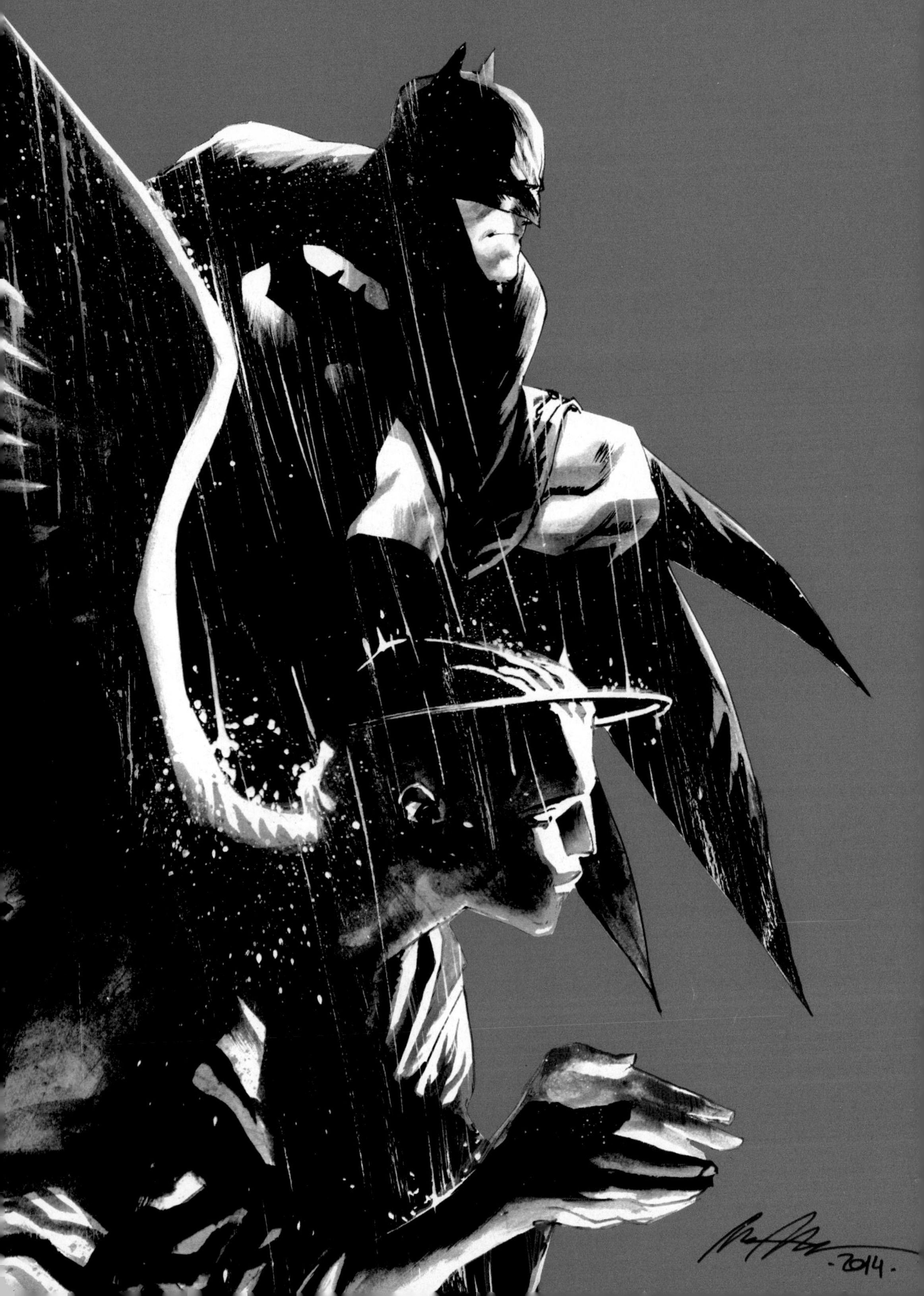
2014

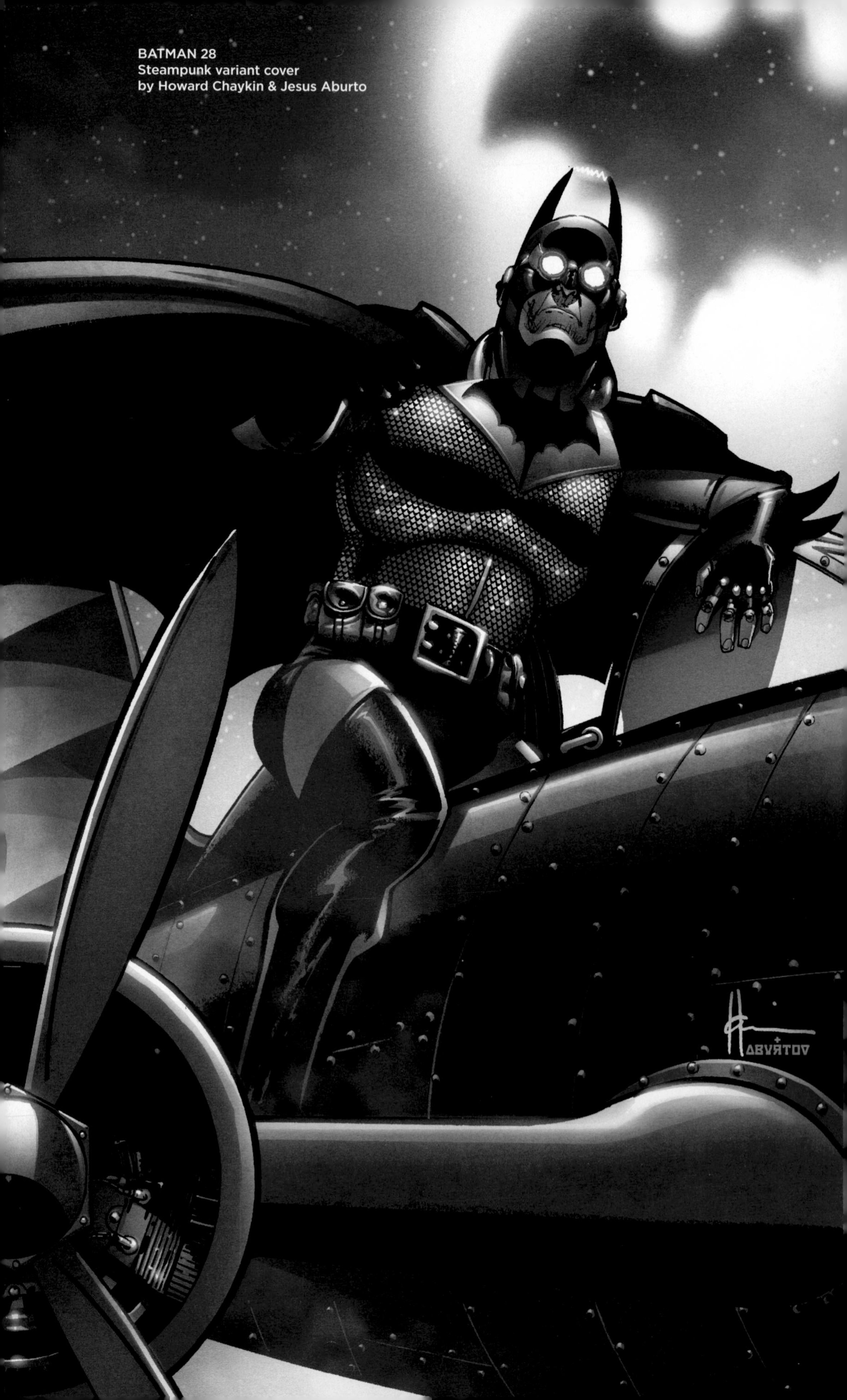

BATMAN 28
Steampunk variant cover
by Howard Chaykin & Jesus Aburto